Dissing Elizabeth

Dissing

Elizabeth

Negative

Representations of

Gloriana

Edited by

Julia M. Walker

Duke University Press

Durham and London

1998

© 1998 Duke University Press

All rights reserved

Printed in the United States of America

on acid-free paper ∞

Designed by Cherie H. Westmoreland

Typeset in Monotype Fournier

by Keystone Typesetting, Inc.

Library of Congress Cataloging-in-Publication

Data appear on the last printed

page of this book.

Honoring

the memory of

Crosby Hall

a room of one's own,

1926–1992

Contents

Acknowledgments

The editor of a collaborative project does not have far to seek for people to thank on the acknowledgments page. The other ten contributors to this collection have my most profound gratitude—especially Peter McCullough, whose antic e-mail correspondence made this work almost fun. Although their names don't appear in the table of contents, the following scholars offered help, advice, support, information, and intellectual energy, without which *Dissing Elizabeth* would never have come into existence: Pippa Berry, Susan Frye, Carol Thomas Neely, and Mary Beth Rose. The advice of my Geneseo colleagues, Laura Doan and Mary Ellen Zuckerman, was both shrewdly and patiently offered throughout the press-choosing phase of the project; Marie Henry offered heroic help in copyediting. At Duke, the constant support of Miriam Angress has been beyond praise, while the primary reader of the collection, Anne Lake Prescott, provided us with enormous(ly) kind criticism and helpful suggestions; her terrifyingly encyclopedic knowledge of all aspects of the Western canon was equalled only by her witty generosity.

Dedicating this collection to the memory of Crosby Hall seems an appropriate acknowledgment in a collaborative work on a powerful woman. Once the home of Richard III and then of Thomas More, Crosby Hall was owned from 1926 until 1992 by the British Federation of University Women. In this metamorphosis it sheltered and nourished many gifted, ambitious, and funny women as they pursued their varied scholarly interests in London libraries, archives, museums, and postgraduate programs. To walk around the corner of Beaufort Street and see the sweep of the Thames from Battersea Bridge down to the confection of the Albert Bridge, to turn through the iron gate off of Cheyne Walk, passing by the sentinel hollyhocks, under the flowering trees, across the shady turf, was to feel "home free" after a day spent sweltering in the North Library. During dinner in More's great hall, beneath the portraits of Winifred Cullin, Virginia Guildersleeve, and Caroline Spurgeon, we fed each other with the daily successes and setbacks in projects as varied as Pepys's letters, pre-Hellenic clay tablets, eye surgery, landscape gardening, and the tombs of Elizabeth I. Then, over weak coffee or fierce tea, we could listen to Rosemary Cowler—Crosby Hall's unofficial Head Girl—tell tales of past decades of scholarship and community, of oilcloth napkin holders and the pronouncements of Dulcie or Ted or Nesta, of the wicked Miss Willisch and of the #19 bus conductor who announced the Beaufort Street stop as: "Crosby 'All, the 'ome of brains an' beau'y."

Nostalgia aside, I never teach the passage on custard and prunes in Virginia Woolf's famous essay without thinking about Crosby Hall meals. Woolf's point, of course, is a culturally significant one, and I would not argue with its larger implications. But I must wonder: if Woolf had actually been part of an impoverished academic community, might she not have felt that the brave persistence of brains and wit rising above dubious mutton and soggy sprouts has more to recommend it than all the port and partridges in the world? True, we can regret the necessity for such bravery, but for most of the women who stayed at Crosby Hall, the academic world required so many more exacting braveries, that the metaphor of food—however powerful—served as comic relief. Rosemary Cowler, Nancy Struever, Barbara Stafford, Claudia Leach, Arlene Jackson, Enid Fuhr, Jane Hubben, Mary Power, Noretta Koertge, Rosemary Welsh, Susan Ferrall Bailey, Jill Cassid, Pamela Walker, and all the other women who shared adventures and ideas across those long tables have given the old stones of Crosby Hall a new historical significance: there, if for too brief a time, a woman could find both community and a room of her own.

J. M. W.

Introduction

The Dark Side of the Cult of Elizabeth

Gloriana, the Virgin Queen, Astraea, Cynthia, Belphoebe, Elissa, "Eliza Queen of Shepherds all," good Queen Bess—the glowing epithets cast their light down the centuries and fill thousands of pages of scholarship devoted to the greatness of Elizabeth Tudor and to the glories of her reign. Not one of the scholars whose essays appear in this collection would question that greatness or diminish those glories. What we seek to illuminate, however, is another, darker discourse, the less famous discourse of disrespect and dissent which also existed from Elizabeth's troubled days as a princess and into the decades after her death. In the 1603 Rainbow portrait, that representation of youthful power painted even as Elizabeth was a dying old woman, the motto reads "non sine sole iris": no rainbow without the sun. This is unquestionably true; there can be no rainbow without the sun, and in that picture the queen is unquestionably the source of light. But where there is sun, there is also shadow. The famous anecdote of Elizabeth hearing a painter explain the techniques of chiaroscuro, then insisting that she be painted in full sunlight in a garden speaks to the queen's own realization that shadows could be dangerous. In these essays we will recover—from the shadows of contemporary documents and artifacts—the contrasting rhetoric of dissent, criticism, and disrespect which permeated all aspects of Elizabeth's life, reign, and posthumous representation.

When I was calling around among Elizabeth scholars, trying to fill in what I perceived as holes in this table of contents, I encountered several versions of the startled response of one scholar whose work on the Tudor court I admired: "Oh!" he exclaimed after I thought I had explained the project to him, "I really wouldn't want to say anything BAD about Elizabeth." This response speaks to two important and easily misunderstood points about the topic and this collection. Elizabeth's perennial popularity—due in part to her undoubted accomplishments and virtues and also growing from her status as a cultural anomaly—has always cast her in an unrealistically golden light; indeed, the tacit assumption in both popular and scholarly studies of the queen was that it was both inappropriate and in distinctly bad taste to speak (very) ill of one who forged such a glorious legend in the face of such great odds. This general feeling survived in scholarly work until the 1980s, in part because there is such a massive amount of positive material to examine in domestic and foreign policy, diplomacy, literary patronage, as well as the still palpable power of that singular personality. While few writers have gone so far as to present a perfect queen, there has always been the assumption that criticism of her was somehow particularly mean-spirited—too simply the product of medieval misogyny or blind religious prejudice.

Certainly that is true of some anti-Elizabeth propaganda. But even here, what we have lost sight of is the cultural context from which such critiques arose. Seldom did any critic of the queen set out simply to "say anything BAD" about her. The critical discourse almost always had a larger point, a cultural and political agenda which dwarfed the individual, even so massive an individual as the globe-straddling Elizabeth of the Ditchley portrait. The most obvious example of this is Catholic discourse on the queen. However sweepingly general, gratuitously nasty, or spitefully specific the rhetoric to and about the queen on the subject of religion became, there was at its heart a fundamental doctrinal and political debate which shook all of early modern Europe, and which indeed still continues today. For this reason we have not included examples of simply or exclusively Catholic rhetoric to and about Elizabeth, turning our attention instead to less canonical sources of criticism and to texts which have been seen as uncritical of the queen, but which need reevaluation.

By using the slang term *dissing* for *disrespect,* I hope to convey two ideas: these negative representations of Elizabeth were often deliberately outrageous and provocative, and even the more subtle forms of criticism drew energy from the existence of the more overt and vulgar documents and artifacts. My second reason for using the term, however, is to mark the collection itself as somewhat at odds with established Elizabeth scholarship. Certainly the opposition to the queen has been discussed in relation to particular issues such as her marriage negotiations, her refusal to name an heir, her favorites, and her religion. What we are doing, however, is to challenge the perception of these moments of opposition as isolated among Protestants or limited to Catholics, and to present them in the dark side of the Cult of Elizabeth, a minority discourse which, although its sources shift continually, was a constant element of the life, reign, and memory of this powerful, successful, and generally popular monarch. The essays in this collection open discussion on neglected texts, lost cultural artifacts, overlooked patterns of discourse, and buried facts— literally buried, as is Elizabeth's body, which was removed to a grave she did not choose and marked by a tomb she did not authorize. This discussion in turn generates a reevaluation of Elizabethan and Jacobean protocols of representation, an examination which will not be limited to the traditionally recognized strategies of praise but which will consider the neglected or unrecognized voices of dissent and disrespect as part of the literary, historical, architectural, and artistic cultural phenomenon of Elizabeth I.

If Elizabeth and her reign have become a canonical subject in the fields of history, literature, and art history, the canonical secondary texts in Elizabethan studies are those of Roy Strong and Frances A. Yates and the history of J. E. Neale. In the last fifteen years it has become fashionable to speak slightingly of these scholarly works, but I think it is important to acknowledge the debt that all scholars in the field owe to Strong and Yates. If we find their analyses of Elizabethan court culture limited to the more positive aspects of public ceremony, we must also recognize that this was their deliberate focus. Looking back at the paradigms of sentimental mythology alternating with venomous misogyny dominating pre-twentieth-century studies of Elizabeth and her reign, we can see that Strong and Yates are relatively stringent in their attempts to document and specifically describe many of the elements that made Gloriana's court spectacular. To call a book *The Cult of Elizabeth* is to set forth a specific topic and thesis; Strong never makes the sweeping claims for a thoroughgoing cultural evaluation attributed to him by many recent scholars.

This is not to say that it is unnatural that many new historicist scholars perceived themselves as being in a paradigm of opposition with the works of Strong and Yates and Neale. When the work of scholars such as Philippa Berry, Louis Adrian Montrose, Leah Marcus, Jonathan Goldberg, Joel Fineman, and Carole Levin began to come out in the 1980s, much of the immediate reaction of the scholarly community was that their insights about Elizabeth's reign constituted simple opposition to Strong and Yates and to Neale's hagiographic history, because these newer scholars were trying to move our eyes off of the fascinating glitter of the spectacle of Elizabethan England and to turn our attention to some of the pragmatic politics and cultural dissonances which also existed in that period. Rather than simple opposition, the historicist scholars were setting up a wider field of study, sometimes in the form of a more complex evaluation of a portrait or icon described by Strong or Yates, and sometimes by suggesting that many aspects of Elizabeth's reign had been slighted, ignored, or simply left outside the parameters set by those earlier scholars. A good example of this is Constance Jordan's analysis of the Siena Sieve portrait, an analysis which goes much further than, but which does not contradict, the work of Strong and Yates on the portrait. Other scholars find themselves in legitimate disagreement with the earlier studies, either in matters of interpretation or because of more thorough archival research, but the element of opposition in the 1980s was more one of perception than of prescription.

What concerns me is that this natural evolution of scholarship—which, like the natural evolution of power dynamics in a family, can sometimes manifest itself as conflict and opposition—has been unnecessarily exaggerated; the artificial construction of seeming oppositions has come to be mistaken for critical analysis. When I recently asked a young British scholar about her work on Elizabeth, she began by saying triumphantly: "It's very anti-Yatesian." Well that didn't tell me much, at least not much about her work. Similarly I was taken aback by the assertions of Helen Hackett in her 1995 book, explaining that she was going to surpass the limitations of Strong and Yates in their analyses of the relationship between the Cult of the Virgin and the Cult of Elizabeth, but that she was going to do so by concentrating on the "literary evidence" of that misinterpreted conflation. Strong and Yates, as we all know, used the visual arts and records of spectacle at least as much, if not more, than they used literature to support their insights. Again, the element of academic opposition seems to obscure, or at least to cloud, the readers'—and in these cases, perhaps the scholars'—view of the real scholarly undertaking.

Some of the blame for such artificial opposition, for scholarly factionalism, must surely lie at the generic feet of introductory rhetoric. As I write this, I am all too aware of the need to define one's project, and I am aware that perhaps the easiest way to do so is to foreground the ways in which that project differs from the work that is already out there. (While pointing out the pit, I do hope I haven't fallen in.) Although many of the scholars in this collection differ quite emphatically with existing work on Elizabeth I, none of the essays is a simple rebuttal of any one view or set of views. All that separates this volume from other historicist studies of the age of Elizabeth is that we have focused on the body of material critical of the queen before, during, and after her reign. Some contributors follow a specific topic through a decade or several decades of that reign. Susan Doran's answer to the question "why did the queen not marry?" spans much of Elizabeth's adult life, and suggests that the answer might lie less in the desires of the queen herself than in the powers of her various advisors. The question of what constituted seditious language in Elizabeth's reign as opposed to the reign of her father is explored by Carole Levin, while Marcy North offers a reading of a private document, Henry Stanford's anthology, a collection of decades of language seditious by any monarch's standards. The set-piece of Christopher Highley's two-decade discussion of anti-Elizabeth discourse in Ireland is an analysis of the ritual destruction of a statue of the queen by the rebel chieftain of Connaught, Sir Brian O'Rourke, and his followers in 1586. The incident foregrounds the complex act of ventriloquism whereby the representatives of the dominant, literary, humanistic culture record the acts of a subordinate, largely oral culture. The ephemeral nature of spoken disrespect is also at the heart of Sheila Cavanagh's argument about the harm done to the reputation of the Princess Elizabeth through gossip about the Seymour incident. Both Highley and Cavanagh confront the scholarly problem of studying language and actions which, by their very nature, have gone essentially unrecorded. From the amorphous non-text of gossip to the very specific text of John Stubbs's *Gaping Gulf* we find many common elements of negative discourse, as Ilona Bell points out in her close reading of the pamphlet which cost its author his right hand. In a fascinating position between the spoken and the written opinion we find the Renaissance sermon, and Peter McCullough's political contextualization of the sermon preached at Elizabeth after the execution of Mary Stuart illuminates many neglected aspects of both the genre and the particular occasion. Literary texts are the focus of essays by Hannah Betts—who suggests that the blazon in poetry from 1588 to 1603 often served as a pornographic representation of the queen's body—and Rob

Content, who links monstrous allusions to Elizabeth in Sidney's *Old Arcadia* to a 1590s cartoon conflating the queen and a giant, unnatural bird of prey. As the work of Montrose, Marcus, and others has elsewhere addressed many of the negative representations of the queen in the work of that most canonical Renaissance writer, Shakespeare, Mary Villeponteaux turns instead to Spenser, who has been considered a canonical supporter of Elizabeth. Villeponteaux unravels the nexus of Elizabeth-figures in book 5 of the *Faerie Queene,* arguing that the rule-usurping Amazon Radigund, not the more positive Britomart, is the primary representation of the political reality of Elizabeth. My own essay follows the dissing of Elizabeth beyond the grave, if not the tomb, comparing the revised tomb in which James marginalized his predecessor with the loving memorials to the late queen in London parish churches; a print and a portrait of the queen from the 1620s exemplify this opposition between discreet royal dissing and populist praise.

In the last two years, as the fruits of historicist scholarship have nourished a new generation of Elizabeth scholars, four book-length studies of Elizabeth I and a collection on the last years of her reign have been published, marking the upsurge of scholarly interest in the queen further represented by critical essays and conference papers too numerous to mention. This collection is both a part of the historicist interest in representations of Elizabeth and a new forum in the rising debate. Existing studies which do mention negative representations of Elizabeth either contextualize the antagonistic references within the more canonical body of praise or treat in detail one isolated example—such as the ambassador's description of the aging queen's habits of dress—as being a product of a particular political agenda rather than as a constant of cultural, social, and political dissent.

In this collection we examine the dissing of the queen over an eighty-year period, from the late 1540s before she came to the throne, continuing after her death, through the 1620s. Ranging over foreign and domestic political issues, religious factionalism, the conflict between free speech and treason, gossip, sermons, art history, architecture, and the literary modes of epic, drama, and lyric, the topics of these essays offer a rich variety of scholarly discussion; the breadth of material here is itself a comment upon the fundamental nature of the cultural disruption generated by the long and well-established rule of a monarch who was also a woman.

History

and

Policy

The Bad Seed

Princess Elizabeth and the Seymour Incident

Sheila Cavanagh

For Elizabeth Tudor, youth cannot have been easy. Always something of a disappointment because of her sex, Elizabeth careened between legitimacy and the precarious disgrace of bastardy, always with an uncertain place in the line of succession. Throughout each of the reigns falling between her birth and eventual accession to the throne, Elizabeth remained vulnerable to a seemingly infinite assortment of competing interests holding considerable influence over her personal and political fates. As a consequence, the status of her title, her household, and her future were continually subject to unpredictable and uncontrollable external forces. Determining whom she could trust and where she should ally herself undoubtedly consumed much of the young woman's attentions.

During this phase of her life, rumors about Elizabeth's behavior and opinions were rampant. The widespread uneasiness about the precarious state of the royal succession—which was enhanced by Edward VI's minority and by the female-dominated pool of candidates who might follow him to the throne[1]—ensured that the most likely future monarchs would be subject to considerable scrutiny and speculation. Furthermore, Elizabeth's lineage and personal history were far from straightforward; therefore, it is not surprising that she would be watched closely and discussed widely. Since the Tudor princess's place in the succession fluctuated even during her father's lifetime, she would never have been able to presume unequivocally that it would be honored after his death. In this climate, there was little room for skepticism about her political intentions, her private allegiances, or her virtue. Consequently, as she matured, her life inevitably generated numerous narratives, based both upon perceived facts and upon speculation, as those in power—or wanting to be—kept a close watch on the politics of succession.

One of the most complex, and most telling, stories which circulated about the young princess concerned her relationship with Thomas Seymour, husband to her father's widow Catherine Parr and brother to the wife Henry married immediately after Elizabeth's mother was executed. The ill-fated Seymour engaged in suspiciously familiar activity with the princess during his wife's lifetime and reportedly sought Elizabeth as a marital partner after Parr's death. Rumors of Seymour's ambitions and transgressions in both these regards were widely circulated;[2] even the young princess admitted to knowing of his marital quest in the testimony she offered after Lord Admiral Seymour's arrest.[3] Here, she acknowledged that her governess, Katherine Ashley, had informed her of Seymour's purported intentions in this arena, and had also insinuated that Seymour saw Elizabeth as an attractive marriage possibility even before his marriage to Catherine Parr:

Kat. Aschlylye tolde me, after that my Lord Admiralde was maried to the Quene, that if my Lorde might haue his owne Wil, he wolde haue had me, afore the Quene. Than I asked her how she knewe that: Than she sayd, she knewe it wel inought, bothe by himselfe and by others. The Place, wher she said this, I haue forgotten, for she hathe spoken to me of him manye Times, and of the wiche I have forgotten divers Times.[4]

Although Elizabeth knew that any hint of her own participation in marital discussions could create political turmoil for her, she did not attempt to hide her awareness of such talk after her servants testified. Presumably, the incidents were so well known that there was little to be gained by attempts at concealment.

Lord Admiral Thomas Seymour played the central role in these tales and in the scandal that accompanied them. For the most part, his execution represented the culmination of official concern about a number of his schemes and plots, including his apparently manipulative and personally ambitious relationships with Edward VI and with Lady Jane Grey.[5] Here, Seymour again focused, at least in part, on marital possibilities and his own related gain, as he attempted to engineer a match between these two. Seymour's effrontery, as we know, ended in death, and Elizabeth's involvement with Seymour constituted only one aspect of the complex saga leading to the lord admiral's 1549 imprisonment and execution on accusations of treason. The charges which led the government, including Seymour's brother, the lord protector, to decide upon death, were many and varied.[6] From the perspective of those seeking to stop Thomas

Seymour's impetuous interference in political affairs, the domestic episode with Elizabeth was only one of many transgressions.

For Elizabeth, on the other hand, Seymour's risks, ambitions, and punishment presumably were secondary. From her perspective, official responses to the incident also demonstrated her vulnerability to stories linking her to transgressions previously attributed to her parents—most particularly to her mother. In addition, the episode bringing Seymour into questionable alignment with the princess underscores the overdetermined role played by narrative in the ongoing shaping of Elizabeth's existence and status. Reluctant depositions combined with plausible and exaggerated rumors kept the young princess in a precarious position, particularly since the stories told by members of Elizabeth's household were considered unreliable. Although she emerged unharmed and even managed to arrange the return of her implicated household staff, the potential danger to Elizabeth was very real. Despite Seymour's central role as target of the investigation, the intense questioning of the princess and her household suggests that Elizabeth's exoneration was not assumed.[7] If complicity with Seymour could be proved, the princess's future might well have been compromised, particularly since the succession was often treated as though it were fluid, despite Henry VIII's instructions to the contrary.[8] While there is no direct evidence to confirm a conspiracy against Elizabeth, the focus placed upon her and her household demonstrates that the government felt sufficient concern to warrant a close investigation in this instance of the young woman's character, political beliefs, and behavior.

The questionable contact between the princess and the lord admiral occurred while Elizabeth was resident in the household of her father's widow. Catherine Parr married Thomas Seymour only a few months after the death of Henry VIII, concluding a match which seems to have been derailed some years previously when the formidable monarch began to show interest in the woman who became his final wife.[9] Elizabeth lived with her stepmother in 1547, while her brother Edward was on the throne. From all accounts, she passed her time there in relative amity until the attentions of Thomas Seymour toward the young girl became excessively familiar.

The scandalous episode that followed emerged from official and domestic responses to a range of anecdotes produced about the potentially compromising relationship between the lord admiral and the young princess. Whether formalized as depositions or circulated privately, these tales became the "evidence" which contributed to the defeat of the ambitious Seymour and which threatened also to bring down Elizabeth. The numerous renditions that have followed in subsequent centuries demonstrate the continuing lure of the tale, with its implications of sexual intrigue and incest, particularly when seen retrospectively in relationship to the "virgin" queen.

The stories, familiar to us through countless renditions in novels and scholarship, certainly contain ample information to give one pause over the intentions and conduct of those involved, even if the stories are only partially true, and even if Frederick Chamberlin overstated the case in his 1922 account: "In the Seymour Affair, fate made Elizabeth the leading character in one of the most daring intrigues ever recorded."[10] According to the depositions provided by Katherine [Kat] Ashley, a longtime member of Elizabeth's household, Seymour regularly appeared in the princess's chamber, dressed in his nightshirt, while the young woman was still in bed. Such familiarity apparently characterized their interactions, to the extent that even a supporter such as Ashley, who later apparently favored the pair's marriage,[11] protested to Lord Admiral Seymour that his behavior toward Elizabeth was unseemly. According to Ashley's testimony, the chamber frolicking between Seymour and the princess either approached too near or crossed the line of decency. Since Ashley was such a strong supporter of the two, it is even possible that she altered and shaped her version in order to put everyone involved in a better light—a likely scenario since she was initially reluctant to testify at all. Although the intentions of those involved cannot be discerned, it seems incontrovertible that there was excessive informality between the pair.

According to Ashley's account, Seymour's unseemly conduct occurred regularly:

After he was maried to the Queene, he wold come many Mornyngs into the said Lady *Elizabeth*'s Chamber, before she were redy, and sometyme before she did rise. And if she were up, he wold bid hir good Morrow, an ax how she did, and strike hir upon the Bak or on the Buttockes famylearly, and so go forth through his Lodgings. . . . And if she were in hir Bed, he wold put open the Curteyns, and bid hir good Morrow, and make as though he wold come at hir: And she wold go further in the Bed, so that he could not come at hir.

And one Mornyng he strave to have kissed hir in hir Bed: and this Examinate was there, and bad hym go away for shame.[12]

Ashley's stories were repeated, corroborated, and expanded upon by other household witnesses. Thomas Parry, Elizabeth's cofferer, for example, gave detailed testimony about events that he either witnessed or heard about which involved the princess and the lord admiral. As part of his tale, he recounted an incident he heard described by Mrs. Ashley:

I do remember also, she [Ashley] told me, that the Admirall loved her but to well, and hadd so done a good while; and that the Quene was jelowse on hir and him, in so moche that, one Tyme the Quene, suspecting the often Accesse of the Admiral to the Lady *Elizabeth*'s Grace, cam sodenly upon them, wher they were all alone, (*he having her in his Armes:*) wherfore the Quene fell out, both with the Lord Admiral and with her Grace also.[13]

According to Parry and others, this incident led Catherine Parr to expel the young princess from the household—an event which cannot have helped Elizabeth's cause when she and her servants were under investigation.

Related stories were told by members of the lord admiral's household. In his testimony, for instance, Seymour's servant Wyghtman discussed the admonitions of Nicholas Throckmorton, who urged Wyghtman to dissuade the lord admiral from any thoughts of a match with Elizabeth. Wyghtman's deposition details this conversation:

[Throckmorton said] My Lorde is thought to be a verye ambitious Man of Honour; and it maye so happen that, nowe that the Quene is goene, he woold be desyrous for his Advauncement to match with oone of the King's Sisters; but in anye wyse in the World, as youe loue him and bear him your good Hearte, if euer youe heare any thing sounding that Waye, worke all that youe canne possiblye to stopp that Intent.[14]

All of the testimony offered from members of both households makes it clear that everyone involved knew that there were rumors of improprieties between Seymour and Elizabeth while Catherine Parr was still alive. They had also all been involved in conversations after Seymour had been widowed where the possibility of marriage between the lord admiral and the princess had been discussed. Consequently, the interrogators received significant corroboration for their suspicions that something improper had probably occurred. At the same time, however, none of those questioned gave any indication that Elizabeth had behaved treasonously. The examiners received no hard evidence that the princess had encouraged any marital negotiations. Nor did they hear anything substantive to suggest that she had encouraged Seymour in his attentions. Nevertheless, Sir Robert Tyrwhit appears to have believed in her complicity, writing to the lord protector, "I do se yt in her Face that she ys guylte."[15]

Despite such suspicions, Elizabeth expressed extreme reluctance in admitting her preferences in the matter of her marriage, even when the questioner asked her to presume the approval of the King's Council. In her interrogation with Tyrwhit, for instance, she demurred from answering such questions directly: "[He] asked me, wether if the Counsel did consente that I shulde have my Lord Admiral, wether I wolde consente to it or no: I answered that I wolde not tel him what my Minde was."[16] Similarly, in her account of discussions with Kat Ashley, she maintains that they never discussed a match which would violate her obligation to the King's Council: "And as concerning Kat. Aschilye, she never avised me unto it, but said alwais (whan any talked of my Marriage) that she wolde ever have me marry, nether in Inglande nor out of Inglande, without the Consent of the Kinge's Majestie, your Grace's and the Counsels."[17]

Throughout her depositions and correspondence, Elizabeth calmly denies wrongdoing on the part of herself or of her staff, saving her vehemence to express outrage against those rumors which she deemed especially scurrilous, particularly those which claimed that she was pregnant:

Master Tirwit and others haue tolde me that ther goeth rumers Abrode, wiche be greatly both agenste my Honor, and Honestie, (wiche above al other thinges I estime) wiche be these; that I am in the Tower; and with Childe by my Lord Admiral. My Lord these ar shameful Schandlers, for the wiche, besides the great Desire I have to see the Kinge's Majestie, I shall most hartely desire your Lordship that I may come to the Court after your first Determination; that I may shewe my selfe there as I am.[18]

Clearly, Elizabeth was most disturbed by the suggestion that she had compromised her honor to such a degree that she was carrying an illegitimate child. When the charges moved from the realm of rumor into the domain of verifiable physical fact, her outrage against them increased. She would obviously realize that this accusation carried the most serious threat against her; she presumably also recognized that she could personally offer proof of this story's falsity, something she could not provide so unequivocally in the case of the other rumors.[19]

At the same time, Elizabeth's response to the stories of her pregnancy also illustrates how she was able to use this unfortunate episode to hone her growing political skills. While the young girl was unable to avoid being implicated in the scandal, she clearly learned some valuable lessons during this incident. At the peak of the crisis, for instance—in February and March of 1549—she wrote to the lord protector, sending letters that expressed contrition and that offered her suggestions for handling the situation.[20] Undoubtedly recognizing that she needed the support of the lord protector and of the King's Council in order to escape significant political or personal harm, she prefaced her requests with markedly conciliatory comments: "I was sorye that ther shulde be anye suche [rumors] aboute me, was bicause that I thogth the people wil say that I deserved throwgth my lewde demenure to have such a one, and not that I mislike any thinge that your Lordeshipe or the Counsel shal thinke good, for I knowe that you and the Counsel ar charged with me; or that I tak upon me to rule my selfe."[21] Similarly, her petition asking that the lord protector intervene on her behalf to help stop the stories being spread about her strikes a tone of humility:

But if it mough so seme good unto your Lordeshipe and the rest of the Counsel to sende forthe a proclamation in to the countries that the[y] refrane their tonges, declaring how the tales be but lies, it shulde make bothe the people thinke that You and the Counsel have great regarde that no such rumors shulde be spread of anye of the Kinges Maiesties Sisters, as I am, thougth vnwordie, and also I shulde thinke myselfe to receve such frendeshipe at your hands as you have promised me, althogth your Lordeship hathe shewed me greate alreadie.[22]

Although Elizabeth was often quite abrupt in her communications during this affair,[23] the demeanor she presents both here and in her insistent assurances that she is concealing nothing from her questioners[24] illustrates her maturing recognition that diplomacy could provide her with the best opportunity for a graceful exit from the scandal surrounding her. In notable contrast to Thomas Seymour, whose brash style helped condemn him, Elizabeth here demonstrates her increasing awareness of the power of modest expression.[25]

Furthermore, the political lessons she learned from this incident clearly stayed with her, as a similarly contrite letter she sent to Queen Mary in 1553 indicates. Here, she quotes the lord protector's dismay at his brother's handling of his affairs as part of her plea not to be sent to the Tower as Mary had ordered:

> I have heard of many, in my time, cast away for want of coming to the presence of their Prince; and, in late days, I heard my Lord of Somerset say that 'If his brother had been suffered to speak with him, he had never suffered'. . . . Therefore, once again, kneeling with humbleness of heart, because I am not suffered to bow the knees of my body; I humbly crave to speak with your Highness.[26]

Although historical records do not indicate what private lessons Elizabeth may have gained from her involvement in Thomas Seymour's downfall, her reference here to the lord admiral's failings suggests that the incident remained a cautionary tale for her for some years. The force of these events, compounded by her apparently strong emotional involvement with Seymour, seemed to have a considerable impact upon her.

Thus the episode clearly provided Elizabeth with numerous important lessons, although she apparently did not suffer long-term political consequences. Ultimately, while her interactions with the lord admiral brought both her chastity and her judgment into question, Elizabeth was not found legally culpable for her role in this household drama. Whispers about her reputed pregnancy lost their intensity. Nevertheless, since rumor alone could be sufficient to shake her security under the right circumstances, the princess remained vulnerable to her interrogators' accusations and conclusions—and to the judgment of future generations.

As indicated above, when the behavior between Seymour and Elizabeth began to cross the line into scandal, Catherine sent Elizabeth away from the household. Notably, she nevertheless stayed on friendly terms with her from a distance. From our vantage point, it is impossible to determine exactly what happened and how those involved interpreted these events privately, but given the continued friendship between Elizabeth and Catherine, it seems probable that the injured wife did not hold her stepdaughter culpable for any improprieties. The openly opportunistic Seymour may well have carried the brunt of whatever anger or blame these episodes provoked in the household where they occurred.[27]

However any contemporary or modern individual might respond to the alleged involvement, from the perspective of the state in the late 1540s Elizabeth's reputed personal entanglement with Seymour, both before and after Parr's death, could not be dismissed readily. Regardless of whether Elizabeth was ever to become queen, her anticipated eventual marriage carried significant repercussions for the realm. Just as an illicit sexual liaison could not be tolerated politically, an unsanctioned marriage or even private marital negotiations would be unacceptable, and in fact were legally forbidden. Accordingly, when rumors of improprieties between Elizabeth and Seymour became known, the state inevitably became involved, as indicated above. Predictably, both the progress of the proceedings and the eventual outcome of the case revolved around the state's response to a series of narrative events, which incorporated Elizabeth's most vulnerable attributes: her family, her virginity, and her sex. The Seymour story sent reverberations throughout the princess's domestic and political spheres, with its suggestions of incest, adultery, and household complicity. Parr's concurrent pregnancy undoubtedly further intensified matters. Since Elizabeth's disputed legitimacy always carried implicit threats against her claim to the throne, these accusations of sexual and familial impropriety held the potential to block her eventual inheritance. If Elizabeth could be identified as a "bad seed," whose behavior was modeled after those presumed failings of her mother which had threatened the kingdom, an alternate line of succession might prevail.[28] A nonvirgin princess, compromised by the husband of her pregnant, then recently deceased, stepmother, might never rule. Though it is far from clear that those questioning Elizabeth were seeking such an end actively, they had ample justification for close scrutiny of the young woman.

For our purposes here, the malleability of accounts offered by Ashley and others, the goals and coercive tactics of the interrogators in this case, and the veracity and reliability of the documents which have come down to us are key points to consider in sorting through the layers of narrative comprising the event. Since neither "ocular proof" nor definitive information about the actions and intentions of those involved was recuperable even at the time, the disposition of the case was inexorably decided in large part by the "spin" placed on the available stories. Inevitably, as the players and their tales sorted themselves out, Elizabeth remained situated on precarious ground.

Given the anxious complexity which characterized the succession question throughout the Tudor era, Elizabeth's particular points of vulnerability during the Seymour scandal were both predictable and unavoidable. Being accused of this brand of familiarity with any man would have been dangerous for the princess, but Seymour's entangled familial tie to the royal teenager broadened the range of possible repercussions awaiting her. The dual specter of adultery and incest already haunted her since birth. As Marc Shell notes, the broad concept of "carnal contagion," which was interpreted with varying degrees of liberality at the time, repeatedly complicated Elizabeth's claim to be the legitimate offspring of Henry VIII: "The argument that the siblings of a sexual mate become one's own sibling tended to make Elizabeth both legitimate by nullifying Catherine's marriage with Henry, and illegitimate by nullifying Anne's marriage with Henry."[29] Henry and others alternately tried to justify the contracting, then the dissolving of his various marital bonds based on shifting interpretations of consanguinity and incest. His marriage with Catherine of Aragon, for example, was initially presented as being encouraged by God's law, then determined to be in opposition to it.[30] Similarly, the king's marriage to Anne Boleyn was transformed from sanctioned into invalid in part by accusing Elizabeth's mother of adultery with her own brother, a charge which, like those leveled later against the princess, offered malleable and suspect testimony in the guise of evidence.[31] In addition, Elizabeth's bastardy was initially reversed inadvertently as part of Henry's maneuvers to marry Anne Boleyn's cousin Catherine Howard. In Bruce Boehrer's presentation of what he terms the "erratic splendor" of the "major" succession acts, the dizzying changes governing Elizabeth's legal status become clear. Boehrer discusses the Succession Acts of 1534, 1536, and 1543, as well as a 1540 statute and Henry's putative last will and testament. As one moves through them chronologically, Henry's marriage to Anne shifts from being deemed "undoubtful, true, [and] sincere" to being reduced to annulment. Similarly, Elizabeth is at varying times officially part of the succession, disinherited, accidentally restored to legitimacy, and legally reinstated to a place in line to the throne.[32]

Seymour's position with regard to Elizabeth within the maze of early modern conceptions of consanguinity staggers the imagination. Brother of one stepmother, husband of another, and uncle of Elizabeth's brother, Thomas Seymour faced numerous consanguinial obstacles barring his way to the unmarried princess. Even before any directly political liabilities could be factored in, Seymour's ambitious plan to join with Elizabeth faced several insurmountable genealogical barriers. The accusations of sexual impropriety with the stepdaughter of his pregnant wife merely accentuated his already untenable circumstances. The likelihood of the King's Council ever approving an alliance between this politically and familially dissonant pair remained negligible, however Seymour might have deluded himself. Although Seymour had been able to secure the young king's support for his secretive marriage with Catherine Parr,[33] he could have no reasonable hope of obtaining the further sanctioning of a subsequent marital alliance with the young princess.

Elizabeth's uneasy situation was intensified by the tenuous quality of evidence which was available to court circles and to those holding legal authority over her. Scanty documentation has survived, and it is unlikely that anything definitive could have existed, apart from the testimony and letters offered or coerced from some of those connected with the scandal. Despite the political ramifications associated with the events in question, their placement within the domestic sphere made it difficult to substantiate any of the incidents or conversations unequivocally. Consequently, there was considerable room available for everyone involved in the household or with the state to manipulate (successfully or not) evidence. Inevitably, the testimony from witnesses such as Kat Ashley, who remained loyal to Elizabeth—but who was facing the wrath of those who imprisoned Seymour due to her supposed role in the questionable activities—was shaped as much or more by domestic and political contingency as by accurate or reliable recollection. As Anne Boleyn had learned, however, dubious recollections could hold considerable legal weight under certain political circumstances.

The personal and political fates of those individuals caught up in the scandal would be largely determined by whose manipulation of narrative worked most successfully. Tyrwhit's suspicions about the stories he was hearing, for example, could easily lead him to discount any claims of the princess's innocence. Elizabeth's inevitable vulnerability in this regard was heightened by the history of sexual scandal attached to the memory of her executed mother, Anne Boleyn. Any young woman occupying Elizabeth's position in the line of succession would be at risk, but the sexual and legal precedents set by Elizabeth's forebears left her particularly ill-equipped to deflect the rumors of incest, adultery, and sexual indiscretion which accompanied the disclosure of Seymour's marital and seductive aspirations. If the stories that came out during the investigation of this affair showed Elizabeth to have inherited a tendency toward the type of sexual misconduct for which her mother ostensibly was beheaded, her subsequent place within the complex configuration of the succession could undergo significant realignment. Regardless of whether or not Anne Boleyn was guilty of the charges against her, she had been duly convicted and executed. Thus Elizabeth was the offspring of an officially condemned incestuous adulterer.[34] Furthermore, roughly contemporaneous physiological beliefs made it unequivocally clear that Elizabeth could easily have inherited her mother's lascivious temperament. As Laurent Joubert wrote in 1578: "It is already evil enough to be conceived by an evil woman and nourished on her blood for nine months in her belly. . . . It is good, therefore, to take them away from these evil mothers as soon as they are born and give them to good and kind nurses, healthy in body and mind, in order to blot out with a better sap the bad constitution imprinted in their bodies from the mothers' bad humors, which could cause similar behavior."[35] Not surprisingly, given the perceived link between parental health and temperament and the state of any offspring, marriage homilies cautioned the wise to give due weight to such qualities when choosing a marital partner, as Heinrich Bullinger illustrates in his 1547 *Christian State of Matrimony:* "Much more shuldest thou haue respect to the condityons of thy spouse, out of whome thou desyrest to plante chyldren. . . . And lyke as plantinge and carefulnesse hath greater power in all growynge thinges, so hath it greter vertue and strength, yea and better frute in the diligente bryngynge up of chyldren."[36] Henry's annulment and beheading of his second wife as well as his intermittent moves to bastardize his youngest daughter provided a legal declaration that he had not chosen this wife wisely or cautiously.

Accordingly, although Elizabeth held a confirmed space in the line of succession at the time of the Seymour incident, there was ample legal precedent for bringing her position under scrutiny. Her purported dalliance with Lord Admiral Seymour offered the perfect opportunity to look again at Elizabeth's personal and political behavior. Notably, even Thomas Seymour is said to have been uneasy about any reminders of Elizabeth's mother. In Thomas Parry's testimony, he reports this conversation with the lord admiral: "No, quoth he [Seymour], that shalbe when I am gon to *Boleyn;* and he said afterwards, no Words of *Boleyn*."[37] Furthermore, as Marc Shell speculates, it is at least conceivable that Elizabeth might have held her own fears about what she may have inherited from her mother: "But what about the adage 'Like mother, like daughter'? Did Elizabeth see, or fear to see, her mother in herself, as in a *glass?* Is that why she pointedly adopted as her own the badge of the sinful Anne Boleyn with its inscription *Semper Eadem*, 'Always the Same,' and retained it even after becoming queen?"[38] While we cannot know what Elizabeth believed or feared about any characterological inheritance from her mother, it seems likely that the princess and her contemporaries at least thought about the implications of this aspect of her background.

Regardless of anyone's qualms—however serious or slight—about the princess's parentage, the accounts that have been preserved of Seymour's involvement with Elizabeth were ripe both for manipulation and for a skeptical reception. The testimony was obtained over a year after the events occurred, predominantly from members of Elizabeth's and Seymour's households, whose own fates could be affected dramatically by the outcome of the proceedings. In addition, those residing with the princess displayed unwavering loyalty to their young charge. As a consequence, considerable pressure to implicate Elizabeth in treasonous activities or collusion was put upon both Ashley as well as upon Thomas Parry. They were imprisoned, questioned repeatedly, and scrutinized closely for errors or conflicting statements. For most of the proceedings, it seemed inevitable that they would never be returned to Elizabeth's household and their futures remained uncertain. Even so, Sir Robert Tyrwhit complained to the lord protector that he did not believe that his interrogation was yielding the truth. Despite the considerable intimidation that the questioners offered, Elizabeth and the browbeaten servants offered Tyrwhit stories which he believed were too similar to be accurate: "I do very beleve that ther hath beyn some secrett Promys, betwyne my Lady, Mestrys Aschlay, and the Cofferer, never to confesse to Deythe; and yf yt be so, yt wyll never be gottyne of her, but ether by the King's Magesty, or ells by yowr Grace."[39] His dissatisfaction with the responses he received prompted further coercion, which led to a more detailed, though inconclusive, narrative from Elizabeth's beleaguered governess. This in turn led to some elaboration from Elizabeth about her perception of the questionable activities, but the accumulated information still lacked sufficient substance with which to condemn Elizabeth easily.

Substance, of course, would not have been essential, if those in power had had specific plans to the contrary. The treason charges against Anne Boleyn, which led to her execution, had drawn their credibility in large part from the intensity of her husband's desire to be rid of her;[40] from the wanton reputation she acquired during her well-known premarital entanglement with Henry; and from rumors of witchcraft which may have been exacerbated by an extra finger on one hand.[41] There were also contemporary stories, which were later revived by anti-Elizabeth factions after the death of Mary Stuart, which claimed that Anne was Henry's daughter as well as his wife.[42] Furthermore, "in this version of her genealogy, Elizabeth is not even Henry's illegitimate, incestuous daughter; she is instead the incestuous daughter of Anne Boleyn by her brother George."[43] In combination with the various other charges of consanguinity which could be used against her,[44] such rumors, stories, and presumptions provided more than enough ammunition to defeat her. As E. W. Ives points out, the holes in the charges against Boleyn are glaring now, and could also have been apparent to an unprejudiced observer at the time, since "eleven of the twenty offences definitely could not have happened, since either Anne or the man involved was someplace else."[45] As Ives also notes, however: "Each allegation was protected by the catch-all addition, 'and on divers other days and places, before and after,' so that even if the specific charge was rebutted, the force of the indictment would remain."[46] In fact, any one of the charges or stories presented could have been twisted adequately to ruin her credibility and depose her as queen; together, they assured Henry of the freedom to move forward with his desired marriage to Jane Seymour.

Elizabeth potentially faced a similar peril, although it is impossible now to ascertain how far her interrogators wished to take these charges and what fate they ideally foresaw for the princess. It seems most likely that they were using this opportunity to test Elizabeth's character and political positioning rather than taking advantage of the Seymour incident in order to fulfill already conceived plans against the princess. Nevertheless, political contingency and the needs of those in power clearly carried far more weight in this matter than Elizabeth's actual activities or intentions concerning Seymour. Since it remained a serious offense for the king's sister to involve herself actively in marital discussions without the consent of the King's Council, this arena of Elizabeth's life provided a volatile space for speculation, concern, and political maneuvering. As a princess with a shady genealogy, Elizabeth was a prime target for a precipitous downfall, if the narrative evidence or its interpretation turned against her.[47]

From this historical distance, the stories appear to be very odd, and probably seemed unusual at the time. Given the political and personal status of the persons involved, the anecdotes relate interactions which are particularly peculiar. This is especially true for the story which tells of Seymour—with Catherine Parr's assistance—slashing Elizabeth's dress, to ribbons: "An other Tyme at *Hanworth,* in the Garden, he wrated with her, and cut hir Gown in an hundred Pieces, beying black cloth; and when she came up, this Examinant chid with hir; and her Grace answerid, She could not do with all, for the Quene held hir, while the Lord Admiral cut it."[48] It is hard to comprehend such a scene, whether or not one puts an innocent interpretation upon it. The story raises numerous interpretive questions, not the least of which concerns the lack of common sense in evidence among the adults in the household. Since Seymour's execution resulted at least partially from his frequent displays of poor judgment in numerous arenas, we might not expect anything different from him, but the apparent complicity here of his wife, the queen, defies understanding, just as Elizabeth's and Kat Ashley's responses leave much room for speculation.

Any interpretation a modern observer might draw obviously results from the sketchiest of information. We do not know how accurate the historical record is; we cannot know exactly what happened; and we have no access to the thoughts and motivations of those who participated. Clearly, any conclusions we can derive remain highly speculative. It is not apparent, however, that those holding power over Elizabeth, Seymour, and the others had much more solid information to go on.

Eventually, Thomas Seymour was executed for treason and Elizabeth suffered no apparent further official harassment because of her poor judgment during her sojourn in Catherine Parr's household. She even successfully lobbied for the return of her household staff, purportedly claiming that "Mestrys *Aschlay* was her Mestrys, and that she had not so demened her selffe, that the Counsell shuld now nede to put eny mo Mestressys unto her."[49] This conclusion seems to confirm that Thomas Seymour was the main target of the investigation and that Elizabeth finally was either deemed not complicit or that the state officials had decided that there was not sufficient profit likely to warrant her further disgrace. Since Elizabeth was a Protestant heir during the reign of a Protestant monarch, it is possible that her religious affiliation made her place in the succession too valuable to jeopardize. In addition, the evidence available against her finally may have lacked sufficient weight to condemn her in the absence of other compelling state reasons to do so. In all likelihood, Seymour's condemnation was considered ample reward for the investigation and there was enough political motivation available to allow the dismissal of Elizabeth's actions as the unwise response of an infatuated teenager.

Nevertheless, suppositions about what "actually" happened have continued to capture countless imaginations. When Gregorio Leti, for instance, wrote his dubious and salacious *Historia o vero vita di Elisabetta regina d'Inghilterra* in 1693, he provided supposed details of the scandal which were reported as factual by numerous subsequent writers over the following centuries. Many of his inventions have become part of the lore regularly repeated about Elizabeth, as Maria Perry notes: "If she [Elizabeth] had made the famous remark ascribed to her by many biographers, 'This day died a man of much wit and very little judgement,' it would have been a wonderful epitaph and an even more wonderful testament to her sang-froid, but the source is the scurrilous seventeenth-century biographer, Grigorio Leti, a man of much invention."[50] Just as Anne Boleyn's story was corrupted during her life by the extensive, erroneous reports of Eustace Chapuys, the imperial ambassador to Henry VIII's court, Elizabeth's history was similarly at the mercy both of her contemporaries and of subsequent writers claiming to have the "true" story of her life and loves. The Seymour incident, with all its juicy tales of sex and incest, provided too rich a lode not to be mined for scandal. A nonvirginal princess, carrying on with her "father/uncle" provided a history which demanded embellishment and repetition.

We can only add to the speculation, of course, by pondering what the

impact of this early incident may have been upon Elizabeth's later decisions regarding love, sex, and marriage. Some connection is probable,
though it inevitably eludes our grasp. The Elizabeth who gave her name
to an age seems, in most respects, to be far removed from the princess who
gave rise to such a scandal. Nevertheless, the rumors begun here were
ready to be assimilated into the countless later stories of her sexual
profligacy, genital deformity, and illegitimate maternity. Then, as now,
the sexual misadventures of the royal family provided titillation for the
realm—and often, for the world.

Notes

I am very grateful to Carole Levin for her valuable comments on this essay and
for sharing her essay in this volume with me prior to publication. I would also like
to thank my husband, as well as Leila Taaffe, Amy Turner, and Jennifer Wolfe,
who made it possible for me to complete the revisions on this essay with their
help in caring for my newborn son.

1. Mortimer Levine, in *Tudor Dynastic Problems, 1460–1571* (New York:
Barnes and Noble Books, 1973), 84–87, among others, details some of the politics
surrounding the succession during this period.

2. G. R. Elton, *Reform and Reformation: England, 1509–1558* (Cambridge:
Harvard University Press, 1977). Elton, among others, places Seymour's marital
ambitions in the context of his numerous political transgressions (346). See also
D. E. Hoak, *The King's Council in the Reign of Edward VI* (Cambridge: Cambridge University Press, 1976), for a discussion of the complex political circumstances surrounding Seymour's death (231–41). John Foxe, *The Acts and Monuments of John Foxe* (New York: AMS Press, 1965), claims that Thomas Seymour
died in large part because Catherine Parr did not get along with the Duchess of
Somerset (6:283).

3. Even though Elizabeth admitted that she knew about Seymour's ambitions
regarding her, Camden claims that she was unaware of them: "It was objected
that he [Thomas Seymour] intended . . . to take the Lady Elizabeth the King's
Sister to Wife. All this she was utterly ignorant of" (William Camden, *The
History of the Most Renowned and Victorious Princess Elizabeth*, 4th ed. (London:
M. Flesher, 1688).

4. Samuel Haynes, *A Collection of State Papers relating to Affairs in the Reigns of*

King Henry VIII, King Edward VI, Queen Mary, and Queen Elizabeth (London, 1740–59), sig. Ddv.

5. See Levine, *Tudor Dynastic Problems*, 79. *The Calendar of the Manuscripts of the Most Hon. the Marquis of Salisbury* (London: Historical Manuscripts Commission, 1883) includes correspondence between Seymour and Grey's parents (55–56).

6. See *Acts of the Privy Council* (1547–1550), edited by John Roche Dasent (London, 1890), 236–38. William Seymour (a descendant) offers a summary of the charges in *Ordeal by Ambition: An English Family in the Shadow of the Tudors* (London: Sidgwick and Jackson, 1972), 236–38.

7. Anne Somerset, *Elizabeth I* (New York: Knopf, 1991), describes the coercive tactics employed by the interrogators (26–27).

8. Levine discusses some of the considerations surrounding efforts to adapt Henry VIII's succession wishes (*Tudor Dynastic Problems*, 88–91). For a related discussion, see John Guy, *Tudor England* (Oxford: Oxford University Press, 1988), 196–99.

9. See Elton, *Reform and Reformation*, 326, 334.

10. Frederick Chamberlin, *The Private Character of Queen Elizabeth* (New York: Dodd, Mead, 1922), 1. For others of the numerous popular accounts of Elizabeth's involvement with Seymour, see Elswyth Thane, *The Tudor Wench* (New York: Harcourt, Brace, 1932), 61–148; Agnes Strickland, *Memoirs of Elizabeth* (Philadelphia: Blanchard and Lea, 1853), 19–39; Elizabeth Jenkins, *Elizabeth the Great* (New York: Coward-McCann, 1958), 25–33; Piers Compton, *Bad Queen Bess* (London: Alex Ouseley, 1933), 30–36; Jennette and Francis Letton, *Young Elizabeth* (New York: Harper and Brothers, 1953), 1–152; Margaret Irwin, *Young Bess* (New York: Harcourt, Brace, 1945), 68–217.

11. Thomas Parry, for example, claims that Ashley supported Seymour's marriage with Elizabeth (Haynes, *State Papers*, sig. Bb2v).

12. Ibid., sig. Cc2.

13. Ibid., sig. Bb2v.

14. Ibid., sig. T.

15. Ibid., sig. T1v.

16. Ibid., sig. Aa.

17. Ibid.

18. Ibid., sig. Aav. Despite Elizabeth's efforts to silence these rumors of a child by Seymour, this talk persisted. See Henry Clifford, *The Life of Jane Dormer, Duchess of Feria* (London: Burns and Oates, 1887), 86–87 for an account of

Elizabeth's purported child by this pregnancy and of Hugh Latimer's homiletic chastisement of Seymour and Elizabeth. (Jane Dormer was a maid of honor for Mary Tudor.) In his sermons preached before King Edward, Latimer admonished Seymour for his many purported failings, including being a "covetous man" (Latimer, *Sermons and Remains of Hugh Latimer*, ed. George Corrie [Cambridge: Cambridge University Press, 1845], 228).

19. See Carole Levin's essay in this collection for a discussion of pregnancy rumors later in Elizabeth's life.

20. Anne Somerset suggests that Elizabeth understood that she could do nothing to help Seymour and decided instead to write on behalf of her servants (*Elizabeth I*, 27).

21. Ellis, *Original Letters* (London: Harding, Triphook, and Lepard, 1825), 156.

22. Ibid., 156–57.

23. See, for example, accounts of her insistence that her staff be returned to her (Haynes, *State Papers*, sig. Ee2v).

24. Ibid., sig. Dd2.

25. While we cannot determine exactly how the Seymour incident may have contributed to Elizabeth's apparently active transformation of her public representation, it appears that she endeavored to present herself as a model young Protestant woman—a choice which may well have been designed to offset any damage caused by this affair. See Alison Plowden, *Lady Jane Grey and the House of Suffolk* (London: Sidgwick and Jackson, 1985). As Plowden and others note, John Aylmer "commented approvingly on her refusal to alter any of her 'maiden shamefastness' while all the other ladies were going about 'dressed and painted like peacocks'" (80). Plowden, among others, also discusses Elizabeth's reputedly modest demeanor during her visits to Edward's court. Plowden also refers to Jane Grey's reported approval of the humility displayed by Elizabeth, whom she contrasts favorably with Mary Tudor (80). In John Foxe's rendition of this last story, Mary is said to go "against God's word" by her affection for finery, while the more demure Elizabeth "followeth God's word" (Foxe, 8:603–4). Foxe also comments on Elizabeth's disdain for "gay apparel, rich attire, and precious jewels" (8:603). See Carole Levin, "Lady Jane Grey: Protestant Queen and Martyr," in *Silent but for the Word: Tudor Women as Patrons, Translators, and Writers of Religious Works*, ed. Margaret Hannay (Kent, Ohio: Kent State University Press, 1985), 96; and Somerset, *Elizabeth I*, 28, for related discussions.

26. See A. F. Pollard, *England under Protector Somerset* (London: Kegan, Paul, Trench, and Trubner, 1900), 344.

27. Susan Bassnett, in *Elizabeth I: A Feminist Perspective* (New York: St. Martin's, 1988), suggests that Parr "did as many other women have done who, because of the strength of their emotions, seem able to ignore a situation in the household involving infidelity or incest, which the exercise of reason would compel them to acknowledge" (24).

28. See Carole Levin's essay in this volume for a further discussion of concerns about possible links between Elizabeth's and Anne Boleyn's behavior.

29. Marc Shell, *Elizabeth's Glass* (Lincoln: University of Nebraska Press, 1993), 13.

30. Henry Ansgar Kelly, *The Matrimonial Trials of Henry VIII* (Stanford: Stanford University Press, 1976), 1–17.

31. Marc Shell argues—controversially—that Elizabeth showed great interest in the subject of incest from an early age: "Of Elizabeth's interest in incest we may be sure. She chose to translate a book, *Le Miroir de l'ame pécheresse*, about incest—a book written by and probably given to her supposedly incestuous mother by Marguerite of Navarre, an author known for her spiritual libertinism and love for her brother" (*Elizabeth Glass*, 19). In "Pearl of the Valois and Elizabeth I," in *Silent but for the Word: Tudor Women as Patrons, Translators, and Writers of Religious Texts*, ed. Margaret Hannay (Kent, Ohio: Kent State University Press, 1985), Anne Lake Prescott questions whether Elizabeth would have had any choice in the decision of what text to translate (64–65), but also suggests that the translation may show influences of Elizabeth's family background (68–71).

32. Bruce Thomas Boehrer, *Monarchy and Incest in Renaissance England: Literature, Culture, Kinship, and Kingship* (Philadelphia: University of Pennsylvania Press, 1992), 44.

33. Anthony Martienssen, *Queen Katherine Parr* (New York: McGraw-Hill, 1973), 228–32.

34. Carole Levin, in *The Heart and Stomach of a King: Elizabeth I and the Politics of Sex and Power* (Philadelphia: University of Pennsylvania Press, 1994), discusses William Allen's assertion in the 1580s that Elizabeth, like her mother, was "monstrous" (80–81).

35. Laurent Joubert, *Popular Errors*, trans. Gregory David de Rocher (Tuscaloosa: University of Alabama Press, 1989), 195. Joubert also remarks upon the impulse for "people [to] look very deeply into the man's and woman's circum-

stances, their ancestry, their blood, and their conduct, so as to have the best lineage possible . . . the sperm has the power to make the children resemble their parents both in body and mind" (192–93).

36. Heinrich Bullinger, *The Christian State of Matrimony* (London, 1547), sig. G7v.

37. Haynes, *State Papers*, sig. Ccv.

38. Shell, *Elizabeth's Glass*, 17.

39. Haynes, *State Papers*, sig. Aa.

40. In *Anne Boleyn* (New York: Basil Blackwell, 1986) E. W. Ives details the political aims he finds fueling Thomas Cromwell's engineering of Boleyn's death sentence and those of her co-defendants (336–408, passim). Retha Warnicke, who attributes Boleyn's downfall to the birth of a deformed child, disputes Ives's conclusions, in *The Rise and Fall of Anne Boleyn* (Cambridge: Cambridge University Press, 1989), 242.

41. Warnicke offers evidence to dispute the tradition which gives Anne Boleyn a sixth finger on her right hand (*Rise and Fall*, 3). Warnicke also discusses subsequent rumors of deformity associated with Elizabeth (240–41). For a related discussion, see Levin, *Heart and Stomach*, 86.

42. See Boehrer, *Monarchy and Incest*, 47, and Warnicke, *Rise and Fall*, 244.

43. Boehrer, *Monarchy and Incest*, 47.

44. Shell, *Elizabeth's Glass*, 8–10.

45. Ives, *Anne Boleyn*, 390.

46. Ibid., 389.

47. See Helen Hackett, *Virgin Mother, Maiden Queen* (New York: St. Martin's Press, 1995). Hackett suggests that Elizabeth's later refusal to marry may have been influenced by "the adolescent trauma of the Thomas Seymour scandal" (53).

48. Haynes, *State Papers*, sig. Cc2.

49. Ibid., sig. Ee2v.

50. Maria Perry, *The Word of a Prince* (Woodbridge, Suffolk: Boydell Press, 1990), 65.

Why Did Elizabeth Not Marry?

Susan Doran

Elizabeth I's virginity has been her most famous attribute since the late sixteenth century. This is understandable, not least because her chastity was celebrated from the 1580s onwards in art, poetry, and drama. But her unmarried state has also attracted criticism. During the first decade of the reign, marriage and childbirth provided the only hope of securing a clear and unchallenged Protestant line of succession to the English throne and of averting the danger of civil war on the queen's death. During the 1570s, when Elizabeth was in her forties and unlikely to bear a child, the country needed her marriage to a powerful prince in order to seal an alliance which might bring an end to its increasingly dangerous isolation in Europe. Yet, despite these considerations, Elizabeth rejected the hand of at least a dozen suitors, including King Philip II of Spain, King Eric XIV of Sweden, King Charles IX of France and his two brothers, Henry and Francis, and an Austrian archduke. By this action, or rather nonaction, she appeared to be betraying her dynasty, her religion, and her realm, especially as she also refused to designate a successor. It was behavior seemingly at variance with her reputation as a monarch traditionally praised for her dedication to national unity and the national interest.

Elizabeth was exhorted to marry time and time again in the early part of the reign. The Privy Council as a body called on her to take a husband in late December 1559 as part of its advice for dealing with the dangers posed by Mary Stuart.[1] In 1559, 1563, 1566, and 1576 her parliaments sent her petitions urging marriage as a way to resolve the succession. Sometime around 1560, Matthew Parker, the archbishop of Canterbury, Edmund Grindal, the bishop of London, and Richard Cox of Ely "thought it our parts for our pastoral office, to be solicitous in that cause which all your loving subjects so daily sigh for and morningly in their prayers desire to appear to their eyes," for they could not "but fear that this continued sterility in your Highness' person to be a token of God's displeasure towards us."[2] During her summer progress of 1565, the Recorder of Coventry greeted her with an oration which included the wish that "like as you are a mother to your kingdom . . . so you may, by God's goodness and justice, be a natural mother, and, having blest issue of your princely body, may live to see your children's children unto the third and fourth generation."

More oblique petitions were also addressed to the queen. Court masques were performed before her in the mid-1560s which focused on the theme of the superiority of marriage over celibacy. In most of them, the goddess Diana representing virginity was trounced by Venus or Juno, the goddess of marriage.[3] As a New Year's gift for 1560, the diplomat Sir Thomas Challoner presented and dedicated to the queen a book in praise of Henry VIII, which ended with the plea that she "bestow the bonds of your modesty on a husband. . . . For then a little Henry will play in the palace for us."[4]

As time went on and childbirth became less likely, Elizabeth's councillors viewed her marriage as a necessary preliminary to a league with the French king. Thus, when the earl of Sussex listed seven advantages to a match with Henry III of France's brother, Francis duke of Alençon, in August 1578, only one related to the possibility of producing an heir, and this was the last one he mentioned; the remainder concerned the beneficial effects that would arise from a dynastic alliance with the house of France.[5]

These petitions and recommendations were always courteous but they often contained a critical note. The 1566 parliamentary petition on the marriage and succession implicitly censured the queen for lack of action despite her promise to marry during the previous session, thereby prompting Elizabeth to reprimand both Houses with the words: "A strange ordere of petycyoners, that wyll make a request and cannot be otherwyse asserteynyde but by the prince's worde, and yet wyll not beleve yt when yt ys spoken."[6] The masques presented before the queen also implied criticism, leading Elizabeth to exclaim after one performance, "This is all against me."[7]

Historians and biographers have always argued that Elizabeth made a conscious decision to reject her subjects' appeals and remain unwed out of personal or political considerations: either an implacable hostility to matrimony or a determination to rule alone. Biographers in particular have focused on the psychological explanations. Some have detected in Elizabeth an antipathy to marriage stemming from an emotional block to any kind of change or an almost pathological inability to take a decision. Others, however, have turned to more complex motives, and have tried to explore the depths of Elizabeth's psyche to discover a cause of her "choice" to remain single.[8] It is certainly easy to find in her childhood experiences a ready explanation for an irrational aversion to marriage. After all, her mother, Anne Boleyn, was executed by her father on a charge of adultery before Elizabeth had reached her third year; Anne's supplanter, Jane Seymour, died soon after giving birth to Prince Edward in 1538; and in 1542, a third stepmother, Catherine Howard, was also executed for adultery. No wonder that some writers have claimed that these early traumas naturally led the young Elizabeth to associate sexual relations with death and develop a hysterical reaction against marriage. They propose, furthermore, that this association was reinforced by the experiences of her troubled adolescence, when she fell victim to the lustful advances and political ambitions of Lord Thomas Seymour, a maternal uncle of the new king, Edward VI. If Elizabeth had been the victim of a degree of sexual abuse and especially if she had found Seymour's advances exciting or even enjoyable, it seems reasonable to infer that she might well have internalized intense guilt at the death in childbirth of Catherine and the execution of Seymour.[9]

According to some historians, these childhood experiences had another important effect in that they taught Elizabeth that "maleness mattered" and left her with a "masculine identification"; after all, had she been born a boy, her mother would not have been destroyed while she herself would have retained her father's affections. As a result, argues Larissa J. Taylor-Smither, Elizabeth came to value and adopt the masculine qualities of dominance, aggression, and fearlessness, which made it impossible for her to assume the subservient role expected of a wife in the sixteenth century.[10]

Psychological theories such as these have proved extremely popular, because they seem to explain not only why Elizabeth did not marry, but also why she appeared to have such an implacable hatred of matrimony in general. Her attempt to curb clerical marriage, her opposition to the marriages of her courtiers and ladies-in-waiting, and her fury when she discovered that their clandestine marriages had taken place despite her wishes, seem to be more readily understandable in the light of some pathological disorder. The uncontrollable rages Elizabeth frequently displayed on such occasions (as when she broke the finger of Mary Shelton on discovering her secret marriage to James Scudamore) only seem to make sense if we accept that her behavior was clinically hysterical and the result of unconscious anxieties stemming from childhood disturbance.

Nonetheless, this kind of psychological speculation is suspect, since it is based on unproved models of human behavior and inadequate evidence. There is no factual information at all to indicate how the deaths of her mother and stepmothers affected the young princess, and it could equally well be argued that their emotional impact was slight. Queen Anne was a very remote figure in Elizabeth's early childhood; the young princess had, moreover, stable surrogate mothers in the persons of Lady Bryan and then Katherine Champernowne, later to be Mrs. Ashley. Attitudes to parenthood and death in the sixteenth century were in any event quite different from those of today, and it is ahistorical to transpose late-twentieth-century sensibilities to the past. Furthermore, in adult life Elizabeth showed herself capable of forming relationships with male courtiers and advisors on a range of levels of intimacy, which suggests that she was not the emotionally stunted woman depicted by many biographers. Finally, Elizabeth's hostility to the marriages of her subjects had their own specific explanations. Antipathy to clerical marriage stemmed from the queen's religious conservatism, while her anger at the secret weddings of her ladies and courtiers often had a political cause. In general terms, she wanted her privy chamber to be apolitical and consequently required her ladies to be free from loyalties to a husband and his kin.[11] By marrying, her ladies were risking their political neutrality; furthermore, when they married secretly (often of necessity), they were demonstrating to their mistress their untrustworthiness and divided loyalties.

For this reason, other historians have generally discarded psychological explanations and tended instead to see Elizabeth's decision to remain unwed as the deliberate, rational response of an intelligent woman to the practical problems of being a female ruler. Marriage, they argued, would inevitably have jeopardized Elizabeth's authority, since sixteenth-century patriarchal society believed that a wife should always defer to her husband when making decisions, given that women were naturally inferior to men and that God had ordained female subordination to men in all private relationships. Accordingly, an unmarried Elizabeth would have been expected to hand over power to her husband or at the very least to follow his wishes over policy.[12] Her refusal to risk this loss of control has been praised by some feminist writers, but others have denounced it. Allison Heisch, for example, complained that Elizabeth represented the typical token woman who accepted "male notions of how the world was or should be organised" and who reinforced rather than eroded "those systems which oppress and exclude women."[13]

It is a mistake, however, to assume that Elizabeth believed that she could deal with the issue of her gender only by remaining celibate, and had to remain unmarried because she did not wish to share her rule with a husband. In his treatise "*An Harborowe for Faithfull and Trewe Subiectes*" (which was written in 1559 as an answer to John Knox's *First Blast of the Trumpet Against the Monstruous Regiment of Women*, the most famous work denying the legitimacy of gynecocracy), John Aylmer, later to be bishop of London, argued against those who said that a married queen regnant should always display uxorial subordination in line with God's law and defer to her husband on all matters of state:

Yea say you, God hath appoynted her to be subject to her husband . . . therefore she maye not be the heade. I graunte that, so farre as perteining to the bandes of mariage, and the offices of a wife, she must be a subjecte; but as a Magistrate she maye be her husbande's head. . . . Whie may not the woman be the husbande's inferiour in matters of wedlock, and his head in the guiding of the commonwelth.[14]

Aylmer saw a queen regnant as two persons, one private and one public. As a wife she would be subordinate to her husband in private affairs, but as a magistrate she would be dominant and could command and even punish her husband if he broke the law. Since her obligations as a wife would not take precedence over her regal responsibility, Elizabeth could thus retain her powers when married.

There were few practical obstacles to this political theory. It was in the obvious interests of all Elizabeth's advisors and servants to exclude her husband from power. The means to do so, moreover, were at hand in the marriage-treaty of Mary I and Philip of Spain, which had fixed clear limits on the king's political power in England, barring him from policy-making and patronage. Consequently, Elizabeth's councillors agreed that any marriage contract negotiated for the queen should be based on this 1553 treaty; as Sir Nicholas Bacon explained, this would ensure that her husband "shall not intermeddell with any parte of the governement of the realme to move any suspicion."[15] The experience of the previous reign was also a reassuring precedent; Mary had not been a weak, dependent woman who had allowed power and authority to slip from her hands into those of her husband. For one thing, she placed difficulties in the way of Philip's playing an effective role in government by denying him a personal patrimony in England, which would allow him to build up an independent patronage base.[16] For another, she made little attempt to push his coronation through Parliament, an investiture which would have enhanced his status as king. Furthermore, all the court rituals and ceremonies of the reign asserted Mary's role as sovereign and emphasized that Philip was merely her consort: her throne was larger than his and placed at a higher level; she was served off gold while he was served off silver.[17] The treaty itself was upheld in every detail. Philip had to pay the total costs of his huge household, and, even when it came to the war against France, the Privy Council did not automatically approve England's participation on the side of Spain but only agreed entry after the French-backed raid on Scarborough Castle. The Marian precedent, therefore, did not suggest that it was necessary for Elizabeth to remain unmarried in order to rule rather than reign.

But some historians argue, in addition, that the decision to remain a virgin gave Elizabeth opportunities to play a role and develop an image, which could help her in a more general way to overcome the obstacle of her gender in asserting her rule.[18] It is often said that she fashioned for herself a public persona as a virginal goddess, which would give her a special mystique as a female ruler and allow her to command the respect and awe reserved for kings. In courtly pageantry she acted out the roles of the *bel dame* of medieval chivalry or the Petrarchan mistress of Renaissance poetry, who was beloved and served by male courtiers without any loss to their honor. In this way, the queen could keep in line male courtiers chafing at the obligation to obey a female monarch. Similarly, through the image of the Virgin Queen she was able to present herself as no ordinary woman, but as an exceptional woman whose purity made her worthy of devotion, even adoration. Her virginity allowed her to be cast in portraits and literature as the moon goddesses, Diana, Phoebe, and Cynthia, as well as Astraea, the virgin who in Virgil's poetry had once presided over the Golden Age and would return again to restore it. Her virginity also enabled her to exploit the coincidence of her birth date, 7 September, with the feast of the Nativity of the Virgin Mary and claim a symbolic kinship with the mother of Christ. These public personae were obviously incompatible with marriage. Quite simply, as Christopher Haigh has explained so succinctly, "how could she admit that she was just the same as the rest, and submit herself to a husband? . . . Elizabeth had refused to be a mere woman, and was not going to be a mere wife."[19]

Elizabeth, however, did not have to remain unmarried and chaste to appear exceptional to her subjects, nor did she need to develop the secular cult of the Virgin to create for herself a special mystique. Instead, she could and did derive a special status as a female monarch by emphasizing her position as the instrument of God's purpose and identifying herself with providential figures in the Bible. Most Protestant publicists described Elizabeth in this fashion. In his treatise of 1559, Aylmer asserted that God had ordained Elizabeth to rule, as a special woman, when he provided for no male heir through the succession: "It is a plain argument that for some secret purpose he [God] myndeth the female should reign and governe."[20] John Calvin too believed that Elizabeth's accession was "ordained by the peculiar providence of God"; although accepting the contemporary assumption that female rule was a "deviation from the original and proper order of nature," he acknowledged that "there were occasionally women," like Elizabeth, who "were raised up by divine authority" to be queen in order to become "the nursing mothers of the church."[21] In John Jewel's *Apology of the Church of England* of 1562 and John Foxe's *Acts and Monuments* of the following year, the authors argued that all the signs of Scripture and history confirmed the providential nature of the queen's rule. Both elitist poetry and popular verses expressed the same argument. From Edmund Spenser's *Faerie Queene* came the lines:

> But vertuous women wisely understand
> That they were borne to base humilitie
> Unlesse the heavens they lift to lawfull soveraintie.[22]

Meanwhile, the verse of the Protestant balladeer John Awdelay proclaimed:

> Up, said this God with voice not strange,
> Elizabeth, thys realme nowe guyde,
> My wyll in thee doo not thou hyde.[23]

Elizabeth also liked to project herself in this providential mold; in her parliamentary rhetoric, for example, she frequently described herself as a woman raised by Providence to be a monarch, one who was thus exceptional in nature, quite unlike other women.[24] The image of the Virgin Queen, in fact, appeared relatively late in Elizabeth's reign. Early royal portraits which deployed emblems of virginity were clearly presenting a marriageable queen rather than one whose power rested on her celibacy. A change began to take place only after 1578. The entertainments performed before the queen at Norwich in the summer of 1578 were possibly the first attempt to lay stress on Elizabeth's special status as a virgin queen, and this was soon followed by a series of some seven Sieve Portraits painted between 1579 and about 1583 in which the queen was depicted holding a sieve, the symbol of Tuccia, a Roman Vestal Virgin, who when accused of breaking her vestal vows had proved her virginity by carrying water in a sieve from the River Tiber back to the temple without spilling a drop. The appearance of this imagery coincided with the unpopular matrimonial negotiations, which had opened with Francis duke of Alençon in the summer of 1578 and were to continue until the end of 1581. Elizabeth herself did not construct it; the patrons of these early representations of the Virgin Queen were some of her subjects who opposed the French match.

Elizabeth herself had early on found a model for active female rule in the scriptural figures of Deborah in the Old Testament, Judith in the Apocrypha, and to a lesser extent Queen Esther. Significantly, all three were married women. Deborah, a providential ruler and the rescuer of the Israelite chosen people from Canaanite idolatry, could readily be identified with Elizabeth in her attempts to uproot popery and build up the Protestant church in England; Judith in her victory over Holofernes was another divinely inspired champion of the true faith against its foes; while Esther, a royal consort not a queen regnant, was a gentler figure who had used her influence and mediatory powers with her husband to abort his chief minister's treacherous conspiracy against her own people.[25] Biblical imagery appeared as early as January 1559, when in one of the coronation pageants presented before the queen, the figure of Deborah appeared and Elizabeth was told: "A worthy precedent, O worthy Queen! thou hast," while the published description of the procession reminded its readers that "God, ofttimes, sent women nobly to rule among men, as Deborah which governed Israel in Peace, the space of forty years."[26] Deborah, Judith, and Esther continued to be portrayed as representations of Elizabeth in pageantry until late in the 1570s; woodcuts and other visual representations identifying Elizabeth with these Old Testament heroines continued well into the 1580s, and it was only then that the imagery of the Virgin Queen grew in popularity. Elizabeth, therefore, had little reason to fear that marriage would end her political power and authority.

Indeed, there is no strong evidence that Elizabeth ever did make a commitment to remain single. William Camden's account of the queen's declaring that she was already married to her realm and swearing an oath of virginity during the 1559 parliamentary session used to be presented as such, but John King has recently questioned the validity of Camden's version of events. He pointed out that Cecil's papers (Camden's source) contain no copy of the speech in question nor any record of the vow described in the *History of Princess Elizabeth*.[27] Furthermore, the queen's formal answer to the MPs about her marriage, which does appear in the records, was totally different in tone from Camden's speech. Yet even if Camden's version can be trusted, Elizabeth's reference to herself as a woman married to her realm and the display of her coronation ring as "the pledge of this my wedlocke" should not be read as a personal statement of an intent to remain chaste. The metaphor of marriage was a conventional rhetorical device to describe a monarch's relationship with her or his realm, and one which was used by both Mary I and James I.[28]

Indeed, at no time during the first half of the reign did Elizabeth rule out the prospect of marriage in her public statements. Certainly her answers to petitions from her House of Commons were often ambivalent, even perhaps obscure, yet they always admitted the possibility of marriage. On 10 February 1559 Elizabeth promised the MPs that if "it may please God to enclyne my heart to an other kynd of life, ye may well assure your selves my meaning is not to do or determyne anie thinge wherwith the realme may or shall have iuste cause to be discontented."[29] In 1563, she told the Speaker: "Yf anie thinke I never meant to trade that [single] lief, they be deceaved; but yf I may hereafter bende my minde thereunto the rather for fullfillinge your request I shalbe therwith very well content."[30] In 1566, she was more direct: "And therefore I saye ageyn, I wyll marrye assone as I can convenyentlye, yf Gd take not hym awaye with whom I mynde to marrye, or my self, or els sum othere great lette happen. . . . And I hope to have chylderne, otherwyse I wolde never marrie."[31]

When discussing her matrimonial intentions with foreign envoys or writing to foreign rulers, Elizabeth made the same point: she preferred a life of celibacy but recognized that marriage might well be forced upon her. In 1564 she wrote to the duke of Württemberg: "Although shee never yet was wearie of her maiden and single life, yet in regarde shee was the laste issue her father lefte, and only of her house, the care of her king-dome, and love of posteritie did ever councell her to alter this course of life."[32] Similarly, in the midst of negotiations with the Archduke Charles of Austria (son of the Holy Roman Emperor, Ferdinand I [1558–64], and brother to Emperor Maximilian II [1564–76]), she told the imperial am-bassador that "she had formerly purposed by all means to remain single, but in consequence of the insistent pressure that was brought to bear upon her by the Estates of her realm, she was now resolved to marry."[33]

Of course it was in Elizabeth's interests to leave open the possibility that she might one day wed, but it is doubtful that her public statements were merely cynical gestures to silence her parliamentary critics or en-courage matrimonial suits for diplomatic gain. In the 1560s, she well knew that marriage and childbirth provided the best route for resolving the thorny issue of the succession. Although there were Protestant claimants in the persons of Catherine and Mary Grey, the granddaughters of Henry VIII's younger sister Mary Tudor, the Roman Catholic Mary Stuart, who had descended from Henry VIII's elder sister Margaret, had the best title by right of heredity.[34] Mary Stuart's claim, moreover, was strengthened during the 1560s by the disgrace of the Grey sisters, caused by the illicit union of Catherine to the earl of Hertford in 1561, the bastardization of their two sons, and the misalliance in 1566 of the dwarfish Mary to a lowly servant of the court, who was reputed to be over six feet tall. As Elizabeth consistently refused to name her heir, and was especially unwilling to exclude Mary Stuart from the throne, a move which might have satisfied her Protestant subjects, she was in no position to reject matrimony as a way of solving the succession problem. Whatever her personal prefer-ences, such freedom of action was not open to her.

On two occasions, moreover, Elizabeth showed a strong interest in marrying. First, after the death of Lord Robert Dudley's wife in Septem-ber 1560, most contemporary observers believed that she was seriously contemplating marriage to her favorite. Then in 1579, she demonstrated a resolution to wed the duke of Alençon; marriage to him was an essential plank in her foreign policy and she was also attracted to his person during his visit to England in the summer of that year. Furthermore, in response to intense pressure from her councillors and parliaments, she showed a readiness to marry two other suitors, though admittedly without the enthusiasm displayed during the Dudley and later Alençon courtships. In the mid-1560s she agreed to open negotiations with the Archduke Charles of Austria as a way to secure a Habsburg alliance and resolve the succession problem. From late 1570 through to the autumn of 1571 she encouraged matrimonial negotiations with Henry duke of Anjou (then heir to the French throne and later in 1574 to become Henry III) in the hope that a betrothal might provide the foundation for an Anglo-French alliance which would protect the realm against Spain. On both these occasions there was no dallying with her suitors for political advantage; on the contrary, Elizabeth exhibited a serious intent to get down to the business of drawing up an acceptable matrimonial contract, and at times was ready to offer concessions on areas of disagreement. Her behavior then was entirely different from that displayed during the protracted matrimonial discussions with the French royal family from August 1572 until 1576. These latter negotiations were designed only for short-term diplomatic gain, as the means for encouraging outward courtesies and extracting political advantages during a period of Anglo-French tension, opened up by the massacre of St. Bartholomew's Day and renewal of religious wars in France. There was no question at all of Elizabeth marrying into the royal house held responsible for persecuting her co-religionists. Throughout the course of the talks, therefore, Elizabeth refused to discuss details of a marriage-treaty before an interview was held with her young suitor, Francis of Alençon; yet at the same time she often placed obstacles in the way of a meeting.[35]

Finding an explanation for Elizabeth's single status in her own personal preference for the single life is therefore unsatisfactory. To understand why all her courtships came to nothing, eyes have to be turned away from the character and gender of the queen, and be directed instead on the matrimonial suits themselves, especially on the sticking-points in the attempts to conclude a marriage contract and on the political tactics employed by the opponents of the various matches to bring about their ultimate failure. With this new focus, the role of the Privy Council rather than the attitude of the queen emerges as crucial to the outcome of the courtships. It is therefore inappropriate to level criticism or blame at Elizabeth for remaining unwed, as far too many historians and biographers have done.

Had Elizabeth's council ever united behind any one of her suitors, she would have found great difficulty in rejecting his proposal; likewise, without strong conciliar backing Elizabeth would not or could not marry a particular candidate. In the case of those men whom she had no particular wish to wed, opposition from within the council allowed her to elude their suits. Thus, it had required concerted conciliar pressure to force her into negotiations for a marriage with the Archduke Charles, and it was only when a significant number of councillors spoke out against accepting Habsburg demands for a private Mass in November 1567 that she felt able to bring the courtship to an end. Similarly, in April 1572 she was able to slip out of the negotiations for a marriage alliance with Francis duke of Alençon on the grounds that her council was divided over whether or not to accept the French terms on religion. As she herself said on several occasions, she was only thinking of marriage to satisfy her subjects, so there was no point at all in taking a husband who would displease a significant number of them.[36] In part such statements provided a convenient excuse to avoid the responsibility for the failure of particular sets of negotiations, but they also contained more than a grain of truth. Furthermore, on the practical side, she needed full conciliar support for a match so that the matrimonial treaty would not run into difficulties when presented to Parliament for ratification.

At other times, however, when Elizabeth appeared to be close to accepting the hand of her favored suitors, first Robert Dudley in the early 1560s and then Francis of Alençon in 1579, the active opposition of some leading councillors convinced her that it would be definitely unwise and perhaps disastrous to proceed with the match. During the course of these courtships she attracted sufficient expressions of disrespect to cause her great concern. Rumors abounded about the propriety of her behavior with both suitors, while questions were raised about the wisdom of her choice of consort. She was all too aware that both Wyatt's Rebellion in Mary I's reign and Mary Stuart's deposition in 1567 had occurred when a queen regnant insisted upon taking a husband against the wishes of her important subjects. Elizabeth was far too cautious and politically adept to make the same mistake. There is every reason to suppose that had her councillors overwhelmingly supported either Dudley in late 1560 or Alençon she would have gone ahead with the wedding.

But why could no suitor ever command the overwhelming support of her councillors? As far as most of the early matrimonial candidates were concerned, the answer is that there was little to recommend any of them. Philip II, who presented his suit in early 1559, was worthy of the queen in terms of dignity and descent, but unacceptable in England as the man held responsible (admittedly most unfairly) for the loss of Calais and the persecution of Protestants during the previous reign. Marriage to him, moreover, was clearly incompatible with the radical changes in religion favored by the queen and her new council. The three younger sons of Henry II were clearly out of the question at the beginning of the reign because of their extreme youth. Even in 1564, when Charles IX was of marriageable age and a suitor for the queen's hand, he was only fourteen to the queen's thirty-one years. While Elizabeth herself was worried that she would look ridiculous at the wedding, like a mother taking her child to the altar, her councillors were more concerned that the young king would be unable to consummate the marriage for several years and that the match would thus fail to resolve immediately the succession problem.[37]

Almost all the remaining early candidates were thought simply not good enough for a reigning monarch. Most were of relatively inferior status—European dukes who were not of royal blood; the duke of Savoy, moreover, had lost his territories to the French, while the duke of Holstein was a mercenary. Even King Eric XIV of Sweden was not a respected monarch in England, for he was the son of a usurper and his throne was elective. The disparagement involved in marrying any one of these men was not insignificant for a queen who had been pronounced a bastard and whose title to the throne was challenged by Mary Stuart and her allies. In addition, although they might meet the requirement of siring an heir, the foreign dukes would bring the queen little or no riches or valuable foreign alliances; on the contrary, there was the strong likelihood that as consorts they would prove a drain on the queen's resources and land her with enemies rather than link her to powerful friends. Even marriage to Eric XIV, who was undoubtedly wealthy, might embroil England in Baltic politics and a war against Denmark, Sweden's historic foe. Nor were there any political benefits to be gained from marriage to James Hamilton, third earl of Arran, despite the Scots' insistence that it would encourage political amity between neighbors, "once so much in discord," and make possible a future union of the two realms.[38] As the Spanish ambassador to France accurately observed in 1560, the Scottish earl would bring the queen only his person, for there was no advantage to be drawn from the match.[39] The Scottish lords were already her allies, the Habsburgs opposed the proposal, and the German Lutherans would be dismayed if she were to prefer a Calvinist husband over a Lutheran. In the longer term, there was no great prospect that an Arran marriage would unite the two realms, as the earl, ten years older than Mary Stuart, was unlikely to succeed her on the Scottish throne.

The Austrian Archduke Charles was probably the most suitable candidate to appear during the first couple of years of the reign, but even he could command little vocal support among Elizabeth's advisors in 1559 when Emperor Ferdinand first offered his son to the queen. Perhaps they were distracted by other political problems or bemused by the variety and number of Elizabeth's suitors. Perhaps too they were in no great rush for the queen to marry, but were content to consolidate their own positions before a foreign consort appeared in England. Hence there was no great pressure on the queen to choose the archduke, or indeed any other of her foreign suitors before 1561.

In the minds of most contemporaries, Robert Dudley was also considered a suitor who was not good enough for the queen. As William Cecil rightly noted: "Nothing is increased by Marriadg of hym either in Riches, Estimation, Power."[40] It was often said that the nobility despised him as a "new man," whose father and grandfather had been attainted for treason, and that they considered the queen's marriage to a commoner as disparagement.[41] Again, such thoughts went beyond the social elitism that was undoubtedly present; Elizabeth's child might well have to compete for the throne against Mary Stuart or any son she might have, and would be at a disadvantage with only one grandparent of royal blood, especially as some Catholics persisted in questioning whether Henry VIII had indeed fathered Elizabeth. The queen's deep affection for Dudley, however, outweighed these obstacles, while his own abilities as a self-publicist and politician helped him gradually to win over many initial opponents of his suit, including the duke of Norfolk and the earl of Pembroke, both of whom petitioned the queen to marry her favorite at a meeting of the Knights of the Garter in April 1562.[42] As a result, Dudley was considered a serious candidate by contemporaries until the mid-1560s and beyond.

Dudley's main handicap in courting the queen was the mysterious death of his wife. Although the coroner's court judged Amy Robsart's fall down the staircase at Cumnor Place to be "death by misadventure," many clearly believed otherwise. Consequently, Elizabeth had good reason to fear that her marriage to Dudley would damage both their reputations: giving credibility to the rumors that she and Dudley had long been lovers, confirming the suspicions that her favorite had conspired to bring about his first wife's death, and implicating her in the murder.[43] Councillors like Cecil and royal servants like Sir Nicholas Throckmorton who opposed the marriage played on her anxiety that a Dudley marriage would impugn her honor, by bringing to her attention the scurrilous comments circulating both at home and abroad about her relationship with her favorite. Calumnies spread in England—that the queen was either pregnant or had borne a child—were brought before the Privy Council, while "dishonorable and naughty reaportes" at the French court were reported home by Throckmorton: "One laugheth at us, an other threateneth, an other revileth her Majestie, and some let not to say what religion is this, that a subject shall kill his wief, and the prince not onely beare withall but marry with him."[44]

Although these concerns about the queen's reputation stimulated opposition to Dudley's suit, hostility to the match also owed much to political self-interest. Most of Elizabeth's councillors and nobles distrusted Dudley as a potential faction leader who would promote his own men and take revenge on the enemies of his father, the late duke of Northumberland.[45] "He shall study nothing but to enhanss his owne particular Frends to Welthe, to Offices, to Lands, and to offend others," wrote Cecil when listing his reasons against a Dudley marriage.[46] No doubt Cecil was also conscious that his own political power would be most at risk if Dudley became royal consort. Like the favorite and unlike his aristocratic colleagues, Cecil had little power base of his own in the early 1560s and his position depended entirely on the queen. Thus, in contrast to Dudley's earliest enemies, Arundel, Norfolk, and Pembroke, Cecil was never won round to the match nor seduced by the belief that it would be preferable for the queen to marry her Master of the Horse than to remain single. He, therefore, worked quietly but consistently behind the scenes to subvert Dudley's Spanish strategy in the late winters and springs of 1561 and 1562. On the first occasion Dudley had tried to secure Spanish support for his marriage to the queen by offering to use his influence on behalf of pro-Catholic policies: the attendance of English representatives at a newly summoned papal council and the admission of a papal nuncio to England. On the second he again approached de Quadra, the Spanish ambassador, and requested Philip II's support for the match, but this time he offered nothing in return "in matters of religion."[47] Cecil was able to foil the first attempt by whipping up an antipapal scare in April 1561 which resulted in the council unanimously vetoing the admission of the papal nuncio, a necessary precondition for Spanish support. He scuppered Dudley's second maneuver by discrediting the Spanish ambassador in the eyes of the queen and once again exposing to Elizabeth the damage that a Dudley marriage would do to her reputation abroad.[48]

Some of the opposition within the council and at court to the later candidates for Elizabeth's hand was also based on political self-interest. In particular, Dudley's hostility to the suit of the Archduke Charles of Austria owed much to his anxieties about his own political future. Despite his admittance to the council in 1562, the extension of his landed base, and his elevation to the peerage as earl of Leicester in September 1564, Dudley's power and influence remained heavily dependent on his role as royal favorite, and he may well have feared that his intimacy with Elizabeth would not survive her marriage to a foreign prince.[49] Furthermore, there was reason to believe that his political rivals, who were promoting the Habsburg match, would benefit from a royal marriage to their favored candidate. The earl of Sussex evidently thought so; during his visit to Vienna in late 1567, he told the Spanish ambassador at the imperial court that "if he concluded the [Archduke Charles] marriage it would help him greatly against his political enemies."[50] Leicester's political position was far more secure during the 1578–79 Alençon matrimonial negotiations; nonetheless, men within the Dudley circle feared that the earl's eclipse would follow the marriage of Elizabeth to the French prince.[51]

It is not therefore surprising that Leicester took the lead in opposing both the Habsburg and French matrimonial projects.[52] In 1564 and early 1565, he secretly encouraged the French ambassador to present Charles IX as an alternative candidate to the Archduke Charles in an attempt to divide the council and take support away from the Habsburg match. When this device failed, he opposed the match in the council on religious grounds, and he may well have been behind the anti-Catholic scare kindled in late 1567 and early 1568 to warn Elizabeth of the dangers in conceding a measure of religious toleration to the archduke.[53] Between 1578 and 1579, his hand can again be detected behind many of the strategies designed to warn Elizabeth off a marriage to Francis duke of Alençon.

On each occasion Dudley was ultimately able to count on the active support of other councillors because of the nationality and religion of the suitors. For the queen and the advocates of the Habsburg and French matches, marriage to a foreign prince was desirable as a means of placing a protective mantle around the realm. A match with the Archduke Charles was expected to bring with it an informal alliance with both the emperor and the king of Spain; matrimony with Henry of Anjou in 1571 and Francis of Alençon in 1579 was intended to bind England and France together in a defensive league against Spain. Yet many at court disliked the prospect of the queen's marrying a foreigner. Besides xenophobic prejudices, they shared a genuine apprehension about the practical political problems that seemed likely to arise from any union between Elizabeth and a foreign prince. Her consort, it was feared, might draw the queen into wars of his own making and expect her subjects to pay their cost; he might take his wife abroad to live in his own territories, leaving England to be governed by a viceroy; worst still, the birth of a male child would put at risk England's national independence. Furthermore, if Elizabeth were to die in childbirth, her husband would act as regent with the authority to rule until the child reached maturity. Even though a number of these concerns could be dealt with in a carefully worded marriage contract, as indeed they had been in Mary I's matrimonial treaty, these alarming prospects influenced many to speak out against Elizabeth's foreign candidates. In a council meeting to discuss the Alençon match, Sir Ralph Sadler voiced the warning that while present history books blamed Mary for losing Calais, future ones would condemn Elizabeth for losing the whole realm to France.[54] Anxieties were also expressed in polemical tracts, such as the 1560 discourse of Thomas Smith directed against the Swedish and Habsburg candidates and the pamphlet of John Stubbs attacking the Alençon project.[55]

The greatest objection of all to the Austrian and French candidates, however, was their Catholicism. In each case, the promoters of the marriage believed that in time Elizabeth's consort would change his religion. Thus, when Cecil reopened negotiations with the Archduke Charles of Austria in 1563, he was under the mistaken impression that the prince was sufficiently flexible to convert to Protestantism soon after the marriage. Similarly, it was hoped that Henry of Anjou would be educated into accepting the Protestant faith once he had been removed from the influence of the ultra-Catholic Guise family, and marriage negotiations with Alençon were only initiated in 1572 because he was held to be "more moderate" and "not so obstinate" in religion.[56] The prevailing view in the council appears to have been that Christian intermarriage was acceptable provided there were sound expectations of a future conversion to Protestantism. They found a theological justification for this position in the teachings of St. Paul (1 Corinthians 7) and Peter Martyr, who had preached that "the unbeleaving is sanctyfied by the faithe of the beleeving, and the cohabitation lawfull for the hope's sake of conversion."[57] Nevertheless, there was a small minority of extreme Protestants, both inside and outside the council, who opposed marriage to a papist on ideological grounds, and a few who bravely expressed concern that the queen might be seduced by her husband to alter her religious views.[58]

Once matrimonial negotiations had opened, difficulties soon arose over the terms on which a Catholic consort could live in Protestant England during the period before the conversion took place. There were three main issues to be resolved. Was the wedding ceremony to follow the Catholic service or the English Prayer Book, and was it to be presided over by a priest or minister? Did Elizabeth's husband have to attend English Protestant services? Would he and his household be allowed to hear the Mass? Attempts to reach agreement on these issues bedeviled all the matrimonial negotiations with a Catholic prince. Henry of Anjou's refusal to make any concessions at all and his insistence both on nonattendance at Protestant services and freedom to hear public Mass ended his suit. Both the Archduke Charles and Francis of Alençon, however, were more accommodating, and after some tough negotiations Elizabeth was able to reach a compromise with them on the first two points, which was satisfactory to the majority of her councillors. It was on the question of the Mass that the council divided. On this issue, both suitors were again more flexible than Henry, in that they agreed to forgo public celebrations of the Mass provided that they and their fellow countrymen could hear it privately.[59] But while this demand seemed reasonable to some councillors, it was totally unacceptable to others.

The division in the council on the issue of the Mass was in part ideological. The councillors who agreed to a limited toleration were on the whole conservative in religion: the earl of Sussex, duke of Norfolk, Lord Howard of Effingham, Sir James Croftes, and Lord Hunsdon. On the other hand, Protestant zealots and Puritan patrons like Sir Francis Walsingham, Sir Walter Mildmay, and Sir Francis Knowles viewed the Mass as extreme idolatry: "The highest treason that can be against the lord's own person." For them and many other Protestants outside the council, there could be no accommodation with idolatry, and they believed that it was Elizabeth's religious duty to take up the sword against this "pagan rite." Any toleration of the Mass would, they feared, "kindle the wrath of God and set fire on church and commonweal."[60]

Nonetheless the council did not always split cleanly along religious lines. Dr. Thomas Wilson, a Marian exile and supporter of an interventionist Protestant foreign policy, gave his support to the Alençon match in 1579, whereas Sir Christopher Hatton, Archbishop Whitgift's patron and a noted conservative in religion, came out as a leading opponent. Wilson's fear of an international Catholic league led him to accept the French match as a necessary evil; Hatton, on the other hand, had more faith in England's power to withstand the international threat but feared the internal consequences of allowing Alençon liberty of worship.[61] Cecil, whose deeply engrained anti-Catholicism reflected an apocalyptic worldview, nevertheless consistently promoted Catholic marriages for the queen on terms that would allow her consort a private Mass.[62] His promotion of the archduke match was mainly motivated by his worries about the succession, while in 1571 and 1579 he advocated a French match as a way to protect England against an international Catholic league. Nor were more self-interested political considerations ever entirely absent from his thinking.

In late 1567 Elizabeth did not need much convincing against the archduke match, for she had her own doubts about agreeing to the Austrian's terms on both legal and political grounds. Conciliar opposition, moreover, bolstered her resolve and enabled her to reject the archduke's request for a private Mass, thereby bringing the negotiations to a close and ultimately keeping intact her reputation as a pious Protestant monarch. Similarly, Elizabeth was unattracted to the Alençon suit in the spring of 1572 and found in conciliar division over his demand for a private Mass under certain restricted conditions a ready excuse for prevarication; had it not been for Cecil she might well have rejected the match altogether.[63] By 1579, however, Elizabeth had changed her attitude to the duke, and was even ready to pass over the issue of the Mass in order to marry him. The overwhelming advantages of the Anglo-French matrimonial alliance seemed to outweigh the dangers of allowing her husband the restricted exercise of his religion; it is also probable that she believed that, once married and under her influence, he would soon cease to hear Mass. On this occasion, therefore, the conciliar opposition to the match had to move into higher gear to persuade the queen against the marriage on these terms.

Led by Leicester and Walsingham, councillors against the match helped to mobilize a widespread propaganda campaign which Elizabeth could not ignore. In the summer and autumn of 1579, London preachers denounced the marriage from their pulpits and organized public prayers against it. Ballads and verses, openly attacking the match, were printed and publicly disseminated. Thousands of copies of John Stubbs's *Gaping Gulf* were published ready for distribution in London and beyond. Several copies of Philip Sidney's appeal against the marriage, *A Letter to Queen Elizabeth,* appeared at court. After a governmental crackdown against sermons and pamphlets, opposition to the match began to be exhibited surreptitiously. Between 1579 and 1581, pejorative references to "frogs" or "toads" appeared regularly in a wide range of printed works as a code for hostility to the match, while at court, allegorical poetry was circulated in manuscript form.[64] Although public anger was directed against Alençon, these works often portrayed Elizabeth in a negative light (Sidney's letter was a notable exception): again and again it was suggested that in her infatuation for the duke she was blind to the dangers to the realm and its religion.

Elizabeth's gender influenced the fears of her subjects to some extent, but not as much as is generally assumed. The marriage of a female ruler obviously exacerbated fears about both "faction" and foreign influences, but these problems existed even when a king or prince was choosing a bride. On almost every occasion that Henry VIII took an English wife, faction reared its head and the marriage resulted in a shake-up of political groupings at court: according to David Starkey, Henry's choice of Anne Boleyn "triggered faction"; his marriage to Jane Seymour in 1536 was accompanied by the destruction of "a whole court faction"; and his decision to annul his marriage to Anne of Cleves and wed Katherine Howard helped seal Thomas Cromwell's fate.[65] In the following century, when James I planned to marry his heir to a Spanish princess, he provoked a political storm which "opened the most dangerous gap between the political 'court' and 'country' " in his reign. According to Thomas Cogswell, many Jacobean men and women feared that "a fecund Infanta could well draw England into the 'empire' just as earlier Habsburg princes had done in the Netherlands and in Spain itself."[66] At the same time, anxieties about the infanta's Catholicism dominated popular concerns, and in 1623, when Prince Charles and the duke of Buckingham traveled to Spain, they ignited an anti-Catholic scare which was not dissimilar to that of 1579.

Obviously, Elizabeth's marriage was a divisive issue in the council and at court; but to what extent, if any, did it create, reflect, or exacerbate "factional" struggles involving Cecil, Leicester, and the Howards? Simon Adams has consistently argued that faction played no part in the politics of the Elizabethan court before the 1590s. He questions the very existence of faction on three main grounds. First, he has found no evidence that either Burghley or Leicester had an exclusive following and operated as faction leaders: "In a number of cases—for example those of Walsingham himself, Henry Killigrew, Robert Beale, William Herle—clear lines of allegiance have been very difficult to draw." Second, he believes that there is little evidence of intense competition over patronage between the leading figures in the court before the last decade or so of the reign. Third, he argues that Cecil and Leicester were "men from a similar political milieu" who shared the same outlook and who "had too much in common for permanent antagonisms to be established." Court politics, he therefore concludes, were less the product of divisions among courtiers than of disputes between "an able, charming yet imperious and idiosyncratic queen and councillors and intimates who generally shared a high degree of social, political and cultural homogeneity."[67]

Adams is certainly correct in emphasizing that the Elizabethan court was not riven in two by the rivalry between Leicester and Cecil. With regard to patronage networks, men seeking favors from the queen solicited help from several important figures at the same time and did not turn to only one for advancement. In the field of policy-making, Cecil, Leicester, and Walsingham frequently cooperated. Finally, as both Adams and Eric Ives rightly point out, there was never a complete breakdown in relations between Leicester and the Howards or Cecil.[68]

Nonetheless, it would be a mistake to conclude that the absence of "faction" in a narrowly defined sense meant that harmony always prevailed in political life. Between 1558 and 1581 personal antagonisms, political rivalries, and policy differences were at least as much a feature of the court scene as cooperation and consensus. Disagreements over the question of the queen's marriage and foreign policy exacerbated personal conflicts among courtiers and councillors, which could easily get out of hand and disrupt political stability. In late 1560 the threat of an armed conflict between Dudley and the earls of Arundel and Pembroke shook the court, while an affray broke out between the retinues of Dudley and Pembroke.[69] In 1562 a meeting of the Knights of the Garter around the time of St. George's Day was disrupted when Arundel and Northampton stormed out in protest after a petition in favor of Dudley's marrying the queen was approved.[70] In January 1566 rival followers of the Howards and Leicester wore distinctive colors to show their group loyalty; four months later "hard words and challenges to fight were exchanged" between Sussex and Leicester, and the queen was forced to intercede between them.[71] In 1579 the divisions generated by the Alençon matrimonial project nearly resulted in a "palace revolution" when Leicester and Walsingham were banished from court and the queen considered bringing some Catholics onto the council. Nor were these disputes always confined to the court. Both the 1563 and 1566 parliaments were affected by divisions within the council on the marriage and succession, while in 1579 preachers and polemicists brought a wider public into the debate on the Alençon marriage.

There is little evidence that Elizabeth encouraged these disputes and divisions by pursuing a "divide and rule" policy which gave her "freedom of action" and turned her into "an umpire to whose judgement the contenders would always have to bow."[72] Too much weight has been placed on the report of the Jacobean Sir Robert Naunton that Elizabeth made and unmade factions "as her own great judgement advised."[73] On the contrary, she usually encouraged rival politicians to work together to formulate and execute policy, and attempted to calm down passions which arose from their disputes. Thus Cecil was brought into the negotiations with de Quadra and Dudley in 1562 concerning England's representation at the Council of Trent, a move which in the event allowed her secretary to outmaneuver both queen and favorite. In 1571 she left the day-to-day negotiations with the French to be handled by Leicester and Burghley in tandem. In October 1579 she tried to obtain the consent of the whole council collectively to the Alençon match; only later did she seek out councillors' individual written views as a way of breaking down the opposition to her plans.[74] On the whole, then, Elizabeth preferred "consensus" politics to "divide and rule"; and the divisions at her court over her courtships were a mark of political failure, not a means for securing freedom of action. Indeed, the marriage issue demonstrates that Elizabeth had less control over politics and policy-making than is usually appreciated; she was unable to impose her will on her council or suppress criticisms of her policies in the court and country.

The courtships were undoubtedly damaging to Elizabeth's reputation both at home and abroad. In the first place, slanders were widely spread about her sexual immorality. During the Dudley courtship "she showed herself so affectionate to him" that gossip questioned or denied her chastity. At the French court in 1571, Henry of Anjou labeled her a whore and eight years later the papal nuncio in Paris accused her of having borne Dudley's illegitimate children. As late as 1590 two Essex villagers declared that Elizabeth and Dudley had stuffed their illegitimate offspring up a chimney.[75] Such allegations suggest that Elizabethan propaganda in the form of her representation as the Virgin Queen had only a limited success. During the Dudley, Archduke Charles, and Alençon courtships, holes were also driven into her carefully constructed image as a wise ruler and Protestant heroine. On each occasion, opponents queried her political judgment in choosing such an unsuitable husband and warned of the danger to religion if the match went ahead. In 1561 tales were spread, and at least one sermon preached, that Elizabeth had promised "to turn Catholic at the instance of Lord Robert" in order to win Spanish support for the match.[76] In the mid-1560s and 1579 fears were expressed that Elizabeth's toleration of the Mass would threaten England's covenant with God and provoke divine vengeance.

On the other hand, the matrimonial negotiations reveal to historians

Elizabeth's great strength as a ruler. Like all successful heads of state she had a highly developed instinct for survival: a sensitivity to public opinion and an awareness of what was politically possible. She listened and acted upon calls to marry but ultimately turned down suits which proved unpopular or divisive. Only briefly during 1579 did her political intuition falter, but even then she soon recovered and stepped back from the brink of the disaster which would surely have accompanied the Alençon marriage. Aware of her own limitations, therefore, she listened to counsel, rejected controversial matches, and in the event remained single.

Notes

1. Petition of the Privy Council drafted by Cecil 28 December 1559, Public Record Office, SP 12/7, fol. 186 (hereafter abbreviated as PRO). To be accurate, the concern here was as much Mary's present claim to the throne as the succession.

2. J. Bruce, ed., *Correspondence of Matthew Parker, Archbishop of Canterbury* (Cambridge: Parker Society, 1853), 129–32.

3. Susan Doran, "Juno versus Diana: The Treatment of Elizabeth's Marriage in Plays and Entertainments, 1561–1581," *Historical Journal* 38 (1995): 257–74.

4. J. B. Gabel and C. C. Schlam, eds., *Thomas Chaloner's "In Laudem Henrici Octavi"* (Lawrence, Kan.: Coronado Press, 1979). I would like to thank Dr. Jonathan Woolfson for this reference.

5. "Notes taken out of a letter from the earl of Sussex 28 August 1578," cited in J. Payne Collier, "The Egerton Papers," *Camden Society* 12 (London: Royal Historical Society, 1840): 74–75.

6. T. E. Hartley, ed., *Proceedings in the Parliaments of Elizabeth I* (Leicester: Leicester University Press, 1981), 147.

7. *Calendus State Papers Spanish, 1558–67*, 404.

8. For hostility to change see Paul Johnson, *Elizabeth I: A Study in Power and Intellect* (London: Weidenfeld and Nicolson, 1974), 112, and for her irresolution see Jaspar Ridley, *Elizabeth I* (London: Constable, 1987), 214. For more complex psychological explanations see L. J. Taylor-Smither, "Elizabeth I: A Psychological Profile," *Sixteenth Century Journal* 15 (1984): 47–70.

9. Alison Plowden, *Marriage with My Kingdom: The Courtships of Elizabeth I* (London: Macmillan, 1977), 160.

10. Taylor-Smither, "Elizabeth I," 47–70.

11. Pam Wright, "A Change in Direction: The Ramifications of a Female Household, 1558–1603," in *The English Court from the Wars of the Roses to the Civil War*, by David Starkey et al. (Harlow: Longman, 1987), 159, 168.

12. Joel Hurstfield, *Elizabeth I and the Unity of England* (London: English Universities Press, 1960), 40; Paula Louise Scalingi, "The Scepter or the Distaff: The Question of Female Sovereignty, 1515–1607," *The Historian* 42 (1978): 59–75; Mortimer Levine, "The Place of Women in Tudor Government," in *Tudor Rule and Revolution: Essays for G. R. Elton from His American Friends*, ed. D. J. Guth and J. W. McKenna (Cambridge: Cambridge University Press, 1982), 109–23; Constance Jordan, "Women's Rule in Sixteenth-Century British Political Thought," *Renaissance Quarterly* 40 (1987): 421–51; Patricia-Ann Lee, "A Bodye Politique to Governe: Aylmer, Knox, and the Debate on Queenship," *The Historian* 52 (1990): 242–61.

13. Allison Heisch, "Queen Elizabeth and the Persistence of Patrimony," *Feminist Review* 4 (1980): 45–56. Susan Bassnett, on the other hand, praises Elizabeth's virginity as a feminist statement in *Elizabeth I: A Feminist Perspective* (Oxford: Berg, 1988), 124–25, 128.

14. Quoted in Carole Levin, *The Heart and Stomach of a King: Elizabeth I and the Politics of Sex and Power* (Philadelphia: University of Pennsylvania Press, 1994), 43. For further discussion of Aylmer's tracts and other writings justifying female rule, see also Amanda Shepherd, *Gender and Authority in Sixteenth-Century England* (Keele, Staffordshire: Keele University Press, 1994).

15. "A discourse of the queen's marriage with the duke of Anjou, drawn out by the Lord Keeper," 1570, in "Egerton Papers," *Camden Society* 12 (London: Royal Historical Society, 1857).

16. D. M. Loades, "Philip II and the Government of England," in *Law and Government under the Tudors*, ed. C. Cross, D. M. Loades, and J. J. Scarisbrick (Cambridge: Cambridge University Press, 1988), 177–94.

17. Sarah Duncon of Yale University, who is working on Philip II as king of England, shared some of her ideas with me, in particular how courtly ritual inversed the traditional gender roles of king and consort during the reign of Mary I. The example of the silver and gold plate comes from D. M. Loades, *The Reign of Mary Tudor: Politics, Government, and Religion in England, 1553–58*, 2nd ed. (Harlow: Longman, 1991), 170.

18. Interest in the portrayal of Elizabeth as the Virgin Queen has grown in

recent years, largely thanks to the work of scholars of literature during the 1980s and 1990s. See for example: Stephen Greenblatt, *Renaissance Self-Fashioning: From More to Shakespeare* (Chicago: University of Chicago Press, 1980), 166–68; David Norbrook, *Poetry and Politics in the English Renaissance* (London: Routledge and Kegan Paul, 1984); Louis A. Montrose, "'Shaping Fantasies': Figurations of Gender and Power in Elizabethan Culture," in *Representing the Renaissance*, ed. Stephen Greenblatt (Berkeley: University of California Press, 1988), 31–64; Philippa Berry, *Of Chastity and Power: Elizabethan Literature and the Unmarried Queen* (London: Routledge, 1989); Susan Frye, *Elizabeth I: The Competition for Representation* (Oxford: Oxford University Press, 1993); Helen Hackett, *Virgin Mother, Maiden Queen: Elizabeth I and the Cult of the Virgin Queen* (London: Macmillan, 1995).

19. Christopher Haigh, *Elizabeth I: Profile in Power* (London: Longman, 1988), 16.

20. According to Levine, "The Place of Women," 112–13, despite Aylmer's acceptance of the legitimacy of gynecocracy, modern feminists would find his views insulting as she shared his contemporaries' misogynist prejudices.

21. Hastings Robinson ed., *The Zurich Letters*, 2nd ser. (Cambridge: Parker Society, 1845), 2:35.

22. Edmund Spenser, *The Faerie Queene*, ed. A. C. Hamilton (London: Longman, 1977), 5.5.25 (p. 562).

23. Elkin Calhoun Wilson, *England's Eliza* (Cambridge, Mass.: Harvard University Press, 1939), 8.

24. Allison Heisch, "Queen Elizabeth I: Parliamentary Rhetoric and the Exercise of Power," *Signs* 1 (1975): 31–55.

25. John N. King, "The Godley Woman in Elizabethan Iconography," *Renaissance Quarterly* 38 (1985): 41–84.

26. "The Passage of Our Most Dread Sovereign Lady, Queen Elizabeth, through the City of London to Westminster, the Day before her Coronation," in *An English Garner: Tudor Tracts, 1532–1588*, ed. A. F. Pollard (New York: Cooper Square, 1964), 365–92.

27. John N. King, "Queen Elizabeth I: Representations of the Virgin Queen," *Renaissance Quarterly* 43 (1990): 30–74.

28. Levin, *Heart and Stomach*, 41–42.

29. For the speech of Elizabeth to the House of Commons see Hartley, *Proceedings*, 1:44–45. A fuller discussion of the two speeches can be found in Frances

Teague, "Queen Elizabeth in Her Speeches" in *Gloriana's Face: Women, Public and Private, in the English Renaissance,* ed. S. P. Cerasano and Marion Wynne-Davies (Detroit: Wayne State University Press, 1992), 63–78.

30. Hartley, *Proceedings,* 112.

31. Ibid., 147.

32. *Somers Tract,* 1:175.

33. Victor Von Klarwill, *Queen Elizabeth and Some Foreigners* (London: John Lane, 1928), 208–9.

34. For the legal claims of the Greys and Mary Stuart, see Mortimer Levine, *Tudor Dynastic Problems, 1460–1571* (New York: Barnes and Noble, 1973), 99–101.

35. For details of all these negotiations, see Susan Doran, *Monarchy and Matrimony: The Courtships of Elizabeth I* (London: Routledge, 1996). It is worth noting here that there were three phases to the Alençon negotiations: January to August 1572; from the St. Bartholomew Massacre of August 1572 until 1576; and 1578 until 1581.

36. See, for example, her answer to the comte de Retz, September 1573, British Library, Cotton Manuscript Caligula E VI, fol. 199 (hereafter abbreviated BL).

37. PRO, SP 31/3/26, fol. 32; Hector de la Ferrière-Percy and Comte Baguenault de Puchesse, eds., *Lettres de Catherine de Médicis* (Paris, 1880–1909), 2:306.

38. 18 August 1560, PRO, SP 52/5, fols. 37–38v.

39. 29 September 1560, Archivo General de Simancas, Estado K 1493 B1 no. 102 (hereafter abbreviated AGS).

40. "De matrimonia Reginae Angliae cum extero Principe," April 1566, in Samuel Haynes, *William Cecil's State Papers* (London, 1740), 444.

41. Klarwill, *Queen Elizabeth,* 189–90.

42. 1 May 1562, AGS, E 8340/234, fol. 158v; BL, Additional MS 48023, fol. 363.

43. 29 October 1560, PRO, SP 70/19, fol. 411; 17 November 1560, Philip Yorke, ed., *Hardwicke State Papers* (1778), 1:145.

44. PRO, SP/12/13, no. 21; 29 October 1560, Throckmorton to Chamberlain, PRO, SP 70/19, fol. 132; 10 October 1560, Throckmorton to Northampton, PRO, SP 70/19, fol. 39.

45. J. H. Pollen, ed., "Papal Negotiations with Mary, Queen of Scots during Her Reign in Scotland, 1561–1567," *Scottish Historical Society* 37 (1901): 61.

46. Haynes, *Cecil's State Papers,* 444.

47. *Cal. S. P. Span. 1558–67*, 178–80, 224–26.

48. Doran, *Monarchy and Matrimony*, 46–52, 58–59.

49. 5 May 1565, *Colección de Documentos Inéditos para la Historia de España*, ed. M. F. Navarete et al. (Madrid, 1842–95), 89:116–17.

50. According to Chantonnay, Sussex said that "seria gran arrimo para el contra sus contrarios, y si no, podria ser que la Reyna pusiese los ojos en persono de quien no viendra bien al dicho conde." 16 October 1567, AGS, E 657, fol. 74b.

51. The November Eclogue of Edmund Spenser's *Shepheardes Calendar*, which lamented the death of Dido, has been interpreted as a general lament for the death of Protestant England and the eclipse of Leicester. Some scholars also view the fable of the oak felled by a husbandmen in the February Eclogue as a warning that the factional struggles surrounding the Alençon match might end in the fall of Leicester. The poem is printed in *Works of Edmund Spenser: The Minor Poems* (Baltimore: Johns Hopkins University Press, 1943), 1:1–120. For a discussion on this work's political importance, see P. E. McLane, *Spenser's "Shepheardes Calendar": A Study in Elizabethan Allegory* (Notre Dame: Indiana University Press, 1961), although he tends to overstate his argument.

52. There is some evidence, however, that during 1571 he worked to forward the matrimonial negotiations between Elizabeth and Henry of Anjou. For a fuller discussion see Doran, *Monarchy and Matrimony*, 123–25.

53. There is no direct evidence for Leicester's role in encouraging preaching against the match, but George Stanley made accusations against him to that effect. 21 January 1568, BL, Lansdowne MS 9, fol. 214.

54. BL, Additional MS 33594, fol. 1.

55. "Sir Thomas Smith's orations for and against the Queen's marriage," in John Strype, *The Life of the Learned Sir Thomas Smith* (Oxford: Oxford University Press, 1820), 184–259; Lloyd E. Berry, ed., *John Stubbs's Gaping Gulf with Letters and Other Relevant Documents* (Charlottesville: University Press of Virginia, 1968).

56. 10 January 1572, PRO, SP 70/122, fol. 50.

57. BL, Lansdowne MS 94, fol. 65.

58. BL, Additional MS 4149, fol. 92v.

59. Charles had in fact not reached any final decision about the Mass, but Sussex, who was conducting the negotiations in Vienna, reported home that this principle had been accepted. For further details see Doran, *Monarchy and Matrimony*, 90–91.

60. Berry, ed., *Gaping Gulf*, 20.

61. For Wilson, see "A Treatise of England's Perils, 1578," *Archiv für Reformations Geschichte* 46 (1955): 243–49; for Hatton, see E. St. John Brooks, *Sir Christopher Hatton: Queen Elizabeth's Favourite* (London: Jonathan Cape, 1946).

62. For Cecil's apocalyptic imagery and anti-Catholicism see M. Thorp, "William Cecil and the Antichrist: A Study of Anti-Catholic Ideology," in *Politics, Religion, and Diplomacy in Early Modern Europe: Essays in Honor of De Lamar Jensen*, ed. Malcolm Thorp and Arthur J. Slavin (Kirksville, Mo.: Sixteenth Century Journal Publishers, 1994), 289–304.

63. Bibliothèque Nationale, Fonds Français 3253, 371–410.

64. For details, see Doran, *Monarchy and Matrimony*, 164–72, and Doris Adler, "Imaginary Toads in Real Gardens," *English Literary Renaissance* 2.3 (1981): 235–60. An example of an allegorical poem which appears to refer to the match is Edmund Spenser's *Mother Hubberd's Tale*. This was probably written sometime between 1579 and mid-1580, though not published until 1591. It is printed in E. Greenlaw et al., eds., *Works of Edmund Spenser: A Variorum Edition. The Minor Poems* (Baltimore: Johns Hopkins University Press, 1943), 1:19–26, 2:107–40.

65. Quotations from David Starkey, *The Reign of Henry VIII: Personalities and Politics* (Hampshire: George Philip, 1985), 29, 128.

66. Thomas Cogswell, "England and the Spanish Match," in *Conflicts in Early Stuart England: Studies in Religion and Politics, 1603–1642*, ed. Richard Cust and Ann Hughes (Harlow Essex: Longman, 1989), 110, 112.

67. Simon Adams's views can be found in a number of articles: "Faction, Clientage, and Party: English Politics, 1550–1603," *History Today* 32 (1982): 33–39; "Eliza Enthroned? The Court and Its Politics," in *The Reign of Elizabeth I*, ed. Christopher Haigh (London: Macmillan, 1985), 55–77; "Favourites and Factions at the Elizabethan Court," in *Princes, Patronage, and the Nobility: The Court at the Beginning of the Modern Age*, ed. Ronald G. Asch and Adolf M. Burke (Oxford: Oxford University Press, 1991), 265–87.

68. Eric W. Ives, *Faction in Tudor England*, Appreciations in History Ser. 6 (London: Historical Association, 1979), 22.

69. Haynes, *Cecil's State Papers*, 365; J. Gough Nichols, ed., "The Diary of Henry Machyn," *Camden Society* 43 (London: Camden Society, 1848), 252.

70. BL, Additional MS 48023, fol. 363; 1 May 1562, AGS, E 8340/234, fol. 158v.

71. *Cal. S. P. Span. 1558–67*, 511, 560–61, 565.

72. Wallace T. MacCaffrey, *Elizabeth I* (London: Edward Arnold, 1993), 360.

73. Quoted in P. Collinson, "The Monarchical Republic of Queen Elizabeth I," in *Elizabethan Essays* (London: Hambledon Press, 1994), 41.

74. *Cal. S. P. Span. 1558–67*, 186–91; Dudley Digges, ed., *The Compleat Ambassador* (London, 1665), 111; Fénélon, *Correspondance Diplomatique* (Paris, 1838–40), 4:59, 93; William Murdin, *Lord Burghley's State Papers* (London, 1759), 322–42.

75. Von Klarwill, *Queen Elizabeth*, 113–14. I. Cloulas, *Correspondance du Nonce en France, Anselmo Dandino (1578–1581)*, Acta Nuntiaturae Gallicae 8 (Paris, 1979), 516; Joel Samaha, "Gleanings from Local Criminal Court Records: Sedition amongst the 'Inarticulate' in Elizabethan Essex," *Journal of Social History* 8 (1975): 69.

76. 5 May 1561, de Quadra to Philip II, AGS, E 815, fol. 5, translated in *Cal. S. P. Span. 1558–67*, 199–203.

The Royal Image in Elizabethan Ireland

Christopher Highley

After England ceded Calais to the French in 1559 as part of the Treaty of Cateau-Cambresis, Ireland became the only overseas territory to which Elizabeth I could realistically claim sovereignty.[1] This territory, originally conquered and claimed for the English crown by Henry II at the end of the twelfth century, and later incorporated as a kingdom by Henry VIII in 1541, was a perplexing mixture of promise and danger to the queen and her subjects. If Ireland figured in the collective imagination of Tudor England as a place of plentiful land and natural resources, of personal self-advancement, and even of greater freedom from the constraints of institutional religion, the queen herself invariably saw her "other isle" as a burdensome liability that, racked by internecine conflict among its diverse ethnic and political groupings, required constant royal attention and treasure. Elizabeth's preoccupation with Irish affairs was most intense in the last decade of her reign, when her former ward and ally Hugh O'Neill, the Earl of Tyrone, galvanized resistance among a coalition of Gaelic and Old English forces to the "Newcomers": the New English planters, administrators, and soldiers whose collective mission was to consolidate, and when possible to extend, the queen's authority in Ireland. With the outbreak of large-scale rebellion in the mid-1590s, O'Neill, with his kinsman and fellow leader Hugh Roe O'Donnell, presented his campaign as driven by large religious and national imperatives. The struggle for religious toleration and an Ireland free of English interference suffered a severe setback, however, at the Battle of Kinsale in late 1601, when Tyrone's confederacy of Irish and Spanish forces was defeated by an English army led by Lord Mountjoy. When Tyrone formally submitted to Mountjoy on 30 March 1603, he remained unaware that Elizabeth had died just six days earlier.[2]

In this chapter I examine responses to Elizabeth among her enemies in Ireland by adumbrating the strategies they employed to contest her authority. However, I want to stress at the outset that personal attacks upon the queen appear to have been infrequent even at the height of Tyrone's rebellion. We can attribute this surprising dearth in part to the fact that many of those in Ireland whom English officials considered rebels or malcontents steadfastly maintained their loyalty to the queen herself. Tyrone, for example, in the years leading up to his open rebellion, persistently defied Sir Henry Bagenal, the English crown's chief representative in the earl's own province of Ulster. In response to Bagenal's efforts to subject Ulster to the rule of a provincial president, Tyrone, instead of denouncing the queen, petitioned her for help. He claimed that his hereditary rights were being threatened, and that he could control Ulster for her more effectively than any English interloper.[3] In this Tyrone was typical of many Irish chiefs and Old English magnates who had no difficulty in reconciling protestations of loyalty to their sovereign mistress with defiance of English deputies, regional presidents, seneschals, sheriffs, and other local officers whom they saw as infringing on their traditional privileges. For many of the queen's disaffected subjects in Ireland, pursuing a strategy of local resistance from a position of formal loyalty was a way of fostering distrust between colonial officials and the Whitehall administration, while at the same time avoiding the full repressive power of the state that total defiance would have been likely to bring down.[4]

Because the display of loyalty to the queen was a valuable form of self-protection, few Gaelic and Old English leaders are on record as defaming Elizabeth or directly repudiating her authority. Most, though not all, of the extant verbal and symbolic attacks upon the queen tend to be anonymous and often collaborative. Assessing these attacks, however, is complicated by the issue of their context, since we know of them largely through the letters and reports of New English officials. By contrast, the texts and artifacts of an indigenous Gaelic culture contain few allusions of any sort to Elizabeth. The verse of the Irish bards composed during her reign is overwhelmingly concerned with the lineage and deeds of Irish and Old English chiefs, with intraclan rivalries, and with the bard's own standing in the patronage network; a few compositions do urge coordinated resistance by the Gaelic Irish to the "newcomers," but without mentioning the queen as a target of hostility.[5] Perhaps, like so much bardic verse, compositions defaming Elizabeth were suppressed by English campaigns against the supposedly subversive practice of "rhyming." Evidence does suggest, however, that Elizabeth was the subject of eulogistic bardic verse by "mercenary" poets hired by administrators in Ireland for propaganda purposes. Lord Deputy Sir John Perrot claimed, for example, that he had "given Money to Rhymers to set forth her Majesties most worthie praises." And among the Irish manuscripts in the British Museum is a poem ostensibly praising "the princess of England" by a bard attached to the powerful Old English loyalist the Earl of Ormond.[6]

Because we are forced to rely largely upon New English sources, we must be alert to the ways in which the testimonies of so-called rebels are filtered by the official/colonial culture. As Carlo Ginzburg writes in a different context, the voices of a dominant culture's "others" reach us (if at all), "strangled, altered, [and] distorted."[7] It is a commonplace of recent ethnographic theory that the complex work of stenography whereby a dominant, literate, humanistic culture records the experiences of a subordinate, largely oral culture can never be a disinterested act of translation. Inevitably, the dominant culture ideologically shapes and re-presents the experience of the observed other. In the case of English reports about Irish resistance to Elizabeth, those reports are likely to tell us less about the material realities of that resistance and its agents than about English projections about Irish attitudes and behavior.

I

If bardic verse exhibited no animus against the queen, works illegally imported into Ireland from the Continent evidently did. Writing to her Irish bishops in 1594, Elizabeth instructed them "to search as well the ships, barques or vessels, as well the shops and houses of any merchant or other person whom you shall suspect for . . . bringing or laying up any such books, ballads, songs . . . [that are] not only repugnant to our ecclesiastical laws, but also seditious to ourselves, our Crown and imperial dignity, and pernicious to our subjects, whereby enormous conspiracies, mutinies and rebellious practices are caused and maintained among the people of Ireland."[8] While few textual traces remain of these imported "books, ballads, [and] songs" that allegedly attacked the person of the queen, there are numerous references in the writings of English observers to " 'unreverend and undecent' speeches [about] Her Majesty"—speeches that may well have been inspired by these illicit materials.[9] We are dealing here with what anthropologist James C. Scott styles "the hidden transcript"—the array of gestures and sentiments to which subordinate groups resort as a way of resisting oppression.[10]

In the memorable phrase of one New English author, "lewd" and "traitorous" words against the queen constituted "mutinous mutterings"—a menacing image that aptly conveys English anxieties about the obscure and undecipherable nature of rebel discourse.[11] As the authorities of Tudor England were aware, the transient and elusive quality of seditious speech made it especially threatening to established order because it was more difficult than printed material to police and prosecute. Subversive speech as well as "any manner of book, rhyme, ballad, letter, or writing containing any false, seditious or slanderous matters to the defamation of the Queen's majesty" were increasingly the target of Tudor legislation, although "distinctions among libel, slander, sedition, and scandal were [still] taking shape in sixteenth- and seventeenth-century English law [and] the terms were still frequently interchanged."[12] In Elizabethan Ireland, where the writ of English law was much weaker, the monitoring and suppression of both the spoken and written abuse of authority was even more difficult than in England. "Is ther no punyshment in *Irelande* for these bould & saucy speaches, may every man use hys tongue, wyth out controulmente?" asks a speaker in Barnaby Rich's dialogue about the state of Ireland written early in James I's reign. The other speaker replies that "thos wordes that in *Englande* would be brought wythin the compasse of treason, they are accounted wyth us in *Ireland* for ordynary table taulke. [The Irish and Catholic Old English] wyll not stycke to belye some of hys Matis most honorable privy counsayll in *Englande* . . . they wyll not forbeare to slandre the kynge hym selfe."[13]

In Ireland as in England, "mutterings" against the queen circulated more freely than printed or manuscript libels and could reach all levels of society; "mutterings" could be understood, embellished, and shared by literate and illiterate audiences alike. Official concern about orally transmitted comments against the queen is epitomized in the authorities' fear of rumors—many of which were spread in Ireland about Elizabeth's illness or death.[14] Such rumors worked inevitably to embolden her enemies and spread uncertainty among her supporters. Reports from Ireland of "rhymes and daily jests" about the queen also suggest how the rebels exploited a tradition of subversive humor and how a rhyming form could ease the memorizing and hence the spread of abusive words. In sixteenth-century Ireland, as in England, rhymes spoken against authority may originally have been written down before gaining a wider oral currency.[15]

Whatever their precise form, rebel "mutterings" invariably shared common concerns as well as a vocabulary of derogatory adjectives and nicknames that focused upon Elizabeth's sex, age, and her status as a heretic. In 1586 an English observer claimed that the rebels in Connaught "made most odious speeches against her Majesty, saying, 'What have we do with that *Caliaghe?* How unwise are we, being so mighty a nation, to have been so long subject to a woman! The Pope and King of Spain shall have the rule of us, and none other.'" "Caliaghe" [*cailleach*], an old woman or hag, was a favorite epithet for Elizabeth among her detractors in Ireland, perhaps because it was a culturally charged word with connotations of magic.[16] Another term for the queen, "pysekytchen," is probably an English rendering of the Gaelic word *phiseogach,* meaning sorceress or charm-worker. English observers who heard the queen referred to as a "Done queen" may have been hearing some sort of play on the Gaelic words *donn,* meaning prince, and *donog,* signifying wretch.[17]

Following Elizabeth's excommunication in 1570, which released Roman Catholic subjects from obedience to her, rebels had a formal religious justification for denying royal authority. During his abortive uprising in 1580, James Eustace, Viscount Baltinglass invoked Elizabeth's illegitimate rule: "Questionless it is great want of knowledge, and more of grace, to think and believe, that a woman, uncapax of all holy orders, should be the supreme governor of Christ's Church."[18]

II

Elizabeth's enemies in Ireland, as well as trying to undermine her authority by spreading malicious words and writings also attacked the very symbols meant to reinforce the sovereign's authority. At home, the queen could project her authority and nurture public affection through civic processions and rural progresses—ceremonies that gave many of her subjects a highly prized glimpse of the royal person.[19] The fact that, like every other English monarch since Richard II, Elizabeth never visited Ireland made the symbolic expression of her authority there even more important. To compensate, royal propaganda was imported from England and also produced in Ireland.[20] A government-sponsored press was operating in Dublin during Sir Henry Sidney's Lord Deputyship, and by 1595 the title of "Queen's Printer" was accorded to one William Kearney whose Dublin press produced schoolbooks as well as a proclamation in both Gaelic and English declaring the Earl of Tyrone a traitor.[21] Despite the innovation of print and the use of a Gaelic font, attempts at disseminating the queen's image and authority beyond the pale of Dublin and the "civil" port towns of the eastern and southern seaboard were inevitably hampered by the lack of a Protestant preaching ministry and of the disciplinary routines established by the regular reading of sermons and homilies.

As in England, where a subject's choice to display the queen's portrait became "a pledge of loyalty" to Elizabeth's regime after the papal excommunication, so in Ireland people's display of portraits and other royal insignia carried immense symbolic value.[22] In 1581, Geoffrey Fenton, the Irish council's principal secretary, urged Sir Francis Walsingham "to send [Her Majesty's] picture. It would be to good purpose to hang by the cloth of state, especially for the great assembly of the country to the parliament."[23] But these most prominent and personal symbols of the queen's authority were also the ones most likely to be defaced or otherwise manipulated by her antagonists. Obscene and "blasphemous" portraits of Elizabeth were displayed in continental Catholic countries; throughout her reign, attempts were made to harm the queen "by stabbing, burning, or otherwise destroying her image." All of these bizarre attempts point to shared assumptions about the magical properties of the royal image and to the belief that "it partook in some mysterious way of the nature of the sitter."[24] The ubiquity of magical and quasi-magical thinking about the power of images in the early modern period is suggested by the remark of the Anglican establishment figure John Jewel that "images do oftentimes vehemently move the mind diuersly to sundrie affections."[25] Jewel's sense of the volatile psychological effects of pictures upon viewers may help to explain the puzzling discovery in a Gaelic rebel's house of "the Queenes picture behinde the doore, and the King of Spaynes at the upper ende of the table."[26] Elizabeth's portrait perhaps hung as a reminder of the rebels' continuing subjection and as a spur to their continued hatred of England and of the great "caliaghe." The relative positioning of the two portraits with the queen's semi-concealed behind the door and the Spanish king's prominently displayed may thus represent the householder's desire both to abase Elizabeth and to register his allegiance to the Catholic Philip.

Disaffected members of the Old English Catholic community were just as likely as Gaelic malcontents to manipulate royal symbols in protest against the acts of the queen and her representatives. In July 1596, for example, William Lyon, the bishop of Cork and Ross, complained to Lord Hunsdon that, during an annual inspection of school books, he had discovered

Her Majesty's style and title torn out of all the grammars, to the number of 74 in one school; the leaf in the grammar quite torn out, which containeth in it, Elizabeth, by the grace of God Queen of England, France, and Ireland, Defender of the faith, &c., and in the end of the leaf, God save the Queen. Whereupon I caused search to be made in all schools within my diocese, and found them all torn out, although they came new from the merchants' shops.[27]

Through this act of violent censorship, the Old English students were enacting their objection not to learning the English language as such, but to the notion that their ancient tongue and the texts that preserved it received authority from a heretical female ruler. When questioned by Bishop Lyon about the missing leaves, two of the teachers invoked the familiar Catholic charge of Elizabeth's illegitimacy, acknowledging her ancestors' right to the "said title," but denying the queen's. For these readers, Elizabeth was an illegitimate teacher and guarantor of meaning.

Elizabeth's adversaries in Ireland, then, might defame her in word and song or strike out against the symbols of her authority; but they could also register their opposition through passive noncompliance with the royal will—a strategy that the authorities found especially frustrating and difficult to counteract. Refusal to take the Oath of Supremacy was widespread among Elizabeth's enemies, while in other gestures churchgoers reportedly would not "so much as open their lips to say Amen, when they hear Her majesty prayed for."[28] And in 1588 the Catholic population of Dublin staged a mass boycott of special thanksgiving services for the queen's safe delivery from the threat of the Spanish Armada.[29]

III

In acts of defiance toward the "newcomers" in Ireland, Elizabeth naturally functioned as a symbolic focus of resentment, a cynosure of Englishness around which individual and collective fantasies of vengeance and liberation were staged.[30] As the rebels' hanging of the queen's portrait behind a door implies, Elizabeth's enemies were adept at manipulating images of her and thereby creating the "caliaghe" as a potent absent presence in their dramas of resistance. Surrogates of the queen could take many forms. A New English treatise written after the Munster revolt of 1598 claimed that "a divelishe preist" who did "spightfully spitte out against" the queen "the most sclaunderous, dishonorable, trecherous, and haynous speaches," had in the process "pulled an auncient old gentlewoman by the throate, and barbarously abused her"![31] But perhaps the most extraordinary example of the rebels' exploitation of royal surrogates occurred in the late 1580s when Sir Brian O'Rourke, the Gaelic chieftain of Connaught, allegedly desecrated a statue of the queen. Sergeant-at-arms John Ball, in late 1586, was the first Englishman to encounter the statue; during an investigation some five years later, Ball recalled how he "was sent into O'Rourke's country, there to receive her majesty's composition, and in the time of my being there at M'Glannagh's town, standing upon a green, I saw the picture (image) of a woman carved in a block, standing upon wheels of small timber. I asked the inhabitants of the town what it was. They told me it was made for a calliagh. I asked who she was. They told me one that denied a carpenter of milk. I demanded where she did dwell. They said on the far side of the water."[32] Ball, who claimed not to know the statue's real identity, was apparently no match for his native informants' seeming-innocent yet duplicitous answers. Their devious reference to the queen as a "calliaghe" denying milk to the needy laborer inverts one of her most cherished public identities as nurturing mother or wet-nurse to her people. Elizabeth extended to her subjects this persona in many speeches and proclamations; but she also acted as surrogate mother in a more practical way to her Irish subjects by fostering the sons of Irish nobility at the English court. According to the New English author Barnaby Rich, the queen was ever "a loving nurse, nay rather a kinde mother, that did still carke and care for [her Irish subjects], with such compassionate love and kindness."[33]

The eventual fate of the image seen by Ball is most fully described in a letter from the Lord Deputy, Sir William Fitzwilliam, to Lord Burghley:

O'Rourke about two or three years since having found in a church or in some other place an image of a tall woman wrote upon the breast thereof QUEEN ELIZABETH, which done he presently fell with such spiteful and traitorous speeches to rail at it, and otherwise so filthily to use it, as I protest unto your Lordship I abhor to remember, and can by no means frame my pen to write. During which time his barbarous gallowglasses standing by played their parts as fast, who with their gallowglass axes striking the image one while on the head, another while on the face, and sometimes stabbing it in the body, never ceased until with hacking, and mangling they had utterly defaced it. And being nevertheless not contented herewith they . . . fastened a halter about the neck of the image, and tying it to a horse tail dragged it along upon the ground, and so beating it with their axes, and railing most despitefully at it they finished their traitorous pageant.[34]

O'Rourke's rite of violence against his "image of a tall woman" both appropriates and retaliates against the image-breaking energies of Protestants.[35] The iconoclasm that swept Reformation England was also a part of the religio-political conflict in sixteenth-century Ireland where, according to Sir John Harington, the "vyolent hewing down [Catholics'] crosses, burning and defasing theyr ymages, rayling in the pulpet on all theyr Saynts and ceremonyes" were familiar sights.[36] Even O'Rourke's isolated province of Connaught in the far west of Ireland was not immune from the image-breaking activities of Protestant Englishmen; indeed, in the 1570s, Lord President Fitton "conducted a campaign of official iconoclasm in Connacht as part of his policy of stamping his authority on that province."[37] In assaulting the statue, then, O'Rourke—a notorious papist who "kept his Christmas according to the Pope's computation" [i.e., the Gregorian calendar]—stages a counterritual that targets in Elizabeth the supreme embodiment of the Protestant cause.[38] Moreover, by constructing the queen as an iconic figure (the original image, perhaps taken from a church, may have been an effigy of the Virgin), O'Rourke also draws attention to Elizabeth's contradictory identity, and hypocrisy, as a ruler who claimed to disown all things Catholic but who drew upon Catholic and especially Marian iconography in the fashioning of her own quasi-religious cult.[39] Whatever the intended symbolic overtones of the attack, the abuse and violence directed against this surrogate Elizabeth became for O'Rourke and his men part of a ritual catharsis in which they could confront and obliterate a usually untouchable figure of oppression.

To what extent, though, can we trust Fitzwilliam's narrative and determine what his motives were in reconstructing the event for his audience? In such a complexly mediated incident where the lines between fact and fiction are uncertain, we cannot disentangle what actually happened from what Fitzwilliam wanted his audience to think happened. Nor can we test Fitzwilliam's account against other, rival accounts since the event appears to be recorded only in official English documents. What is clear is that Fitzwilliam's narrative is no bland, unadorned rendition of the "facts" written in the colorless prose of a bureaucratic report but, on the contrary, a highly embellished and rhetorically skillful textualization of an event that apparently intrigued all who encountered it.[40]

Fitzwilliam's rhetorical design is to portray the desecration of the statue in terms of assorted theatrical and oratorical practices. O'Rourke's ranting at the statue functions as a kind of prologue, a verbal overture to the dramatic entrance of "the barbarous gallowglasses" who then play their scripted parts in the drama. Their repeated stabbings of the statue symbolize a kind of gang rape of a queen who styled herself a *virgo intacta*, "an unspotted virgin" whose bodily borders served as a metonymy for the geographical and political borders of her island nation.[41] With the subsequent strangulation of the effigy, the scene of the playhouse is displaced by that of the gallows and, then, by the spectacular context of the "pageant." When the effigy is finally dragged behind a horse, Elizabeth suffers a final indignity—one that parodies both a royal progress and the fate of a common traitor conveyed to execution on a horse-drawn hurdle.[42] Fitzwilliam's narrative derives its authority, then, from its artful design and imaginative appeal rather than from any claim to direct or indirect experience of the event: indeed, he never claims to have witnessed the event nor does he reveal the sources of his knowledge.

In the narratives of Fitzwilliam, Ball, and others, O'Rourke's attack on the statue is, as we would expect, routinely denounced; but the denunciations disguise more conflicted impulses and responses. Fitzwilliam's carefully honed description reveals, I would argue, a level of imaginative involvement resonant not of a routine attention to the incident but of an almost voyeuristic excitement. And as the retelling of the incident in various documents of the period suggests, others shared this (guilty) fascination. Indeed, O'Rourke's act of *lese majeste* entered the collective memory both in and out of Ireland, ostensibly as an emblem of native barbarism. Even fourteen years later Sir John Harington could refer to the Irishman who "trayled Queen Elisabeth's picture at his horse tayle," confident that his audience, Lord Mountjoy and Robert Cecil, would recognize the allusion.[43]

O'Rourke's "treason of the picture" (as other accounts referred to it) exercised a continuing fascination for English observers on both sides of the Irish Sea because it provided a displaced enactment of their own disaffection toward the queen and their own literally unspeakable desires for freedom from female rule.[44] In a revealing footnote to the attack, Sir Richard Bingham, the governor of Connaught and O'Rourke's major adversary, was accused by George Castell of conniving in O'Rourke's action. Castell alleged that, far from vigorously prosecuting the Irish chief for his assault on the queen's image, Bingham had furnished the image from his own house.[45] Whether or not Castell's charge was just, the fact that he made it implies that he believed his audience capable of suspecting the fealty of the queen's own commanders in Ireland. Bingham's superior, Lord Deputy Sir John Perrot, was the most notorious commander to be charged with disloyalty and treason while serving in Ireland. At his trial in 1592, Perrot was accused of seeking "to deprive, depose, and disinherit the queen's most excellent majesty from the royal seat, to take her life away, to make slaughter in her realm, to Raise rebellion in England and Ireland."[46] Perrot had allegedly "been a confederate and maintainer of notable rebels," including Sir Brian O'Rourke, whose attack upon the improvised image of the queen Perrot had heard of but failed to punish. The charges against Perrot were probably mostly fabricated, but the fact that they were given credence required the preexistence of a latent suspicion about the intentions of powerful officials in Ireland.[47]

Disaffection with Elizabeth's handling of Irish policy, particularly with her sensitivity to Old English opinion and her reluctance to prosecute large-scale war, was widespread among the cadre of New Englishmen who took up posts in Ireland from mid-century. Another New English "garrison hardliner" like Bingham was Barnaby Rich, whose posthumous description of Elizabeth as "a loving nurse, nay rather a kinde mother" to her Irish subjects turns out to be not a royal compliment but a sarcastic denunciation of what he saw as her abiding weakness.[48] Rich wrote elsewhere that "by overmuch clemency [in Ireland, Elizabeth] defeated her selfe."[49] Rich's alienation from the queen's Irish policies, his disgust at her preference for pardons over punishment, was articulated more or less explicitly and with different degrees of emphasis by many of his contemporaries, including Edmund Spenser, Richard Beacon, and the numerous anonymous authors who contributed proposals and position papers to the government in Dublin and London. In fact, the "dissing" of Elizabeth in Ireland was as much a part of a collective New English discourse as it was of the words and deeds of her declared Irish enemies.[50]

Notes

1. The treaty required that France return Calais to English control after eight years or forfeit 500,000 crowns. But as historians point out, the English apparently realized in 1559 that this agreement would never be honored and that Calais had been permanently lost.

2. Colm Lennon, *Sixteenth-Century Ireland: The Incomplete Conquest* (New York: St. Martin's Press, 1995), 300–302.

3. See Hiram Morgan, *Tyrone's Rebellion: The Outbreak of the Nine Years War in Tudor Ireland* (London: Royal Historical Society, 1993), 46–48, 76–80.

4. See Mary O'Dowd, "Gaelic Economy and Society," in *Natives and Newcomers: Essays on the Making of Irish Colonial Society, 1534–1641*, ed. Ciaran Brady and Raymond Gillespie (Dublin: Irish Academic Press, 1986), 139–40.

5. For examples, see Eleanor Knott, *The Bardic Poems of Tadhg Dall O Huiginn, 1590–1591* (London: Irish Texts Society, 1926), 2:1, 16, 18. For another poem of incitement to a Gaelic chief, see Standish Hayes O'Grady, *Catalogue of Irish Manuscripts in the British Museum* (London: British Museum, 1926), 1:412–20. For general discussion, see Nicholas P. Canny, *The Elizabethan Conquest of Ireland: A Pattern Established 1565–76* (Hassocks: Harvester, 1976), 137–39, and Bernadette Cunningham, "Native Culture and Political Change in Ireland," in Brady and Gillespie, eds., *Natives and Newcomers*, 148–70.

6. See Standish Hayes O'Grady, *Catalogue of Irish Manuscripts*, 1:544, and Eleanor Knott, *The Bardic Poems of Tadhg Dall O Huiginn*, 1:xviv–xlv. For discussion, see Michelle O Riordan, *The Gaelic Mind and the Collapse of the Gaelic World* (Cork: Cork University Press, 1990), 140–43, 152–57. Also on the English

employment of bards, see Nicholas Canny, *Kingdom and Colony: Ireland in the Atlantic World, 1560–1800* (Baltimore: Johns Hopkins University Press, 1988), 20–22.

7. Carlo Ginzburg, *Ecstasies: Deciphering the Witches' Sabbath*, trans. Raymond Rosenthal (New York: Pantheon, 1991), 10.

8. Constantia Maxwell, *Irish History from Contemporary Sources, 1509–1610* (London: Allen and Unwin, 1923), 136–37.

9. *Calendar of State Papers Relating to Ireland, of the Reign of Elizabeth, 1586–1588*, ed. Hans Claude Hamilton (Nendeln, Liechtenstein: Kraus Reprint, 1974), 505. In August 1599, William Treffry wrote to Robert Cecil from Fowy in Ireland that he had seized from an "Irish bark . . . great quantities of rapiers and other munition for the war." And "in a hogshead of salt" he had also discovered "a barrel of Papistical books, as well English as Latin, composed by sundry English seminaries and others"—materials in the Counter Reformation propaganda war for the bodies and minds of the peoples of Ireland (*A Calendar of the Manuscripts of the . . . Marquis of Salisbury*, 24 vols. [London: Historical Manuscripts Commission, 1883–1976], 9:326–27).

The queen, of course, was not the only target of verbal abuse in Ireland. The Irish, it was claimed during Essex's campaign, "have made two Irish terms of scorn against the Earl of Essex; one, that he never drew sword but to make knights; the other, that he came like a hasty messenger, that went away before he had done his errand" (*C.S.P. Ireland 1599–1600*, 260).

10. James C. Scott, *Domination and the Arts of Resistance: The Hidden Transcript* (New Haven: Yale University Press, 1990); also see his *Weapons of the Weak: Everyday Forms of Peasant Resistance* (New Haven: Yale University Press, 1985), chap. 2.

11. *The Supplication of the Blood of the English Most Lamentably Murdered in Ireland, Cryeng Out Of The Yearth For Revenge (1598)*, ed. Willy Maley, in *Analecta Hibernica* 36 (Dublin: Irish Manuscripts Commission, 1994), 80.

12. Penry Williams, *The Tudor Regime* (Oxford: Clarendon Press, 1979), 389–92; M. Lindsay Kaplan, "Slander for Slander in *Measure for Measure*," *Renaissance Drama* 21 (1990): 47 n. 1.

13. Edward M. Hinton, "Rych's *Anothomy of Ireland*, with an Account of the Author," *PMLA* 55 (1940): 91.

14. *Calendar of the Carew Manuscripts Preserved in the Archiepiscopal Library at Lambeth, 1575–1588*, ed. J. S. Brewer and William Bullen (Nendeln, Liechtenstein: Kraus Reprint, 1974), 432; "daily rumours" are mentioned in *Cal. Carew*

Mss. 1601–1603, 170. Also see *The Supplication of the Blood of the English*, ed. Maley, 89. William Lyon claimed that the bards "spread false tales among [the queen's] subjects" (*C.S.P. Ireland 1596–97*, 17).

15. For England, see Martin Ingram, "Ridings, Rough Music, and Mocking Rhymes in Early Modern England," in *Popular Culture in Seventeenth-Century England*, ed. Barry Reay (London: Croom Helm, 1985), 166–97; Adam Fox, "Ballads, Libels, and Popular Ridicule in Jacobean England," *Past and Present* 145 (1994): 47–83; and Alastair Bellany, " 'Raylinge Rymes and Vaunting Verse': Libellous Politics in Early Stuart England, 1603–1628," in *Culture and Politics in Early Stuart England*, ed. Kevin Sharpe and Peter Lake (Stanford: Stanford University Press, 1993), 285–310.

16. *Cal. Carew Mss 1575–1588*, 431. It was reported in 1575 that the Earl of Kildare had called Elizabeth "the callioght of England" (quoted in Canny, *Elizabethan Conquest*, 153).

17. Hinton, "Rych's *Anothomy of Ireland*," 77. Also see *Focloir Gaeilge-Bearla*, ed. Niall O Donaill (Richview: Browne and Nolan, 1977). I wish to thank Terry Odlin for assistance with translations.

18. *Cal. Carew Mss 1575–88*, 289.

19. Compare Richard A. McCabe, "Edmund Spenser, Poet of Exile," *Proceedings of the British Academy* 80 (1993): 81.

20. In October 1576, William Gerrard, the Lord Chancellor of Ireland, requested Sir Francis Walsingham to have printed and sent over to Ireland "300 or 400" copies of the "meetest" laws in the form "of proclamations." These would then be publicly proclaimed twice yearly by English judges on circuit throughout Ireland (*Cal. of Carew Mss 1575–1588*, 55).

21. E. R. McClintock Dix, *Printing in Dublin Prior to 1601* (Dublin: C. O. Lochlainn, 1932); David B. Quinn, "Government Printing and the Publication of the Irish Statutes in the Sixteenth Century," *Proceedings of the Royal Irish Academy 1943–1944*, vol. 49, sec. C, pp. 45–130.

22. Roy C. Strong, *Portraits of Queen Elizabeth I* (Oxford: Clarendon Press, 1964), 8.

23. *C.S.P. Ireland 1574–85*, 297.

24. Strong, *Portraits of Queen Elizabeth*, 32, 40.

25. Quoted in Strong, 37.

26. *Cal. Carew Mss 1589–1600*, 430.

27. *C.S.P. Ireland 1596–97*, 17. Sir John Dowdall informed Burghley in 1595 that "every town is established with sundry schools where the noblemen and

gentlemen's sons of the country do repair; these schools have a superstitious or an idolatrous schoolmaster, and each school overseen by a jesuit, whereby the youth of the whole Kingdom are corrupted and poisoned with more gross superstition and disobedience than all the rest of the Popish crew in all Europe" (*C.S.P. Ireland 1592–96*, 487–88).

28. Maxwell, *Irish History*, 135, 147. For noncompliance as a general strategy, see Scott, *Weapons of the Weak*, 31–34.

29. *C.S.P. Ireland 1599–1600*, 355; Maxwell, *Irish History*, 153.

30. On the way in which Gaelic resistance in the later sixteenth century developed from general hostility against the "newcomers" to a specific rejection of a "heretic sovereign," see Wallace T. MacCaffrey, *Elizabeth I: War and Politics, 1588–1603* (Princeton: Princeton University Press, 1992), 347.

31. *The Supplication of the Blood of the English*, ed. Maley, 50.

32. *C.S.P. Ireland 1588–92*, 336. Hiram Morgan sees the sudden "discovery" of the incident so long after its occurrence as motivated by the need to justify a government assault upon O'Rourke ("Extradition and Treason Trial of a Gaelic Lord: The Case of Brian O'Rourke," *Irish Jurist* 22 [1987]: 294).

33. *A Short Survey of Ireland* (London, 1609), sig. A2r. Quoted in John P. Harrington, "A Tudor Writer's Tracts on Ireland, His Rhetoric," *Eire-Ireland* 17 (1982): 99.

34. *C.S.P. Ireland 1588–92*, 143. The episode can also be followed in the same volume at pp. 141, 273, 336, 404–5, 408, 432, and 440. Also see, "Offences of Sir Bryan O'Rourke," in *The Egerton Papers*, ed. J. Payne Collier (London: Camden Society, 1840), 144–57, esp. 147–48.

35. On patterns of early modern religious violence, see Natalie Zemon Davies, "The Rites of Violence," in *Society and Culture in Early Modern France* (Stanford: Stanford University Press, 1985), 152–88.

36. Sir John Harington, *A Short View of the State of Ireland*, ed. W. Dunn MacRay, in *Anecdota Bodleiana*, vol. 1 (Oxford: James Parker and Co., 1979), 19. For further context, see Alan Ford, *The Protestant Reformation in Ireland, 1590–1641* (Frankfurt, 1985).

37. Colm Lennon, *Sixteenth-Century Ireland*, 319 and 137–38.

38. *C.S.P. Ireland 1588–92*, 141.

39. See Frances A. Yates, *Astraea: The Imperial Theme in the Sixteenth Century* (London: Routledge and Kegan Paul, 1975), and John N. King, "Queen Elizabeth I: Representations of the Virgin Queen," *Renaissance Quarterly* 43 (1990): 30–74. Leah Marcus points to the dialectic between licensed and un-

licensed icons of female authority during Elizabeth's reign. While visiting a Catholic household in Norwich in 1578, the queen and the local people witnessed a spectacle in which royal officials, having discovered an icon of the Virgin Mary, held it aloft opposite the queen, and then ritually burned it. Marcus argues that the episode stages the use of ceremony against ceremony, a process by which the dangerous associations of the cult of a Protestant queen were aired and exorcised through the treatment of a Catholic icon (*Puzzling Shakespeare: Local Reading and Its Discontents* [Berkeley: University of California Press, 1988], 83–87).

40. For a discussion of the consciously crafted nature of apparently nonliterary historical documents, see Natalie Zemon Davis, *Fiction in the Archives: Pardon Tales and Their Tellers in Sixteenth-Century France* (Stanford: Stanford University Press, 1987).

41. *Cal. Carew Mss. 1589–1600*, 105.

42. John Bellamy, *The Tudor Law of Treason: An Introduction* (London: Routledge, 1979), 187.

43. MacRay, ed., *A Short View of the State of Ireland*, 14. In an undated letter among the Bagot manuscripts, Richard Broughton noted that O'Rourke had "made a picture of the queen in wax, tied it to a horse tail, and his gallowglasses trailed it in pieces." The reference to a wax image suggests how the details of the episode could be subtly altered in subsequent retellings (*Historical Manuscripts Commission, 4th Report* [London, 1873], 336).

44. My thinking on this matter is influenced by the work of Louis Montrose, especially his discussion of courtiers' "frustrated desire for mastery over the sovereign mother / mistress," in "The Elizabethan Subject and the Spenserian Text," in *Literary Theory / Renaissance Texts*, ed. Patricia Parker and David Quint (Baltimore: Johns Hopkins University Press, 1986), 326.

45. *C.S.P. Ireland 1588–92*, 273.

46. *A Complete Collection of State Trials and Proceedings for High Treason and Other Crimes and Misdemeanors from the Earliest Period to the Year 1783*, ed. T. B. Howell (London, 1816), 1:1316.

47. Ibid., 1:1323–24. The attack is recounted on 1324. For a nuanced account of the place of the statue incident in Perrot's downfall, see Hiram Morgan, "The Fall of Sir John Perrot," in *The Reign of Elizabeth I: Court and Culture in the Last Decade*, ed. John Guy (Cambridge: Cambridge University Press, 1995), 109–25, esp. 118–20.

48. Brendan Bradshaw, "Sword, Word, and Strategy in the Reformation in Ireland," *Historical Journal* 21 (1978): 483.

49. Barnaby Rich, *A New Description of Ireland* (London, 1610), 103.

50. See Richard Beacon, *Solon His Follie, or A Politique Discourse, Touching the Reformation of Common-Weales Conquered, Declined or Corrupted* (Oxford: Oxford University Press, 1594). An especially lurid New English tract that registers deep misgivings about the queen is *The Supplication of the Blood of the English*, ed. Maley. For recent accounts of the "dissing" of the queen and her Irish policies among New English writers see, for example, Clare Carroll, "Representations of Women in Some Early Modern English Tracts on the Colonization of Ireland," *Albion* 25 (1993): 379–93; Christopher Highley, " 'A Soft Kind of War': Spenser and the Female Reformation of Ireland," in *Shakespeare, Spenser, and the Crisis in Ireland* (Cambridge: Cambridge University Press, 1997); and Maley's introduction to *The Supplication*, where he remarks that the author's "resentment [of the queen] is barely submerged beneath the frequent protestations of loyalty" (9).

"We shall never have a merry world while the Queene lyveth"

Gender, Monarchy, and the Power of Seditious Words

Carole Levin

In 1536 Thomas Syson, or Sheton, abbot of the Leicestershire house of Garendon, got into trouble for his seditious statements that included a series of prophecies he was making. In the sixteenth century the authorities found prophecies to be dangerous and uncontrollable, as they were a means to focus popular dissent on how different England might be from what the government planned. Prophecies were clearly defined, hostile forms of social commentary and protest. So were rumors, which were also rife in sixteenth-century England. By the sixteenth century, the term *rumor* had powerful and negative connotations, such as "loud expression or manifestation of disapproval or protest" about a person "noted or distinguished."[1]

Syson was upset by the religious changes Henry VIII caused in his search for a wife who could give him a male heir. Syson claimed that though the Church was having trouble now, by 1539 it would be as strong as ever it had been. As for Henry VIII, he was "cursed of God's mouth, for he roots up the churches as the mole roots up the molehills." Syson expected bishops and a queen to be burned in the near future, and Henry presumably punished by God for his blasphemy, but once "this is past we shall have a merry world." Over fifty years later some would have said that the merry world Syson had prophesied had still not come to pass. In 1591 John Feltwell, a laborer of Great Wenden, decided to "pray for a king." One of his neighbors asked him why he would do that, as "we have a gracious queene already, wherefore would you praye for a kinge?" Feltwell's answer demonstrates another side to the anger and anxiety over Tudor rule, this time aimed at Henry's daughter Elizabeth. "The Queene was but a woman and ruled by noblemen. . . . so that poore men cold gett nothinge. . . . We shall never have a merry world while the Queene lyveth." Five years later Edward Ewer echoed this sentiment when he said that it "would never be a merrye worlde till her majestie was dead or killed." He was sentenced to hang, though we do not know whether it was for these seditious words, since he was also convicted of stealing a horse.[2]

In sixteenth-century England two rulers especially stand out for their success in presenting themselves to their people and creating a personal monarchy. Eric Ives argues that Henry VIII's reign "was the apogee of English personal monarchy." G. R. Elton suggests that actually Henry was even more successful at this self-creation than Elizabeth. "In its most restricted sense, personal monarchy perhaps reached its apogee in Henry VIII. At this task of personal projection he was better than his father, who had been a better and abler king; more successful even than his daughter, who died with court and country emerging from the spell she had cast."[3] Yet despite this success, both also had serious problems: with the succession, with disputes over religion, and with the economy. Though Henry VIII's and Elizabeth I's popularity proves the success of their self-presentations, both also had to deal with seditious words and dangerous rumors. Many of these seditious statements had to do with the sexual behavior of the sovereign. Elizabeth was particularly vulnerable to such attacks, being not only a woman, and unmarried at that, but the daughter of Henry VIII, who went through six wives, and Anne Boleyn, whom people called whore and harlot, and who was executed for committing adultery with five men, one of whom was her own brother. The seditious statements against Elizabeth not only stand in counterpoint to those said of her father, but of her mother as well. There were even suggestions that Anne Boleyn was a witch. The accusation of adultery encouraged this belief, since many people believed that witches indulged in wild sexual behavior, including incest. Henry VIII claimed that he was seduced into his second marriage by witchcraft. For at least some of their subjects, there was no opportunity for a "merry world" while either Henry VIII or Elizabeth reigned.

It is no wonder these seditious statements were so upsetting, and were often taken quite seriously, since, as Francis Bacon pointed out, rumor and treason were often siblings. We can well understand how the Tudor government would take *words* as well as actions very seriously. Speaking subversive words to someone else was in fact an act potentially dangerous to the existing order. The Act of 1534 made it treason for anyone to call the king a heretic, a schismatic, a tyrant, an infidel, or an usurper of the crown, not only in writing but also by spoken word.[4] Neither Henry VIII nor Elizabeth had a standing army or a very elaborate, effective police structure. Much of the authority with which they ruled came from the way they were able to convince the people of their sanctity and power, rather than from brute force. People of the sixteenth century were also well aware of the power and influence of what words could do. As Barbara Rosen points out, the great interest in words during the Tudor age demonstrates a new awareness of "the meaning of meanings, the numberless contradictory possibilities of experience contained in a single word."[5] Words, indeed, were thought to have great potential power—the very fact of a curse was enough to destroy someone, as those who believed in witchcraft were all too aware. One proof of witchcraft was mischief following anger, a witch cursing someone and then evil chance, such as the death of a child or failure of a crop, befalling them. It is striking that Syson sees Henry being cursed from God's own mouth. Seditious words, if used in conjunction with witchcraft, could even harm or kill the sovereign. Moreover, in using seditious words against the sovereign, people were expanding the way they used words against neighbors and others they knew; the courts in early modern England had many examples of slander litigation.[6] As Deborah Willis contends, Elizabeth's conflicts with Mary I while she was a princess, and even more her conflicts with Mary Stuart once queen, "eerily repeat aspects of village women's quarrels."[7] Rumors allowed a disruption of social relations, and presented, Dermot Cavanagh suggestively argues, "a counter-image of authority."[8] Rumors allowed the expression of doubts about the sovereign's right to her or his subjects' obedience. Rumors were also more dangerous because they were extremely difficult to trace to a source. This essay considers seditious words about both Henry VIII and Elizabeth and examines the significance of gender in analyzing how both monarchs were regarded.

The fifteenth-century War of the Roses left a strong sense of insecurity in the sixteenth century, and many people saw a male heir as a political necessity. For Henry, this desire for a son became an obsession, and though one would well imagine the lack of a male heir would also upset the English people, much of the seditious comments of the 1530s had to do with Henry divorcing Catherine of Aragon[9] to marry Anne Boleyn and the subsequent break with Rome. Henry's daughter Elizabeth, on the other hand, refused to name an heir, claiming that God would provide a stable succession for England when the time was right. The seditious comments, especially of the 1580s and 1590s had to do not only with resentment over a woman's rule but also with a woman who refused to deal with the succession.

In certain ways it is ironic that the seditious words against Elizabeth so often reflected concern over the lack of a king, because though Henry VIII himself was very upset by the possibility of no male heir, most of the seditious language of the 1520s and 1530s does not reflect this concern as a national preoccupation. In fact, much of the seditious language of the 1530s supported Catherine of Aragon and condemned Henry for putting her aside, even though the continued marriage of Henry and Catherine meant that the heir would be Mary, a female. Yet when a woman actually ruled, though deeply loved and supported by many of her subjects, there was also much unrest over female sovereignty. The upset over Elizabeth's refusal to deal with problems of the succession manifested itself as criticism of Elizabeth as a *woman* ruler and a wish for a king, an attitude that is hardly prefigured in the seditious words uttered under her father.

For Henry VIII the decade of the 1530s was the most tumultuous in terms of religious change and fear over the succession. As a result, it was also a decade of seditious words uttered against the sovereign. The antagonism to Henry's divorce in the 1530s strongly suggests that the break with Rome was far more traumatic for some of the English than the idea of a female heir. One key reason for this may well have been that from the time Mary was a small child there were marriage negotiations going on. As a result, for many people the expectation would have been that Mary and her husband would rule after Henry, though in 1525 during marriage negotiations Henry was hesitant to state unequivocally that Mary was his heir and that England was her dowry.[10] Still, part of the anxiety manifested during Elizabeth's reign had to do with her refusal to marry.

With a system of hereditary monarchy, succession was always a crucial issue. When Henry VIII married Catherine of Aragon upon his accession to the throne in 1509, he did so with the expectation that he and Catherine would have sons. But all Catherine's sons died—only Mary survived. On

November 10, 1518, Catherine's last child, a girl, was born dead. The Venetian ambassador reported the deep vexation the people of England expressed over this news. By 1525, if not earlier, Henry, his council, and his people had to accept the fact that Mary was the heir, though Henry was obviously doubtful. And in the mid-1520s there was even more severe worry about the succession when there were a number of risks to Henry's life. In March 1524 Henry forgot to put his visor down in a joust with the Duke of Suffolk. Suffolk's lance struck Henry's helmet less than an inch from the king's exposed face. (This, of course, was how Henry II of France died in 1559.) Henry also almost drowned while he was out hawking in 1525. And there were attacks of both the plague and the sweating sickness in London in 1525 and 1526. With the pope's refusal to annul his marriage, Henry had limited choices. Clement VII offered Henry VIII several desperate remedies, such as a dispensation that would allow him to have two wives at once. Erasmus, for one, thought this was not the worst possibility; he wrote perhaps jokingly to Juan Luis Vives in 1528, "Far be it from me to mix in the affair of Jupiter and Juno [his names for Henry and Catherine], especially as I know little about it. But I should prefer that he should take two Junos than put away one."[11] Yet it is hardly surprising, given the dubious nature of the suggestion, that Henry refused to consider it. Henry wanted one undisputed wife who could give him a son for an heir.

Though it was not in fact true, some people in early-sixteenth-century England believed that a woman could not succeed to the crown. "By English law," the Venetian ambassador wrote in 1531, "females are excluded from the throne."[12] Given England's one long-ago and unhappy experience with a potential queen back in the twelfth century—Matilda—one might have expected the English people to thoroughly support Henry's quest for a male heir. And certainly historians today make that assumption. For example, J. J. Scarisbrick argues that "English experience of the queen regnant was remote and unhappy, and Henry's conventional mind, which no doubt accorded with his subjects', demanded a son as a political necessity." More recently Antonia Fraser has suggested, "It was a situation to arouse atavistic uneasiness in a country where memories of civil unrest, rebellions by claimants to the throne, had by no means died away."[13] Yet there were few reports of seditious comments about the succession in the 1520s. Margery Stone reported a conversation she had heard that was an attack on the legitimacy of the Tudor line. Sir Robert Sherrard apparently told Agnes Clifton, who passed it on to Stone, that Henry VIII was "not worthy to wear the crown, for . . . the father of King Henry VIII was a horsegroom and a keeper of horses." During the trial of the duke of Buckingham one of the pieces of evidence against him was that a monk had prophesied that Henry "would have no issue male of his body." Also at the time of the trial, John Stede claimed that "if the duke of Buckingham had lived three years longer, he . . . should have worn the crown."[14] Henry's lack of a male heir no doubt was one of the reasons for the execution of Buckingham, but there are still only a few reported comments about concern over the succession in the 1520s. In the next decade there was a very large number reported, and those of the 1530s often supported Catherine as queen, even though logically this meant a female heir. Some of those arrested were quite explicit in recognizing this consequence. John Snappe of Horsington told his drinking companions that he would bestow his life "upon my Lady Mary's title against the issue that should come" from Henry's marriage to Anne Boleyn.[15] Such comments were not only hostile to Catherine's replacement Anne Boleyn, but to the man doing the replacing, Henry himself.

In July 1533 James Harrison, parson of Leigh in Lancashire, reacted violently to the proclamation of Queen Anne: "I will none for queen but Queen Catherine; who the devil made Nan Bullen, that whore, queen?"[16] In 1534 Richard Stopes hoped that Catherine would again occupy her old place as queen of England.[17] Despite the fact that it was obvious to all that Catherine would have no more children, a number of people in England felt great loyalty to her; this loyalty for Catherine also translated into hostility toward Anne and toward Henry.

A drunken spinster, Margaret Chanseloer (at least she later claimed to be drunk at the time), called Anne Boleyn a "goggle-eyed whore." Rauf Wendon told Sir Thomas Gebons that Anne was a "whore and a harlot," and he trusted that she "should be burned in Smithfield, and [that] . . . would be the end of queen Anne." Later the same year Mrs. Amadas echoed this thought with the prophecy that "shortly after my Lady Anne should be burned, for she is a harlot." Seditious words were aimed not only against Anne but against Henry himself. Marjorie Cowpland called Anne Boleyn a "strong harlot" for whom Henry VIII turned extortioner, knave, and traitor. George Taylor exclaimed that if only he had Henry's crown, "I would play football with it." In July 1533 Sir William Ap Lli, a priest in Wales, was reported for his "outrageous words against" Henry VIII. He "wished to have the king upon the mountain in North Wales." There "he would souse the King about the ears till he had his head soft enough."[18]

Some people were even more explicit than Ap Lli in the harm they wished for the king. A man at Walden in Essex said he wished that the king would fall from his horse and break his neck. The priest John Hale in 1535 prayed of Henry VIII that his "death I beseech God may be like the death of the most wicked John, sometime King of this realm, or rather to be called a great tyrant than a king." In medieval/early modern England many people believed that John had been murdered by a monk, and the authorities perceived Hale's statement as an open incitement to kill King Henry. Hale was found guilty of treason and executed.[19]

Some even blamed Henry—not Catherine—for the lack of healthy male issue. John Gurle, master of Manton College, was convinced that Henry VIII had such great difficulty in siring children because he "did occupy with so many whores and harlots."[20] There was so much comment over Henry's sexual behavior that authorities saw slights against the king where they may not have been intended. A ballad singer composed a story about "a King" who goes out riding and meets an attractive woman and promptly seduces her. Authorities were concerned enough that the singer had to explain himself. He protested that this was a fantasy, and not intended to refer to Henry, but he was told he should not make up such stories about kings.[21]

Even some of those who tried to defend the king sometimes did so by also denigrating him. William Hoo, vicar of Eastbourne, tried to exculpate the king from responsibility in the divorce and the reformation, but his explanation sounded almost like a condemnation. "They that rule about the King make him great banquets and give him sweet wines and make him drunk, and then they bring him bills and he putteth his sign to them."[22] Henry contributed to this point of view, by always blaming his advisors if things went wrong.

Even after Henry's third wife, Jane Seymour, gave Henry the son he so craved, there were still strange mutterings that centered on the birth of the prince and Edward's role in life. In November of 1538 Richard Swann, a young serving man of Hounslow, passed on to some people a prophecy that he had heard about the birth of Prince Edward, to the effect "that he should be killed that never was born." He knew it meant the prince because a lady had told the king at the time of Edward's birth "that one of the two must die," whereupon Henry had ordered the child to be saved by being "cut out of his mother's womb." When asked where he heard this strange tale, Swann responded, conveniently enough, that a stranger told him. Swann's story, while not true, certainly captured Henry's passion to have a son and his belief that women, especially wives, were always expendable. It also hardly made the king appear to be caring about his wife in her most trying moment. This story was echoed many years later in Samuel Rowley's play, published in 1605, with its suggestive title of Henry's power and ego, *When You See Me, You Know Me*.[23]

There were further prophecies circulating in the 1530s that included not only Henry but Edward. In 1539 John Ryan, Roger Dicons, and John Wessell all were drinking together. Dicons offered a toast to King Harry and Prince Edward, saying he trusted to see each of them reign to a ripe old age. Ryan agreed that Edward would eventually succeed Henry, explaining he had been assured this in a prophecy he had heard. But the prophecy also stated that Edward would be "as great a murderer as the King his father is, and that he must be a murderer by kind, for he murdered his mother in his birth." Ryan was apparently imprisoned for this imprudent statement.[24]

There were also attacks on the sanctity and special nature of the king. A gunner in the navy was reported in September of 1539 for suggesting that if the king's blood and his own were side by side in a saucer, no one would be able to tell the difference.[25] Blood is intensely personal and it was something that powerfully resonated to people of the sixteenth century, different from the painful connotations today. A powerful curse was "by God's blood," which was the way "bloody" got into the language as a popular saying. Blood was the most intimate way to know God. One of the major struggles between Catholics and Protestants was over who had access to the wine of the communion supper, which Catholics wholeheartedly believed to be the blood of God. Was it only priests or should all believers participate? By stating that there was no difference between his blood and that of the king, the gunner was denying the king's sanctity, Henry's role as God's representative on earth.

The immense changes in religion and the worry over the succession may well have provoked these statements, but so did Henry's behavior, with the public repudiation of his popular, if no longer fertile, first wife. Perhaps most striking are the attacks on Henry's potency and sexual behavior, though the verbal violence and threats of attack and murder must have also deeply disturbed those in power. For Henry, having a male heir to succeed him was of such primary importance it became one of the guiding forces of his reign. Though there are certainly other reasons as well for his six marriages, desire for a son was certainly of first importance especially in the early ones. His much publicized divorce from Catherine and the execution of Anne Boleyn for adultery must have made Henry seem fair game to the many who were disaffected and wanted to criticize the king. We can see it in Europe as well. Charles V's sister, Mary, Regent of the Lowlands, Queen Dowager of Hungary, and niece of Catherine of Aragon, commented after the execution of Anne Boleyn and Henry's immediate marriage to Jane Seymour that "when he is tired of this one he will find some occasion of getting rid of her. I think wives will hardly be well contented if such customs become general."[26]

Elizabeth handled many aspects of her life and reign differently than had her father. Elizabeth effectively conveyed her love for her people and encouraged their love for her. Yet many of the English still had great difficulty with the concept of a woman ruler, though of course this would have in fact been the logical outcome—the reign of Mary—if Henry had not put aside his first wife. Elizabeth could not always control the way people responded to her. Together with the love and respect she inspired, there was hostility toward her as an unmarried female ruler whose position transcended the traditional role allotted to women in English Renaissance society. This hostility was expressed in the many rumors and antagonistic comments that circulated about Elizabeth.

Elizabeth's approach to the succession was completely different from her father's. She refused to name an heir at all, and stated that God would provide for the succession, perhaps with a much better ruler than any child of hers could be, "peradventure more beneficiall to the realme then suche ofspring as may come of me. For although I be never so carefull of your well doinges and mynde ever so to be, yet may my issue growe out of kynde and become perhappes ungracious."[27] Elizabeth, though she played with courtship for over twenty years into her reign, was at best ambivalent about actually marrying. She could lose power to a consort,

and her council was always divided on whom she should actually marry.
Perhaps also the lessons of her father's wives, their trouble having sons
and their subsequent fates, made her wonder if she would have trouble
conceiving a son or surviving childbirth if she did. By primogeniture, the
obvious heir was her cousin Mary Stuart, but naming her Catholic cousin
as heir to the English throne, either while she was queen of Scotland or
during the subsequent time Mary was the enforced "guest" of the English
after her abdication, would have created many other problems. After
Mary's execution in 1587, Mary's son, the Protestant James, was a more
appropriate heir, but Elizabeth, as she stated in a moment of candor, did
not want to play the setting sun to an heir who would look like the rising
sun. Yet while Henry's search for a son and repudiation of his wives and
their daughters caused insecurity, Elizabeth's refusal to name an heir also
caused great anxiety for the English. And one can well understand this
concern. Had Elizabeth died earlier with no settled succession, England
might well have been plunged into civil war.

But though Elizabeth handled the succession very differently than had
Henry, and unlike her father never married at all, her relationship with
her favorites, especially with Robert Dudley, appointed Master of the
Horse at the beginning of her reign and then elevated to earl of Leicester,
provoked even more sexual innuendo than the statements about her father. As with those aimed at her father, these comments included not only
seditious words from her subjects but malicious gossip in the courts of
Europe. After the mysterious death of Dudley's wife Amy Robsart in
1560, when she was found dead with her neck broken at the bottom of
some stairs, the courts of Europe buzzed with gleeful comments about
Dudley's relationship with his queen. Mary Stuart, still the young queen
of France, proclaimed that Elizabeth was about to marry her horsekeeper,
who had murdered his wife to make room in his bed for the queen. In
England itself the event provoked much gossip. Thomas Lever wrote to
Francis Knollys and William Cecil on September 17, 1560, about "the
grevous and dangerous suspition, and muttering" in Coventry about
Amy's death. He hoped there would be some way to alleviate these
suspicions, because if not the "displeasure of God, the dishonor of the
Quene, and the Danger of the whole Realme is to be feared."[28]

We will never know exactly how Amy Robsart died, though modern
historians consider it most unlikely that Robert Dudley had her murdered

with or without the connivance of Elizabeth. Nor can we ever know the exact nature of Elizabeth's relationship with him. But what is more important than the nature of their relationship was what people in England believed it to be. The gossip about Robert and the queen continued throughout Elizabeth's reign, and concerned government officials noted many instances of it. A generation earlier rumors and scandal about Elizabeth's mother helped to destroy Anne Boleyn.[29]

In the court records of those arrested for seditious words, hostility toward Elizabeth provoked as much verbal violence, and wishes for her demise, as had been provoked by her father. But in Elizabeth's case, the hostility intertwined with attitudes about a woman in power. Given society's restrictive views about what was appropriate female behavior, Elizabeth was in some ways far more vulnerable than her father, or even than her sister Mary, daughter of a popular and devout queen. The seditious words from Henry's reign had categorized Anne Boleyn as a whore. In the hostile criticism of Henry and Anne's daughter, we find the same labeling of her, and those who criticized Elizabeth's sexual behavior also denied that she was competent to rule. The seditious words about Elizabeth mark her not only as Henry's daughter but very much as Anne's as well.

Elizabeth was sensitive about any references to what her father had done to her mother. When in late 1586 James VI tried to convince Elizabeth not to execute his mother, he had his envoy William Keith tell Elizabeth that "King Henry VIII's reputation was never prejudged but in the beheading of his bedfellow." Elizabeth was furious that James would imply a parallel between Mary Stuart and Anne Boleyn, and would raise a subject she considered taboo. Keith told James that Elizabeth took such "chafe as ye would wonder."[30]

Elizabeth's government took the seditious statements about her, and attacks on her legitimacy and right to rule, very seriously. The 1559 Parliament made it treason for anyone to "maliciously, advisedly, and directly say . . . that the Queen's Majesty that now is, during her life, is not or ought not to be Queen of this realm." Simply to "hold opinion" of this view was also treason. The treason act of 1571 reaffirmed this definition of treason. Many of the people arrested in the reign of Elizabeth had gossiped about the queen in malicious ways. In Mary's reign Parliament passed a law against sedition in 1554; Parliament made this law even more stringent in 1581. The 1581 statute demonstrated again the fear that something could happen to Elizabeth, a catastrophe particularly when there was no settled succession. The act "against seditious words and rumours uttered against the Queen's most excellent Majesty" was aimed especially at those who "not only wished her Majesty's death, but also by divers means practised and sought to know how long her Highness should live, and who should reign after her decease."[31] There were rumors of Elizabeth's imminent death throughout her reign, but they became more intense as she grew older. England was drifting toward war, and there was still no settled succession. In 1584 Jeffrey Leeche "declared the Queen would not live half a year." Fifteen years later William Crowsyer stated that "her majesty was dead, and that an army was in the field about London."[32] The death of the queen without clear succession could easily lead to chaos and civil war. Prophesying the sovereign's death was treason, but these statements suggest not only potential malice but extreme anxiety.

Like her father, Elizabeth was strong willed and determined. Once she was queen, she intended to live her life as she wanted within the confines of rule. And this meant promoting in rank and openly flirting with such favorites as Robert Dudley. Though Elizabeth always claimed that there was nothing dishonorable about her relationship with Dudley, she was also determined to decide for herself how to set the parameters of that relationship, and to openly express her feelings for him. These public displays of affection led many people to express the belief that Dudley was her lover, and that they even had children together. Some even argued that this was the reason Elizabeth left court to go on progress—to hide her pregnancies.

Though from the very beginning of her reign there were rumors about Elizabeth's love affair with Dudley and that she was pregnant by him or had children, the rumors about Elizabeth's illegitimate children became even more intense in the last two decades of Elizabeth's reign, as did attacks on her rule. By the late 1570s and early 1580s Elizabeth, already in her late forties, was now too old to bear a child, and she still refused to name a successor. Anxiety was even more acute as the relationship with Spain deteriorated and open conflict became more and more likely. At court people worried desperately about her health, seeking reassurance from one another that she would survive. In the countryside, these worries took on a different form. The attacks on Elizabeth reflect on another level the fears over the succession and the antagonism toward a queen who refused to provide for her people's future.

Some of the attacks on Elizabeth had to do with her title and her right to the throne. For example, in 1577 Mary Clere, an Ingatestone spinster, declared Elizabeth was base born and Mary Stuart had a better claim to the throne. Clere was brought to trial and executed. Soon after, Randall Duckworth, a laborer in the village of Bradwell, stated that "this is no good government which we now live under and it was merry England when there was better government and if the queen die there will be a change." He was made to stand in the pillory with a paper on his head. In 1580 Vicar John Pullyver stated that "some did saie that we had no quene"; he was placed in the pillory.[33]

Other seditious statements had to do more specifically with her sexual behavior. In 1580 an Essex laborer, Thomas Playfere, stated that Elizabeth had two children by Lord Robert; he claimed he had seen them when they had been sent out of the country in two of the queen's best ships. The next year Henry Hawkins explained Elizabeth's frequent progresses throughout the countryside as a way for her to leave court and have her illegitimate children by Dudley—he claimed that she had five. Hawkins said of Elizabeth, "She never goethe in progress but to be delivered."[34]

As the 1580s progressed, and England moved toward war with Spain, the attacks became even more brutal. In April of 1585 Jeremy Vanhill, a laborer, publicly stated, "Shyte uppon your Queene; I woulde to god shee were dead that I might shytt on her face." This was a direct, vivid, and violent statement of hostility. Vanhill wished "that the Queene were as sicke as Peter Aveger then was." Aveger was so ill he died that night. The authorities took Vanhill's ravings seriously; he was hanged for what he said, a far more serious punishment than was usually given.[35] In 1586 Joan Lyster of Cobham argued that "the Counsayle makes a foole of the Queenes Majestie, and bycause she is but a wooman she owght not to be governor of a Realme." In September 1589 Cecily Burche, a spinster of London, was sentenced to stand in the pillory for publicly saying that "she trusted in god to see the blodd run thorrowe the streetes as water runneth in the Thames. And she trusted to see a newe prince to raigne over us."[36] The same year Thomas Wendon claimed that "Parson Wylton spake openly in church . . . that the Queen's Majesty was an arrant whore" since "the Queen is a dancer, and Wylton said that all dancers are whores."[37]

There were also further rumors of supposed children. In 1590 a widow named Dionisia Deryck claimed that Elizabeth "hath already had as many children as I, and that two of them were yet alive, one a man child and the other a maiden child, and the others were burned." We do not know exactly how many since the records do not state how many times Deryck herself had given birth. The father of the queen's children, claimed De-ryck, was Dudley, who had "wrapped them up in the embers which was in the chamber where they were born." The same year Robert Gardner or Garner told a similar story; Leicester "had four children by the Queen's Majesty, whereof three were daughters alive, and the fourth a son that was burnt." Both Deryck and Garner stood in the pillory for their indiscretions.[38]

Henry Collins, a servant, was committed to prison in the Marshalsea in 1592 for saying he would kill Elizabeth. Another prisoner there, Gratian Brownell, said that there were many prisoners who felt that way, and "some one would make an end of her one day, and then all those commit-ments would be void, and all would be well." In October 1598 the laborer Thomas Farryngton publicly stated that "the Queenes majestie was Ante-christ and therefore she is throwne downe into hell." Farryngton was placed in the pillory and his ears were cropped. In 1598 Edward Fraunces also made a remark that connected misogyny and sexual politics. Fraunces called Elizabeth "base born," and wished "that Her Majesty had been cut off twenty years since, so that some noble prince might have reigned in her stead."[39] The last decade of Elizabeth's reign was difficult. Not only was Elizabeth elderly and still refusing to name an heir, but the conflict with Spain was not entirely resolved in 1588, and in the last decade of the sixteenth century there was inflation and misery caused by poor harvests. Focusing on Elizabeth's failure as a woman—the wish for a noble *prince*—was an easier way to deal with these anxieties. It is hardly a wonder that at these crisis times there were also accusations for witchcraft, another way to focus and scapegoat anxiety, and again aimed overwhelmingly at women.

These rumors and slanders are but a small part of the way the English regarded their monarch in the sixteenth century. There was also great love for both these Tudor rulers. And even more serious problems. Both

Henry and Elizabeth also had to deal with actual revolts—such as the 1537 Pilgrimage of Grace and the 1569 Rising of the North. There were attempts to kill Henry VIII and Elizabeth using magic. While Elizabeth herself showed no personal fear of magical plots against her, members of her government were desperately afraid she would be the victim of image magic.[40] Even more seriously, there were also a number of conspiracies to assassinate Elizabeth and place her cousin Mary Stuart on the throne. But the words of disaffected English people, usually with no plan to carry out any threat to the monarch, are interesting in reflecting anxiety over religion, the succession, and, significantly, gender and power.

While there were certainly rumors and seditious words about Henry VIII, despite the catastrophes of his reign, they were not as specific in the gendered nature of their attack as those made toward Elizabeth. And ironically they were at their most intense in the 1530s, when Henry was attempting to provide a son, a male heir, for his people, not in the 1520s, when his only heir was a daughter. In the 1530s Henry in a sense opened the door to such commentary by his public putting aside of his popular first wife and then the even more public villification of his second, even though his stated motives were to provide England with a male heir. But though Henry was attacked by some seditious commentary, his various wives were also able to deflect some of that concern. And it seems that for some of the English people, the possibility of a woman ruler in the future was not so horrifying, perhaps because they did not really believe it would happen. By 1553 that possibility was a reality, and five years later Henry's youngest daughter was on the throne. Elizabeth was the child of Henry and the woman denounced for her supposed sexual promiscuity, Anne Boleyn; as a woman ruling alone Elizabeth represented deeply felt concerns about rule, stability, women's roles, and sexuality. We can hardly be surprised that Elizabeth, the unmarried queen, was so attacked.

In many ways Elizabeth was a successful queen loved by many of her people. But there were also, especially toward the end of her reign, serious problems and deep areas of dissatisfaction. The seditious statements about their queen allowed people to vent their frustration over the lack of a settled succession and also to denigrate Elizabeth by dismissing her as a whore and an incompetent female, and perhaps to imply the view, certainly believed in by her father in his obsessive search for a son, that a woman could not rule.

Notes

Versions of this paper were presented at the Mid-Hudson Medieval and Renaissance Studies Group at Vassar College and at the Patristics, Medieval, and Renaissance Conference at Villanova University. I appreciate the thoughtful feedback in both instances. I want to thank Kristin Elliott for her research assistance and I am especially grateful to Ilona Bell, Jo Eldridge Carney, Katherine French, and Retha Warnicke for their help in working through these ideas.

1. *The Oxford English Dictionary*, prepared by J. A. Simpson and E. S. C. Weiner, 2nd ed. (Oxford: Clarendon Press, 1989), 14:241. Dermot Cavanagh makes this point in " 'Possessed with Rumours': Popular Speech and King John," *Shakespeare Yearbook* 6 (1996): 176.

2. G. R. Elton, *Policy and Police: The Enforcement of the Reformation in the Age of Thomas Cromwell* (Cambridge: Cambridge University Press, 1972), 71–72. *Calendar of Assize Records: Essex Indictments, Elizabeth I*, ed. J. S. Cockburn (London: Her Majesty's Stationery Office, 1978), 373; *Calendar of Assize Records: Kent Indictments, Elizabeth I*, ed. J. S. Cockburn (London: Her Majesty's Stationery Office, 1979), 402, 431. Some of the issues about Elizabeth and sedition in this essay are also discussed in Carole Levin, *The Heart and Stomach of a King: Elizabeth I and the Politics of Sex and Power* (Philadelphia: University of Pennsylvania Press, 1994), chaps. 4 and 5.

3. Eric Ives, "Henry the Great?" *The Historian: The Magazine of the Historical Association* 43 (Autumn, 1994): 8; G. R. Elton, *Henry VIII: An Essay in Revision* (London: Historical Association, 1962), 12.

4. John Bellamy, *The Tudor Law of Treason: An Introduction* (London: Routledge, 1979), 32.

5. Barbara Rosen, ed., *Witchcraft in England, 1558–1618* (Amherst: University of Massachusetts Press, 1991), 37.

6. Laura Gowing, "Language, Power, and the Law: Women's Slander Litigation in Early Modern London," in Jenny Kermode and Garthine Walker, eds., *Women, Crime, and the Courts in Early Modern England* (Chapel Hill: University of North Carolina Press, 1994), 26–47.

7. Deborah Willis, *Malevolent Nurture: Witch-Hunting and Maternal Power in Early Modern England* (Ithaca: Cornell University Press, 1995), 16.

8. Cavanagh, " 'Possessed with Rumours,' " 183.

9. Or, more technically, annulling the marriage.

10. David Loades, *The Politics of Marriage: Henry VIII and His Queens* (Stroud, Gloucestershire: Alan Sutton Publishing, 1994), 35.

11. Erasmus, *Opus epistolarum,* 7, ep. 2040, p. 471, cited in Lacey Baldwin Smith, *Henry VIII: The Mask of Royalty* (Boston: Houghton Mifflin, 1971), 104; Preserved Smith, *Erasmus* (1923; New York: Dover Publication, 1962), 281.

12. *Venetian Calendar of State Papers,* 4. 300, in A. F. Pollard, *Henry VIII* (London: Longmans, Green, 1905), 144. For more on the question of legality and arguments over women's rule, see Amanda Shephard, *Gender and Authority in Sixteenth-Century England* (Keele, Staffordshire: Keele University Press, 1994).

13. J. J. Scarisbrick, *Henry VIII* (Berkeley: University of California Press, 1968), 150; Antonia Fraser, *The Wives of Henry VIII* (New York: Alfred A. Knopf, 1993), 93. See also, Richard Rex, *Henry VIII and the English Reformation* (New York: St. Martin's Press, 1993), 7.

14. *Letters and Papers of the Reign of Henry VIII,* ed. James Gairdner and R. H. Brodie (London: HMSO, 1864–1932), III: pt. 1, 1284 (p. 491), 1313, 1356. Hereafter cited as *L&P.*

15. *L&P,* VII: 497; David Loades, *Mary Tudor: A Life* (Oxford: Blackwell, 1989), 93.

16. Henry Ellis, ed., *Original Letters Illustrative of English History,* 2nd ed. (London: Harding, Triphook, and Lepard, 1825), 2: 42 44; G. R. Elton, *Policy and Police: The Enforcement of the Reformation in the Age of Thomas Cromwell* (Cambridge: Cambridge University Press, 1972), 278.

17. Elton, *Policy and Police,* 65.

18. *L&P,* VI: 733, 790, 923; VII: 1609; VIII: 196, 278, 727, 844; Elton, *Policy and Police,* 11–12 n. 4.

19. Jasper Ridley, *Henry VIII: The Politics of Tyranny* (New York: Fromm, 1986), 307; *L&P,* VIII: 609.

20. *L&P,* XII: pt. 1, 126; Elton, *Policy and Police,* 10. In fact, for a Renaissance king, Henry VIII had relatively few mistresses, though many wives.

21. Elton, *Policy and Police,* 307–8.

22. *L&P,* XI: 300; Elton, *Policy and Police,* 12.

23. For more on Rowley's play, see Jo Eldridge Carney, "Queenship in Shakespeare's *Henry VIII:* The Issue of Issue," in Carole Levin and Patricia A. Sullivan, eds., *Political Rhetoric, Power, and Renaissance Women* (Albany: State University of New York Press, 1995), 189–202.

24. *L&P,* XIV: pt. 2, 73, 102; Elton, *Policy and Police,* 59, 62.

25. *L&P*, XIII: pt. 1, 595; XIV: pt. 2, 165; Elton, *Policy and Police*, 308.

26. *L&P*, X: 965.

27. T. E. Hartley, ed., *Proceedings in the Parliament of Elizabeth, 1558–1581* (Leicester: Leicester University Press, 1981), 44–45.

28. William Murdin and Samuel Haynes, eds., *A Collection of State Papers Relating to Affairs in the Reign of Queen Elizabeth from 1542 to 1596 left by William Cecil, Lord Burghley* (London: William Bowyer, 1740–59), 362.

29. See Retha Warnicke, *The Rise and Fall of Anne Boleyn* (Cambridge: Cambridge University Press, 1989), for a full discussion of this issue.

30. R. S. Rait and A. I. Cameron, *King James's Secret* (London, 1927), 60–61, 69, cited in Anne Somerset, *Elizabeth I* (New York: Knopf, 1991), 435.

31. Lacey Baldwin Smith, *Treason in Tudor England: Politics and Paranoia* (Princeton, N.J.: Princeton University Press, 1986), 137; G. W. Prothero, ed., *Select Statutes and Other Constitutional Documents Illustrative of the Reigns of Elizabeth and James I,* 4th ed. (Oxford: Clarendon Press, 1913), 23; William Camden, *The History of the Most Renowned and Victorious Princess Elizabeth,* 4th ed. (London: M. Flesher, 1688), 28; Christopher Haigh, *Elizabeth I: Profile in Power* (London: Longman, 1988), 18; Joel Samaha, "Gleanings from Local Criminal-Court Records: Sedition amongst the 'Inarticulate' in Elizabethan Essex," *Journal of Social History* 8 (Summer, 1975): 64–65.

32. *Calendar of State Papers, Domestic Series, of the Reigns of Edward VI, Mary, Elizabeth, James, 1547–1625,* ed. Robert Lemon and Mary Anne Everett Green (London: Longman, Brown, Green, Longmans, and Roberts, 1856–72), 2:206; 5:296. Hereafter cited as *CSP, Domestic.*

33. Samaha, "Gleanings from Local Criminal-Court Records," 68–69.

34. Louis Adrian Montrose, "The Elizabethan Subject and the Spenserian Text," in *Literary Theory/Renaissance Texts,* ed. Patricia Parker and David Quint (Baltimore: Johns Hopkins University Press, 1986), 311; F. G. Emmison, *Elizabethan Life, Vol. I: Disorder* (Chelmsford: Essex County Council, 1971), 42–43; *Calendar of Assize Records: Essex,* 195; *CSP, Domestic,* 2:12.

35. *Calendar of the Assize Records: Kent,* 246. The scatological motif was echoed a decade and a half later. In 1599 Mary Bunton was whipped and placed in the stocks after she said, "I care not a Turde for the Queene nor hir precepts." *Calendar of the Assize Records: Kent,* 445.

36. *Calendar of the Assize Records: Surrey Indictments, Elizabeth I,* ed. J. S. Cockburn (London: HMSO, 1980), 282, 345.

37. *Calendar of Assize Records: Essex,* 195.

38. Emmison, *Elizabethan Life*, 42; Samaha, "Gleanings from Local Criminal-Court Records," 69.

39. *Calendar of the Assize Records: Essex*, 373; *Calendar of the Assize Records: Kent*, 402, 431, 440; *CSP, Domestic*, 3:282, 5:136–37. Fraunces made these comments after he had failed to seduce Elizabeth Baylie. His "line" to Baylie was that, since the queen had lovers and even three illegitimate children, why did she refuse him.

40. Rosen, *Witchcraft in England*, 52.

Pamphlets

and

Sermons

"Souereaigne Lord of lordly Lady of this land":

Elizabeth, Stubbs, and the *Gaping Gvlf*

Ilona Bell

Flattering Glosses and Manifest Depraving of Her Majesty

On 17 August 1579 François, Duke of Anjou, Monsieur Frère du Roi, arrived in Greenwich having come to England "secretly" to court the queen. On 18 August 1579 or thereabouts a thousand copies of *The Discoverie of a Gaping Gvlf whereinto England is Like to be Swallowed by an other French mariage* were secretly printed in London.[1] Elizabeth, as yet unaware of this latest assault on her sovereignty, seemed genuinely charmed by her French frog, as she affectionately dubbed Monsieur.[2]

The Discoverie (meaning the action of disclosing or divulging something that has been hidden; the finding out or bringing to light something which was previously unknown) was a carefully planned political act, calculated to blow wide open the "secret" of Monsieur's visit. It is also an archetypal example of dissing the queen. Though published anonymously, the treatise was written by John Stubbs, a graduate of Trinity College Cambridge, a lawyer and member of Lincoln's Inn, and the brother-in-law of the influential Puritan minister Thomas Cartwright. *The Gaping Gulf* galvanized public opposition to the marriage by arousing the country's deepest fears.

The cataclysmic title plays upon the free-floating anxieties of a small island nation, open to attack from all sides. ("Gaping" means splitting or rending asunder; "gulf" means: a body of water; an abyss; the depths.) Images representing the French marriage as a violation of the country's boundaries abound. The match would "open a gate of losing all that is left" of "those dominions which we have lost" (Berry 58); it "opens all the ports to foreign enemies" (Berry 77). Stubbs portrays the proposed marriage as equivalent to inviting a member of the enemy forces to be England's gatekeeper: "I would be loath that either France or Spain should have such a porter here to let them in at a postern gate as Monsieur is" (Berry 38). England must take steps to shore up "the naturally bridling bands of the sea, wherewith God hath compassed us about," lest the country be deluged and torn asunder. For "the surest girths which hold us in our saddle are the peace and good order of our land" (Berry 88).

As feminist anthropologists and historians explain, an obsessive concern with boundaries and invasions typically occurs when there is an "actual change in the functions and structure of the family, alterations in the lines that divide the family from other social institutions, redefinitions of public and private space, and, most especially, changes in relations between the world of men and the world of women."[3] Stubbs's alarmist rhetoric plays upon the gender unconscious—inciting fears that the queen's female body is threatening the social order.[4]

While the queen's advisors hesitated, fearful of arousing her anger during the Duke's visit, *The Discoverie* began circulating in London and was soon making its way to other parts of the country. William Page, a London gentleman, sent fifty copies to a friend in Cornwall with instructions to distribute the book to friends. Sure enough, the queen's fury was phenomenal. She issued a proclamation banning the "lewd, seditious book of late rashly compiled and secretly printed and afterwards seditiously dispersed into sundry corners of the realm."[5]

The proclamation created an immediate stir, which is described by Bernardino de Mendoza, the Spanish Ambassador, in a letter to Philip II, dated 25 September. "A printed book has recently been published here setting forth the evils arising from a union with the French," Mendoza writes. "As soon as it was published the Queen prohibited its possession under pain of death, and great efforts were used to collect all the copies, and to discover the author, in order to prevent the circulation of the facts before Parliament meets" (Berry xxvii). The speed of the queen's reaction, the severity of the punishment, and the elaborate mechanism for retrieving every copy already in circulation made the proclamation all the more notable, as Mendoza explains in another letter, written two days later: "As the proclamation was only dated two days before its promulgation (which was carried out with great ceremony), people are attaching a great deal of importance to it, and saying that it was advisable to cut short the sensation caused by the book, in order to effect the marriage" (Berry xxvii).

The tract raises a number of serious objections to the proposed marriage. First, Stubbs argues, as a Catholic, Monsieur would become a catalyst for civil resistance to the English church. Second, he claims that a French match would alienate England's Protestant allies abroad, encouraging foreign plots against the queen and the church. Third, Stubbs believes the marriage would be detrimental to the queen. At her age, moreover, she was unlikely to survive the dangers of childbirth. Moreover, there were serious concerns about Monsieur's health. Having recovered from smallpox, he contracted tuberculosis which eventually killed him. Moreover, he was believed to have syphilis—the AIDS of the sixteenth century—which, prior to antibiotics, was a disfiguring, highly infectious, and often fatal disease.[6] Stubbs alludes to the French pox as God's punishment for a licentious, sinful life.

Stubbs's argument provides more than enough reasons for Elizabeth's anger. To begin with, the vicious, public attack on Alençon was not only a personal insult to her and the duke, but also a diplomatic nightmare which threatened to undermine the extraordinary efforts Elizabeth had made to establish an alliance with France as a hedge against Spain. The claims that Monsieur could not possibly be in love with a woman twenty years his senior, coupled with the argument that she was too old to bear a child, were no doubt a blow to Elizabeth's vanity, eager as she was throughout her reign to create an image of perpetual youth. Most modern scholars agree, however, that the religious issue was paramount: "In the proclamation, Elizabeth refers to the book as being 'lewd and seditious,' lewd in touching upon the personal life of both Alençon and her, and seditious in rousing the people to a fear that she would restore Catholicism and make France an ally," Berry explains, before venturing to offer a rare opinion. "And I suspect that it is the last reason, more than any other, that caused Elizabeth's prompt action" (Berry xxxix). There can be no doubt that Stubbs, who was an ardent Puritan and skilled polemicist, saw the French marriage as a grievous threat to the English church.[7] Yet I believe that the queen was less outraged by Stubbs's militant Protestantism—for the years of hesitation over one suitor after another show that she also feared domination by a Catholic husband—than by his overt paternalism and barely concealed antifeminism.[8]

In her proclamation, the queen condemns *The Discoverie* for "interlacing of flattering glosses towards Her Majesty to cover the rest of the manifest depraving of Her majesty and her actions to her people," and disseminating a "heap of slanders and reproaches of the said prince, bolstered up with manifest lies and despiteful speeches of him"—all "under pretense of dissuading Her Majesty from marriage with the Duke of Anjou, the French king's brother" (Berry 148). Yet the treatise is clearly a carefully reasoned argument, written because Stubbs thought the marriage was not in the queen's or the country's best interest. Stubbs even argues that marriage is the most important matter even to a private person that he can do all his life long. How much more consequential marriage must be for a prince! Why then does the queen's proclamation describe the proposed marriage as a "pretense" to "cover" up "slanders" against the duke and attacks on "Her majesty and her actions to her people"? To answer that, we need to place *The Discoverie* in the context of the ongoing marriage debate which, I believe, Elizabeth had come to see as a "pretense" for the most serious of challenges to her majesty.

The Marriage Debate

Marriage was the one major political question where Elizabeth's female sex could not be finessed. Parliament passed a statute which granted first Mary and then Elizabeth the same authority as a man: "the kingly or regal office of the realm, and all dignities, prerogative royal, power, preeminences, privileges, authorities, and jurisdictions thereunto annexed, united, or belonging, being invested either in male or female, are and ought to be as fully, wholly, absolutely, and entirely deemed, judged, accepted, invested, and taken in the one as in the other."[9] Yet the system of sovereignty was for all practical purposes predicated on a male body. If the king's wife died in childbirth, he could remarry, but if Elizabeth died in childbirth, what then? Primogeniture meant that the king's wife was generally not next in line to inherit her country's throne, but Monsieur was his brother's heir. If he inherited the French throne, would he leave Elizabeth behind, or would he take her with him, leaving England in the hands of a viceroy? The king rules over his subjects as the husband rules over his wife and children, but who rules over whom when the king is a married woman? If Elizabeth's husband rules over her in marriage, how can she then rule over her subjects? But if she rules over him, what then?

"Subuersion of good order, of all equitie and iustice," Knox argued. Stubbs and many Englishmen seemed to agree.[10]

The first three parliaments pressed the queen to marry; in one parliamentary speech after another Elizabeth responded that she would marry only if moved to do so by God. While boldly assuring Parliament that she would "never in that matter conclude anything that shall be prejudicial to the realm," she also insisted that she would make her own decision, in this matter above all: "it being unfitting and altogether unmeet for you [Parliament] to take upon you to draw my love to your liking or frame my will to your fantasies."[11] To protect her freedom of choice, Elizabeth took a vow "to see and know the man who was to be her husband."[12] As she told the foreign ambassadors, she had no intention of marrying unless a suitor appeared "pleasing her so much as to cause her to desire what at present she has no wish for."[13]

The queen's marriage was again a key issue when the second Elizabethan parliament was convened in 1563. The country was still reeling from Elizabeth's recent bout with smallpox. Parliament was more anxious than ever to settle the succession and safeguard the reformed church. A parliamentary delegation was sent to the queen with a petition, stating that only her immediate marriage could prevent "the unspeakable miseries of civil Wars, the perillous intermingling of Foreign Princes with seditious, ambitious, and factious Subjects at home, the waste of noble Houses, the slaughter of People, subversions of Towns, intermission of all things pertaining to the maintenance of the Realm, unsurety of all men's Possessions, Lives, and Estates, daily interchange of Attainders and Treasons."[14] The doomsday rhetoric sounds very much like *The Discoverie of a Gaping Gvlf whereinto England is Like to be Swallowed*—with one significant difference. Parliament attributes these "great dangers" to Elizabeth's unmarried state, whereas Stubbs attributes the looming cataclysm to the proposed French marriage. Married or unmarried, the queen's female body seems to pose an "unspeakable" threat to the body politic.

Elizabeth assured the 1565 parliament that she was willing to marry if the obstacles to a match could be resolved, but she did not budge from her earlier conditions. Marriage negotiations with the Austrian archduke heated up, but soon came to naught because the duke's brother, the Emperor Maximilian, thought Elizabeth's "resolve to marry no one whom she has not previously seen" was "entirely novel and unprecedented, and we cannot approve of it."[15] The emperor, moreover, would not allow his brother to "be excluded from all share in the governance." To be "nothing more than a shadow or figurehead in the realm" would be "derogatory to the dignity and esteem not only of His Love, but also of our glorious House of Austria."[16]

In 1570 the French requested permission for the duke of Alençon to court the English queen, but he was more than twenty years younger, and the English responded less than enthusiastically. Negotiations continued in 1572, but the queen's interest flagged when England and France signed the Treaty of Blois, a mutual defense pact against Spain. There was a hiatus between 1573 and 1575 because the duke was warring with his brother and virtually under house arrest. When the brothers signed a truce in November 1575, "the French ambassador set afoot anew the French marriage," as Burley wrote to Lord Cobham. Although Burley expected "nothing" of the French "but dalliance to use us to their advantage," he nonetheless felt "earnestly moved to seek her Majesty's marriage as far forth as I may."[17] Burley's tone runs the gamut: his initial skepticism is tempered by his own earnest desire for the queen's marriage, only to be qualified by pragmatic considerations ("as far forth as I may"). Finally, Burley throws up his hands: "God send her to marry without respect of any my particular liking." Burley was certain that his own "particular liking" was of no consequence; only God could induce Elizabeth to desire what she had never yet been earnestly moved to seek.

Negotiations dragged on, reaching a climax in 1579. By this time, Elizabeth was forty-six years old, and the French marriage was beginning to look like the last chance for her to marry and produce an heir of her own flesh. Yet the marriage raised a number of serious questions. Would Monsieur's Catholicism become a catalyst for plots against the queen and the English church? Would he try to gain control of the government, placing his people in positions of power? Or would he bankrupt the English treasury for his own personal ends? Would he inherit the French throne, deserting Elizabeth and subjecting England to French rule? These political, financial, and religious concerns were serious enough to give everyone, including the queen, pause. Elizabeth's advisors were also concerned about discrepancies in age and power which she was unwilling to confront. Would Monsieur willingly spend the rest of his life humoring an aging queen, more than twenty years older than he? Was Elizabeth already too old to bear a child? If she failed to produce a child and heir, would Monsieur seek to annul the marriage, as Elizabeth's own father had done? Elizabeth had been the most desirable woman in Europe for almost two decades, and her standards were as high as her visibility. Monsieur was a younger brother with limited assets and no power. Moreover, his eyes bulged; his complexion was deeply scarred by smallpox; his nose was large, heavily veined, and disfigured, probably by syphilis. His mother devalued him. His brother, the king, distrusted him, and at times, even warred with him. His contemporaries mocked him, calling him dwarfish. Was this the man, Elizabeth's advisors wondered, to make the queen "desire" a marriage she had evaded for nearly two decades?

In March 1578/9, Burley wrote a memo or "Memoryall for the Queen's Majestie tochyng the matter of her marryage" to the French duke. The list of objections, followed by answers "to every one of them in order," begins with the two issues Burley saw as the most important: (1) Elizabeth's long-standing reservations about marriage; (2) doubts about Monsieur's attractiveness as a suitor. In response to the first, Burley reasserts Elizabeth's insistence that she would make her own decision, guided by God: "Her majestie is to take councell therin only of God & of her awne harte." If, on the one hand, she decides "not to marrye then the hole matter is at an ende." If, on the other hand, she resolves to marry, then there was no reason to fear that she would be discontented as a result. As for the second point, "the dyffyculte in choyce of suche a persone as in all respectes myght contente her Majestie's mynd and satysfye her Iee [eye]," Burley offers virtually the same answer: "Her harte is to be gyded only by God's directyon & her awne, so in this cas is her [eye] also." Referring once to her mind, twice to her heart, and four times to her eyes, Burley supports Elizabeth's own declaration that she alone could decide whether a particular suitor was intellectually, emotionally, and physically attractive. No one—neither Burley, nor the Privy Council, nor the ambassadors, nor Parliament—can counsel the queen "by cause no man can knowe the inward entencyon of her harte or contentatyon of her Iee but God and her selfe, nether can eny man gyve councell thereon but leave that to God and herself."[18] Only god and the queen know her thoughts and feelings, Burley concludes; therefore, God alone is in a position to counsel her.

Having addressed these two fundamental issues, Burley's memo proceeds to work through a long list of additional concerns. To those who fear the queen is too old to conceive a child or to survive the dangers of childbirth, Burley responds that Elizabeth's healthy complexion and perfectly formed body prove she is well suited for childbearing. Furthermore, he points out, the Duchess of Savoy bore a child when she was even older than Elizabeth. But, Burley concludes, any attempt to predict the odds is beside the point: if God wants Elizabeth to marry and produce an heir, it will be done. If God believes Elizabeth needs Monsieur as a helpmeet, God will provide another heir for the French throne. Monsieur may try to bring England to his own "possessyon & subyectyon," but that too "resteth in the hand of God."[19] Moreover, any possible conflicts over which throne a son of theirs might inherit would not arise for years to come.

Burley argues that it is the Privy Council's charge and Parliament's responsibility to think about what is best for the queen, now and as long as she shall live: "Consyderyng howe muche we be bound to have care of her suerty ther is no accydentall & uncerten perrell that maye come after her dathe which is to be respected before her awne persente suertye or to be better loked to to be prevented then the perrells which in her awne lyfe may growe to her self." The queen's immediate welfare is more important than any potential perils that might or might not materialize at some much later date.

Burley's memo is remarkable for the sheer persistence with which it reiterates the position Elizabeth repeatedly set forth, in her parliamentary speeches, her conversations with foreign ambassadors, and negotiations with Parliament over the terms of the marriage treaty. Point by point, his carefully argued position paper supports the queen's right to make her own decision—with God's guidance, of course: "Besydes yt is fyrmely to be hoped for that God beying the Auter of her majestie's marryage, by puttying of it into her harte for so good a purpose, wyll also preserve and prosper her in all thyngs that dependethe thereupon."[20]

On May 3 Elizabeth asked Burley to report to the Privy Council that negotiations with Monsieur had reached a turning point: "Her Majesty had always refused to conclude marriage without an interview," but "Monsieur had at last agreed and given Simier commission to assent thereto, provided he might first see what the Articles to be agreed upon for the Covenant of Marriage should be."[21] In response, the Privy Council asked whether her majesty wished them to discuss the whole question of the marriage, or only the new demands. Elizabeth directed the council to limit their discussion to the new articles only. Apparently, she had already made up her mind to proceed.

After much negotiation back and forth, a marriage agreement was drawn up stipulating that Elizabeth would continue to rule the country in the future as she had in the past: "After the marriage was consummated, he shall enjoy the Title & honour of a King, but shall leave the disposing of matters full and whole to the Queene. . . . The Queen onely shall beare the superiority." The French proposed that he be given "a joint authority in the giving of Benefices, Offices, Lands, &c." but the English were vehemently opposed to giving him any kind of political power. An agreement was reached that Monsieur "shall leave the disposing of matters full and whole to the Queene."

To allow Elizabeth the freedom of choice without which negotiations could not proceed, it was agreed that Monsieur would come to England secretly so both parties could see whether a "mutual liking" would develop. The French requested and received reassurances that Monsieur could withdraw without losing face should no such liking occur. In return, the English requested and received reassurances that Elizabeth could call off the match without damaging relations with France: "A re[s]eruation also was added apart by it self, signed with the hands of all the Commissioners in these words: 'Queen Elizabeth is not bound to consummate the marriage, untill she and the Duke shall clearly satisfie one another in certaine points, and shall thereof certifie the French King in writing within six weeks.'"[22] Finally, Elizabeth agreed that Monsieur could receive Mass in private, but it was decided "that the question of religion should remain in suspense until an interview had taken place, when if there should be a mutual liking it should be finally settled, and if there were no such liking the cause of breaking off the marriage should be imputed to the difference on matters of religion."[23]

Queen Elizabeth signed a safe conduct on 7 July 1579. She had finally succeeded in negotiating the conditions she had been fighting to defend ever since the beginning of her reign: (1) to decide for herself, guided by God but moved by her heart and eyes, whether or not to marry; (2) to rule the country herself, with God's guidance, whether or not she married. Or so it seemed when *The Discoverie of a Gaping Gvlf whereinto England is Like to be Swallowed by an other French mariage* was published.

Our Eve

The Discoverie prophesies what Elizabeth's subjects most feared: that her chosen suitor, marrying her for his own personal gain, would turn traitor, encouraging plots against the reformed church, plundering the treasury, mastering the queen, and opening the gates to foreign invasion, leaving Elizabeth's subjects to be "gouerned by him that shal be her gouernor." It also denies out of hand the conditions Elizabeth had spent the better part of her reign defending.

The argument begins with a biblical trope: "they have sent us hither not Satan in body of a serpent, but the old serpent in shape of a man, whose sting is in his mouth, and who doth his endeavor to seduce our Eve, that she and we may lose this English paradise" (Berry 3–4). The comparison to Eve flatters Elizabeth by describing her as the paradisial ideal of womanhood, but it also epitomizes what Elizabeth saw as "the manifest depraving of Her majesty and her actions to her people." Depicting Monsieur as Satan is bad enough but representing Elizabeth as the cause of all our woe is far worse. There was no one else in Paradise but Adam and Eve: if "she and we may lose this English paradise," then she is not only England's spouse and helpmeet but also the reason Paradise was lost. In the arsenal of Renaissance antifeminism, Eve is the weapon of choice: the archetypal symbol of female weakness, vanity, greed, and willfulness. The mere mention of Eve is enough to insinuate what cannot be stated overtly: that women need to be ruled by men.[24] Since it would be treason to suggest that as a woman Elizabeth is too weak, vain, passionate, irrational, greedy, willful, and easily duped to rule the country, Stubbs quickly adjusts the metaphor, acknowledging that Elizabeth is not only "our Eve" but "also our Adam and sovereign lord or lordly lady of this land" (Berry 4). But if Elizabeth is both Adam and Eve, once she eats the apple that is the end of England's earthly paradise.

Stubbs's image of Elizabeth as "our Adam and sovereign lord or lordly lady of this land" sounds a lot like Elizabeth's own rhetoric. In her coronation address, Elizabeth attempted to alleviate the problem of her sex by citing the medieval theory of the king's two bodies: "and as I am but one Bodye naturallye Considered though by his permission a Bodye Politique to Governe."[25] The theory posits that the monarch's corporeal body, weak because mortal—and in Elizabeth's case, supposedly even weaker because female—becomes in spirit the king's eternal—and male—body politic. Elizabeth claimed that as "the minister of his Heavenly Will in this office now commyttcd to me," she could rule the body politic with her eternal male soul. The theory provided a useful justification when it came to negotiating peace treaties or distributing subsidies and monopolies—whenever power and knowledge could be equated with majesty. But marriage posed a distinct challenge to the theory, as the Scottish ambassador pointed out when he said, "Madam, I know your stately stomach: ye think if ye were married, ye would be but Queen of England, and now ye are King and Queen both; ye may not suffer a commander."[26]

The similarity between Elizabeth's rhetoric of the king's two bodies and Stubbs's lasts only as long as the subordinate clause: "Who because she is also our Adam and sovereign lord or lordly lady of this land, it is so much the more dangerous" (Berry 4). Elizabeth argues that although she had "the body of a weak woman" she also had "the heart and stomach of a king." Stubbs uses the metaphor, but inverts the meaning, relegating her male sovereignty first to a dependent clause ("Who because she is . . .") and then to a mere modifier of her female body ("or lordly lady"). Elizabeth claimed that her female weakness was infused with an inner strength that came directly from God; Stubbs uses the trope of the king's two bodies to argue that the male body politic was only as strong as the queen's female body natural: "The one her natural body, such as other private ones have, the other her body politic or commonweal body, which is her body of majesty, nothing can be harmful to one but the same is full of harm to both."

The sensational, highly symbolic title implies that the country is about to be swallowed or split asunder to satisfy someone's voracious appetite: "gaping" means not only rending asunder but also opening the mouth wide and yearning for; moreover, "gulf" means not only a body of water but also a voracious appetite. One needn't look too hard to discover whose appetite Stubbs had in mind when he attacks her need "to have her particular liking and heart's contentation in this match, in respect of that life she must lead with a husband, so as she may say within her self, 'I am gladly satisfied in this choice'" (Berry 69). Stubbs's remarks about Elizabeth's "particular liking" and "contentation" "gladly satisfied" allude to Elizabeth's own repeated declaration that she would only marry a suitor capable of arousing her liking and satisfying her desire. Indeed Stubbs mocks what both Burley and Elizabeth go to great lengths to defend: "He should hardly be the man, that choice man of choice in all respects to content both eye and mind" (Berry 69). The pounding rhetorical iteration—"that choice man of choice"—scorns the very notion that Elizabeth should be allowed to make such an important choice for herself. The queen is deceiving herself, Stubbs warns—allowing passion to cloud her reason, all to marry a man whose own motivations are entirely political and self-seeking.

Elizabeth may be the king, but when it comes to choosing a husband, Stubbs argues, she is like any other helpless daughter—sorely in need of patriarchal guidance. Her government, her advisors, and her subjects must all "learn of every parent or other whatsoever that hath a loving care of their daughter . . . it is a faithless careless part, to leave her helpless in her choice of the person and personal conditions of her husband to her own only consideration" (Berry 69–70). Since she has no father or brother, she can only receive the guidance Stubbs believes she needs from her advisors, her parliament, and her male subjects.

Using his power over the queen to place his supporters in positions of power, Monsieur will gain control of the government. In the end, both the queen and her subjects will be ruled by her husband; therefore, the decision should be made by "the whole land" which must be able to "say, I have chosen such a Lord as I dare put in trust with my Queen, for so much as it also is to be married with her, and in sort to be governed by him that shall be her governor."

From the very outset of the treatise, Stubbs places the blame on the queen's advisors: "knowing Her Majesty's wisdom sufficient to teach her, in such a matter as this, neither to trow [trust] a Frenchman nor once hear speak a daily hearer of Mass (for she may know him by his hissing and lisping), but that some English mouths professing Christ are also persuaders of the same" (Berry 4). Speaking directly to Elizabeth, Stubbs urges: "Show yourself a zealous prince for God's gospel to the end; foresee, in a tender love to the people . . . continuance of the truth among them. . . . Keep this sin from you. . . . The Lord endue you with wisdom" to supply flatterers' lack of duty with "extraordinary counsel in your own breast" (Berry 30). The Privy Council is full of flatterers who are afraid to give Elizabeth the guidance Stubbs believes she needs. Therefore, Stubbs argues, Elizabeth can only avoid making a disastrous decision if she receives "extraordinary" guidance from God—guidance above and beyond what a male monarch ordinarily needs and receives.

Stubbs praises Elizabeth for redeeming England from a foreign king, which he sees as a great accomplishment, second only to restoring the reformed church. Yet he also describes Elizabeth as a helpless, dumb creature: "We shall find the Church notably undermined by the Pope; the very foundations of our commonweal dangerously digged at by the French; and our dear Queen Elizabeth (I shake to speak) led blindfold as a poor lamb to the slaughter" (Berry 4). While the pope is actively undermining the church, and the French are purposefully "digging" away, Elizabeth is "led blindfold" to the slaughter, without knowledge or volition.

Surveying the long history of royal marriages between England and France, Stubbs concludes that the ancient, inbred hatred between the two countries is all the more dangerous in this case since, for the first time, the French partner is a king who "as owner [will] possess our queen." If the queen loves him, she will willingly bow to him. If not, then she must fear him. Either way, Stubbs concludes, Monsieur will use his power over the queen to "thrust in at door such counselors in whose mouth he may speak." Although the marriage-treaty specifically denied Monsieur any such authority, Stubbs nonetheless claims that Monsieur would rule the country through his "promoted creatures" (Berry 40).

Much as the relentless piling up of biblical comparisons all go to prove that Elizabeth cannot be allowed to make her own choice of a husband, the seemingly endless list of historical precedents and future contingencies all come down to the same basic problem. Stubbs, who is incapable of seeing Elizabeth's female body except in terms of conventional gender roles, assumes that she must either be ruled by her husband or by her advisors. If Monsieur inherits the French throne, he will return to France, taking Elizabeth along to where she will be subordinated to her sister-in-law, or he will return to France, leaving Elizabeth alone and disgraced. Either way, Stubbs assumes that Elizabeth's honor and status are completely dependent on her husband.

Ultimately, Stubbs denies Elizabeth the power she fought so hard to establish: "In this marriage our Queen is to be married, and both she and we poor souls, are to be mastered" (Berry 58). Since her first parliamentary speech, Elizabeth maintained that she alone would decide whether or not to marry, and that she would continue to rule the country whether or not she married. Again and again, she insisted that as God's divine representative on earth, she would be guided by God to make the right choices, for herself and her subjects. It is this hard-fought right that Stubbs challenges when he questions Elizabeth's judgment, criticizes her counselors for not giving her sufficient guidance, and urges every one of her subjects to join him in advising the queen. To the queen, Stubbs's policy of "offering to every meanest person authority to determine affairs of State" was "a thing most pernicious in any estate." And that, I believe, is why the queen decided to outlaw the book to "maintain that devotion of love" between the queen and her subjects, and why she charged Stubbs with trying "to diminish her majesty's credit of her good people."

God Save the Queen

To appease the queen's fury, John Stubbs, along with Singleton, whom Camden describes as the printer, and William Page, who dispersed the copies, were charged with treason under an act passed by Philip and Mary against the authors of seditious writings. Singleton was pardoned, but Stubbs and Page were found guilty and sentenced to have their right hands cut off—a dire, if symbolically apt, form of punishment.[27] Elizabeth's advisors disapproved. Her lawyers resisted. Two judges who declared the verdict illegal were imprisoned. But most important of all, her subjects were appalled.

Upon being brought to the scaffold, Stubbs delivered a long speech, praying for "grace, that the loss of my hand do not withdraw any part of my duty and affection toward her Majesty" (Berry xxxv). Camden, who was in the crowd, later described the events. Stubbs's right hand was "cutt off with a cleauer, driven through the wrist by the force of a beetle [mallet]." Still reeling from the blow, with blood pouring from the open wound, Stubbs "put off his hat with his left and sayd with a loud voice, *God save the Queen*; the multitude standing about, was altogether silent, either out of horror of this new and unwonted punishment, or else out of pity towards the man being of most honest and unblameable report, or else out of hatred of the marriage, which most men presaged would be the overthrow of Religion."[28]

The courtly gesture and the words of homage, expressed so forcefully at a moment of extreme pain, are not only a remarkable expression of loyalty and courage; they are also a brilliant political act. Before the verdict, Stubbs defended his innocence. Having been found guilty, it was his duty to accept the court's judgment. In saying "God save the queen," Stubbs concedes the position adopted by the Privy Council and attacked by *The Discoverie of a Gaping Gulf*, the position set forth in Elizabeth's parliamentary speeches and Burley's "Memoryall for the Queen's Majestie tochyng the matter of her marryage" to the French duke: "Her majestie is to take councell therin only of God & of her awne harte." At the same time, he demonstrates his extraordinary devotion to the queen, making his punishment seem all the more cruel and unwarranted.

According to MacCaffrey, "this episode" reveals "new energies at work within the English political order which were to have a permanent place within its structure. A deep anti-Catholic prejudice, as much a xenophobic phenomenon as a theological one, had taken deep root within important strata of the English political nation. It was a latent force but easily aroused and immensely powerful."[29] To my mind, this episode reveals two additional forces at work within the English political order, one new, one old. First, *The Discoverie* brings to light a deep-seated distrust of female rule which had taken root within an important strata of the English political nation. Second, *The Discoverie of a Gaping Gulf* dramatizes the nascent power of print to sway public opinion and influence the political process. By addressing the argument not only to the queen but also and primarily to the people, Stubbs uses the press to deny Elizabeth the freedom of conjugal choice which she had so zealously defended from the outset of her reign. In the end Monsieur was no more able to win the combined approval of Parliament, Privy Council, church, country, and queen than were the queen's earlier suitors. Regardless of what Elizabeth may have privately desired, public opposition, aroused by the treatise, the proclamation, and cinched by Stubbs's punishment, made the French marriage so unpopular as to be ultimately inconceivable.

That Elizabeth and the Elizabethan system of justice turned a perfectly good right hand into a useless stump because they didn't like what it wrote about her is not a pretty story.[30] Yet, with his chillingly apt surname and his severed stump or stub, John Stubbs provides a haunting sign of the lengths to which Elizabeth felt compelled to go to cut off the attempt to undermine her hard-won authority.

Notes

1. The text is quoted from *John Stubbs's Gaping Gulf with Letters and Other Relevant Documents,* ed. Lloyd E. Berry (Charlottesville: University Press of Virginia for the Folger Shakespeare Library, 1968). All further references to this volume will be cited parenthetically. Berry's edition is an invaluable source of information about Alençon's courtship, Stubbs's life, the publication of *The Gaping Gulf* and the trial, and literary associations, though his account is more factual than interpretive. Most modern historians recount the events and judge the severity of the punishment, but do not analyze the treatise itself, the notable exception being Wallace MacCaffrey, who devotes several pages to Stubbs's position, both in *Queen Elizabeth and the Making of Policy, 1572–1588* (Princeton: Princeton University Press, 1981), 255–66, and in *Elizabeth I* (London: Edward Arnold, 1993), 202–5. "Its central arguments were shrewdly considered, comprehensive, and very knowledgeable," MacCaffrey concludes in *Queen Elizabeth and the Making of Policy,* p. 256. "Indeed they were so well informed—and so close in content to the actual Council debates—that the Queen had some ground for her suspicion that someone in the Council was behind Stubbs."

2. For further information, see the *Salisbury Manuscripts* (London: Her Majesty's Stationery Office, 1888), 272.

3. Carroll Smith-Rosenberg, "Writing History: Language, Class, and Gender," in *Feminist Studies/Critical Studies,* ed. Teresa de Lauretis (Bloomington: Indiana University Press, 1986), 48–49.

4. As Mary Douglas writes in *Natural Symbols: Explorations in Cosmology* (New York: Pantheon, 1970), 70, "Interest in [the body's] apertures depends on the preoccupation with social exits and entrances, escape routes and invasion. If there is no concern to preserve social boundaries, I would not expect to find concern with bodily boundaries."

5. *Tudor Royal Proclamations,* vol. 2, *The Later Tudors: 1553–1587,* ed. Paul L. Hughes and James F. Larkin (New Haven: Yale University Press, 1969), 445–49.

6. Conyers Read, *Lord Burghley and Queen Elizabeth* (London: Jonathan Cape, 1960), 217, writes: "Stubbs spoke with Puritan bluntness. The Queen, he said, was too old to think of marriage, and as for the Duke, he was rotten with debauchery. . . . Sidney was more discreet. He said nothing about the Queen's age, a little by innuendo about Alençon's personal attributes, much about his nationality, his religion and the 'unhealthiness of his whole race.' " Neville Williams, *Elizabeth the First: Queen of England* (New York: E. P. Dutton, 1968), 201, comments, "Stubbs did not pull his punches."

7. Jasper Ridley, *Elizabeth I* (London: Constable, 1987), 209, offers a particularly useful summary of the reasons for the queen's anger: "She was indignant at Stubbs's attack on Anjou, the brother of a King with whom she was at amity, for it was the recognised custom of sovereigns to forbid publications and sermons which criticized foreign Princes, even those with whom their relations were unfriendly. . . . She was also personally affronted by the abuse of Anjou, with whom she was at least a little in love, and by Stubbs's reference to her age and inability to have children. But what she most resented was that it was, in her view, a seditious attempt by the Puritans to interfere in matters which did not concern them, and to influence her decision about her marriage and her foreign policy."

8. To my knowledge, Susan Bassnett, *Elizabeth I: A Feminist Perspective* (New York: St. Martin's Press, 1988), 49, is the only modern scholar to foreground the question of gender: "The publication of Stubbs's pamphlet sent Elizabeth into a rage. That she often lost her temper is well documented, but she had a particular hatred of scurrilous misogynous pamphlets." Carolly Erickson, *The First Elizabeth* (New York: Summit Books, 1983), and Anne Somerset, *Elizabeth I* (London: Weidenfeld and Nicolson, 1991), mention related issues, but they both emphasize the personal over the political. "*The Gaping Gulf* was monarchical insult of a high order," Erickson writes, p. 307: "Stubbs's condescension toward Elizabeth was as maddening as his language was offensive; he assaulted her sovereignty, her judgment, and her statecraft as well as her nubility—and the latter alone was enough to warrant severe punishment." For Somerset, pp. 312–13, the treatise was "literate and well argued," but "in places its tone was nothing short of offensive. Not only did Stubbs stress the likelihood that the Queen was too old to be successfully delivered of a child, but he stated that it was unthinkable that Alençon could love a woman so many years his senior, and went on to abuse the Duke and his brothers in the coarsest possible terms."

9. The text is reprinted in *Tudor Constitutional Documents A.D. 1485–1603*, ed. J. R. Tanner (Cambridge: Cambridge University Press, 1922), 123–24.

10. John Knox, *The First Blast of the Trumpet. Against the Monstruous Regiment of Women* (London, 1558), 9. Knox goes on to argue, p. 10, that "men subject to the counsel or empire of their wyues were vnworthie of all publike office."

11. J. E. Neale, *Elizabeth I and Her Parliaments*, vol. 1 (1953; London: Jonathan Cape, 1957), 49.

12. Great Britain, *Calendar of Letters and State Papers Relating to English Affairs, Preserved Principally in the Archives of Simancas*, vol. 1, Elizabeth, 1558–1567, ed. Martin A. S. Hume (London, 1892; Nendeln, Liechtenstein: Kraus, 1971), 73. Hereafter cited as *CSP Sp*.

13. *CSP Sp*, 1:123.

14. Simonds D'Ewes, *The Journals of all the Parliaments. During the Reign of Queen Elizabeth* (London, 1682), 81.

15. Victor von Klarwill, *Queen Elizabeth and Some Foreigners* (New York: Brentano's, 1928), 239. For a more detailed analysis of the role these stipulations played in the marriage negotiations, see my essay, "Elizabeth I—Always Her Own Free Woman," in *Political Rhetoric, Power, and Renaissance Women*, ed. Carole Levin and Patricia A. Sullivan (Albany: State University of New York Press, 1995).

16. Klarwill, *Queen Elizabeth and Some Foreigners*, 241.

17. *CSP Sp*, 1:110.

18. *Salisbury Manuscripts*, 239.

19. Ibid., 240–41.

20. Ibid., 240.

21. Ibid., 253.

22. William Camden, *The historie of the . . . princess Elizabeth*, trans. R. N[orton] (London, 1630), 3:5–6.

23. *Salisbury Manuscripts*, 253.

24. Elizabethan law defines a traitor as anyone who dares "say, publish, maintain, declare, or hold opinion that" Elizabeth Tudor "ought not to be Queen of this realm" (reprinted in *Tudor Constitutional Documents*, ed. J. R. Tanner, 411).

25. Quoted in Allison Heisch, "Queen Elizabeth I: Parliamentary Rhetoric and the Exercise of Power," *Signs* 1 (1975): 33.

26. J. E. Neale, *Queen Elizabeth I* (London: Jonathan Cape, 1934), 125.

27. Modern historians are eager to pronounce judgment. Christopher Hib-

bert, *The Virgin Queen: Eliȥabeth 1, Genius of the Golden Age* (Reading, Mass.: Addison-Wesley, 1991), 196, writes that "the defendants, as was usual in such cases, were all sentenced to have their right hands cut off." Neale, *Queen Eliȥabeth I,* 243, argues that the sentence was unexceptionable but ill-advised: "Measured by the offense and the age the sentence was not vicious, but it was certainly tactless and unmerciful. . . . Elizabeth's good sense had deserted her." "Its nature is a measure of royal wrath," MacCaffrey writes in *Queen Eliȥabeth and the Making of Policy,* p. 257: "The penalty was an unusual and brutal one." Paul Johnson, *Eliȥabeth I: A Biography* (New York: Holt, Rinehart, and Winston, 1988), 257, is much harsher: "Elizabeth's savagery on this occasion, for which she must take sole responsibility, was uncharacteristic and wholly indefensible." Williams, *Eliȥabeth the First,* p. 202, remarks, "Elizabeth's popularity was at a very low ebb."

28. Camden, *The historie of the . . . princesse Eliȥabeth,* 3:10. As Berry notes in *John Stubbs's Gaping Gulf,* xxxvi, the fact is confirmed by Stubbs's letter to Hatton.

29. MacCaffrey, *Queen Eliȥabeth and the Making of Policy,* 266.

30. Apparently, Stubbs convinced the queen of his loyalty, for he became a polemicist for the government and a member of Parliament. He signed his letters, "John Stubbe, Scaeva," meaning left-handed. He is probably alluding to the mythical Roman hero Caius Scaevola who tried to murder Lars Porcena, who was besieging the city. When Scaevola was condemned to burn at the stake, he put his right hand into the flames. Porcena was so impressed by Scaevola's courage that he pardoned him and called off the siege.

Out of Egypt

Richard Fletcher's Sermon before Elizabeth I after

the Execution of Mary Queen of Scots

Peter E. McCullough

Despite a revolutionary return to "historicism" in studies of early modern English literature, the most prominent, indeed the most culturally significant, literary genre in Tudor-Stuart Britain—the sermon—continues to be ignored in scholarship as well as in the classroom. Ironically, a refusal to take religious expression seriously, as more than a diffused "social energy" in the period, has obscured the sermon's relevance for one of New Historicism's pet projects: revealing the political at work in the literary.[1] And in few places was the sermon more politicized than in the pulpit that stood at the center of the nation's power-structure, the royal court. New Historicism can also be justly chided for an obsession with elite culture that gives the impression that the court engineered a kind of political hegemony through the art forms that flourished there. But the court pulpit gives the lie to these assumptions, for the sermons preached from it offer some of the best evidence of political opposition administered in the sugared pill of verbal artifice from the heart of the supposed ideological monolith that was the Tudor-Stuart court. I have treated the religious and institutional dimension of court preaching in some detail elsewhere.[2] Here, however, I would like to offer a closer literary reading of one court sermon—the hitherto ignored sermon preached before Elizabeth I by Richard Fletcher shortly after the execution of Mary Queen of Scots—to demonstrate how the sermon could deploy sophisticated verbal strategies to comment on a sensitive political matter, even to the point of criticizing the sovereign in her presence.[3]

But before texts, contexts. An important body of revisionist historiography has called attention to the geography of the early modern court itself, emphasizing spacial and architectural restrictions that guaranteed that "the key to political power at court remained access to the sovereign."[4] Building on this work, literary scholars have suggested that the distance imposed by the restriction of the queen's contact with suppliants and suitors, and the related fact that she was the pinnacle of the court's patronage system, produced an iconographic "conceptualisation of the Queen as on another plane, above and beyond." Hence the proliferation of poetic tropes in which the speaker addressed the queen as a semidivine "mediatrix and dispenser of God's graces."[5] Of course decorum and convention insisted that this elevation of the monarch be literally observed whenever the queen appeared in public, most familiarly in the raised and canopied chair of state that dominated the presence chamber. But nowhere did the literary project of metaphorically elevating the queen meet the literal elevation of the queen's person more dramatically than in the chapels royal. For here, ministers appointed to preach before the queen and court addressed a sovereign who sat not in the chapel stalls with the courtiers, but in an elevated gallery, known as the chapel closet, over the west end of the chapel.[6]

The court pulpit, then, was a crucial point of access to the queen for an influential segment of the educated elite. The royal chapels were physically and spatially designed to contain that contact within an idealized Elizabethan world picture, one in which Elizabeth and her courtiers, arranged hierarchically under a ceiling painted to evoke the heavens, embodied "the cosmic dance reproduced in the body politic."[7] But the men who filled the court pulpits were not a unison chorus singing anthems to Gloriana. Rather, the patronage systems that provided court preachers guaranteed that the queen could be just as likely to hear a critic of her or her court than a panegyrist of the same. Of course, criticism was expected to be couched in careful terms of deference and compliment. As the venerable dean of St. Paul's Alexander Nowell summarized it, "he had no other way to instruct the queen what she should be, but by commending her"—and Nowell had learned the hard way, having been shouted down by the queen during a Lent sermon against religious images in 1565.[8] Some preachers never learned Nowell's lesson, and there were some infamous frontal attacks on the queen from her pulpit. Most famous was the nonconformist Edward Dering's 1570 drubbing of Elizabeth for her less-than-zealous efforts to further reformation in England—a sermon that, with sixteen editions before the queen's death, was by far the most popular Elizabethan court sermon in print.[9]

Not surprisingly that sermon earned Dering the queen's contempt. Entertaining as Dering's attack may have been (indeed, is) to read, his is not representative of pulpit advice to Elizabeth. More common, and from a literary point of view more sophisticated, were those sermons that manifested not only Dean Nowell's advice to sugar the pill of blame with praise, but also exploited the coded speech of biblical exempla and exegetical tradition to electrify the chapel with an obvious, but safely distanced, application to the royal person or matters of state. Few moments in the reign could have been more daunting in the court pulpit than the days of Elizabeth's guilty rage after the execution of her kindred queen, Mary Stuart. But such was the lot—undoubtedly not left to chance—of one of Elizabeth's few favorites among the royal chaplains, Richard Fletcher, in the dark February of 1587. The sermon he preached before his angry mistress only days after the execution at Fotheringhay is in itself an important document for the historiography of Elizabeth's dealings with Mary. But a close reading of the sermon also reveals how pulpit oratory could use biblical allusion, typology, and iconography to safely advise and rebuke the queen at a time when she had cut herself off from all other institutional forms of counsel.

Richard Fletcher (d. 1596) needs first to be remembered as part of a family notable for its literary accomplishments and its commitment to evangelical, anti-Catholic Protestantism. His father, also Richard, was deprived by Mary in 1555, the year the man who ordained him, Nicholas Ridley, was burned in Oxford. In 1583, father and son, identifying themselves as "spectatores presentes," contributed an account of a 1555 Dartford martyrdom to the third revision of Foxe's "Book of Martyrs."[10] Another brother, Giles (1549–1611) became a noted lawyer, ambassador, and author and was father of the Spenserian poets Phineas (1582–1650) and Giles the younger (1588?–1623), both of whose work influenced Milton's *Paradise Lost*. The most notable of Richard's nine children was his younger son, the dramatist John Fletcher (1579–1625). Richard Fletcher himself was patronized first by Archbishop Parker, who introduced him to the queen's favor as early as 1575, whereupon followed an impressive ecclesiastical career as dean of Peterborough (1583), bishop of Bristol (1589), Worcester (1593), and London (1594), as well as Lord Almoner, a court post that carried with it the privilege of preaching before the queen on major feast days. His was one of the most successful careers of any preacher at Elizabeth's court, and perhaps the closest any Elizabethan churchman came to the Jacobean model of a court preacher-prelate epitomized by Lancelot Andrewes. According to Sir John Harington, he possessed two virtues requisite for the queen's pulpit, a "comly" person and "courtly" speech. And more to the point for our purposes here, "he could preach well and speak boldly, and yet keep decorum. He knew what would please the queen, and would adventure on that though that offended others." But Fletcher ended his life in disgrace, and he is still best remembered for two seeming indiscretions: his ministry at the trial and execution of Mary at Fotheringhay in 1586–87, and his injudicious second marriage to a rich widow in 1595. In the former he acted very much in accord with the wishes of the lords of the council. Significantly, it was Fletcher's marriage, not his role at Fotheringhay, that earned him Elizabeth's contempt, leading to temporary suspension from episcopal duties and banishment from court.[11] He died suddenly in 1596, leaving nine children and substantial debts. Memorials to the queen on the family's behalf were pressed by Fletcher's brother, Giles, as well as Francis Bacon and the Earl of Essex, who cited Elizabeth's "displeasure and indignation" as the cause of his "untimely and unlook'd for death."[12]

But when the crisis over Mary Queen of Scots reached its climax with the discovery of the Babington Plot in June 1586, Fletcher was comfortably settled in his first church dignity as dean of Peterborough and, as a favored royal chaplain, had every right to expect further preferment. Mary's final prison, the castle at Fotheringay, Northamptonshire, lay within the diocese of Peterborough only a few miles up the River Nene from Fletcher's cathedral, and it was Fletcher who served as chaplain throughout the official proceedings that began with Mary's trial in October 1586 and ended with her execution on 8 February 1587. He was probably chosen not simply as a local church dignitary but more specifically as one of Elizabeth's chaplains.[13] In November, with sentence passed and only the lack of a royal warrant keeping Mary's neck off the block, Lord Buckhurst and Clerk of the Council Robert Beale visited Mary to urge her preparation for death, and offered the spiritual counsel of either the bishop or the dean of Peterborough.[14] On the evening of 6 February, when Beale finally did deliver Elizabeth's warrant to Fotheringhay, Fletcher, already in place for the last act, was dining with Mary's keeper, Sir Amyas Paulet. The following day, the earls of Kent and Shrewsbury

showed the warrant to Mary and offered her a final chance to confess her
guilt and reject popery. Mary having been deprived of her own Roman
Catholic chaplain, Kent this time offered to call for Fletcher, who, according to Mary's physician, he hyperbolically described as "des plus doctes
de l'Europpe."[15] Mary of course refused to hear Fletcher, as she did again
more dramatically on the scaffold the next day. Fletcher had carefully
prepared, "by the direction of the LL. com[m]ission[er]s," a series of
exhortations "to have bene vttered to the Q of Scott[es] at the place &
tyme of hir execuc[i]on," which, no sooner had Fletcher begun, he "was
by hir interrupted, and refused to be hearde."[16] Catholic propaganda,
beginning with the first eyewitness accounts by Mary's servants, cast
Fletcher as an unfeeling zealot ("La scène était horrible, scandaleuse"),
and Mary as a paragon of restraint under pressure ("Monsieur le doyen,
lui répondit doucement la reine . . . retirez-vous d'ici"). Admittedly,
Fletcher had tried his best to fulfill the duty given him; when Mary turned
her back on him, he moved to the other side of the scaffold to look her in
the eye once more. Shrewsbury put an end to the stand-off by instructing
Fletcher to leave his exhortations and lead the commissioners in prayer
instead.[17] After the executioner's ax had fallen for the second and fatal
time, it was Fletcher who broke the silence in the hall with the loyal
exclamation, "So perish all the Queen's enemies!"[18]

Elizabeth, of course, was not so enthusiastic. The story of her crisis of
conscience leading up to the execution and her guilty rage afterwards has
been told and retold many times.[19] But for a consideration of Fletcher's
sermon and the light it may shed on events immediately following Mary's
death several elements bear reemphasis. The first is the sincerity of Elizabeth's grief—her postmortem fury was not feigned for policy's sake.
Stunned, if not genuinely surprised, by the news of the execution, Elizabeth was, in Neale's summary, "overwhelmed by a sense of irrevocable
tragedy and the infamy of a sacrilegious deed." And as a more recent
historian trenchantly concludes, "Elizabeth was in agony about Mary's
death which stands in stark and instructive contrast to Mary's cheerful
willingness to countenance hers."[20] Even more to the point for Fletcher
was the fact that his queen's anger was directed at her council, and in
particular at those she deemed most responsible for the act. Secretary
Davison, who secured the queen's warrant for the execution, was the
public scapegoat. And Elizabeth not only berated her council, but even

refused to receive letters from her trusted Lord Burghley or to allow him to enter her presence for weeks after the execution.[21]

How remarkable, then, to possess a copy of "A Sermon preached before the Queene immediatly after the execuc[i]on of the Queene of Scott[es] by the Deane of Peterburghe" (49v). But how much more remarkable to find in that sermon not palliative flattery but rather, through the skillful use of veiled biblical speech, a defense of the execution, a stiff rebuke of the queen's own foolish pity, and a call for her to pursue similar policies against all other Catholics. The sermon survives in a small sixteenth-century commonplace book, now St. John's College Cambridge MS I.30, containing not only the court sermon but also accounts of Mary's trial, execution, and funeral, the sermon preached by Fletcher before the commissioners at her trial, and extensive notes and meditations on theological subjects.[22] No corroborating evidence survives to supply a more specific date and place of preaching than the manuscript heading's "immediatly after the execuc[i]on." But since outside Lent Elizabeth routinely heard sermons only on Sundays, 12 and 19 February, the Sundays immediately following the execution on Wednesday, 8 February, seem the most likely dates.[23] During this time, Elizabeth had retired to Greenwich, which would place Fletcher's sermon in the chapel there, the smallest and most intimate of the Tudor chapels royal.[24]

But before following Fletcher into the pulpit we must attend, as he did, to the politics of choosing a scriptural text for a sermon. Annabel Patterson's influential work on censorship has called attention to how early modern authors could employ deliberately ambiguous language to allow "explicit address to the contentious issues of the day" without incurring punishment by authority.[25] Some have objected to Patterson's exaggeration of the power of pre-print licensing to influence what authors wrote and booksellers published. Print historian Sheila Lambert, for example, pours contempt on "the notion of coded discourse," asking, "what purpose can be served by codes that everyone can understand?"[26] Both sides, however, have not given sufficient attention to the sermon, whether spoken, written, or printed, as a paradigmatic site for the so-called "hermeneutics of censorship."[27] A sophisticated sermon like Fletcher's that chose to comment on matters of state employed a signifying strategy not unlike allegory: the literal sense of the sermon was presented to the auditors in the narrative terms of a biblical story, while the author-preacher left the symbolic, or "allegorical," application of that biblical narrative to the political sphere safely to the listener (or reader). Herein lies one of the many reasons for the popularity of the sermon with Elizabethan audiences. Hearing or reading a sermon could be not only entertaining, edifying, even dangerous, but also dynamically participatory when preachers, like poets, invited listeners to a game of anticipating and decoding meanings they chose only to imply. And this gamefulness in the pulpit began with the preacher's selection of a biblical text for the sermon that played with audience expectations about what was appropriate for both the auditory and the occasion at hand. The most conventional approach would be to pick a text suited to a liturgical season or state occasion and expound it accordingly. Conversely, preachers often chose the most bizarre or seemingly inappropriate text possible only to show with exegetical *sprezzatura* that it was eminently suitable after all, as when Thomas Drant took the titillating fragment from Genesis 2.25, "And they were both naked," and wittily descanted on the frailty of flesh, abuse of apparel, and the need for the nation to be "clothed" militarily.[28]

Auditories, then, were expected to participate in a mutual game of interpretation that began the instant a preacher ascended the pulpit and declaimed his text. And this tacit understanding underwrote any preacher's attempt to use the veil of a biblical verse or story to comment safely on matters of state. The court was one audience well-trained in this interpretive game. A rare comment on the unspoken rules of this game came in Lancelot Andrewes's sermon before King James on the anniversary of the Gowry Conspiracy in 1616. After declaiming his text relating the discovery of the plot against King Ahasuerus (Esther 2.21–23), he admitted, "I speake, before understanding hearers: and (I know) there was not eny but upon the reading of the Text, his conceipt did lead him presently, who was meant by *King Ahashuerus* . . . and so made the comparison, with your owne selves, before I could make it."[29] And in 1593, with anxieties about the succession running high, the archbishop of York, Matthew Hutton, took the court's breath away when he declaimed his text from Jeremiah 27.5, *The kingdomes of the earth are mine, and I do giue them to whom I will.* According to Harington, "taking the sence rather then words of the prophet, there followed first so generall a murmur . . . as I haue neuer obserued either before or since."[30] There was a well-conned "hermeneutics of censorship" at least in chapels and churches in early modern England. But much more is at work here than authors' fear of official reprimand; hearing a sermon, like reading, was a collaborative act between author and public, and veiled speech was as much part of the fun—a convention, a decorum—as it was a reaction to threats of state censorship.

The courtiers assembled in Greenwich chapel to hear Fletcher must have been apprehensive about how or even if the preacher would touch the subject of Mary's execution—an act that had inspired revelry in the city, outcries from foreign ambassadors, and sent the councillors responsible flying for cover. And there in the pulpit was the man who had officiated at Fotheringhay. The text Fletcher declaimed could only have increased the tension:

The Angell of the Lorde appeared to Ioseph in Egipt in a dreame, sayeng arrise, and take vpp the childe and his mother and returne into the Lande of Israell for they are deade that sought the chyld[es] Lyfe. (49v)

What interpretive possibilities lay before Fletcher's auditory upon hearing this text? No doubt the allusion to "they who are dead" begged some sort of application to the execution. And certainly they would have known the narrative context of these verses (Matthew 2.19–20), including the introductory clause carefully omitted by the preacher, "But when Herode was dead." Clearly enough, Fletcher was to preach on the angel's message to Joseph that the holy family could return from its flight into Egypt because Herod, who had sought Christ's life in the massacre of innocents, was safely dead.[31] Contemporaries would also know this story as one rich in typological associations, first in the traditional Christian reading of Joseph's leading the holy family out of Egypt as a recapitulation of Moses's and Israel's exodus from Egyptian slavery, with both stories in turn figuring Christ's deliverance of humanity from its slavery to sin.[32] But to this had also been added the Protestant reading of Roman Catholicism as a latter-day Egypt out of which Elizabeth had led the chosen people of England, in which both Pharaoh and Herod were established types for Roman Catholic oppressors.[33] The text thus begged a typological connection between Herod and Mary Queen of Scots, both safely dead. But Fletcher refused to make that application immediately, instead exploiting ambiguities in the biblical text to frustrate, even to invert, easy correspondences with the present.

Ignoring the more obvious concern of both his text and the times with the death of a tyrant, Fletcher instead opened his sermon with an emphasis on events antecedent to his chosen text: on the flight into Egypt rather than the return into Israel. Of particular concern to the preacher was the irony that the faithful, indeed the Saviour, should need to fly from the wicked, that Egypt, the land of slavery, should become the land of refuge. In an extended anaphora, Fletcher cataloged biblical sinners who properly fled from justice: "Let Adame flye that hath broken & transgressed the Lawe. . . . Let Cayne that murtherer flye . . . let Sheba flye that traytor. . . . Let Ionas flye. . . . Let the wicked flye," concluding with the angry *rogatio,* "But why shoulde Iosephe flye, who is a iuste man and Marie who is a pure and undefiled virgin; and christe who is an Innocente and Lambe w^{th}oute spotte." His answer was an arresting one:

Though ye^e righteous maye sometyme stande and staye in the testimonie of theire Innocencie, and simplicitie of a dove yet must they sometyme flye in the wisedomme of a serpent. It ys Christ[es] owne doctryne, & heavenlye direction: If they p[er]secute you in one citie, flie into another. (52v)

Arresting, because in a sermon inviting application to Mary Queen of Scots, Fletcher's elaboration of the metaphor of a flight to safety must have summoned up memories of Mary's own flight into England in 1568. Her hopes for recapturing her throne dashed at the battle of Langside, and faced with a probable return to imprisonment, Mary had fled in a fishing boat across the Solway Firth on the night of 16 May, cherishing the hope that Elizabeth would welcome her with affection as well as protection: "If they persecute you in one citie, flie into another."[34] But what does this potential parallel do to the political valence of Fletcher's chosen text? Is Mary Herod or Joseph? Is England Egypt or Israel?

Clearly Fletcher would not leave Christ on Mary's side in his typological equation, but the temporary ambiguity seems deliberate and serves a larger purpose. Fletcher had consciously played with an iconographic type—the flight of the righteous—that, in context, had two potential antitypes: both Mary and Elizabeth. Lessons drawn from Scripture by Fletcher—"hee that loveth daunger shall perishe in his daunger," "vse the meanes of safetye offered by god: for thou shalt not tempt the Lorde thy god"—could have been used to justify Mary's flight into England. But since 1570 and the discovery of Mary's involvement in the Ridolfi Plot,

precisely the same lessons had been applied to Elizabeth as justifications
for executing her sister queen: to "flee" from danger, Elizabeth must kill
Mary.[35] The potential duality of Fletcher's iconography recapitulated in
metaphor the moral and political double-bind created for Elizabeth and
England by the crisis over the Scottish queen: Elizabeth herself was of two
minds, wanting Mary dead politically but alive theoretically; the government was split, with its sovereign insisting on preservation, its council and
parliaments demanding execution; and the moral arguments for and
against execution could cancel one another out as each side could argue
that justice was mercy and vice versa; even Elizabeth herself, as we shall
see, in her replies to parliamentary petitions for execution, could only
speak in null-sets, in casuistical answers that tried to have it both ways,
famously remembered as her "answers-answerless."

But if the dominant tenor of Fletcher's ambiguous "flight" conceit was
that Elizabeth was the virtuous refugee, what or where was her Egypt?
Was it the state of danger into which she had "fled" by refusing to execute
Mary? If so, Fletcher was telling his queen to her face that she had turned
England's promised land into "Egipt the oude [sic; "oulde"] and invete-
rate fornace of Israell[es] affliction," a haven for the servants of the
Roman pharaoh. The preacher, however, moved on to limit the ambiguity
by first moralizing that God cared for his chosen people even in Egypt: "It
ys all one for god[es] providence to protecte at Memphis, in Egipt, and at
Bethelem in Iurye his grace to his seru[a]ntes ys wanting in no place"
(53r). But more dramatically, in the sermon's first direct address to the
royal closet, Fletcher retracted the prior application of Egypt to England
in order to score the first of a series of points against the woman facing
him at the opposite end of the chapel. Addressing the closet without the
conventional deferential request for verbal access, Fletcher said, "But you
are not in Egipte but in Canaan, you are not at Babylon, but at Ierusalem
the citie & sanctuarye of peace" (53v). He told Elizabeth that, like Joseph,
she had already been brought by God's hand out of Egypt and was safely
delivered into Israel. Fletcher here insinuated for the first time the
primary application of the biblical text to contemporary events. With
the explicit application of Joseph's example to the person of Elizabeth,
Fletcher paid the queen a rather conventional iconographic compliment.
Joseph, with Mary and Jesus as "his charge" (58r), was symbolically the
guardian of the nascent church. Elizabeth, similarly, was defender of the

faith, guardian of the true church in England. But Elizabeth was not simply equated with Joseph, she was contrasted to him. She, like Joseph, had received news that her promised land was now free of a tyrant's murderous threat to herself and her church; but, unlike Joseph, she mourned the death of her Herod and languished in a mental and spiritual Egypt, needing to be told that she was in fact in Israel.

Instead of an extended direct rebuke, however, Fletcher registered criticism of the queen's fault through panegyric praise of its opposite: celebration of past deliverances that had been properly acknowledged pointed up how the present one was dangerously spurned. The power of Fletcher's prescriptive praise, however, depended upon a fluency with biblical allusion that today requires some reconstruction. Much like a metaphysical poet works and reworks an image or conceit, expanding and transforming it in the course of a lyric, Fletcher embroidered the image of angelic annunciation from his biblical text to replay Elizabeth's accession and the deliverance from the Scottish queen as analogous miracles. To set the stage, Fletcher first invoked biblical personæ who had received messages or ministrations from angels: Abraham, Lot, Zechariah and Elizabeth, Joseph and Mary, the shepherds, Christ in the wilderness, the disciples at the tomb, Peter in prison. To this noble number Fletcher then added his queen in her deliverance by the "ministerie of holy angell[es]" from another Marian Egypt—the captivity imposed upon her as a young woman by her half-sister Mary Tudor (54r–v).

The miraculous transformation of the young Elizabeth from prisoner to princess was a stock part of Elizabeth's mythography, perhaps initiated by herself, but given wider currency by Foxe. According to Foxe's account of her imprisonment by Mary Tudor at Woodstock, the captive "wrote these Uerses with her Diamond in the glasse windowe. Much suspected by me: / Nothing prooued can be. / Quoth Elizabeth, prisoner." Foxe then cast Mary's death and Elizabeth's accession as a dénouement from romance, with the Protestant heroine "erected out of thrall to Libertie, out of daunger to Peace and quietnesse . . . briefly, of a prisoner made a Princesse, and placed in her throne Royal."[36] But in the hands of godly preachers in ensuing years, replaying Foxe's myth of deliverance could become criticism, not praise. As Patrick Collinson has shown, the failure to render sufficient thanks and appreciation for God's mercies was a ground-bass of prophetic Protestant indictments of worldliness and calls for further reformation. The English Israel had been singled out by God for deliverance from Romish tyranny, and any hint of a relapse into false religion was a betrayal of the nation's election.[37] So, any perceived failure on Elizabeth's part to live up to the promise of her deliverance from Mary Tudor's Rome inspired remembrances of that deliverance as a form of chastisement. Edward Dering in his infamous 1570 sermon reminded the queen (echoing Foxe) that she could say, "I haue bene a prisoner, I am a Princes," and should therefore "take heede, flee far away from al vnthankfullnes."[38] Elizabeth had been delivered from prison, and was now herself prison keeper to another princess who was only too eager to reverse their respective roles yet again.

Fletcher too replayed Elizabeth's accession, but in a cleverly chosen biblical vocabulary that furthered several of his sermons' controlling conceits. He admonished that "ye Angell of the Lorde delyu[er]ed you as miraculously as eu[er] he dyd S^t. Peter," alluding to the apostle's deliverance from prison (Acts 12). Fletcher's auditory would have known that Peter had been imprisoned not only by another Roman tyrant, but by another Herod.[39] And Peter's deliverance was another angelic one: "The angel of the Lord was there present, and a lyght shyned in the habitation: and he smote Peter on the syde, and raised hym vp, saying, Aryse vp quickly. And his chaynes fel of from his handes" (Acts 12.7). In Fletcher's Elizabethan retelling, God's angel is first given the satisfaction of smiting the queen's enemies "in the hynder part[es]." He then proceeded to strike the sleeping prisoner-princess "on the syde wth his right hande," loosed her chains, and allegorically led her out through the "Iron gate that yo[ur] enemyes would have rampered against yo[u]re most iuste and naturall succession" (54v–55r). Fletcher's angelic deliverance of Elizabeth stands in a line of iconographic descent from Foxe that anticipates Thomas Heywood's sentimental and nostalgic *If You Know Not Me, You Know No Body* (1605), where angels in dumbshow defend the sleeping prisoner-princess from murderous friars and place in her hands an English Bible.[40]

But Fletcher's redaction of St. Peter-in-chains not only recalled the queen to her miraculous providential accession in 1558, but through its parallels in imagery recalled Elizabeth to the text and the event at hand — the angel's message that her Herod was dead. Like Peter, "when Ioseph is at rest, and layed into his bedd and place of forgetfulnes, then dothe god[es] Angell bringe hym glade tydyng[es] of delyueraunce" (55r). And the admonitory tone in Fletcher's treatment of these exempla becomes ever clearer if we remember that these angels are no Raphaelesque *putti*, but soldiers in the heavenly host who, as Milton properly conceived them, spoke with gravity and urgency and knew when to show their might. Neither Peter nor Joseph was gently roused, but rather knocked or shouted out of bed: "and he smote Peter on the side," "Arise and take the young chyld and his mother." And if Elizabeth was the sleeping Peter or Joseph, who then were the angels? Surely in the dramatic sense of the chapel space, Fletcher played the angel to Elizabeth's Joseph. It was a pulpit commonplace to claim, as Dering did, that God spoke directly through his preachers.[41] The implicit application of Fletcher's biblical text to the times allowed him to take the part even more explicitly. He stood in the Greenwich pulpit as a "mercurie and messenger of god" (63v) sent, if not from heaven, then from Fotheringhay, to strike the queen on the ear with the message of her Herod's death and to recall her from the sleep of false pity.

But Fletcher was careful to remind Elizabeth that other angels had actually made the deliverance from Mary possible. She had, he maintained, been "warned and infourmed of yo[ur] enemyes secret maliciousnes by ye Angell of god, by divine and miraculous intelligence, the manye detections of theire manyfoulde designement[es] have sealed yt vnto you" (55v). Did Elizabeth have angelic spies? Certainly no cherub, but certainly an intelligencer, was the man who actually sprang the trap that snared Mary for the block, Sir Francis Walsingham. The spymaster had managed to route Mary's correspondence across his own desk, providing the proof of her complicity in the Babington Plot that finally forced Elizabeth to allow her trial.[42] And here recourse to an Old Testament story—Elisha's divination of the secret war councils of King Ben-Hadad (II Kings 6)—allowed Fletcher safe opportunity to laud the men whom Elizabeth now refused to allow into her presence, the very men who in the nation's eyes had saved her life. "In the tente[s] of the kinge of Aram," Fletcher ventured, "yt ys sayde as sometyme in the dayes of Elizens the prophete who ys yt y^t betrayethe oure councell vnto the kinge of Israell." The wicked king's counsellors answered, "It ys none of thy serua[u]nt[es], it is Elisa the prophet, it is the Angell of the Lorde" (55v). Mary's councils had been betrayed not by one of her own, but by Elizabeth's Elisha, her divining angel, Walsingham.[43]

Having shown, in the typological terms of Moses's and Christ's flights from Egypt and Peter's deliverance from prison, the queen's own life to be a succession of deliverances that recapitulated England's escape from popery, Fletcher concluded the sermon's first half with a pointed admonition to the queen. After cataloging the many blessings she had received, he cautioned that a false sense of security wrought by them "maye make a fulnes, and so a forgetfulnes of that whiche brought you oute of Egipte." "But if yoᵘ doe forgett hym," he continued, eyes trained on the royal closet, "then, audi virgam: beare the rodd and heare yo[ur] punishement," a quotation of the prophet Micah's condemnation of the Israelites' unthankfulness for God's having "broght thee vp out of the land of Egypt" (Micah 6.4, 9). Then, using the language of the psalmist, he reminded Elizabeth of her family's escape from its own Egypt. Psalm 45, known by the prayerbook title taken from its opening Latin phrase, *Eructavit cor meum* (Coverdale's "My heart is inditing"), was one of the three psalms specially appointed to be read on Christmas. As such it not only would have been familiar, but it fit admirably into the Christmas-Epiphany themes of Fletcher's text from Matthew.[44]

But only an understanding of the exegetical and liturgical tradition surrounding Psalm 45 makes any greater sense of its place in Fletcher's sermon. In fact, it is a crowning elaboration of the image and theme of Elizabeth's deliverance from her Egypt, for Psalm 45 was believed to be a royal epithalamion for Solomon's marriage to an Egyptian princess. Commenting on the tenth verse the Geneva headnote explained that the princess is called by her spouse to *"renou[n]ce her people & the loue of her countrey and giue her selfe wholly to her housband,"* and the gloss on the same verse adds, "Vnder the figure of Pharaohs daughter he sheweth yᵗ yᵉ church must cast of all carnal affections to obey Christ onely." Fletcher, then, worked within the established iconographic tradition of Elizabeth as the church, the *sponsa Christi*, but with a keenly critical edge.[45] As he had already shown in Foxeian terms, Elizabeth had been repeatedly delivered from Egypt. Here she comes out of Egypt yet again, this time arrayed as a royal bride converting to true religion through her marriage with Solomon, a type of Christ. Hence Fletcher's harsh redaction of images from Psalm 45.10 that follows: "Forgett therfor yo[ur] self and yo[ur] fathers house forgett yo[ur] hono[ur], and yo[ur] glorie . . . and let not your life be precious in yo[ur] sight to keepe in remembraunce . . . the mercie & lovinge kyndenes of yo[ur] god and ouʳ gracious god toward[es] You"

(57r–v). Her father's house was Pharaoh's house, the house of false religion, and she dallied there, mourning one of its unreformed daughters instead of rejoicing in her own marriage to the truth.

In the second half of his sermon Fletcher turned to the angel's "oracle": "*Surge:* Aryse and take the Childe, and his mother and returne into the lande of Israell" (57v). First he again deliberately crossed the expected typological applications to Elizabeth and Mary, and even more significantly, made his only explicit reference to a contemporary personage by name. Joseph, Fletcher said, was to be commended for heeding the angel's instruction to remain patiently in exile until summoned. Unlike "our runnagates & seedemen of sedition," Joseph made no attempt to take Christ and "sett him vpp in Israell" without God's warrant. Here Fletcher inverted, or even parodied for ironic effect, his own text. For the "Christ" that the Roman Catholic false-Josephs, or "seedemen of sedition," wished to plant in "Israell" was of course not Elizabeth, but her alterego, Mary Queen of Scots, and that "w[th]oute the testimonye of god and the warr[a]unte of the Angell." Mary and the Catholic plotters fell short of "that apostolicall pietie" shown by St. Paul, who, when accused by his fellow Jews before the Roman governor Festus, maintained that he "was constrayned to appeale vnto Caesar: not that I had ought to accuse my people of." Paul had been innocent of sedition yet refused to call for Caesar's revenge against his false accusers.[46] But Fletcher's "monstrous apostatates [*sic*] not successo[ur]s of the apostels" cried to their papal Caesar not only for "vengeaunce" and "excom[m]unication" of their countrymen—an allusion to the 1570 papal excommunication of Elizabeth and subsequent Jesuit missions[47]—but also for his "shopp of vulcane" to "frame devyses to overthrowe christian kynge Iames" (59r–v).

In a sermon that studiously avoided anything but veiled allusion to contemporary figures, reference by name to Mary's son, the twenty-year-old James VI, demands further attention. Herein lies another of Fletcher's savvy political ploys. Nearly every parliamentary argument since 1572 justifying Mary's execution had been based on Mary's threat to Elizabeth's own life.[48] At least in their official rhetoric, those clamoring for Mary's death never cited any concern for James's sovereignty as one of their reasons for dispatching his mother. On the contrary, until 1586 he was widely regarded as an ally of France and Spain, with many Catholics holding onto hopes for his conversion.[49] Indeed the only mention of him in the final English parliamentary prosecution of his mother came in a November 1586 committee speech dismissing him in unflattering terms as unlikely, for lack of intellectual or military power, to continue his mother's machinations against England.[50] Why then would Fletcher displace the threat of Mary Stuart and her religion from Elizabeth to James? Perhaps Scottish ears were addressed, for after the execution James was crying foul, and his people had taken to the streets to denounce Elizabeth as a murderous Jezebel. Perhaps Fletcher suggested—unlike any English propagandist before him—that England had done Scotland and its king a favor by executing its fallen queen. But Fletcher intended his sermon primarily for Elizabeth's ears, and it must have been for her benefit that James was written into it. On a purely emotional level, Fletcher could assuage some of Elizabeth's guilt by simply transferring justification for the execution from an English to a Scottish context—implying, in short, that Elizabeth and her government had not acted out of hostile self-interest, but a charitable concern also for a neighbor prince. Moreover, one of the shrewdest amendments Elizabeth had made—against the inclinations of both the council and Parliament—to the 1584 Act for the Queen's Safety was to exempt James from any penalties should his mother be found guilty of plots against Elizabeth. In short, Elizabeth had protected James's crown and safeguarded his claims to her own— something she knew the young king valued more than his mother's life.[51] Fletcher's flattering invocation of "christian kynge Iames" is one of the earliest examples of a radical shift in propaganda against Mary Stuart following her execution that tempered attacks on her in tacit acknowledgment of her son's likely accession to the English throne.[52] The preacher paid a discreet compliment to an Elizabethan piece of policy that put James forever in Elizabeth's debt.

From this digression Fletcher returned to his text with "but let vs heare the Angell" (60r). Thereupon followed one of the most rhetorically heightened passages in the sermon, as Fletcher, retelling the angel's message to Joseph in a kind of free-indirect discourse, strategically blurred the distinctions between the biblical personæ, the angel and Joseph, and their counterparts, himself and the queen. "What neede have you to be awaked, and styrred vpp. wch have taken vppon yo^u the tuition of Christe, the care of his churche," he asked. Amplifying his point, Fletcher reminded the queen that rulers who fell into a sleep of false security would be roused by God's prophets. Two biblical vignettes in particular, both of which had long pedigrees in anti-Marian propaganda, deftly criticized the queen for her lassitude, justified her council's actions, and validated Fletcher's own present efforts to counsel his prince. He first evoked the picture of King David in his chamber lamenting the death of his traitorous son Absalom. As early as 1572, in the bishops' petition for Mary's execution, this story had been deployed as an exemplum of how filial affection could blind the magistrate to the threat of a traitor.[53] In October 1586 the queen's commissioners heard Fletcher, in his pretrial sermon, parody how David had "entreated the captaines . . . be good to a traytoure . . . spare the ladd Absolom," and conclude, "See the preposterous pittie toward[es] a rebell: spare him, that will not spare his father."[54] One month later, to conclude the opening salvo in the parliamentary prosecution, Sir Christopher Hatton had intoned, "*Ne periat Israell periat Absolon*" — Absalom must perish lest Israel perish.[55] And Absalom had conveniently perished without the lifting of a royal finger: God providentially caught his curly locks in an oak, and the king's loyal retainer Joab finished the job. At court after the execution of Elizabeth's Absalom, Fletcher lauded the biblical event as "the most righteous and honorable execution of Iustice that euer was in Israell." He hardly needed to apply the exemplum to the present.

But now another portion of the same biblical story was much more pertinent to the queen and court than Absalom's death, and that was the rebuke of David's "soroweinge and lamentynge" by Joab, "his faythfull counselor." Here again, by the careful deployment of a biblical narrative, and without direct application, Fletcher could press the queen not only to leave off her misguided mourning, but to accept as God given the advice of her now-banished councillors. With subtle but significant additions to the biblical text (here given my italics), Fletcher hit his mark with a simple quotation of Joab's advice to David (II Samuel 19.5–8):

Surge: aryse and speake comfortablye to thy serv[a]unt[es] *that have done thys thinge,* wch if thou doe not, I sweare vnto thee by god, there will not one man abyde wth thee this nighte. *Thou wilte loose the hart[es] and love of all thy faythefull subiect[es],* and that wilbe worse vnto thee then all the evill that euer befell thee from thy youthe hitherto. (60v–61r)

The opening imperative of course quoted the angelic annunciation to Joseph from Fletcher's primary text, and reiterated not only a formal but also a thematic motif: the events of biblical history literally spoke to events in contemporary history in patterns of providential symmetry. Joab had begged David to arise and "speake comfortablye" to his subjects, to tell them publicly that Absalom's death was a blessing to Israel. But Fletcher's emendation turned the populace in general into the very specific few who had "done thys thinge." Fletcher, like Joab, sought royal endorsement for dispatching a traitor. And the fact that the men responsible were either in the Tower or not allowed into the queen's presence ironized, without any elaboration by Fletcher at all, Joab's threat that David's court would be void of his loyal retainers that night. And Fletcher's final and most overt addition to the scriptural narrative turned some of Elizabeth's own rhetoric about the dilemma of Mary Stuart back on its begetter. In her November 1586 "answers-answerless" that declined action on two parliamentary petitions for Mary's execution, Elizabeth had softened the blow of her equivocations by professing to "acknowledge the greatest argument of youre true hartes, and great zeale to my safetie . . . so shal my bonde be strongar tied to gretar care for all your good." And, she insisted, "there was never anie Prince more beholding unto her subiectes then I to youe, so was there never prince, more willing to do youe good then I in my mynd, though I may fayle in the means."[56] To those who—justifiably—considered Mary a grave threat to queen and country, Elizabeth was choosing a perverse way to repay their loyalty and do them good. Fletcher, by inserting her own vocabulary of "hart[es]," "love," and "faythefull subiect[es]" in Joab's advice pointed up precisely this disparity between her words and her deeds.

But it was here at this crucial juncture, where direct criticism of the sovereign lay so close to the surface of the sermon, that Fletcher showed the kind of literary skill that earned him Harington's approbation for being able to "speak boldly, and yet keep decorum." As if Joab's advice to David were not daring enough, Fletcher next reached for a New Testament exemplum, assuming for himself the voice of none other than Christ, and stopping only just short of aligning Elizabeth with the archetypical traitor, Judas. Fletcher struck the set of David's chamber, and replaced it with the Garden of Gethsemane in this remarkable passage:

If Iesus christe be in the garden prayeinge and groninge in spirite before the throne of god wythe dropp[es] of sweate, lyke bloude, beware yt be not sayde vnto yo^u as vnto Peter, Ieames & Iohn: sleepe henceforthe, and take yo[ur] reste: beholde the son[n]e of man ys betrayed vnto the hand[es] of synners: Aryse lett vs goe hence: Awake thou that sleepest, and stande vpp from deathe, and christe shall gyve thee light: tempus est It ys tyme for vs to awake oute of synne. (61r–v)

Fletcher here cast Elizabeth as one of the negligent disciples; Christ, who had committed his cause to the vigilance of their prayers, had to rouse them with news of his own betrayal. Elizabeth, similarly, had slept while her charge, the church, lay unprotected from the plots of a she-Judas. In the chapel royal at Greenwich it was Christ again, though symbolically in the person of a minister of his body on earth, who told the sleeping royal disciple to awake. Fletcher's call, "Aryse lett vs goe hence" was a small masterpiece of functional ambiguity in court pulpit admonition. First, it concluded Fletcher's quotation from the Gospel account, Christ's "Ryse, let vs be going" (Matt. 26.46). As such, it was safely distanced from the dangerous present. But the call also stood at the beginning of a direct address to the queen in Fletcher's own voice. Christ's voice merged with Fletcher's own, the biblical world merged with the temporal, and the exemplum itself walked into the present with Fletcher leading the queen by the hand out from Gethsemane.

Having raised his queen from her sleep of security, Fletcher invited her to take on one of the biblical roles associated with her since the accession. He called to the court, "stirre vpp and awake yo[ur] selues wythe that notable Iudge of Israell: Surge Debora, surge Baracke: Arise Debora arise Baracke: Arise prynce, aryse counsell, and aryse people, and let yo[ur] enemies be scattered" (61v). But Fletcher's was not simply a panegyric to the heroic female judge of Israel.[57] Instead he emphasized the collaboration that was required for Deborah's victory. She had exhorted her general, Barak, to battle, but he would attack the Syrians only in her company; only with this union of spiritual and civil power were the armies of Israel triumphant, inspiring the refrain of Deborah's song that Fletcher wove into his own call: "Vp Debora vp: get thee vp, and syng a song: aryse Barak, and leade the captiuitie captiue thou sonne of Abinoam" (Judges 5.12). Fletcher offered a similar vision that urged prince, council, and people to march in step against the common enemy. It was, of course,

a vision that contrasted painfully with current political realities: whereas
Deborah had joined hands with Barak and her people and rejoiced in
her victory, Elizabeth was estranged from her council (was Burghley
Fletcher's Barak?) and her people, and lamented, instead of lauded, their
victory. The preacher called for a biblical story, indeed for a received
iconographic image of Elizabeth, to be made flesh, in an attempt to make a
scriptural text write contemporary history. Here was a chance to reify the
iconic metaphor of the Elizabethan Deborah, or, put another way, an
opportunity for the Elizabethan regime's apologists to write contemporary history as a recapitulation of sacred history. Perhaps Fletcher and the
earl of Kent had even been busy scripting events in biblical terms on the
scaffold at Fotheringhay. Their exclamation after Mary's decapitation,
"So perish all the Queen's enemies," paraphrased the climactic exclamation of Deborah's victory song: "So peryshe all thyne enemies, O Lorde"
(Judges 5.31). But try as her ministers might, Elizabeth was spoiling the
play by refusing to act her part.

Fletcher knew that he would never convince Elizabeth to sing *Te
Deum*'s over Mary's execution. Understanding his audience—unlike
many godly preachers of Dering's stripe—Fletcher took a pragmatic turn
in his peroration that deflected attention from the painful situation at hand
in order to salvage something of worth from it. Returning to his text, the
preacher again asked Elizabeth, as Joseph, to take up Christ, to "aryse,
and take hym vpp, and establishe him in Israell" (62v). How was she to do
this? Not by celebrating or dwelling upon the events at Fotheringhay, but
by putting them behind her. Herein lies another stroke of genius in
Fletcher's choice of text. Clearly he could have preached an entire sermon
on any of the biblical stories that more closely paralleled the execution,
such as the death of Jezebel (2 Kings 9.30–37), or Judith slaying Holofernes (Judith 8). But instead Fletcher turned to a text not about endings,
but new beginnings. The text would allow him not to exacerbate the
queen's lamentations, but lead her out of them. "Returne into the Lande
of Israell" became Fletcher's concluding refrain, forcing Elizabeth to look
away from the Egypt of the Mary Stuart crisis to the Israel of a secure
England. If Elizabeth could never have been persuaded to accept the role
of Judith holding a Scottish Holofernes's head, she should, Fletcher's
strategy seems to have run, have been willing to accept that of Joseph
returning with the Christ child to Israel. "Gyve mee leave I do most

humbly praye & besseche yo[ur] most christian maiestie," Fletcher asked
in the sermon's only direct supplication, "to stirr you vpp . . . to the
spreadynge of his gospell." And in petitions that anticipated parliamentary legislation pursued that very month, Fletcher pressed the queen to
support Protestant evangelism in Ireland and the "coulde partes" of
northern England where the people remained "frozen in their dregg[es]"
of popery (62v–63r).[58] Fletcher moved beyond the execution of a queen
to the execution of policy.

The "last thinge to be considered" from the preacher's text—"the
reason whie Ioseph shoulde returne wth his charge into his native cun-
trie"—might have been an occasion to revisit in upsetting detail the death
of Elizabeth's Herod. Fletcher, however, diffused that tension by descant-
ing on the collective threat of all Roman Catholics as a "Herod." This
strategy allowed the preacher to touch the matter of the execution without
actually saying as much, and distanced the queen from the horror and
guilt of the deed by sublimating it into a metaphor for a general attack on
Roman Catholicism. Thus Fletcher's observation that "herod the better to
compasse his crueltie gave yt oute, that if christe coulde be founde hee
woulde com[m]e and worshipp him" undoubtedly referred to Mary's
feigned protestations of filial affection and duty to Elizabeth. But the
"worshipp of the tyraunte" (63v) could also apply to conformist or
recusant English Catholics who likewise insisted that their faith did not
compromise their allegiance to their sovereign. So Fletcher could simultaneously dismiss the whole lot, couching a tacit justification of the execution in a conventional denunciation of popish dissimulation: "Theire
fawninge ys but flatterie, and theire pretended piety nothinge ell[es] but
treacherie" (64v). Here again Fletcher exploited an ambiguity found in
the biblical text itself. As he explained, "the texte sayethe, not onely herod
was dead, but y[e] Angell sayed they are deade" (65r). "They" or "their"
could function as a dignified plural for a single antecedent—Herod, and
by application, Mary—or as a true plural referring to all those loyal to the
tyrant. But pressing his political advantage, Fletcher kept both in play by
insisting that to have killed the single tyrant was also to have killed his (or
her) followers.

Next Fletcher urged the queen to accept another iconographic role
long used for her, but now brought to an almost uncanny consummation.
What did the Assyrians do, he asked, "which laye at the siege of poor

Bethulia, but flye and be confounded: when holofernes theire chyefe captayne lyethe headles by the hande of Iudithe" (65v). Since early in her reign, Elizabeth had been cast as a Protestant Judith beheading a Roman Catholic Holofernes.[59] But now iconography came too close to life, and Elizabeth wanted anything but to be reminded that she really had struck the head from Holofernes's shoulders. So Fletcher deftly moved away from the execution itself by calling again for those around Judith, her generals and counsellors, to seize their advantage against Holofernes's dismayed minions: "ffollowe therefore vppon them . . . you elders, & men of Bethulia, for god hathe delyuered them into yo[ur] handes" (65v). Not only was Elizabeth to rise up from her bed of foolish grief, she and her scattered elders were to pursue their newly scattered enemies. This was how Elizabeth, as a latter-day Joseph, could be a true Christ-bearer: to mount a "chariott of Iustice," and ride out against those who had sought her life and Christ's life in her church. Thus serving as Christ's guardian, Fletcher promised Elizabeth, in conclusion, she would "appeare wth hym, in glorie" when he returned at the last day (67v).

Fletcher's sermon calls for further comment in the light of recent work on Elizabeth's iconography, since its choice of biblical types for the queen complicates some assumptions about gender and representations of Gloriana. Perhaps the best treatment of religious imagery applied to Elizabeth is Helen Hackett's recent study of Elizabeth and the cult of the Virgin Mary. One Marian attribute she very logically finds applied to Elizabeth is that of the church's (or Christ's) nursing mother.[60] This trope so perfectly fit the needs of those celebrating a female head of the English church that it became a commonplace, especially in the pulpit. Another of Elizabeth's chaplains, Richard Eedes, best summarized the iconographic point in a sermon he preached before her in 1594: "God hath honored her . . . so far beyond other princes, as to make a *virgin Queen the best nurce* of the religio[n] of him, who had a *virgin to his Mother*."[61] Seen in this context, then, Fletcher's typological alignment of Elizabeth not with Mary but with her spouse Joseph may be a radical iconographic shift, or it may suggest our own ahistorical exaggeration of the importance of gender in sixteenth-century representations of Elizabeth. Elizabethan preachers, it must be said, had no qualms about celebrating Elizabeth as the antitype of male types from the Bible. In sermons preached at her own court, Elizabeth appeared far more frequently as a latter-day David or

Solomon than in the more gender-correct guise of Judith or Deborah.[62] We do need to remember that moral or political attributes were of more importance than gender when choosing biblical personæ as types illustrating royal virtues and vices. Hence, as we have seen in Fletcher's sermon, Elizabeth's accession could be retold in terms of Peter's deliverance from prison without any anxieties about making the queen appear "unnaturally mannish" because of congruities more important than gender between the biblical narrative and the historical event.[63]

But even with these considerations allowed, Fletcher very self-consciously, even aggressively, avoided both the feminine and the Marian in his treatment of Elizabeth. Hackett has demonstrated how Marian imagery deployed to praise Elizabeth depends on "specific political circumstances"; Fletcher's sermon is an example of how such political circumstances could inspire the pointed avoidance of otherwise expected imagery as a way to criticize the queen.[64] As we have seen, the Virgin, and by Elizabethan extension, the Virgin Queen, was an established iconographic type for the church itself or its nurse. But under the threat of Mary Stuart and her papistical plotters, Fletcher thought Elizabeth's church needed a guardian, not a nursemaid. Thus enter Joseph as Elizabeth's biblical type and exemplar. "Christe is yo[ur] charge," Fletcher insisted, but added also "Marie that fostereth hym, and all that professe hym w^{th}in yo[ur] kyngedom[m]e hath almightie god committed to yo[ur] protection" (62r). Fletcher actually entrusted Elizabeth with the paternal protection of one of her maternal iconographic images. Crudely put, the preacher told the queen to be a man. But to have said so in so many words would have destroyed his fragile rapport with the occupant of the royal closet. Instead, the deliberate ambiguity of a biblical image with obvious but only implied potential for application to the queen left the interpretive responsibility with the auditory, not the preacher. Surely Fletcher's sermon, and many others like it, provide some answer to skepticism about the existence and cultural viability of "codes that everyone can understand."

But how did Fletcher's sermon, preached to such a privileged auditory, fit into the state's public handling of the execution? As J. E. Phillips has shown, Burghley orchestrated a very detailed and careful propaganda campaign after Mary's execution, a campaign based on an official account of the deed written specifically to justify it to other European governments. In Phillips's sum, Burghley pressed four points: that Mary was executed for treason, not religion; that the execution was not regicide since Mary forfeited sovereignty and regal status upon entering England; that Elizabeth was reluctant to execute Mary, and did so only under pressure from her council and Parliament; and that as God's lieutenant, Elizabeth had no choice but to do his will.[65] These may have been the government's international aims, but they were in large not Fletcher's. His departure from the public propaganda line proves not only how profoundly estranged the queen was from her ministers, but how crucial the court sermon was in this case as perhaps their only viable means of advice and rebuke to her. On one point, Fletcher pursued Burghley's public propaganda line without variation, that being the insistence that in moral-political terms the queen "was forced to act against her sister queen or be punished for neglect of duty."[66] As we have seen, Fletcher devoted the majority of his sermon to recalling Elizabeth to her duty as Christ's guardian, which meant leaving Egypt and accepting as meet and right the justice executed in Israel. Fletcher even threatened that if she did not succor her subjects thus, "the Egiptians shall succoure them and you shalbe forsaken. . . . [G]od shall send delyveraunce by some other meanes, and thou, and thy fathers house shall perishe" (62r). But there was irony even in this, the sermon's one point of agreement with the public justification of the execution. While Burghley tried to convince the wider world that Elizabeth had been duty-bound to take Mary's life, Fletcher had the job of trying to convince the queen herself of her own government's position.

With respect to Mary's regal status, Elizabeth never accepted her subjects' insistence that Mary had ceased to be a queen; regicide was regicide, and she knew what kind of precedent she would set by executing a sister queen. Fletcher, probably knowing this to be the ultimate source of his queen's despair, skirted the sovereignty issue. Whereas parliamentary pronouncements as early as 1572 had declared Mary "nowe iustely no queene," Fletcher did not comment directly upon the status of Elizabeth's adversary.[67] Here his biblical text again did the critical work for him. Mary's type in Fletcher's text was a king; but Herod the Great was no ordinary king. Not only was he an archetypical tyrant—one who feigned devotion to the truth, tricked the Magi, massacred the innocents—he was also a puppet king, servant of usurping Rome in the Promised Land. Also at play in the typological imagination was probably Herod the Great's son, Herod Antipas, who before beheading John the Baptist was rebuked by him for marrying his brother's wife (Mark 6.18). This "whordom of Herode," familiar from the official homily against adultery, squared perfectly with Mary's reputation as both Roman Catholic whore and incontinent wife.[68] So Fletcher subtly dethroned his Mary in the persona of Herod, who like Mary was at once usurper, tyrant, alien, apostate, and adulterer, and thus deserved to die. But more to the point, Herod had been struck down by divine intervention. Matthew's gospel gives no cause for Herod the Great's death after the massacre of the innocents, but familiar to all was the fate of his grandson Herod Agrippa in Acts 12.23: "The Angel of the Lord smote him . . . so that he was eate[n] of wormes." The Geneva gloss maintained, "his grandfather also was eaten of lise."[69] Fletcher therefore could hold Herod up as an exemplar of a threat removed, but one removed by God himself, and without the nasty business of a state execution. Not only did the use of Herod as exemplum obscure the question of regicide, it obscured, or distanced, the whole question of Elizabeth's culpability by simply inviting her to return to an Israel cleansed and purged by no act of her own, "for they are deade that sought the chyld[es] Lyfe."

Burghley may have wanted to convince Catholic Europe that the execution was an act of civil justice, but Fletcher, like most of England, saw it in sectarian terms: at Fotheringhay the axe had been laid in the trunk of popery in England. Yes, Mary had sought Elizabeth's life, but her planned treason was religious, for in seeking Elizabeth's life she sought the Christ Elizabeth protected in England's Protestant church. Fletcher could not separate civil from religious motives; instead he saw plots against Elizabeth tricked out in all the popish whore's frippery:

They seeke yo[ur] lyfe, and the lyfe of yo[ur] chylde Iesus It ys all theire practise to worke theire designement[es] by all man[ner] of shewe and meanes whatsoeu[er] gyvynge of faythe, swearinge vppon bookes, eatinge of consecrated host[es], receavinge of sacrament[es], celebratinge of mariage settinge forthe of tryumphes, makinge of leagues, wytnessinge at baptisme Invytyng to feast[es], reconcilinge to god, confession of synnes, absolution of preist[es], all are cou[er]ed wyth pretence of holynes, and religion, and all to vpholde, and houlde vpp the whore of babilon w'h all hir detestable enormities. (64v–65r)

But on no point did Fletcher depart more dramatically from Burghley's official accounts than in his treatment of Elizabeth's grief over the execution. Burghley—like Edmund Spenser—actually seized on Elizabeth's postexecution grief and anger as a way to exonerate her, to convince Europe that she had not acted rashly, even that she had not made up her mind before her ministers forced her hand. Elizabeth, in her government's international propaganda, was a pitiable victim of events beyond her control.[70] But in her own household chapel, Elizabeth's favorite chaplain rebuked her for precisely this reluctance to take responsibility for the execution. Rather than excusing, or using as an excuse, her guilty rage, Fletcher had stigmatized it as a politically dangerous, morally culpable lounging in Egypt while her redeemed Israel waited anxiously for her return.

Sadly we know nothing of Elizabeth's response to Fletcher's sermon. We do know from his rapid climb up the ecclesiastical ladder that if she did take offense it did not last long. I hope I have shown that Fletcher's was no flattery, nor even a subtle scolding, but in an artful way a firm rebuke of the queen's behavior after the deed was done. But Fletcher's continued favor at court, like Burghley's eventual return to good graces, shows that criticisms of Elizabeth couched in literary form—"negative representations"—were often constructive engagements in political discourse and not merely vilifications of the queen.

Notes

The author gratefully acknowledges the president and fellows of Trinity College, Oxford for the research fellowship that enabled this project and for access to the college's Chadwick-Healey collection of early printed Bibles and prayerbooks; the president and fellows of St. John's College Cambridge for permission to quote manuscripts in the college's Old Library; and the reader for Duke University Press with such keen Latinity and respect for Francis Walsingham.

1. There are of course welcome exceptions to this complaint; the most challenging are perhaps Debora K. Shuger, *Habits of Thought in the English Renaissance: Religion, Politics, and the Dominant Culture* (Berkeley: University of California Press, 1990), and her *The Renaissance Bible: Scholarship, Sacrifice, and Subjectivity* (Berkeley: University of California Press, 1994). See also the essays collected in Richard Strier and Donna B. Hamilton, eds., *Religion, Literature, and*

Politics in Post-Reformation England, 1540–1688 (Cambridge: Cambridge University Press, 1996).

2. P. E. McCullough, *Sermons at Court: Politics and Religion in Elizabethan and Jacobean Preaching* (Cambridge: Cambridge University Press, 1997).

3. Fletcher's sermon, which survives in St. John's College Cambridge (hereafter SJCC) MS I.30 (described below), has to my knowledge gone unnoticed since its citation by the antiquarian Edmund Venables in his article on Fletcher for *DNB* vol. 7 (1889).

4. Pam Wright, "A Change of Direction: The Ramifications of a Female Household, 1558–1603," in David Starkey et al., *The English Court from the War of the Roses to the Civil War* (London: Longman, 1987), 159. See also Simon Thurley, *The Royal Palaces of Tudor England* (New Haven: Yale University Press, 1993).

5. Helen Hackett, *Virgin Mother, Maiden Queen: Elizabeth I and the Cult of the Virgin Mary* (Basingstoke: Macmillan, 1995), 129; see also Stephen W. May, *The Elizabethan Courtier Poets: The Poems and Their Contexts* (Columbia, Mo.: University of Missouri Press, 1991), 9–14.

6. Thurley, *Tudor Royal Palaces*, 195–205; McCullough, *Sermons at Court*, chap. 1.

7. E. M. W. Tillyard, *The Elizabethan World Picture* (New York: Vintage, 1944), 106.

8. Ralph Churton, *The Life of Alexander Nowell* (Oxford, 1809), 92; Patrick Collinson, *The Religion of Protestants* (Oxford: Oxford University Press, 1982), 34–35.

9. Edward Dering, *A Sermon Preached before the Quenes Maiestie* (1570); for this sermon, see McCullough, *Sermons at Court*, chap. 1; and Collinson, *A Mirror of Elizabethan Puritanism: The Life and Letters of "Godly Master Dering,"* (London: Dr. Williams's Library, 1964), 16–17.

10. John Foxe, *Actes and Monuments* (1583), 1679–80.

11. Sir John Harington, *A Supplie or Addicion to the Catalogue of Bishops, to the Yeare 1608* (Potomac, Md.: Porr'ua Turanzas, 1979), 54.

12. Harington, *Supplie or Addicion*, 50; Thomas Birch, ed., *Memoirs of the Reign of Queen Elizabeth*, 2 vols. (1754), 2:113–14, 150, 171, 224.

13. The heading of Fletcher's sermon identifies him as "Deane of Peterborough, and one of hir maiesties Chaplaynes" (SJCC, MS I.30, fol. 3r).

14. *Journal de Dominique Bourgoing Médecin de Marie Stuart*, in M. R. Chantelauze, *Marie Stuart Son Procès et Son Exécution* (Paris, 1876), 547. Mary re-

counted the offer to her counsellor, the archbishop of Glasgow, with contempt. See Alexandre Labanoff, *Lettres, Instructions, et Memoires de Marie Stuart*, 7 vols. (London, 1844), 6:467. The diocesan was Richard Howland, friend and client of Whitgift and Burghley.

15. Bourgoing, *Journal*, in Chantelauze, *Marie Stuart*, 573.

16. SJCC, MS I.30, fol. 38v.

17. Chantelauze, *Marie Stuart*, 411–12.

18. Although accounts of this exclamation vary in detail, two of the most reliable accounts of the execution concur on Fletcher's words: "Then M[r] Deane said w[th] a lowde voyce soe p[er]ish all the Quenes enymies and afterwardes the E of Kent . . . sayd such an end of all the Quenes and the gospells enemyes" (Bodl. MS Tanner 78, fol. 131[v]); "one of the executioners . . . bid God saue the queene: And the Deane said and soe p[er]ish all her Enimies' . . . my Lo: of Kent . . . said . . . This be the End & reward of all that hate the gospell and her Ma[ts] government" (Bodleian MS Ashmole 830, fols. 15[v]–16[r]). These accounts are inaccurately reprinted in Mary M. M. Scott, *The Tragedy of Fotheringay* (London, 1895), 249–63.

19. For a succinct account, see J. E. Neale, *Queen Elizabeth I* (London: Jonathan Cape, 1934), 257–82.

20. J. E. Neale, *Elizabeth I and Her Parliaments*, 2 vols. (London: Jonathan Cape, 1969), 2:143; Jenny Wormald, *Mary Queen of Scots: A Study in Failure* (London: Collins and Brown, 1991), 186.

21. The council wrote abjectly seeking the queen's grace on 12 February; as late as 25 February Burghley was still denied access. *HMC Salisbury*, 3:220–21; Neale, *Parliaments*, 2:141.

22. The manuscript is written in the same secretary hand, one that the donor, eighteenth-century antiquarian Thomas Baker, speculated was Fletcher's own. However, the hand is decidedly not that of Fletcher's holograph in letters calendared in *HMC Salisbury* (4:446; 5:32, 167, 171). It is very possibly that of BL MS Cotton Caligula D.I.196, a letter from Fletcher dated 3 September 1587. If this latter is holograph, Fletcher used a hand different from that of the Salisbury letters (1593–95). I am preparing an edition of the texts in the manuscript relating to Mary Queen of Scots. Foliation here is my own, and subsequent references to Fletcher's sermon appear in the text.

23. During Lent, which in 1587 began on 1 March, three sermons per week were preached before the queen and court. Fletcher was appointed to preach three times during the Lent series on 10 and 24 March, and 7 April (Westminster

Abbey Muniment Book 15, fol. 15). These dates seem too late to be described as "immediately" after the execution. For the Lent series, see McCullough, *Sermons at Court*, 2:2.

24. The chapel was built by Henry VII, and according to a report of James I's renovation, had been left unaltered since Mary Tudor's time. See Howard Colvin, gen. ed., *A History of the King's Works*, 4 vols. (London: HMSO, 1962–83), 4:97–118.

25. Annabel Patterson, *Censorship and Interpretation: The Conditions of Writing and Reading in Early Modern England* (Madison: University of Wisconsin Press, 1984), 11. Consonant with Patterson's view is Christopher Hill, "Censorship and English Literature," in *The Collected Essays*, vol. 1, *Writing and Revolution in Seventeenth-Century England* (Brighton: Harvester, 1985), 32–71.

26. Sheila Lambert, "State Control of the Press in Theory and Practice: The Role of the Stationers' Company before 1640," in Robin Meyers and Michael Harris, eds., *Censorship and the Control of Print in England and France 1600–1910* (Winchester: Saint Paul's Bibliographies, 1992), 5.

27. In her treatment of Donne's sermons, Patterson does not pursue her own claims about the potential for the use of veiled speech in sermons, focusing instead on Donne's attempts to limit meaning after their delivery (*Censorship*, 92–105).

28. Thomas Drant, *Two sermons* (1570?), sig.I.i^r–Lviij^r.

29. Lancelot Andrewes, *XCVI Sermons* (1629), 845.

30. Harington, *Supplie or Addicion*, 170.

31. Fletcher's quotation follows most closely, but not exactly, the Bishops' Bible. Throughout the sermon his biblical quotations seem to be memorial, with a preference for the Bishops' over the Geneva, and for the Coverdale (prayerbook) version of the Psalms. Cf. his quotation of Jer. 8.22 in the translation unique to the Bishops', or "Treacle" Bible: "ys there anye treacle sayethe the prophet At Gilead" (fol. 53r). Unless otherwise noted, I quote from the Bishops' Bible and Coverdale Psalter.

32. Cf. the Geneva gloss on Mat. 2.15: "That which was prefigured by the deliuerance of the Israelites out of Egypt, w^c were Christs Church and his bodie, is now verified, and accomplished in the head Christ."

33. Cf. the retelling of the Exodus in terms of the Tudor succession by Fletcher's early patron, bishop Richard Curteys, in *A Sermon preached before the Queenes Maiesty at Richmond* (London, 1575), sig. Cviij^v–Dj^v. There seems to have been little concern to distinguish the three rulers called "Herod" in the New

Testament. As members of the same family who all persecuted Christ and his followers, they formed a composite type often treated as the same wicked tyrant. For Pharaoh and Herod, see Foxe, *Actes and Monuments,* 2101, 2115, 2116.

34. Wormald, *Mary Queen of Scots,* 173–74. See also Antonia Fraser, *Mary Queen of Scots* (London: Weidenfeld and Nicholson, 1969), 366–76. The "doctryne" Fletcher quotes is from Christ's commission to his Apostles in Matthew 10 (here vv. 16 & 23).

35. Cf., for example, the bishops' 1572 case for execution, and Job Throckmorton's 4 November 1586 speech in Commons: T. E. Hartley, ed., *Proceedings in the Parliaments of Elizabeth I,* 3 vols. (London: Leicester University Press, 1981–95), 1:274–82; 2:228–32.

36. Foxe, *Actes and Monuments,* 2096, 2097.

37. Patrick Collinson, *The Birthpangs of Protestant England: Religious and Cultural Change in the Sixteenth and Seventeenth Centuries* (Basingstoke: Macmillan, 1988), 17–18.

38. Dering, *A Sermon,* sig. Bij^{r-v}.

39. Peter was imprisoned when "Herode the King stretched forthe his handes to vexe certayne of the Churche" (Acts 12.1); this was Herod Agrippa, grandson (not nephew, as Geneva gloss) of Herod the Great.

40. John Pearson, ed., *The Dramatic Works of Thomas Heywood,* 6 vols. (1874), 1:228.

41. Dering, *A Sermon,* sig. Biij^v.

42. Wallace MacCaffrey, *Elizabeth I* (London: Edward Arnold, 1993), 347–50; Neale, *Parliaments,* 2:104.

43. There is a possible pun on "Elisa"—Eliza, Elizabeth—an idiosyncratic spelling of "Elisha" ("Eliseus" in Bishops' Bible).

44. The flight into Egypt and massacre of the innocents (Mat. 2.13–18) was read on Innocents' Day, 28 December; and the coming of the Magi to Herod and the holy family on Epiphany, 6 January. See John Booty, ed., *The Book of Common Prayer, 1559* (Washington: Folger Shakespeare Library, 1976), 32, 88, 93–94.

45. For Elizabeth as the church, see Hackett, *Virgin Mother,* 60, 136.

46. Acts 25.10–11, 28.18–19.

47. The argument placing Mary in the sequence from Elizabeth's excommunication to the Jesuit mission launched in 1579 was well rehearsed. See, for example, Sir Walter Mildmay's Commons speech against Mary, 3 November 1586, in Hartley, ed., *Proceedings,* 2:226–27.

48. The Parliament of 1572 took as its "first and cheif" business the queen's

safety; the primary product of the 1584 session was the Act for the Queen's Safety; and the 1586 sentence of execution was the fruit of what Hatton described as "the summary cause . . . of this parliament . . . to provyde for the safetie of our most gracyous sovereigne." Hartley, ed., *Proceedings*, 2:317; Neale, *Parliaments*, 1:244, 272, 277; idem, *Parliaments*, vol. 2, chaps. 2–3 and 132–33; Hartley, ed., *Proceedings*, 2:214.

49. James Emerson Phillips, *Images of a Queen: Mary Stuart in Sixteenth-Century Literature* (Berkeley: University of California Press, 1964), 104–5.

50. Hartley, ed., *Proceedings*, 2:233–38. This speech was not used by Neale (*Parliaments*, 2:198).

51. Neale, *Parliaments*, 2:52–53, 135.

52. Phillips, *Images*, 121–22, 199–208.

53. Hartley, ed., *Proceedings*, 1:278–79.

54. SJCC, MS I.30, fol. 10r.

55. Hartley, ed., *Proceedings*, 2:217; Neale, *Parliaments*, 2:107, 143.

56. Hartley, ed., *Proceedings*, 2:252, 269–70. These speeches were carefully revised by the queen herself for publication in R. C[ecil], *The copie of a letter to the right honourable the Earle of Leycester* (1586); cf. Neale, *Parliaments*, 2:114–21, 126–29.

57. For Elizabeth as Deborah, see Elkin C. Wilson, *England's Eliza* (Cambridge, Mass.: Harvard University Press, 1939), chap. 2, passim.

58. For the session of February 1587, stage for the puritans' "great effort to revolutionize the Church," see Neale, *Parliaments*, vol. 2, chap. 3.

59. Wilson, *England's Eliza*, uses Judith as little more than a chapter title; see instead John N. King, *Tudor Royal Iconography* (Princeton: Princeton University Press, 1989), 225–27.

60. Hackett, *Virgin Mother*, 136.

61. Richard Eedes, "The principall care of Princes to bee Nurces of the Church," in *Six Learned and Godlie Sermons* (1604), fol. 89v. Eedes's sermon, not used by Hackett, is one of the best Elizabethan treatments of the key text, "Kings shall be thy nursing fathers, and Queenes thy nursing mothers" (Is. 49.23).

62. Lancelot Andrewes, for example, could feminize male pronouns in royal psalms to praise Elizabeth, but also use male pseudonyms for her, including Prince Alkum and Zerubbabel, and return frequently to David and Solomon as her exemplars. See Nicholas Lossky, *Lancelot Andrewes the Preacher, 1555–1626* (Oxford: Oxford University Press, 1992), 102–15.

63. Hackett, *Virgin Mother*, 164.

64. Ibid., 11.

65. Phillips, *Images,* 123–25, 131–33.

66. Ibid., 126.

67. Hartley, ed., *Proceedings,* 1:283.

68. *Certayne Sermons appoynted by the Quenes Maiestie* (the "First Book of Homilies," 1559), sig. Uii^r.

69. Cf. Foxe, *Actes and Monuments:* "Antiochus and Herode, although the Children of GOD whom they so cruelly persecuted, layd no hand vpon them, yet they escaped not vnpunished of Gods hand" (2115).

70. Phillips, *Images,* 124–25, 136, 140. Spenser, of course, famously captured all the painful ambiguities of Elizabeth's position in *The Faerie Queene,* book 5, especially 9.50 and 10.4. See the lucid commentary by Thomas P. Roche Jr.—particularly on the crucial 5.9.50, in his edition (Yale, 1978; Penguin, 1981), 1204–5.

The

Power

of the

Poets

"The Image of this Queene so quaynt"

The Pornographic Blazon 1588–1603

Hannah Betts

The Earl of Leicester died in 1588 having distinguished himself as Elizabeth I's longest-serving and best-loved favorite. Shortly after this event, a pornographic narrative was written that described Leicester's abortive efforts to gain entry into heaven.[1] In it Leicester is attacked for a combination of insatiable sexual and political appetites that are claimed to have motivated his career at court. The narrative concludes with an incident in which he is punished for his transgressions by means of "the member wherewith he had most offended," his penis. Accordingly, Leicester is condemned to a future spent gazing into the vagina of a fiend disguised as a former mistress.

Now there was no doubte made but that this pleasant sight . . . would . . . geve him such an edge that he could not forbeare, especialy haveing bene all his lief a valient cavilere in armes, to geve a charge with his lance of lust against the [ce]nter of her target of proffe, and rune his ingredience up to the hard hiltes into the unserchable botome of her gaping g[u]llfe . . . It was ordained that every smale t[o]wch of the cheane should drowen the member of his virillitye in the bottomeless barrell of her virginnitye, through which runeth a felde of unquenchable fier which at every gioneing to gether did so hisse his humanytye, that he was in continuall danger to lose the tope of his standard of steele. (157)

Leicester, one of the principal inventors of the chivalric fantasy through which the virgin queen was celebrated, is compelled to reenact this fantasy in its starkest sexual terms. The queen's favorite is destined to wield his lance for all eternity in the service of fathomless and terrible virginity.

This short but fascinating sexual satire offers a paradigm for the role of pornography in late-sixteenth-century English culture. Most immediately, it suggests the ability of this kind of writing to reflect the political metaphors of the Elizabethan court in a way that compromised the queen's own virginal iconography. In this instance, this critique was confined to the relatively private sphere of the manuscript text. However, in the years following 1588 a series of published works appeared that, although less graphic than the Leicester narrative, nevertheless began to implicate the queen in contexts that were sexually and, by extension, politically compromising. As in the quotation that supplies my title, these printed texts rejected the qualities of the virgin queen in favor of heroines whose presentation reflected the vernacular sense of the word *queen:* the prostitute and traditional heroine of pornographic literature.[2]

Since its origin as the ancient genre constituted by "writing about prostitutes," pornography has evolved into a notoriously problematic category. Traditional definitions have focused on the content and purpose of pornography, identifying it as sexually explicit material designed for erotic arousal. More recently, a number of feminist critics have drawn attention to the fundamental structures of pornographic representation and to their complicity with larger systems of patriarchal oppression.[3] Such analyses have emphasized the objectification of female characters within pornography, together with a corresponding elevation of masculine subject positions both within and without the text. This structure involves a basic identification between the male reader and the fictional protagonist, a relationship mediated through the reader's desire to enact an analogous possession of the female object. By extension, it can also imply a larger community identified through a shared enjoyment of the female body, such as a cinema audience or literary readership.[4] It is primarily with this structural reading of pornography that I will be concerned in the present article. According to these interpretations, the female character appears only as a vehicle for the creation of male identity, reduced to a catalog of physical parts or bodily functions. Clearly, individual responses to pornography are not confined within the limits of this gendered system. Nevertheless, as a basic structure it remains fundamental to pornographic writing. Similarly, attempts to distinguish erotica from pornography, even where the former is characterized as presenting a more "positive" female image, present no significant disruption to this gendered scheme. As a result, such distinctions will not be the subject of this investigation.

As the Leicester narrative confirms, Renaissance culture inherited the ancient tradition that associated pornography with social satire. Recently, Lynn Hunt has argued that Renaissance pornography invariably included elements of political critique, whether this agenda was stated, implied, or even subsequently inferred. Before its transformation into a commercial industry during the nineteenth century, pornography was "linked to free-thinking and heresy, to science and natural philosophy, and to attacks on absolutist political authority."[5] At the same time, it could also appear in support of a wide range of conservative arguments. Paula Findlen's account of Italian erotica testifies to this flexibility. In it she contends that pornography's place in early modern culture reflected its ability to provide "a sensitive measure of shifting social hierarchies and the vicissitudes of intellectual and political culture in the complex network of republics and courts that composed Renaissance Italy."[6] As Findlen demonstrates, this measure operated through a satirical reversal of accepted social hierarchies, most obviously through pornography's obsession with "grotesque rather than courtly bodies."[7]

Of course the nation state was equally susceptible to the contingencies occasioned by fluctuating social hierarchies. Moreover, these pressures were considerably more likely to be rendered in pornographic form where a 'courtly body' was itself the focus of patronage at court and of political interests throughout the country. In her creation of the role of unmarried, female monarch, Elizabeth I encouraged the dependent relationship between prince and subject to be played out as a romantic courtship. The result was the conflation between sexual and political registers that has traditionally been recognized as the dominant language of the late Tudor court. This Petrarchan political idiom celebrated the queen as the ultimate, unattainable "courtly body." As has been demonstrated by a series of influential studies, the expression of desire for this body became an accepted metaphor for articulating a variety of forms of social ambition.[8] The "cult" of Elizabeth was not a performance confined to its star player. Instead it invited, indeed depended upon, a supporting cast of subjects, each defining himself as suitor to his monarch.[9]

Although there has been considerable attention to the eroticized language of Elizabethan panegyric, the negative potential of this rhetoric has remained largely unexamined. In this essay it will be my contention that this sexualized language could be negatively adapted in terms that also offered opportunities for masculine self-invention. I will argue that during the 1590s a current of sexual imagery emerged within English poetry that reflected a hostile perception of Elizabethan government. This register reversed the language of Petrarchan politics back against its subject, transforming the courtly body into a series of grotesque sexual manifestations.

The focus for this transformation was the blazon, the erotic compendium of the female body. The blazon had been a feature of English poetry since the fourteenth century. Following the publication of Tottel's *Miscellany* (1557), the panegyric catalog grew in popularity as one of many techniques associated with Petrarchan poetics.[10] In the early Elizabethan period the coincidence between this vogue and the reign of a female monarch found various expressions, most obviously in Spenser's partial inventory in the "Aprill" Eclogue of *The Shepheardes Calender* (1579).[11] In Lyly's *Euphues and his England* (1580) Euphues anticipates the creation of a monarchal blazon with some zeal, but it was not until the turn of the 1590s that a full catalog of the queen appeared in print.[12] Nevertheless, just as the blazon's potential as monarchal encomium was finally realized, the device also showed signs of becoming sexually explicit to a degree unprecedented within its Elizabethan history.

Over the course of the 1590s the blazon continued to appear both in its traditional panegyric mode and in its new sexually descriptive forms. In addition to these more physically detailed catalogs, the blazon was also presented within a series of pornographically charged situations. Although the queen was never overtly associated with these scenarios, some connection with her was repeatedly implied. Indications of this connection include: an aggressive hostility toward female virginity and chastity; the depiction of queens or Petrarchan heroines engaged in various forms of sexual activity; images of sexual encounters that debunk courtly practices; and references to Elizabeth in sexually compromising contexts. Collectively these descriptions represent a small but significant example of a counter-discursive response to the rhetorical practices of the Elizabethan cult. As elsewhere in early modern Europe, pornography functioned as an effective means of social satire.

These blazons were also implicated in circumstances that replicate the homosocial conditions of the pornographic experience: the organization of masculine identity around the objectified female body. The catalog's enactment of the speaker's possession of his mistress's body formed the primary stage in this process. At a wider level, the writers that generated the pornographic blazon transformed this possessive relationship into an expression of group identity. Although in no sense a coherent movement, these men shared certain ambitions and generational similarities that identify them as examples of the "alienated intellectuals," "aspiring minds," or "transitional men" that have been judged characteristic of the late Elizabethan period.[13] The majority were university men. Most went on to be associated with the Inns of Court: the training ground for the political establishment that also generated the counterestablishment stereotype, the juvenile wit. Although a diverse group by way of politics, religion, and profession, these writers were united as members of an educated class eager for social promotion. The court provided a natural focus for these aspirations. Nevertheless, as the administration drew to a close, it was also an environment in which professional opportunities were increasingly limited.[14] Where the courtier poet used an erotic involvement with the female body as a means of expressing a political investment in Elizabethan government, so these writers parodied this idiom as a means of demonstrating a combination of ambition and social disaffection.

The idea that manuscript culture could support intellectual communities is, of course, a familiar argument. As Harold Love has summarized, manuscript circulation "was often a mode of social bonding whose aim was to nourish and to articulate a corporate ideology."[15] In fact, as Love acknowledges, communal feeling of this sort was also possible within print culture. A variety of literary and social relationships were fostered in and around published texts, while certain genres became associated with particular audiences and groups of writers. It was within one such example of a flexible but cohesive group atmosphere that the pornographic blazon emerged.

I

The principal Elizabethan text in which a communal identity was proposed for English literature was also the platform for the publication of a more sexually suggestive blazon of Elizabeth I. George Puttenham's *The Arte of English Poesie* (1589) demonstrates the practical techniques required in support of its aim to promote the status of vernacular poetry. Throughout the text this objective is consistently translated as a desire to impose coterie literary attitudes on a mass audience. *The Arte* made publicly available rhetorical devices that had largely been confined within a court-based manuscript culture. In disclosing such strategies, Puttenham made the courtly idiom accessible to a nonaristocratic audience whose literary ambitions were more market-place orientated. At the same time, this audience was also taught to emulate the social dynamics of court literature. Puttenham was a squire's son who had been educated at Cambridge and the Middle Temple. His paradigm for the contemporary poet, the "Courtly maker," was derived from the class he subsequently sought to occupy: the "Noble men and Gentlemen of her Maiesties owne seruauntes."[16] The subtext of Puttenham's manual was that the aspirations of the published author could be achieved by reproducing the social investments of the courtier poet, most immediately his relationship with Elizabeth I.[17]

The Arte contrives to simulate the courtier's intimacy with the royal person. The queen is a constant presence within the treatise, frequently addressed in the vocative, in incidental bursts of apostrophe and repeatedly referred to by way of example.[18] Rehearsing tactics for the creation of a language to articulate Elizabeth's princeship, and her subjects' relationship to it, is a fundamental element within the text. Interestingly, this relationship is often expressed in physical terms. Puttenham's monarchal roundel anticipates the paradigmatic image for the blazonic depiction of the female genitalia during the 1590s, that of a park or natural landscape (99–100). Its central conceit involves the conflation between royal territorial dominion and the queen's own body. As a gendered landscape Elizabeth is "most spatious," her authority originating in her breast and reaching to her very "fardest part." A "Monarchie large and wide," she surrounds and sustains her dependents, literally incorporating a populace "imparked" as if "heards of deere." Significantly, she herself also figures as a character within this landscape. Here she presides in the midst of a nation that surrounds her with the intimacy of a court

> Where she allowes and bannes and bids
> In what fashion she list and when,
> The seruices of all her men. (99)

In this second capacity, the queen plays her familiar role as Petrarchan mistress, with the conventional, sexually charged authority over her servants.

Puttenham's roundel suggests that Elizabeth's authority was a phenomenon that could be exaggerated or diminished according to its representational context. This flexibility was understood to be a function of the disparity in prestige between her "two bodies": the first a public symbol of nationhood, the second merely a female body divested with an unusual degree of power.[19] The ramifications of this paradox for her suitability as a literary topic were self-evident: the queen occupied a fluctuating and ambiguous rhetorical status.

Puttenham's blazon, his "*Icon.* or Resemblance by imagerie," testifies to these qualities with more ambivalence (244). Within the catalog exposure of the monarchal body is used to realize the goal of courtly accessibility. Crucially, this accessibility is characterized as a form of sexual availability. The most striking imagery in the catalog focuses on the mouth and breasts, areas of the body that denote privileged sexual contact. The description of the mouth explores ways in which this contact might be interpreted:

> Two lips wrought out of rubie rocke,
> Like leaues to shut and to unlock.
> As portall dore in Princes chamber:
> A golden tongue in mouth of amber. (244)

In this passage Puttenham draws attention to issues of access that are both sexual and political. The 'private' connotational force of that initial act of sexual penetration, the kiss, is here emphatically politicized. The erotic aspect of the image is combined with a diplomatic register that emphasizes the mouth's ability to facilitate or deny access according to the terms in which court etiquette represented access to the monarch.[20] The return to the more conventional imagery of the final line is colored by this language and the reader evaluates the worth of the "golden tongue in mouth of amber" according to both its sexual and political connotations. Taken in this context, the royal tongue implies a combination of favors, from a return to the fantasy of monarchal embrace, to the urgent political imperative for basic communication with the queen.

The concluding lines of the catalog take the accessibility of the monarchal body to an extreme:

> Her bosome sleake as Paris plaster,
> Helde vp two balles of alabaster,

Eche byas was a little cherrie:
Or els I thinke a strawberie. (244)

As in the roundel, the status of the royal physique suffers a sudden diminishment in scale. The stately exorbitance with which Elizabeth's features have been associated elsewhere in the inventory—silver, ebony, gold, ruby, and amber—is immediately negated in the account of her succulent nipples. The impropriety of the description is further compounded by the fact that the roundel had identified the queen's breast as the very source of her authority, from which issued the rays "Of her iustice, bountie and might" (100). In the blazon this emblem of royal beneficence is transformed into an image that suggests the tasting or biting of the royal nipples in an erotic context. Political intimacy with a sexual edge has rapidly degenerated into actual sexual contact.

The issues of access implicit within the poem's final image can be illuminated by comparison with contemporary accounts of Elizabeth's habit of strategically revealing her bosom as she grew older.[21] This gesture, a form of self-display made available to a limited audience, had a political currency as the dramatization of the queen's youth and virginity. Had Puttenham's blazon retained its original situation as one of the "Partheniades," or "virgin songs," that he apparently presented to the queen as a New Year's gift in 1581–2, then it would have remained part of a sanctioned coterie discourse in which this kind of symbolization was accepted and understood.[22] That the poem went on to appear in the context of Puttenham's packaging of court culture for a popular audience has the effect of profoundly destabilizing the poem's erotic content. In Puttenham's blazon the queen's body is made available, a metaphor for textual circulation that imitates and enacts sexual exposure.

II

Puttenham's inventory was immediately followed by the publication of the most famous blazon of Elizabeth I: the catalog of Belphoebe in *The Faerie Queene* (1590).[23] Spenser's blazon confirmed Puttenham's argument that the published poet could manipulate a fictional intimacy with the royal body as a means of advancing his professional status. Through his ability to re-create the queen's body as a Petrarchan icon, Spenser nominates himself as Elizabethan England's first laureate and identifies his readership as a community encompassing the entire nation.[24] Nevertheless, even given the degree of his professional interest in the royal blazon, Spenser's portrait shares much of Puttenham's ambivalence concerning social investment in the monarchal body.

This ambivalence is focused not on the mouth or breast, but on the description of Belphoebe's genitalia. The vulva is conveyed as a euphemistic space within the catalog, according to the blazon's conventional use of *occupatio,* or emphasis by means of apparent avoidance, to describe the genitalia. As Louis Adrian Montrose has famously remarked, in this instance this space represents not only the sexual organs themselves, but is the virgin warrior's "symbolic locus of royal power," in a style consistent with other examples of Tudor iconography.[25] Significantly, it is this combination of symbolic and material properties that exposes Belphoebe to sexual misinterpretation. The immediate spectators of the blazon, Braggadocchio and Trompart, are representatives of the court arriviste who seek to reinvent themselves by assuming the outward signs of aristocratic status.[26] On seeing Belphoebe, Braggadocchio accurately surmises that developing a relationship with her will guarantee his status at court.[27] Nevertheless, he dramatically misunderstands the nature of this relationship, interpreting her body as an invitation to sexual rather than political intimacy—a misreading that culminates in attempted rape.

The narrative context of Spenser's blazon suggests the problems inherent in a political rhetoric that celebrated a commitment to virgin authority through the metaphor of sexual service. As his account makes clear, these problems were particularly frustrating for those whose social position made their need to invest in the structures of court patronage most urgent. Similar responses to the issues of power and sexuality explored in the blazons of Spenser and Puttenham emerged in the 1590s from among men, like Braggadocchio, who were excluded from or seeking to insinuate themselves into the social and political establishment. Where Spenser's catalog had denoted the vulva by means of an empty space, so these writers began to describe the material constituents of this space in some detail. As a result of this practice, the blazon became considerably more sexually explicit, conforming both in terms of its content and structural premises to the category of pornography.[28]

During the period 1589 to 1603 a number of blazons were published that feature accounts of the female genitalia, typically using geographical metaphors. These catalogs convey the sexual organs in graphic, predominantly tactile detail, as soft, smooth, moist, slippery, and downy. They also use gustatory imagery to depict the vulva as a place of delicious tastes, alternately sweet, nourishing, or intoxicating. At the same time, the blazon began to be used to represent female characters of a more active sexual disposition.[29] The recurrent victim of these new catalogs was the Petrarchan mistress. Several of these blazons occur in the context of her apparent pain or humiliation. Elsewhere either hers is the body suffering exposure, or she is displaced by heroines who resemble her, but whose sexual proclivities imply a critique of her behavior. Remarkably, these innovations took place within the device that Spenser twice advocated as the principal mode of royal panegyric. Given this situation, this denigration of the Petrarchan mistress could hardly take place without implicating this figure's ultimate cultural referent, the queen herself.

The initial examples of this phenomenon were associated with the Inns of Court, the legal training centers that provided an unofficial finishing school for the Elizabethan gentleman. Within Elizabethan culture the Inns functioned as an establishment satellite. Close to the center of power but distinct from it, their members generated a radicalism contained by their social ambition. This compromise between subversion and aspiration was never more apparent than during the final years of the sixteenth century when the numbers of educated young men seeking preferment rose dramatically. The frustrations of this situation found expression within the Inns' vigorous literary system, most obviously in noncourtly genres such as the epigram and the Ovidian elegy.[30] A hostility to courtly practices became one of the chief characteristics of the Inns' style, representing its members' simultaneous enthrallment with and distaste for court culture. As Arthur Marotti has commented, this hostility was registered as "a kind of moral or satiric disengagement from the courtly world, a stance of (sometimes openly cynical) criticism of its rules, of its styles, and of its (deliberately exaggerated) corruptions.[31] An immediate focus for this disengagement was a critique of the love rhetoric that supplied the central idiom of the court.

These anti-courtly tendencies were reflected within the rich manuscript culture native to the Inns, but they were also apparent in the printed literature connected with this environment. The epyllion, the Ovidian minor epic, provides the strongest evidence of this occurrence.[32] Within the epyllion the mechanisms for social bonding produced within scribal circulation were replicated in the public arena of print. The writers of the epyllion fostered a close affinity with the juvenile audience of the Inns and the universities. They characterized their poetry as the work of ambitious youth and dedicated it to young men whom they addressed in terms of friendship. The epyllion's erotic subject matter enforced this group identity, providing a focus for their self-identification as a literary avant-garde. In 1590 Spenser fulfilled Elizabethan culture's expectations of a blazon of Elizabeth I, creating a chaste Petrarchan icon as the expression of his ambition to become the nation's poet. However, from 1589, these writers dismantled the panegyric blazon as a means of generating a coterie-style audience who would read its remnants factionally.

Thomas Lodge's *Scillaes Metamorphosis* (1589) was dedicated to an audience identified as the author's peers, "the Gentlemen of the Innes of Court and Chauncerie."[33] The poem was designed to ingratiate itself with this readership, from its references to Oxford and to a university education, to its overriding theme of male solidarity. It is within this larger structure of male bonding that Glaucus, the amorous sea-god, blazes his mistress's body in ostentatiously sexual terms (stanzas 48–54). The first English epyllion features a catalog that includes a challenge to the device's traditional circumlocution of the genitalia.

> But why alas should I that Marble hide
> That doth adorne the one and other flanke,
> From whence a mount of quicknèd snow doth glide;
> Or els the vale that bounds this milkwhite banke,
> Where Venus and her sisters hide the fount,
> Whose lovely Nectar dooth all sweetes surmount. (st. 53)

Glaucus's description provided a template for the sexually explicit catalog.[34] The pudendum is conveyed in a straightforward figurative device that includes reference to the 'mons veneris' and to the "vale" produced between the labia. Beneath the labia, Glaucus indicates the entrance to the vagina, the fluidity and sweetness of which both contribute to the cunnilingual idea that it might be tasted.

Scillaes Metamorphosis is not by any means an overt discussion of

Elizabethan politics. Nevertheless, the violent retaliation against female chastity carried out in the poem does suggest a certain hostility toward the cult of virginity by which the regime was characterized. Moreover, its conclusion makes clear that this aggression toward female chastity is to be regarded as a strategy of self-presentation for the new poet. The hero, who began the story wandering aimlessly along the banks of the Isis, emerges from the poem as a professional author. Glaucus rewards the speaker for his role in humiliating Scilla by teaching him sonnets and advising him on an appropriate career path. The young poet's first commission is to compose the erotic verse itself, specifically the admonitory narrative of Scilla's punishment. Having established his reputation in this manner, he will be able to abandon erotic themes in pursuit of more prestigious literary subjects. In *Scillaes Metamorphosis* publication of the sexualized female body is represented as a new vehicle for authorial ambition.[35]

William Shakespeare's adaptation of the blazon in *Venus and Adonis* (1593) relies upon a related approach. Shakespeare was neither an Inns nor a university man, but his first publication was calculated to appeal to this audience. Like Lodge, Shakespeare used the epyllion to draw attention to his literary aspirations. The poem's dedicatory material emphasizes that it is at once an inaugural and a transitional moment within his career: both the "first heire" of his invention and a promise of "some grauer labour."[36] The poem was an instant commercial success, running to at least ten editions during its author's lifetime. As Gabriel Harvey remarked, it was particularly popular among "the younger sort," many of them members of the Inns and the universities.[37] As in Lodge's poem, this audience was invited to enjoy the spectacle of female sexual humiliation. Unlike Scilla, Venus is emphatically nonvirginal. Nevertheless, her sexuality is as unwelcome to the poem's juvenile hero as Scilla's had been to his predecessor and contrived to be equally as ridiculous to its male reader.

Venus is the poem's sexual aggressor. She is senior to her conquest, more substantial in build, and perspires with sexual excitement. It is she who assumes the proactive, conventionally masculine role within the courtship, manipulating the range of seduction ploys available to the Petrarchan lover. In turn, Adonis adopts the position of love-object, advancing the traditional excuses of the reluctant virgin. Not only does the poem reverse the gender roles normally assigned to the courtly romance, but it also characterizes its heroine as a queen.[38] The combination of these features is suggestive. In *Venus and Adonis* Shakespeare implies a satirical shifting of the parameters for the language in which court patronage was conducted. In place of a structure in which the aspiring youth courted his queen, Shakespeare creates a fantasy in which a voracious empress is forced to plead for the attentions of her younger lover.[39]

Venus's connection with Elizabeth is further supported by the imagery that she deploys in her self-blazon. Significantly, the catalog adapts Puttenham's metaphor for the relationship between the queen and her "imparked," deerlike subjects. Here, however, the physical space occupied by this animal has become considerably less ambiguous. Puttenham's subtle exposition of the conflation between Elizabeth's eroticism and her authority is superseded by a blatant proposition that reinterprets her ability to encompass as a sexual phenomenon.

> I'll be a park, and thou shalt be my deer:
> Feed where thou wilt, on mountain, or in dale;
>   Graze on my lips, and if those hills be dry,
>   Stray lower, where the pleasant fountains lie.
>
> Within this limit is relief enough,
> Sweet bottom grass and high delightful plain,
> Round rising hillocks, brakes obscure and rough,
> To shelter thee from tempest and from rain.
> (ll. 231–38)

Shakespeare's insatiate queen directs the reader's attention to areas of her body that offer unambiguously sexual forms of sufferance, in particular, her vagina.

In *Parthenophil and Parthenophe* (1593) Barnabe Barnes used the pornographic blazon to reinvent the sonnet sequence as Ovidian verse: an imposition of Inns' style upon what was perceived as being the paradigmatic courtly genre.[40] As a consequence of this policy, the sexualized female body acquires a key structural position within the text. Where in other sequences there is an assumption that the sonnet mistress has at least some cerebral qualities to attract her suitor, in Barnes's poetry there is a monomania about the body that can only be sated in physical consummation. This narrative obsession is advertised in the sequence's title. Parthenophe, derived from the Greek term for "virgin," is pursued by Parthenophil, meaning "virgin-lover," or given the coital preoccupation of the text, "virgin-seducer."[41] Parthenophil's relentless antagonism toward female chastity is manifested throughout the text. Various instances occur in which Parthenophil fantasizes about forcing his reluctant mistress to engage in sexual intercourse.[42] This culminates in the sequence's climactic scene in which Parthenophe, overcome by black magic, is conveyed to her lover naked, weeping, and riding on the back of a goat, following which she is ritually deflowered (sestine 5).

The sequence's sustained hostility toward virginity was in obvious opposition to the dominant ideology of the late Elizabethan court. The text parades rather than resists these implications. The nation's most famous virgin is subtly implicated in the sequence's compromising narrative intrigue. Canzon 2, which includes a dedication to the queen as the "flower of loues, and pure virginitie," is followed by two of the most defiantly sexual pieces in the collection. Ode 3 is a blasphemous prayer to the Virgin Mary for her intercession in the seduction of Parthenophe; ode 4, an invocation to Bacchus to provide a lusty erection to entertain her during this act. The juxtaposition of these poems with praise for the queen's chastity necessarily qualifies the way in which her sexuality is subsequently interpreted. No less provocative is the sequence's closing dedication to Bridget Manners, daughter of the fourth duke of Rutland, and one of the queen's most esteemed maids of honor (pp. 133–34).[43] Barnes, addressing Manners in his capacity as author, claims to offer in his work a representation of her own matchless features, the same features that within the text provide Parthenophil with his argument for rape. Any further link between Parthenophe and this member of the virgin entourage is avoided. Nevertheless, the fact that Barnes considered his poems an appropriate tribute to the "Pride of chast Cynthias rich crowne" (p. 133) is remarkable.

The blazon is the focus for the text's rapacious attitude toward the virgin body. Within Barnes's catalogs the sexual organs receive a studied level of attention. Most immediately, they are the subject of an entire madrigal in terms reminiscent of the description in *Scillaes Metamorphosis:*

> I dare not speake of that thrise holy hill,
>> Which spread with siluer lillyes lyes,
>> Nor of those violettes, which voyde vaynes fulfill,
>> Nor of that maze on loues hill toppe,
> These secrets must not be surueyde with eyes,
>> No creature may those flowers croppe,
>> Nor bath in that cleare fountaine,
> Where none but Phoebe, with chast virgines wash,
>> In bottome of that sacred mountaine:
> But whether now? thy verses ouerlash. (madrigal 26)

In fact, Barnes dares to convey the genitalia in some detail in *Parthenophil and Parthenophe,* albeit while making concessions to the device's traditional recourse to sexual euphemism. Ostensibly, stanza 5 of canzon 3 refers to the cleavage; however, the localizing details that it includes make the genital connotations of this area striking. The preceding verse closes with a statement that the eventual possessor of this region will be privileged above all men, a trope that the catalog more usually applies to the claimant of virginity (4.14–15). The location itself is described in the metaphor of hill and vale previously associated with the genitalia (5.1–2). The moisture produced in this region is said to animate the "dead," a traditional erectile pun, and has its source in a place specifically "betweene, or vnder" Parthenophe (5.3–7). References to "loues mountes" and to the downy softness of this feature confirm its implied relocation within the catalog (5.10–11). The function of this ambiguity is that it allows Barnes to offer a suggestive account of the experience of the vagina during the sexual act. The tactile imagery that dominates the second half of the stanza provides a rhapsodic elaboration of the qualities of wetness, softness, and smoothness (5.8–15). This innuendo is confirmed in the poem's concluding verse. Here the speaker declares that although the "straitely skirted" character of his mistress keeps him frustrated, he is determined to live "through vertue of her eye" (8.5–9); an "eye" that has been surreptitiously celebrated in the fifth stanza.[44] Similar equivocation occurs in the next poem, ode 16. Here the logic of the catalog, and certain

aspects of the hellish place described, all suggest that "Loves place of tor-
ture" is as likely to be the sexual organs as the heart, the area with which it
is formally identified. Accordingly, the blazon once again concludes with
the speaker's desire to be allowed access to his mistress's genitalia with the
aim "That I might dye, before I dye." The goal that unites these catalogs is
ultimately realized in the act of rape.

The social conditions that generated these published inventories bear
comparison with the circumstances determining the circulation of explicit
catalogs within manuscript culture during the same period. Like the
printed blazon, these poems were instrumental in securing their authors'
status among a juvenile readership. The graphic nature of John Donne's
catalogs gave them a currency as among the most coveted examples of
Inns of Court manuscript culture and their creator a reputation as one of
its principal wits.[45] Similarly, the inverted blazon featured in Thomas
Nashe's "The Choise of Valentines" (1595) contributed to the pornographic credentials of a poem that was popularly associated with its
author's name as "Nashe's Dildo."[46] Although they appeared within traditional coterie environments, these blazons are not significantly more
explicit than their printed counterparts. Donne's accounts of the female
anatomy are more vituperative and Nashe's blazon appears amidst more
obvious pornographic action, but like Lodge, Shakespeare, and Barnes,
their catalogs are distinguished by being focused on the "Centrique
part."[47]

What is different about these poems is that they correspond still more
obviously with the category of social satire. Donne's blazons are characterized by a satiric antifeminism that implicates the female body in contemporary discourses of class and commerce.[48] Nashe's poem takes this
policy a stage further, situating the blazon in the traditional category of
pornography as a form of writing about prostitutes.[49] In both contexts, the
sexually explicit blazon is the vehicle for an exposé of contemporary
morality that has wider applications as a form of cultural critique. This
more overtly satirical approach could be contained within the coterie
groups sustained through scribal circulation. However, as the decade
drew to a close, there were indications that analogous communities might
be generated within print culture; a situation that could not be tolerated
by the political establishment.

III

The late 1590s has long been recognized as one of the most unstable periods in English history.[50] While a case can be made for the nation's relative prosperity compared with the rest of Europe at this time, there was much local evidence to support the apocalyptic anxieties that emerged as the end of the century approached.[51] The political pressures caused by war, famine, disease, and mounting economic crisis were exacerbated by indications of the queen's growing decrepitude. In these circumstances, the decline of Elizabeth's material body gave new currency to its metaphorical association with the body politic. From its inability to symbolize the ultimate reward of courtiership, to Elizabeth's increasingly garish attempts to simulate her former appearance, the queen's body became the living emblem of her exhausted government. The succession issue, in particular, focused attention on the limitations of the aging monarchal body. More immediately, it was also a chief source of the political faction that characterized the closing years of the regime.

The prospect of the queen's death and the rapid demise of her chief officers created a power vacuum at court that produced a climate of faction and political intrigue.[52] At the same time, there were indications at a national level that the prevailing economic crisis might provoke some form of civil insurrection.[53] The government reaction to these issues was characterized by acts of state intervention where previously it had shown some leniency.[54] One of the reflections of this policy was the administration's increased interest in the activities of the publishing industry, an interest principally directed toward the production of satire. Following the publication of the first three books of Joseph Hall's *Virgidemiae* in 1597, there had been a dramatic rise in the output of satirical literature. Like Hall, the writers associated with this vogue adopted a Juvenalian style in which moral and social corruption were discussed in a way that implicated contemporary figures and, ultimately, the government itself.

The state response to this challenge came in the Bishops' Order of 1599, in which the archbishop of Canterbury and the bishop of London ordered the Stationers' Company to withdraw a series of offending publications.[55] Interestingly, the critical debate surrounding the bishops' ban has revolved around an argument as to whether their action was motivated by a desire to restrict pornography or satire. The presence of *Caltha Poetarum* (1599), Marlowe's Ovidian *Elegies* (1594/5?) and two antimarriage treatises in the list of censored works has traditionally been used to characterize the entire exercise as a move against the spread of pornography.[56] More recently, Richard McCabe has made a convincing case against this interpretation, arguing that the suppression of satire was the bishops' main objective.[57] However, the very fact that this confusion has existed draws attention to the place of pornography in late Elizabethan satire. McCabe's observation that there is no reason why the obscenity of these works "should be more objectionable in satire than elsewhere" overlooks the fact that national politics were dominated by the iconography of militant virginity.[58] Although the pornographic elements within these works were not the primary cause of their censorship, it is reasonable to assume that they made their satirical content seem considerably more urgent.

The majority of the authors named in the Bishops' Order were associated with the universities or the Inns of Court. Joseph Hall had studied at Cambridge, while John Marston and Sir John Davies both progressed from Oxford to the Middle Temple. Tailboys Dymoke, who appeared under the pseudonym of Thomas Cutwode, was entered at Lincoln's Inn in 1584. Christopher Marlowe's audience was characterized by Nashe as being made up of courtiers and members of the Inns.[59] Both Nashe and his archenemy Gabriel Harvey were Cambridge men, albeit of a very different status. Of the writers not identified by name, Everard Guilpin, creator of *Skialetheia* (1598) and Thomas Middleton, the author of *Microcynicon* (1599), were both members of Gray's Inn.

Once again, the blazon provided a vehicle for the production of politically charged erotica within this environment. The most significant appearances of the device within the Bishops' Order publications are in *Caltha Poetarum: Or The Bumble Bee* (1599) and John Marston's *The Metamorphosis of Pygmalions Image* (1598). Elsewhere it features as one of the repository of forms available to the contemporary satirist. The first part of Hall's *Virgidemiae* (1597) contains a satire of the "loue-sicke Poet" who, although he may be base, has a passion that inspires him with "high thoughts."[60] This courtly paradigm is disrupted by the fact that the object of his desire is socially undistinguished, ugly, and likely to be sexually promiscuous. Nonetheless, this "dunghill drudge" is celebrated in the

rhetoric of monarchal encomium as "Lady and Queene, and virgin de-
ifide." Accordingly, she is referred to in blazonic terms, despite conforming to the counterblazonic stereotype of being "sootie-blacke, or
bery-browne." Guilpin's *Skialetheia* (1598) and Davies's *Epigrammes*
(1595/6?) both use the counterblazon to describe painted city prostitutes. Guilpin argues that the metropolitan women who exhibit themselves in a similar fashion ultimately expose the corruptions of Elizabethan manhood:

> Then how is man turnd all *Pygmalion*,
> That knowing these pictures, yet we doate vpon
> The painted statues, or what fooles are we
> So grosly to commit idolatry?[61]

Middleton's *Micro-cynicon* (1599) pursues this subject to its furthest
extreme. His penultimate satire depicts a transvestite prostitute who ma-
nipulates a blazonic style beauty to transform himself into one of London's many counterfeit "Virgins," and thus to beguile a still more deluded
Pygmalion.[62] The perversity of these blazons, and their insistence on
the impulse to commit idolatry "grosly," interrogate the conventions of
courtly veneration from whence the English catalog derived. Openly
satirical, with heroines who are prostitutes, or who share some of the
characteristics of prostitutes, they relocate the blazon in the context of
pornographic writing.

John Marston's censored epyllion takes Pygmalion himself as its hero.
As I have sought to establish, the affinity of the epyllion with satire had
been a defining element within the genre. *The Metamorphosis of Pygmalions Image* carries this affinity to its logical conclusion as an Ovidian
poem that offers a parodic vehicle for a range of literary forms, including
Petrarchism, the epyllion, and its own principal genre, the satire itself.
The poem contains no actual description of the sexual organs, but satirizes
the fixation with this area both of its hero and the blazon. The catalog
occupies seven of the poem's thirty-nine stanzas.[63] Within the inventory
the pudendum is indisputably the major focus. Pygmalion is struck dumb
on discovery of "Loues pauillion" (st. 9), revealing the true goal of his
erotic monomania. Significantly, the catalog itself suffers a similar crisis.
The blazon is suspended where it encounters the vulva and does not
recommence for three stanzas, fundamentally disrupting the balance of

the inventory. Far from observing the decorum that requires a disingenuous *occupatio* of this area, the poem, like its hero, cannot pull itself away from the genitalia.

The stanzas immediately following the catalog develop this rhetorical ineptitude into the material for an Ovidian narrative. Having inventoried his icon, Pygmalion attempts to have intercourse with it. Interpreting its silence as consent, he takes the vulva as his first place of assault

> presuming to discouer
> The vale of Loue, where *Cupid* doth delight
> To sport, and dally all the sable night. (st. 16)

The desire to look at the genitalia has devolved into an impulse to "discouer" it by more practical means. The poem's analysis of the motivations determining the blazon could not be made more obvious: the device's primary objective is not literary but sexual. This pornographic function is confirmed at the end of the poem. Here any reader seeking titillation through a report of sexual action is invited to put himself in Pygmalion's position and use his imagination (st. 33–36). The blazon reappears in summary form as a rhetorical aid designed to stimulate this masturbatory fantasy (st. 37, ll. 5–6).

Given a lack of contrary evidence, it is fair to surmise that Marston's parody of Elizabethan poetry's tunnel-vision was considered subversive because of its implications for the political language of Petrarchan veneration. The scale of these implications can be assessed by comparing the poem with an earlier study of courtly idolatry, Lyly's *Endimion* (1591). In Lyly's play Endimion learns to regulate his desire for the goddess Cynthia, transforming sexual attraction into a reverence with the appropriate degree of distance. In contrast, Marston's poem flamboyantly disrupts the careful boundaries imposed upon Petrarchism as a modus vivendi. Like Endimion, Pygmalion rejects earthly women in pursuit of a feminine ideal. Unlike Endimion, Pygmalion's inappropriate lust is given a concrete sexual reward. Lyly portrays a Petrarchan mistress who is revered and whose body connotes abstract metaphysical qualities. Marston invents a Petrarchan inflatable doll, to be viewed and fornicated with at the caprice of her poet-inventor. Unlike Lyly, whose play was submitted for royal approval prior to publication, Marston maximizes print's capacity for sensationalism to earn his place in the satiric vogue.[64]

The political relevance of the erotic narrative in *Caltha Poetarum* is still more obvious, even where its overall meaning remains uncertain. Its impropriety as a published text is equally apparent. The poem represents the more exotic end of the market in slander and libel that flourished at the turn of the century. Attributed to one Thomas Cutwode, *Caltha* is a pornographic political satire in which, as its commendatory verse establishes, "Persons of good worth are ment."[65] Leslie Hotson rediscovered the identity of these persons for the twentieth-century reader.[66] According to Hotson, the poem is in part a record of the troubled relationship between Henry, 2nd Earl of Lincoln and his relatives the Dymokes, as composed by Tailboys Dymoke. On this basis, Hotson speculated as to the identities of the principal characters: the protagonist, the bumble bee, is Dymoke himself; Caltha, the Marigold, "one of Queen Elizabeth's maids of honour"; Diana, unsurprisingly, represents the queen.[67]

If we accept Hotson's reading, then Dymoke's poem is the most fantastically erotic vision of Elizabethan court politics to survive from the period. The Lincolnshire garden that provides the poem's opening location is populated by a series of plants representing royal houses, monarchs, and court flatterers. Even less distinguished flowers wear ruffs and assume loverlike or melancholy personae. The activities in which these courtiers engage are unashamedly sexual. The narrative teems with coital symbolism and with tales of erotic exploits. Honey is extracted from blooms in compromising circumstances; a tumescent mandrake root assails a virginal flower; the hero damages and successively restores his "sting"; and even the goddess of love is the victim of sexual assault. Diana herself is not excluded from these events, boasting the creation of a penis as her most unseemly adventure.

Indeed, virginity, even monarchal virginity, is an ambiguous, peculiarly sexualized condition within the poem. When the bee first enters the story he is fresh from taking honey from the "damaske Rose," the Tudor rose itself (st. 38). This activity has left him saturated with "virgin waxe," a substance that protects him against Cupid's shaft by acting as a "soueraigne salue" (st. 44). This phrase had previously appeared in *The Faerie Queene* to describe the sexual restorative that Belphoebe refuses to yield both to Timias and "to all th'vnworthy world."[68] In Dymoke's poem this monarchal "salue" is widely available. Similarly, although Caltha eventually becomes Diana's handmaid, she is not by any means a typical virgin. Before her transformation into human form she too is happy to allow her suitor access to her "virgin waxe." This process is described in obviously sexual terms. Caltha spreads herself before the bee who, after much frantic activity, "begins to find and stir his sting" (st. 60) as

> in her circle vp and downe he hops,
>   and feeds apace and doth refresh his flank,
> And with her wax he stores his spindle shank. (st. 61)

Were these redefinitions of virginity an insufficiently negative reflection on Elizabeth I, the blazon at the poem's center is an erotic reworking of Spenser's catalog (st. 94–102). Like Belphoebe, Caltha is an ameliorated version of the amazon, complete with buskins, baldrick, and hunting weapons. As in Spenser's catalog, she has long, golden hair, and a white hunting outfit, and is bedecked with jewels. Both descriptions use the architectural image from the *Song of Songs* in which the thighs are compared to stone pillars. Belphoebe's limbs support a temple of the gods around which people celebrate in tribute.[69] Caltha's thighs maintain her own saintly body:

> Her thighes like pillars of faire Allablaster,
>   that do support the body of this Saint:
> Where men must kneel them down & Idolaster
>   vnto the Image of this Queene so quaynt,
> That *Caltha* she may pittie their complaint,
> And heare their happie Orysons and prayer,
> When as her priest and people do come there. (st. 99)

Unlike Belphoebe, Caltha also has a full mouth made for kissing and breasts that are apples of temptation. Most significantly, her genitalia is not covertly indicated, but is elaborately described as a "blessed country" full of cunnilingual enticements; a region in which the speaker hopes to live and, more appropriately, to die (st. 97). Dymoke's heroine is a "quaynt" queen in the vernacular sense of both terms.[70] Like Nashe, Guilpin, Middleton, and Davies, he consigns the blazon to the category of writing about prostitutes. Incredibly, he does this while alluding to the device's association with monarchal panegyric. Caltha is an emphatically regal whore. If, as the poem's title instructs, she is the "Marigold of the poets" then, unlike her Spenserian sister, the poets she unites are satirists rather than encomiasts.

Robert Chester's *Loves Martyr or Rosalins Complaint* (1601), although not one of the suppressed texts of the Bishops' Order, provides an appropriate conclusion to an account of the blazon's revised role in the "cult" of Elizabeth. Like *Caltha Poetarum*, Chester's poem is an allegorization of court politics as an erotic narrative. Nevertheless, rather than being a satire, *Loves Martyr* is an admonitory fiction that invents a political mythology for the close of the reign. That Elizabeth is signified by the figure of Rosalin, the eponymous phoenix, seems certain. Within the poem the phoenix is assailed by Envy and Malice, a situation that Anthea Hume has connected with the wave of antiroyal slander generated by the Essex Rebellion. Chester's remedy to this crisis is the loving relationship that the phoenix shares with the turtle, an event that symbolizes a reunion between the queen and her loyal subjects.[71]

In accordance with this conciliatory theme, Chester returns the royal blazon to its panegyric context. However, even when restored to an encomiastic setting, the device bears the legacy of its recent past. Chester's catalog is arranged according to marginal titles that offer a guide to the inventory of the royal body.[72] The pudendum, emphasized by its appearance in two stanzas rather than the single verse attributed to every other feature, is indicated not by name but by the word "Nota" (pp. 13–14). The accompanying description identifies this area as being "Of more then most, and most of all beloued" (p. 13). The account that follows adapts the geographical metaphors of the pornographic blazon:

> There is a place in louely paradize,
> From whence the golden *Gehon* ouerflowes,
> A fountaine of such honorable prize,
> That none the sacred, sacred vertues knowes,
>> Walled about, betok'ning sure defence,
>> With trees of life, to keepe bad errors thence. (pp. 13–14)

In the course of a decade the blazon's depiction of the monarchal genitalia has undergone a transformation from Spenserian ellipsis to Chester's emphatic exhortation: "Mark."

IV

Chester's appropriation of the characteristics of the pornographic blazon within an encomiastic context reflects the device's wider development during the 1590s. The rise of the more explicit blazon with satiric connotations had taken place in the context of a continuing tradition of conventional blazons of praise.[73] This simultaneity between the panegyric and pornographic blazons corresponded with the wider relationship between cult and countercult in late Elizabethan England. By transforming virginal authority into the political orthodoxy of the post-Armada period, the Elizabethan administration reinvented the perceived weakness of the queen's body as its defining asset. One consequence of this paradox was that the rhetorics of praise and blame generated around Elizabeth were forced into proximity. Every celebration of the queen's eternal reign invited a counterdiscourse in which her waning authority could be more accurately represented.

There is a sense in which the royal physique contained its own satire during this period, as the distance between Elizabeth's real and ideal bodies grew ever wider. The French ambassador, André Hurault, Sieur de Maisse, gave a by now familiar account of the queen's appearance that exemplifies this situation.[74] A diplomatic blazon, his catalog combines both blazon and counterblazon, panegyric and satiric bodies. Heavily bejewelled, attired "strangely" in a fairy-tale costume of silver gauze, the queen's body is the splendid facade that we recognize from the "masque of youth" phase of her later portraiture. Her garlanded red wig is worn long to signify virginity and she keeps the front of her gown open, frequently making a gesture that exposes "the whole of her bosom, and passing low."[75] De Maisse even closes his first paragraph with the panegyric blazon's evasive reference to the lower regions of the body, promising that although the queen's bosom appears wrinkled, "lower down her flesh is exceeding white and delicate, so far as one could see." By the second paragraph, however, the mask has begun to crack.

As for her face, it is and appears to be very aged. It is long and thin, and her teeth are very yellow and unequal, compared with what they were formerly, so they say, and on the left side less than on the right. Many of them are missing so that one cannot understand her easily when she speaks quickly. Her figure is fair and tall and graceful in whatever she does; so far as may be she keeps her dignity, yet humbly and graciously withal.[76]

The coincidence between the pornographic and encomiastic blazons in late Elizabethan literature reflected the conflation of extremes acted out upon the royal body itself.

Notes

Earlier versions of this article were delivered at the Women, Text and History seminar, All Souls College, Oxford, and at the M.L.A. Convention, Chicago, 1995.

1. The anonymous and untitled text appears in a manuscript in the British Library, Sloane MS 1926, fols. 35–43v. It is reproduced in D. C. Peck, " 'News from Heaven and Hell': A Defamatory Narrative of the Earl of Leicester," *English Literary Renaissance* 8 (1978): 141–58. Subsequent references are to this edition and are within the text.

2. The words "queene" and "quaynt" had established sexual meanings in the early modern period. "Quean" had been used as a synonym for *hussy* or *harlot* from the thirteenth century—a sense that preponderated in the sixteenth and seventeenth centuries. "Quaint" was a term applied to the vagina from the fourteenth century onwards. See Gordon Williams, *A Dictionary of Sexual Language and Imagery in Shakespearean and Stuart Literature*, 3 vols. (London: Athlone Press, 1994), 3:1127, 1125. The quotation is from Thomas Cutwode, *Caltha Poetarum: Or The Bumble Bee* (London, 1599), stanza 9. See section 3 herein.

3. See Andrea Dworkin, *Pornography: Men Possessing Women* (London: Women's Press, 1981); Susanne Kappeler, *The Pornography of Representation* (Cambridge: Polity Press, 1986); Catherine A. MacKinnon, *Toward a Feminist Theory of the State* (Cambridge, Mass.: Harvard University Press, 1989): 195–214; Catherine Itzin, ed., *Pornography: Women, Violence, and Civil Liberties* (Oxford: Oxford University Press, 1992). Dworkin's and Kappeler's studies are a particular influence on the description that follows.

4. My account of the pornographic structure is also obviously indebted to studies of the homosocial textual dynamic. See Eve Kosofsky Sedgwick, *Between Men: English Literature and Male Homosocial Desire* (New York: Columbia University Press, 1985); and Jonathan Goldberg, *Sodometries: Renaissance Texts, Modern Sexualities* (Stanford, Calif.: Stanford University Press, 1992).

5. Lynn Hunt, "Introduction: Obscenity and the Origins of Modernity, 1500–1800," in Lynn Hunt, ed., *The Invention of Pornography: Obscenity and the Origins of Modernity, 1500–1800* (New York: Zone Books, 1993), 9–45; quotation on p. 11. For a further account of pornography in Renaissance culture, see David O. Frantz, *Festum Voluptatis: A Study of Renaissance Erotica* (Columbus: Ohio State University Press, 1989).

6. Paula Findlen, "Humanism, Politics and Pornography in Renaissance Italy," in Hunt, ed., *The Invention of Pornography*, 49–108; quotation on pp. 53–54.

7. Ibid., 59.

8. See Arthur F. Marotti, " 'Love is not Love': Elizabethan Sonnet Sequences and the Social Order," *Journal of English Literary History* 49 (1982): 396–428; Philippa Berry, *Of Chastity and Power: Elizabethan Literature and the Unmarried Queen* (London: Routledge, 1989), 61–165; Catherine Bates, *The Rhetoric of Courtship in Elizabethan Language and Literature* (Cambridge: Cambridge University Press, 1992). See also a series of articles by Louis Adrian Montrose, including "Celebration and Insinuation: Sir Philip Sidney and the Motives of Elizabethan Courtship," *Renaissance Drama*, n.s., 8 (1977): 3–35; " 'Eliza, Queene of shepheardes,' and the Pastoral of Power," *English Literary Renaissance* 10 (1980): 153–82; "Gifts and Reasons: The Contexts of Peele's *Araygnement of Paris,*" *English Literary History* 47 (1980): 433–61.

9. Susan Frye has analyzed the ways in which a variety of social groups defined themselves through their relationship with Elizabeth I, and the queen's role in supporting or contesting these structures. See Susan Frye, *Elizabeth I: The Competition for Representation* (New York: Oxford University Press, 1993).

10. The range and cultural significance of the Elizabethan blazon is far wider than has been generally suggested, as I seek to demonstrate in the larger study of which this is a part. For accounts of the English blazon see Patricia Parker, *Literary Fat Ladies: Rhetoric, Gender, Property* (London: Methuen, 1987), 126–54; and Jonathan Sawday, *The Body Emblazoned: Dissection and the Human Body in Renaissance Culture* (London: Routledge, 1995), 197–212.

11. *The Shepheardes Calender,* in *The Works of Edmund Spenser,* ed. Edwin Greenlaw et al., variorum edition, 11 vols. (Baltimore: Johns Hopkins University Press, 1932–57), vol. 7, the "Aprill" Eclogue, ll. 37–99.

12. *Euphues and his England,* in *The Complete Works of John Lyly,* ed. R. Warwick Bond, 3 vols. (1902; Oxford: Clarendon Press, 1973), 2:203–5.

13. The respective sources for these terms are: Mark H. Curtis, "The Alienated Intellectuals of Early Stuart England," *Past and Present* 23 (1962): 25–41;

Anthony Esler, *The Aspiring Mind of the Elizabethan Younger Generation* (Durham, N.C.: Duke University Press, 1966); and Richard Helgerson, *Forms of Nationhood: The Elizabethan Writing of England* (Chicago: University of Chicago Press, 1992). Curtis's study identifies a class of underemployed young professionals in the late Tudor and early Stuart periods. Esler describes an aspirational, but largely frustrated courtier class coming of age in the 1590s. Helgerson contends that the cross-cultural invention of nationhood during the period was "a concerted generational project" produced by men with an unusual degree of social and economic mobility (1).

14. See Curtis, "Alienated Intellectuals." The queen's refusal to fill vacancies as they emerged in the Privy Council and her reluctance to reinforce the nobility created similar pressures at a different social level. See Linda Levy Peck, "Peers, patronage and the politics of history," in John Guy, ed., *The Reign of Elizabeth I: Court and Culture in the Last Decade* (Cambridge: Cambridge University Press, 1995), 87–108, esp. 88–98.

15. Harold Love, *Scribal Publication in Seventeenth-century England* (Oxford: Clarendon Press, 1993), 181.

16. *The Arte of English Poesie*, ed. Gladys Doidge Willcock and Alice Walker (Cambridge: Cambridge University Press, 1936), 61. All subsequent references are within the text.

17. Recent discussions of *The Arte* have focused on the text's reflection of similar issues relating to social mobility. See Louis Adrian Montrose, "Of Gentlemen and Shepherds: The Politics of Elizabethan Pastoral Form," *English Literary History* 50 (1983): 415–59, esp. 433–52; Barry Taylor, *Vagrant Writing: Social and Semiotic Disorders in the English Renaissance* (New York: Harvester Wheatsheaf, 1991), 127–50; Rosemary Kegl, "'Those Terrible Aproches': Sexuality, Social Mobility, and Resisting the Courtliness of Puttenham's *The Arte of English Poesie*," *English Literary Renaissance* 20 (1990): 179–208.

18. The queen is directly addressed on pages 4–5, 46, 58, 298–99, and 307–8. Instances where she is referred to by way of example include pages 96, 97, 98–99, 99–100, 164, 177, 182, 193, 215, 215–16, 217, 223–24, 244, and 256. A woodcut portrait of the queen that faces the opening of book 1 seems to have served as Puttenham's dedication to the *Arte*.

19. For the classic account of the "king's two bodies" theory see Ernst H. Kantorowicz, *The King's Two Bodies: A Study in Mediaeval Political Theology* (Princeton: Princeton University Press, 1957). Marie Axton has analyzed the theory's place in debates over the accession of Elizabeth I. Marie Axton, *The*

Queen's Two Bodies: Drama and the Elizabethan Succession (London: Royal Historical Society, 1977). For a critique of the "two bodies" model and a suggestive reading of its place in Renaissance criticism, see David Norbrook, "The Emperor's New Body? *Richard II,* Ernst Kantorowicz, and the Politics of Shakespeare Criticism," *Textual Practice* 10, no. 2 (1996): 329–57.

20. David Starkey has led a series of critics in examining the implications of access to the monarch throughout the early modern period. David Starkey et al., *The English Court: from the Wars of the Roses to the Civil War* (London: Longman, 1987).

21. The accounts of this phenomenon occur in the diary of the French ambassador, André Hurault, Sieur de Maisse, in the year 1597. See *A Journal of all that was Accomplished by Monsieur de Maisse Ambassador in England from King Henri IV to Queen Elizabeth Anno Domini 1597,* ed. G. B. Harrison and R. A. Jones (London: Nonesuch, 1931), 25 and 36–37. Lisa Jardine has raised doubts concerning the areas of the body actually being described in these passages. Nevertheless, she concedes that there does appear to have been some breach of decorum involving "gestures of revealing." Lisa Jardine, *Reading Shakespeare Historically* (London: Routledge, 1996), 21–25; quotation on p. 164, n. 14. Paul Hentzner's description of the queen in 1598 also refers to her exposed bosom, specifically associating it with virginity: "her bosom was uncovered, as all the English ladies have it till they marry." *Travels in England during the Reign of Elizabeth,* ed. H. Walpole, trans. R. Bentley (London: Cassell and Co., 1889), 47.

22. I follow the Walker/Wilcox estimate for the date of the presentation of the "Partheniades." The blazon, "A ryddle of the Princesse Paragon," appears as number 7 of the "Partheniades" and runs to some fifty-eight lines. The printed catalog is a selective version of this longer poem. Frederick J. Furnivall and W. R. Morfill, eds., *Ballads from Manuscripts,* 2 vols. (London: Ballad Society, 1868–73), 2:77–79.

23. *The Faerie Queene,* in Greenlaw, *Works,* 2.3.21–31. Of course, Belphoebe represents only a partial aspect of the queen's character and is one of a series of depictions of Elizabeth within the text.

24. Ralegh confirms this achievement in his poem "A Vision vpon this conceipt of the *Faery Queene.*" See *The Faerie Queene,* ed. A. C. Hamilton (London: Longman, 1977), 739.

25. Louis Adrian Montrose, "The Elizabethan Subject and the Spenserian Text," in Patricia Parker and David Quint, eds., *Literary Theory/Renaissance Texts* (Baltimore: Johns Hopkins University Press, 1986), 303–40; quotation on p. 327.

26. See, for instance, the description of Braggadocchio at 2.3.4–5.

27. See 2.3.39.

28. Robert Merrix has identified the blazon's place in what he terms Elizabethan "soft-core" pornography. See Robert P. Merrix, "The Vale of Lillies and the Bower of Bliss: Soft-core Pornography in Elizabethan Poetry," *Journal of Popular Culture* 19, no. 4 (1986): 3–16.

29. Examples of both types of blazon will be included in the account below.

30. John Carey and Arthur Marotti have both provided detailed accounts of the Inns of Court as a literary milieu. See John Carey, "The Ovidian Love Elegy in England," (D.Phil. diss., Oxford, 1960), 349–77; and Arthur F. Marotti, *John Donne, Coterie Poet* (Madison: University of Wisconsin Press, 1986), 25–34.

31. Marotti, *John Donne*, 33.

32. For an account of the epyllion see William Keach, *Elizabethan Erotic Narratives: Irony and Pathos in the Ovidian Poetry of Shakespeare, Marlowe, and Their Contemporaries* (New Brunswick, N.J.: Rutgers University Press, 1977).

33. For the dedication, see *Scillaes Metamorphosis*, in *The Complete Works of Thomas Lodge*, ed. Edmund W. Gosse, 4 vols. (1883; New York: Russell and Russell, 1963), 1:3. All other references are to Elizabeth Story Donno, ed., *Elizabethan Minor Epics* (London: Routledge, 1963), with subsequent references within the text.

34. The blazonic account of the genitalia in Robert Greene's *Menaphon*, published the same year for a largely similar audience, presented a similar model. *Menaphon: Camillas Alarum to Slumbering Euphues*, in *The Life and Complete Works in Prose and Verse of Robert Greene*, ed. Alexander B. Grosart, 15 vols. (London: Private circulation, 1881–86), 6:128.

35. "Beauties Lullabie," one of the verses published in conjunction with *Scillaes Metamorphosis*, makes a similar connection between authorial ambition and the sexualized catalog. Its preface situates the poem in the context of professional literary rivalry. The object of this rivalry, the accomplished blazon that follows, is distinguished by a description of the genitalia even more lavish than that in Lodge's epyllion. "Sundrie sweete Sonnets," in Gosse, *Works*, 1:39–41.

36. *Venus and Adonis*, in *The Riverside Shakespeare*, ed. G. Blakemore Evans (Boston: Houghton Mifflin, 1974). The dedication to the earl of Southampton appears on p. 1705. All subsequent references are within the text.

37. Quoted in Katherine Duncan-Jones, "Much Ado with Red and White: The Earliest Readers of Shakespeare's *Venus and Adonis* (1593)," *Review of English Studies*, n.s., 44, no. 176 (1993): 479–501; 490.

38. Venus is referred to as queen in lines 251, 503, 523, 607, and 1193.

39. As Duncan-Jones has illustrated, the analogy between Venus and Adonis and the erotically charged relationship between Elizabeth and her subjects was recognized, albeit bizarrely literally, by at least one contemporary reader. See Duncan-Jones, "Much Ado with Red and White," 479–90.

40. Barnes was not a member of the Inns of Court, although he had been at Oxford. Like Shakespeare, he was part of the circle of writers associated with the earl of Southampton.

41. See *Parthenophil and Parthenophe: A Critical Edition*, ed. Victor A. Doyno (Carbondale: Southern Illinois University Press, 1971), xxiv–xxv. All subsequent references are within the text.

42. The rape fantasies in sonnets 23 and 43 are obvious examples. Sonnet 43 concludes with an imaginative image in which Parthenophil envisages entering his mistress's body as wine in order to be expelled as urine and "passe by pleasures part."

43. Manners is not Barnes's only dedicatee, but hers is certainly the most indecorous tribute that he makes.

44. For the use of the word "eye" to refer to the vagina in Elizabethan literature, see Williams, *Dictionary*, 1:453–54.

45. Donne uses the blazon in "The Comparison," "Loves Progress," "The Anagram," and "To his Mistris Going to Bed." *The Elegies and The Songs and Sonnets*, ed. Helen Gardner (Oxford: Clarendon Press, 1965). "To his Mistris" and "Loves Progress" were still considered inappropriate for a public audience in 1633 when Donne's poems were first published. For Donne's self-creation as an Inns of Court author see Marotti, *John Donne*, 34–95.

46. "The Choise of Valentines," *The Works of Thomas Nashe*, ed. Ronald B. McKerrow and F. P. Wilson, 5 vols. (1958; Oxford: Basil Blackwell, 1966), 3: ll. 99–122.

47. "Loves Progress," l. 36.

48. For a discussion of the place of antifeminism within the *Elegies* see Marotti, *John Donne*, 44–66. See also Carey's account of the socioeconomic conditions in which this fashionable misogyny emerged; Carey, "The Ovidian Love Elegy," 349–77, esp. 360–77.

49. As Carey notes, Nashe's heroine represents "the extravagantly dressed, proud London woman persistently berated by the satirists and satirical dramatists as a symbol of the economic prosperity of the citizen class." Carey, "The Ovidian Love Elegy," 157.

50. Peter Clark, ed., *The European Crisis of the 1590s: Essays in Comparative History* (London: George Allen and Unwin, 1985). See, in particular, R. B. Outhwaite, "Dearth, the English Crown and the 'Crisis of the 1590s,'" 23–43; and Peter Clark, "A Crisis Contained? The Condition of English Towns in the 1590s," 44–66. John Guy has argued that the years from 1585 onward were so distinctively negative that they can be characterized as Elizabeth's "second reign"; "Introduction: The 1590s: The Second Reign of Elizabeth I?," in Guy, *The Reign of Elizabeth I*, 1–19.

51. In a tribute to Elizabeth written shortly after her death Francis Bacon remarked on the widespread anxiety experienced during these years: "the name and government of Elizabeth was assailed with a variety of wicked libels, and there was a strange ferment and swelling in the world, forerunner of some greater disturbance." See "In Felicem Memoriam Elizabethae, Angliae Reginae," in *The Works of Francis Bacon*, ed. James Spedding, Robert Leslie Ellis, and Douglas Denon Heath, 7 vols. (London: Longman, 1857–59), 6:314.

52. See Paul E. J. Hammer, "Patronage at Court, Faction and the earl of Essex," in Guy, *The Reign of Elizabeth I*, 65–86.

53. See Clark, "A Crisis Contained?"; and Jim Sharpe, "Social Strain and Social Dislocation, 1585–1603," in Guy, *The Reign of Elizabeth*, 192–211.

54. See Clark, "A Crisis Contained?," 56–61.

55. For the terms of the Bishops' Order, see Edward Arber, ed., *A Transcript of the Registers of the Company of Stationers of London; 1554–1640*, 5 vols. (London: Stationers' Company, 1875–77; Birmingham: Stationers' Company, 1894), 3:677–78.

56. See, for example, John Peter, *Complaint and Satire in Early English Literature* (Oxford: Clarendon Press, 1956), 149–50.

57. Richard A. McCabe, "Elizabethan Satire and the Bishops' Ban of 1599," *The Yearbook of English Studies* 11 (1981): 188–93.

58. Ibid., 190.

59. Cited in J. W. Saunders, *A Biographical Dictionary of Renaissance Poets and Dramatists, 1520–1650* (Totowa, N.J.: Barnes and Noble Books, 1983), 106.

60. *Virgidemiae*, in *The Collected Poems of Joseph Hall*, ed. A. Davenport (Liverpool: Liverpool University Press, 1949), book 1, satire 7.

61. Everard Guilpin, *Skialetheia* (London, 1598), satire 2. See also *Epigrammes*, in *The Poems of Sir John Davies*, ed. Robert Krueger (Oxford: Clarendon Press, 1975), "In Gellam.26."

62. T. M., *Micro-cynicon: six snarling satyres* (London, 1599), satire 5.

63. *The Metamorphosis of Pygmalion Image,* in *The Poems of John Marston,* ed. Arnold Davenport (Liverpool: Liverpool University Press, 1961), st. 6–12. All subsequent references are within the text.

64. *Endimion* does include more critical reflections of the Elizabethan cult, in a way that relates to, but is also at a discrete remove from, the portrait of Cynthia. See, for instance, arriviste squire Sir Tophas's counterblazons of the aged witch Dipsas. *Endimion,* in Bond, *Works,* 3: 3.3.52–60 and 5.2.94–100.

65. Thomas Cutwode, *Caltha Poetarum: Or The Bumble Bee* (London, 1599), "G. S. in commendation of the Authour," sig. A8. All subsequent references are within the text. Together with Hall's *Virgidemiae,* the poem received an eleventh-hour reprieve from the bishops' bonfire.

66. Leslie Hotson, "Marigold of the Poets," *Transactions of the Royal Society of Literature,* n.s., 17 (1938): 47–68.

67. Ibid., 59–61.

68. *The Faerie Queene,* in Greenlaw, *Works,* 3.5.50.

69. Ibid., 2.3.28.

70. See note 2 above.

71. See Anthea Hume, "*Love's Martyr,* 'The Phoenix and the Turtle,' and the Aftermath of the Essex Rebellion," *Review of English Studies,* n.s., 40, no. 157 (1989): 48–71.

72. Robert Chester's "Loves Martyr, or Rosalins Complaint," ed. Alexander B. Grosart (London: New Shakespeare Society, 1878), pp. 10–14. All subsequent references are within the text.

73. The appearance of the device within the sonnet sequence during this period offers an obvious index of this continued encomiastic tradition.

74. See Harrison and Jones, ed., *A Journal of all that was Accomplished,* 25–26. Lisa Jardine has drawn attention to the limitations of de Maisse's account (see note 21 above). While it is apparent that his portrait creates an idiosyncratic and sexually ambiguous image of Elizabeth, it remains equally clear that the queen herself is engaged in a complex act of image creation.

75. Jardine amends the translation of "bosom" to read "throat"; Jardine, *Reading Shakespeare Historically,* 163–64 n. 13.

76. Paul Hentzner's description of Elizabeth in her sixty-fifth year reflects a similar compromise between the magnificent and the grotesque. Walpole, *Travels,* 47–48.

Queen Elizabeth Compiled

Henry Stanford's Private Anthology and

the Question of Accountability

Marcy L. North

Rumors that Queen Elizabeth I had given birth to, reared secretly, or even murdered several illegitimate children surfaced frequently during her reign in tavern gossip and in polemical Catholic literature.[1] The seditious implications of such rumors were exemplified by the illegal *Leicester's Commonwealth* (1584), which claimed that Robert Dudley planned to crown his own illegitimate child after Elizabeth's death by falsely asserting Elizabeth's maternity.[2] Those who were caught libeling the queen with seditious rumors faced imprisonment, loss of ears, and even death. The medium of the libel, whether it was speech, writing, or print, might determine the harshness of the punishment but did not affect the basic definition of the crime. A 1581 act of Parliament condemned all who maliciously spoke "any false seditious and slaunderous Newes Rumors Sayengs or Tales againste our said moste naturall Soveraigne Ladye" or who dared to "devyse and wrighte printe or setforthe, any manner of Booke Ryme Ballade Letter or Writing, conteyning any false sedicious and slaunderous Matter to the Defamacion of the Queenes Matie."[3] The illegality of almost all media of libel against the queen underscores the daring of a poem that appears in a commonplace book compiled by Henry Stanford at the turn of the sixteenth century. Although private manuscripts offered collectors and writers a safer medium than print for the transmission of illegal texts, Stanford's inclusion of a libelous poem claiming Elizabeth's maternity nevertheless raises questions about *how* a particular manuscript medium such as a commonplace book offered its protection. Was the inaccessibility of the manuscript to a broader public and to authorities enforcing libel laws its only advantage? Or is it possible that the pattern and process of manuscript collecting also created a protective frame for seditious expression? The following essay pursues these questions by tracing the accidental narrative of *Henry Stanford's Anthology* as it absorbs and contains criticism of the queen and disperses responsibility for the seditious implications of its critical texts.

On folio 51 of Henry Stanford's 63-folio anthology, an anonymous poem denounces a very powerful woman's claim to virginity. After several lines deceptively praising the nameless woman's wisdom and influence, line 6 suddenly asserts that "even she" has "lost her maidenhead & daughters .3. to all ye world brought forthe." The long list of her accomplishments serves at this point to fuel the reader's outrage and to confirm the moral weakness of even the most powerful of women:

> She y^t was thought so full wth wisdom fraught, y^t all ye world might go to her
>   to scole
> & he y^t at no tyme by her was taught, is taken yet by som but halfe a foole
> She y^t taught princes how ther states to weld & y^r imbassadours what to doe
>   & say
> she y^t for sober & devout was held & clerckes & preistes taught how to
>   preache & pray
> she y^t so many yeares refusd to wed, & boasted what virginitie was worthe
> Even she I say hath lost her maidenhead & daughters .3. to all ye world
>   brought forthe
> wch Ile averre on Churche & on Churchesteple are bastardes bred right
>   children of ye peo[ple.][4]

The libel's subject needs no name; "Elizabeth Tudor" would have been every reader's guess. Not surprisingly, the libel's author also remains unnamed, for this work could not have been transmitted safely in Elizabethan England without great discretion. Even when the references to Elizabeth are read as unintentional, they remain provocative, for the poem does nothing to deny that its subject is Queen Elizabeth, and no poet in her reign could have composed these lines naively. The wit of the poem turns on the certainty that the reader will mistake its subject for the queen.

However easy it is to identify the poem's subject, the queen's anonymity remains an important impetus within the poem, magnifying the connection between the female subject and the queen. The absent name advertises the need for secrecy, and the absence of *any* name points to the name that would be most dangerous to write. The subject's anonymity also suggests identification with the queen in another way, in that the exaggerated terms by which the subject is praised would act as simple rhetorical tropes, as a kind of false praise, if applied to anyone below a queen. The anonymity of the female figure allows the reader to ask, in the fashion of solving a riddle, if there is any woman who *literally*, rather than figuratively, fits the description in the first five lines. Only one woman in Elizabethan England both "taught princes how ther states to weld" and "boasted what virginitie was worthe." With Elizabeth as the literal subject of the poem, the author's anonymity takes on new meaning as a protective device and tool for necessary discretion.

The libel's authorial anonymity, however, does not stand out in the larger context of *Henry Stanford's Anthology*, for most of the 338 poems and prose pieces surrounding the text on Elizabeth are also anonymous. A few texts are libelous enough to warrant protective anonymity, but the majority are politically benign and would not have posed a threat to an author or compiler. The many courtier poets included in the anthology indicate that class expectation and coterie discretion lie behind some instances of name suppression, but editorial style and accidents of transmission explain the anonymity equally well. The broader compilation does not tell us explicitly why the libel against Elizabeth is anonymous, and it is this very silence that provides me with the context for the following discussion of accountability in a personal compilation. The compiler's freedom to record literature critical of his sovereign depends on a process of compilation which disperses responsibility for sedition and exploits the ambiguity of intellectual property. The pervasive anonymity of the anthology as a whole proves significant to the establishment of this freedom, even though it functions somewhat differently than the protective or discrete anonymity of the individual pieces.

Henry Stanford compiled his anthology during a three-decade period at the end of and following Elizabeth's reign. The manuscript contains a smattering of poems that focus thematically on Elizabeth, most of which appear to have been copied during her reign.[5] These pieces vary in perspective from the malice of the rumor-based libel to the devotion and deference of dedicatory verse, but together they suggest Stanford's distinct interest in Elizabeth's politics and in the implications of her unmarried state. The libel stands out as one of the most dangerous texts in the manuscript, though there are several that could not be printed legally. A poem pleading with Elizabeth to consider her lack of husband and natural heir, "[W]hiles deep conceipt renowned queen presentes vnto my mynd," marks the milder end of a spectrum of criticism and serves in this essay as a contrast to the libel. The presumptuousness of this plea from the people invites censure even though Elizabeth reluctantly tolerated some discussion of her marital status in Parliament and at court. These two critical poems appear in Stanford's anthology without any attention to their seditious or critical content, and they blend into the heterogeneity of the whole with ease, taking their places next to love lyrics, political libels, anti-Martinist poems, and verse by Elizabeth herself.

To determine the extent to which these critical poems were treated as risky possessions within the private sphere of a personal anthology, one must consider how the qualities of the "private" and "personal"—their association with elite culture, individual use, and secrecy—create space for seditious and critical ideas. Whether one understands the compiler's accountability as a claim to and responsibility for a text's expression or as the possession of a material text, the private material context works to mute the claim and hide the possession. The simplest explanation is that when a text is inaccessible to a broad public, it is less visible to the authorities enforcing libel laws and, not coincidentally, less of a public threat. Yet this explanation demands that one treat a particular manuscript context as a final haven for a poem, as an end point in its transmission history when it has retreated from the world where illegal texts are smuggled and traded. Likewise, it requires that one read privacy as the sole agent of protection when privacy is more likely an occasional and accidental consequence of a broader dynamic in the transmission and compilation process.

Clearly, manuscripts were not always subject to the censorship and restrictions of the press. The exact relationship between the privacy of manuscript circulation and freedom of expression, however, remains difficult to articulate for a period when the boundaries of the private sphere differed somewhat from our own.[6] The 1581 act of Parliament, for instance, includes the "letter" among the generic mediums of libel for which one could be indicted, though this genre was sometimes used for "private" communication. Ruth Hughey points out that it was illegal as late as 1594 to *own* copies of the poem "Why doe I vse my paper ynke and pen," which describes the Jesuit Edmund Campion's 1581 martyrdom.[7] This poem circulated in both manuscript and print. "Private literature" is an ambiguous term that has come to mean both what was composed or compiled for personal use and what was kept private or secret from others. While Stanford's anthology certainly falls into the former category, there is no evidence that it was a secret manuscript or that Stanford relied on its inaccessibility for protection. Stanford's freedom to compile criticism of the queen cannot be explained adequately by labeling his compilation "private." Although Stanford surely understood the illegality of the texts he compiled, he found protection in the social and political confusion created by the act of compilation, a process that allows accountability for a presumptuous plea for the queen's marriage and a dangerous libel to be shared among several real and implied parties of writers and readers. It is not simply that sedition and disrespect are enclosed or focused within a boundary where they can be controlled.[8] Rather, a text such as Stanford's renders ambiguous the accountability for its individual expressions by embracing less individuated forms of authorship and text transmission.[9] The compiler may have imagined only a small number of readers for his manuscript originally, but the compilation itself points to many more participants as it blurs the lines between compiler, author, conveyer, and reader, and as it reminds one that texts *do* travel beyond their first "private" expression.

The two poems that have inspired this essay, the libelous "She y^t was thought so full wth wisdom fraught" and the presumptuous "Whiles deep conceipt renowned queen presentes vnto my mynd" engage in complex dialogues with the other texts in Stanford's anthology. These dialogues tend to emerge, disappear, and reemerge when one reads these poems through their anonymity and in light of their placement within the whole, for both anonymity and compilation require the reader to draw the lines that connect and divide individual works. The libel against the queen is followed by an anonymous poem, probably a riddle, mocking images of tyranny and kingship. "Aetos is a cruel and bloudie king" (pp. 188–89, f. 51) reemphasizes the potential instability of monarchy that the libel first introduced by prophesying the inevitable downfall of the tyrant: "famin at ye last shall kill his hart."[10] When one reads these poems as a developing dialogue, the sedition of the libel becomes more acute. The compilation process that creates dialogues such as this one asks the reader to reimagine authoring as a communal construction of meaning. In terms of accountability, for instance, the author is not clearly responsible for the new context in which the compiler places his or her work and the compiler is not entirely responsible for the content of the individual pieces. Likewise, the author of the libel may not be responsible for the poem that follows it even though the two poems work together to create a certain impact. Indeed, "accountability" may be an insufficient and overly proprietary term for what is manipulated by the compilation process. Although "accountability" comes close to describing the social obligation, intellectual control, and duty to assume consequences that one observes in the relationship between owner / author / reader and text, it also implies that there is a clear set of standards that determine who is responsible for what. Such standards had not been legislated or clearly articulated in the late sixteenth and early seventeenth centuries, especially outside the realm of print.

The freedom to include criticism in manuscript compilations was partially enabled by this lack of standards, but one could also say that the compilation process demonstrates why such standards were impractical. Compilation narratives constantly shift perspective and boundaries and thereby shift the potential identity and location of those who control and take responsibility for the included texts. Similarly, the collective nature of Stanford's anthology—the fact that many authors, patrons, gatherers, and conveyors of poetry make the whole possible—obscures the distinction between private and common domain literature. The anthology encloses critical texts within a circle, a household, a limited group, but it also frees the included texts from their dependence on the identity of an individual author. Like the anonymous songs, riddles, and maxims which appear frequently in commonplace books, the critical texts belong to the community, however open or closed that community is. The private manuscript seems to promise those threatened by its contents that the texts will remain restricted, but the anonymity of those texts, their freedom from clear attribution, allows them to circulate with more impunity than attributed texts can. The predominant anonymity of Stanford's anthology and its shifting political perspectives frame the texts criticizing and praising Elizabeth in a careful (and seemingly careless) ambiguity. Each text can claim affiliation with the safety of the private realm or with the anonymity of the commonplace and public sphere.

Henry Stanford's social position lends credence to this theory, for he compiled his anthology from the edge of an inner circle of courtiers and seemed to reach in and out, having access to some close-kept texts but relying just as often on a more public transmission of materials. Stanford served as tutor to William Paget, son of the recusant Baron Thomas Paget, in the 1580s and was later employed by the prominent Carey family which included among its members Henry Carey, first Baron Hunsdon, his son George Carey, second Baron Hunsdon, Elizabeth Spencer Carey, and George's and Elizabeth's daughter Elizabeth Carey Berkeley.[11] Stanford's social and professional position as tutor and retainer in these important families afforded him some access to court and coterie literature. Steven W. May speculates that Stanford may have had connections to John Astley, Sir Henry Lee, Sir Philip Sidney, and many of the court poets of the late 1580s and 1590s.[12] These connections, however, were probably not personal or direct. Stanford only rarely ascribed poems obtained from court circles, and if he had insider's knowledge of these authors, he did not advertise it explicitly. Several of his source texts seem to have been very good copies, though Stanford most likely received them through his employers and their contacts rather than from the authors themselves. He copied the courtly poems, along with other lyrics, satires, and riddles as they became available to him. This familiar compilation method points initially to availability and literary taste as motivations for the compiler's selections,[13] but Stanford's interest in political issues of Elizabeth's reign also influenced his selection, though the variety of his inclusions does not point to a single vision of Elizabeth.

Stanford's employment with the Paget and Carey families must have exposed him to a relatively broad range of opinion about Elizabeth. Stanford saw one employer, Thomas, Third Baron Paget, accused of recusancy and treason and the other, Henry Carey, first Lord Hunsdon, situated in relatively secure favor as Elizabeth's lord chamberlain, a position which Carey's son, George, would also assume in 1597.[14] As a member of the Paget household, Stanford found himself subjected to the harsh investigation of Lord Paget that led to the family's loss of fortune. There is some evidence that this association and the Catholic traditions in his own family caused Stanford trouble later in his career as well. A letter to Walter Bagot from April 1599 shows Stanford defending himself against rumors of recusancy. His connection to the Careys at this time afforded him some safety from these allegations, but this connection also magnified the potential damage the allegations could cause: "Lyving wth my lord chamberlain as a dayly folower & hauing so many yeares byn hys only houshould chaplain, to be proscribed as a recusant cannot greatly touche me, which can so manifes[t]ly disproue yt, but soundethe to my Lorde reproache to haue any suche about hym."[15] The political paradox in Stanford's having more security against false accusations because of his association with a powerful courtier but also more concern about them also plays itself out in his personal anthology.

The Carey family's prominence and close ties to Elizabeth required Stanford to maintain a clear position of loyalty to the queen. Although a personal manuscript seems an unlikely place to advertise one's loyalty, Stanford included several texts that reflected the government's perspective on recent crises and that hinted at a self-conscious compilation practice, perhaps an effort to imitate the responsibilities and privileges of his employer or a less deliberate tendency to gather texts that interested his employer or circulated within the household. Among the works supporting the queen are a verse account of the traitor William Parry's downfall (p. 82, f. 27v) and a series of satirical poems condemning religious factions in response to the Martinist controversy of the late 1580s and early 1590s (pp. 111–14, ff. 34–34v), all of which call attention to writing as a tool that exaggerates or deflates political crisis. In the least satirical of the anti-Martinist poems, an anonymous author mourns the dissension around him and implicates "writing" for its power to "display" discontent and to fuel the country's religious debates:

> What sonnes? What fathers? sonnes & fathers fighting?
>   alas our welfare, alas our health
> what moates? what beames? & both displaied in writing?
>   alas the Churche, alas the common welth
> (pp. 113–14, f. 35, ll. 1–4)

As the poem bewails the *ad hominem* tactics of the Martinist controversy, it reminds the reader of the dangerous potential of the libel against Elizabeth, which similarly attempts to divide queen and kingdom through a written display of her supposed wrongs. In stanza 2, the author expresses wonder that such strife could happen "vnder suche a Queene," making Elizabeth the focal point of peace rather than a participant in the strife:

What at this tyme, what vnder suche a Queene
   Alas that still our fruict should so be greene
What? wanton calves? what? lost our former loue
   alas our pride alas our mutabilitie
(ll. 5–8)

The poem cleverly advocates the queen's position on religious debate by situating her outside of the disagreements. Even in the final stanza when the author calls on queen, nobles, clergy, and commoners to "bear ioyntlie on an others weaknes," the queen initiates, by her position in the first line of the stanza, the unity of all estates within the church:

bear gratious Soveraign, Europes matcheles mirrhour
   bear noble lordes renowned counsail gevers
bear cleargie men for yours ill all ye error
   bear common people commonlight beleevers.
     bear ioyntlie on an others weaknes so
     that thoughe we wither yet ye Churche may grow
(ll. 13–18)

The several works supporting the queen's political perspective balance Stanford's anthology rather than eclipsing the other positions. They point to a compiler who was sensitive to the expectations of his employer and seemingly appreciative of the government's defenders. Nevertheless, one cannot assume that they represent Stanford's politics any more accurately than the libel does.

Stanford also had access to texts opposing the queen's policies and critical of the queen and her favorites, and his association with the Careys may have given him a protective license to collect and transmit these texts. A satirical comment on royal monopolies, probably copied very late in Elizabeth's reign during Stanford's employment with the Careys, contains a relatively mild threat of sedition, but resembles the libel in the way that it dramatically names the wrong in the second to last line:

Calamus pontificis[16] men say it growes in Rome
   And yt hath powr to sweepe vp gold as it were wth a broome
But we haue flowres in England here, wch doe subdue yt quight
The Calamus pontificis against them hath no might

Carnasions[17] of Elizabeth her subiectes many saue them
against the fowle Epilepsie & happie are they that haue them
Doe you not know what flowers I meane ye Queenes small shinking[18] letters
They set fooles forward now & then sixe miles before ther betters.

(p. 190, f. 51)

In this poem the queen is at the very center of a problem that threatens to disrupt an idealized meritocracy (or aristocracy, depending on one's reading of "betters"). The poem does not necessarily disapprove of favor, as long as favor is granted to those who deserve it. The poem's wry tone and antipapal images, however, build toward the identification of the queen's flowers in a way that leaves the queen under critical scrutiny for misuse of her powers. She has not preserved a system that distinguishes fools from their betters. If the Careys were the source of Stanford's interest in Elizabethan politics, their influence and protection allowed him to collect an incredible variety of perspectives and may have even encouraged the particular view of this poem, the fear that the queen's favors to a few threaten an older economic system.

The larger organization of Stanford's anthology demonstrates how the processes and accidents of compilation interact with the political perspective of individual texts to limit the private compiler's accountability. Stanford's anthology divides into two sections which May has labeled "domestic" and "public." The domestic section contains a series of poems predominantly by Stanford's students and other youths in his employers' families. George Berkeley, the son of Elizabeth Carey and Thomas Berkeley, is named in the headings to over a dozen poems, most of them New Year's gifts to his relatives. This section of the anthology records specific coterie or family events; the authors are named more for their participation in a coterie exchange than for their authorship. In every case, Stanford had a direct relationship to the included author.

The domestic section of Stanford's book, with its many commemorative names, is followed at its close by a poem headed "Anonymus" (p. 71, f. 20v), the only poem in the manuscript that calls explicit attention to its anonymity. Even though the poem may be a late addition to the blank leaves that separate the sections, its position at the end of the domestic section signals that the section to follow will establish very different relationships between compiler and author and between compiler and text

than those holding previously. It is within the public section that the many
pieces about and by Elizabeth I appear, beginning on folio 28 with her
1575/76 speech to Parliament in which she cleverly confronts her subjects' anxiety about her marriage prospects and the succession. Although
the term "domestic" works well to describe Stanford's collection of his
students' works, the term "public" is misleading here, even for a text as
seemingly public as a Parliament speech. Many of the less dangerous
"public" works were originally written for specific coterie events and
occasions with private audiences.[19] The Parliament speech, for instance,
was not printed during Elizabeth's reign and would only have reached a
general public by word of mouth or by manuscript.[20] Another clearly
occasional work is a poem headed "to ye Q. by ye players 1598" in which
the poets wish the queen an exceedingly long life:

As the diall hand tells ore / ye same howers yt had before
   still beginning in ye ending / circuler account still lending
   So most mightie Q. we pray / like ye diall day by day
   you may lead ye seasons on / making new when old are gon.
that the babe wch now is yong / & hathe yet no vse of tongue
   many a shrouetyde here may bow / to y^t empresse I doe now
   that the children of these lordes / sitting at your counsell bourdes
   may be graue & aeged seene / of her y^t was ther father Quene
   once I wishe this wishe again / heauen subscribe yt wth amen.
(p. 162, f. 46)

This text reminds one again of the peculiar difficulties in using the terms
"public" and "private" to describe a text or a context, for the poem
acknowledges its own publication—its performance. Yet if the play to
which this poem refers was performed before the queen, the particular
audience would have been a somewhat limited and elite group. Even in
the so-called "public" section of Stanford's anthology, many of the works
retain some quality of their coterie or private origins.

This second section of Stanford's anthology differs from the previous
one in its interesting juxtaposition of texts. Outside of a few clusters of
maxims, riddles, and poems by Stanford himself, the items have not been
gathered and organized by genre or by subject. The variety of love lyrics,
political poems, satires, advice poems, and other texts discourages a
reader from making any grand distinctions between literary works and

partisan commentaries on political issues. Beginning on folio 27, for instance, one finds two Sidney lyrics followed by a poem to accompany the gift of a book and then by a lyric (one of the few that is not anonymous) attributed to "W.R." The verse against the traitor William Parry begins on 27v and is immediately followed by a poem in praise of a lover. Queen Elizabeth's 1575 / 76 speech starts next on folio 28, and beneath the last few sentences of the speech on folio 29 Stanford has copied a widely circulated verse beginning "The state of fraunce as now yt standes," which attempts to sort out the many players in a political game of primero.[21] The narrative that these texts create, which asks us to see literature and events in a complicated historical network, is not simply the result of accident, for Stanford exercised some control in choosing the texts. But neither is the narrative entirely Stanford's. To understand how the material genre complicates Stanford's accountability for the criticisms of the queen, one must observe how the juxtaposition of unrelated texts remains open to two interpretations, one of which involves seeing the text as the record of an occasion.

The fact that most of these works are anonymous does not detract from their power as occasional, coterie, or political literature even though anonymity is part of the dynamic of the compilation narrative. The contents of these works often reaffirm the occasion, and when the contents do not, the surrounding texts, by their dissimilarity to the poem in question and by the conspicuousness of their own specific occasions, encourage the reader to imagine an occasion outside of the text. When one reads the lines in praise of a lover's beauty, "her eyes are of cristall her nose white as mylke / her cheekes are of roses her skyn soft as silke / her lippes are of Corall her teeth are of pearl / her tongue is of sugar ah delicate girle" (p. 83, f. 27v, ll. 11–14), after a satire on the downfall of William Parry, and before Queen Elizabeth's Parliament speech, one is more likely to imagine the lyric in a coterie or political context, as a plea for favor, for instance. On the other hand, the miscellaneous nature of the compilation context may have the opposite effect of reaffirming the detachability of each piece of work and discouraging a consideration of the text's occasion.[22] From this perspective, the diversity of the compiled works calls attention to their status as collected texts rather than to their individual social uses. Queen Elizabeth's Parliament speech is, like the lyric poem, included as a piece of literature.[23] Whether a reader decides to interpret the diverse collected context as one that accentuates the possibility of a past occasion or absorbs the occasion into a collection depends on how that reader intends to use the poem in question. A reader wanting to demonstrate his or her inside knowledge about court circles might read the context one way while a reader looking for song lyrics might read it another way. This diverse context continually opens itself up to the possibility that its items will be excerpted again or reappropriated for other immediate social uses.

The dual interpretation of the collected context points to another difference between the first and second sections of Stanford's anthology. In the first section, the detachability of the poems and their occasional quality appear to overlap completely without ever detracting from each other, perhaps because the headings and dates that Stanford places above or below these poems record the occasion even when they do not record the author's name. More likely, however, the qualities overlap because the act of compiling coheres so well with the original coterie events. Recording these events is in itself a coterie act, a bringing together of the same people who wrote and read these works. A reader does not need to perform a dual reading of the texts in order to consider them both excerpts and occasions. In the public section of the manuscript, the bringing together of writers creates a very different assemblage from what might be imagined as the original coteries for the individual poems. The records of various literary and political occasions that appear side by side in the manuscript establish an improvised collected context for each poem that sometimes points toward occasional specificity and sometimes away from it.

The anonymity of most of the second section of Stanford's anthology guarantees the flexibility that the compilation process creates. The contents of the poems suggest a variety of anonymity conventions, from authorial discretion meant to protect the author of illegal literature to coterie discretion enacted to preserve class boundaries. With the complexity of "occasion" in mind, one can analyze the silent juxtapositions of anonymity conventions in a sequence that includes the presumptuous plea to the queen to ask how anonymity influences the compilation narrative. Rather than defining "coterie" as an immediate circle of readers established by social class or educational affiliation, the juxtapositions in Stanford's anthology point to overlapping and slightly looser social circles based on political faction, religious sentiment, and libertine values. Yet none of these coteries is as pervasive as that constituted by the exercise of authorial discretion. The circle of authors created by the compilation process has discretion as a common link even though each act of discretion possibly excludes a different group of readers. This loose coterie based on anonymity is able to absorb the most dangerous texts and factions by making them a small part of the whole, and paradoxically, by both isolating them and situating them in the chance narrative of the compilation.

The series that frames the plea to the queen is revealing. After two lover's laments, one at the bottom of folio 43v and one at the top of folio 44, Stanford copies a poem that is more about the dangers of friendship than about love. The anonymous author bewails the friend who pretends loyalty but works secretly against him.[24] In the first stanza, the poet blames himself for trusting in a flatterer:

> In choise of frendes what chance had I to choose on of sirenes kynd
> > whose harpe whose pipe whose melodie could feed myne eyes & make me blind
> > whose pleasant voyce mad me forget that in great trust was great disceit.
> (p. 153–54, f. 44, ll. 1–3)

In the second stanza, he develops his topic into a general maxim:

> In trust I see is treason found & man to man disceitfull is
> > and wheras fortune doth abound of flatterors ther doth not misse
> > whose painted speache & outward show as frendes do seme but be not soe
> (ll. 4–6)

In the third and fourth stanzas, the poet addresses the deceiver directly, accusing him in line 10 of being a "traitour":

> Oh fauell false thou traitour born what mischeife more mightest thou deuise
> then thie dere frend to haue in skorn & him to wound in sondrie wise
> yet still a frend pretendst to be & art not so by proofe I see.
> (ll. 10–12)

Whether one reads this poem as a complaint about the personal or political complexities of friendship, or something of both, flattery and a "pleasant voyce" are identified as the mask behind which treason lurks. True friendship requires a kind of honesty that defies the "painted speache & outward show." This antiflattery poem establishes the immediate collected context for the poem that follows, in which the speaker complains to the queen that she has neglected to marry, produce an heir, and guarantee the succession:

> whiles depe conceipt renowned quene presentes vnto my mynd
> thie statly race & birth sprong forth from passing princely kynd
> three titles doe I note in the & twain I see do fail
> the want wherof wth me alas doth Brittain land bewail
> A daughter to a mightie king the heauens do the alow
> a princes sister & a neipce, the world & we advow
> but princes wife nor mother yet thou wilt vouchsafe to be
> thoughe euery name of euery wight is wished vnto the.
> O let such glittering glorie peirce thie pure vnspotted brest
> that thie renown may be preferd aboue the starres to rest
> but yf thie constant virgins mynd such passing prayse forsake
> yet at the least regard the plaint thie pensiue people make.
>
> (p. 154, f. 44)

The poem at first depicts Elizabeth as a woman whose worth is determined by her relationship to a father, brother, uncle, husband, and son. The queen would hardly have found these roles flattering, though she emphasized them upon occasion when they helped her to secure power and the confidence of the people. The consolatory acceptance of her virginity at the end of the poem is not necessarily complimentary either, since it sets up the final unspoken plea for some confirmation of an heir. Yet despite its derogatory images, the poem is written in a plain and straightforward style, using a language very different from the style that the previous poet associated with treason. Elizabeth did not appreciate this kind of explicit and direct advice any more than she did the coy messages in her courtiers' poems and entertainments,[25] but the compilation narrative encourages the reader to interpret these critical lines as the words of a friend. The anonymity of both poems allows the reader either to make a connection between the poems, assuming a similar author or coterie group, or to separate the poems from each other and to read them through the compilation process as pieces detached from their social environment and placed in a collection. In either reading, the presumptuousness of the second poem is tempered by the anonymity of its context, and Stanford's responsibility seems no more than that of his reader, who has the power to determine one poem's relationship to the next.

One can widen the context of the presumptuous poem so that it encompasses an even greater variety of opinions of the queen's affairs. One of the works included in this broader context is a poem sometimes attributed to Elizabeth herself,[26] which appears at the top of folio 44v just two items away from the plea to the queen. The voice in the poem is one of an older poet answering to the temptations of a more youthful suitor with the understanding that certain joys are behind him or her. The first stanza captures this quality:

> now leaue & let me rest, dame pleasure be content
> go chuse among the best my doting dayes be spent
> by sundrie signes I see thy proffres are but vain
> & wisdom warneth me that pleasure seaketh pain
> & nature that doth know how tyme her steps doth trie
> giues place to painfull woe & biddes me learn to die
> (pp. 155–56, f. 44v)

As with the libel against Elizabeth, the poem's subject is not named. Unlike the libel, however, this poem does not point immediately to Elizabeth as a subject, though once her name is attached to the text as it is in Harleian MS 7392, the poem seems to make reference to the Anjou courtship, where a mature Elizabeth seriously considered marriage to a much younger man. Stanford's anonymous version of this poem does not necessarily lose all association with Elizabeth, for the text can still stand as an answer and balance to the poem pleading with the queen to marry. Even anonymously, the lines from the disillusioned older lover present an alternative mature perspective of love, and it seems probable from the urgency of the plea to the queen that she was not young at the time of that poem's composition. Elizabeth was certainly not young when Stanford collected the plea. Even if Stanford and his readers were not aware of its tenuous association with the queen, the poem to the younger suitor acts as the counterpart of the plea simply because it deflates the political implications of the plea and grants the older subject a more personal choice, as the final stanza indicates:

And all the fancies strange that fond delight brought forthe

I do intend to change & count them nothing worthe

    processe worn

for I by prooffes [am taught] to know ye skyll

what might haue byn forborn in my yong reacheles will.

by wch good proofe I fleete from will to witte again.

in hope to set my feete in suretie to remain

(ll. 34–39)

Elizabeth often framed her answers to the marriage question by distin-
guishing the political from the personal,[27] and one could read the plea and
this anonymous lament together as parts of that ongoing debate about
queenship. The dialogue between these two texts complicates the accountability of the author or compiler, for it is a very different thing to be
accountable for either of these pieces individually than it is to be accountable for the two of them together. The combined message of the dialogue
is one of dilemma and limited choices, but of still finding some power to
speak for oneself. This message is a far cry from the presumptuous voice
of the first poem and the resigned voice of the second, both of which have
become actors in a larger dialogue that absorbs some of the criticism in
the plea for marriage; the poems form an imagined coterie around a
particular argument without advocating any one side or faction.

The plea for the queen's marriage can also be read in isolation, however, as a text copied separately with no relation to the texts around it, and
this potential reading must be kept in mind even when the dialogue seems
most intentional, for this isolation creates the space for future dialogues.
While the plea's inclusion in the whole might indicate the compiler's
privileged access to texts of a certain political opinion, the absence of a
name, heading, or other contextualizing devices suggests that the text
could also have come to the compiler already detached from its origins.
The context created by bringing together unrelated texts diminishes the
force of the poem's politics. The lack of authorial names in the Stanford
anthology makes all of these readings possible for the critical text, which
can be included so easily in the private manuscript, not only because the
private manuscript will remain out of reach of the objecting authorities,
but because anonymity and the compilation process leave open to the

reader some of the responsibility for excerpting, grouping, and re-grouping—responsibility for the creation of contexts—that is necessarily part of interpretation.

This reading process does not need to be one in which Stanford himself participated. Imagining a later and less informed reader sheds light on how the transmission of commonplace literature changes the dialogues within the manuscript. The second part of Stanford's manu-script envelops a third section, a small cluster of what May believes are Stanford's own poems.[28] The enclosed section (pp. 191–201, ff. 51v–54) begins with three hymns and ends with nine sonnets all based upon a conceit in which the poet asks the addressee to "place" or imagine the author in various famous and faraway cities and lands in order to prove that, even there, his devotion to the addressee would be constant. Judging from the way a numbered collection of riddles and epigrams from the "public" section surrounds them, these hymns and sonnets were probably added to the manuscript early in the compilation process.[29] If these poems are indeed Stanford's, they warrant attention for the way the possible interpretations of their anonymity alter as the compilation evolves. Stan-ford may have intended this section to work as a single-author cluster which needed no attribution because the work was his own and because he planned to keep it within a familiar circle of readers. It is not unusual in early personal anthologies to find compilers neglecting to ascribe the poems and to name the poets with which they are most familiar. Once the second miscellaneous section had encroached upon the Stanford cluster, however, the potential interpretations of Stanford's anonymity changed.

The carefully numbered riddles, satires, and witty stories that sur-round Stanford's poems were probably copied from one text, and judging from the politically dangerous and morally adventurous contents of the pieces, they were almost surely anonymous before they reached Stanford. Both the poem against royal monopolies and the libel against Elizabeth appear in this series. Among the most interesting of the politically sugges-tive works is a prose prophecy of a Catholic tyrant's succession to the English throne in 1602. According to the prophet, a "popes sonne w^{th}out ever drawing sword shall make all or most part of Cristendom subiect vnto him. . . . He shall come into England greatly welcommed of many and not a few of our bishops prelates Clergie." After the tyrant abuses "many of the richer sort as of ye poorer," and after the "death of many

Innocentes & effusion of muche bloude vpon ye Earth he shalbe over-
thrown & chased away" (pp. 184–85, f. 50). It is difficult to gauge the
implications of this piece without knowing exactly when it was written
and when Stanford took an interest in it, but May guesses that the entire
series was transcribed very late in Elizabeth's reign, which would make
the prophecy another expression of fear about the succession.[30] Elizabeth,
like several of the monarchs before her, had banned political prophecies
such as these early in her reign.[31]

The context which the libel, the prophecy, and the other potentially
dangerous poems create for the Stanford cluster alters a reader's perception of Stanford's anonymity. Instead of assuming that a name was unnecessary for Stanford's own poems, one is tempted to read in his anonymity
a fear of being associated with or identified as the anonymous author of
the numbered libels and riddles. Ascriptions within Renaissance manuscripts and books often announced the beginning or end of a group of
poems from a subscription or heading, and misinterpretations of the
boundaries of clusters occurred easily. At the same time that Stanford's
anonymity protects him, it also implicates him in the authorship of anonymity and in the design of the larger anonymous cluster into which his
lyrics have been absorbed. Stanford has essentially the same "signature"
as the author of the seditious libel against Elizabeth. So while the modern
textual scholar has good evidence that the Stanford cluster was copied
into the text before the numbered riddles and libels, it is fruitful to
imagine the experience of a less informed reader who does not look for
the signs that mark clusters and chronology. It is this reader who reads
anonymity through the overlapping of conventions and interpretations
and who can carry this complexity of authorial presentation to the next
text he or she reads or writes. Whether this early reader has gained access
to Stanford's text as an insider (a member of the Carey family, for instance) or as an outsider who has stumbled upon Stanford's anthology
after his death, he or she will recognize anonymity as a signature with
potential meanings in a particular textual space and social context. That
one meaning of anonymity reflects upon and sometimes determines another is the very nature of this convention, which, because of its similarities of appearance and its functional differences, can alter its message
for a new reader or new context.

The compilation process in *Henry Stanford's Anthology* allows one to read poems critical of Queen Elizabeth as voices in a dialogue rather than as voices in rebellion. The responsibility for these particular poems is absorbed into the consistent anonymity of nearby clusters and into the variety of perspectives on Queen Elizabeth. Yet these poems can also be read as excerpts severed from their occasions and production origins with little connection to the texts that surround them. The responsibility for their composition and inclusion seems variously assigned to the author, the compiler, the accidents of text transmission, and the reader who partially creates the narrative and the politics of compilation. The juxtaposition of anonymous texts, whether Stanford intended it or not, renders ambiguous the anthology's statements about Queen Elizabeth and allows for the freer expression of a critical perspective, though not without some sacrifice of political impact and individual political perspective. In a heterogeneous anthology like Stanford's, the accountable party that the text asks its readers to imagine changes as the readers move from one item to the next and from one grouping of texts to the next. Stanford's accountability for the libel against the queen and the presumptuous plea for her marriage, like the authors' and readers' accountability, depends on the stability or flexibility of the lines his readers draw around a "work" or idea.

Notes

1. Carole Levin discusses the prosecution of several individuals for malicious gossip about the queen in *"The Heart and Stomach of a King": Elizabeth I and the Politics of Sex and Power* (Philadelphia: University of Pennsylvania Press, 1994), 66–90. Anne Somerset also describes a 1560 case in which a woman was jailed for a malicious rumor about Elizabeth's maternity; see *Elizabeth I* (New York: Knopf, 1991), 130–31.

2. *The Copie of a Leter, Wryten by a Master of Arte of Cambrige* (1584), commonly known as *Leicester's Commonwealth*, STC 19399, 100–101.

3. "An Acte against sedicious Wordes and Rumors uttered against the Queenes moste excellent Majestie," 23 Elizabeth c. 2, 1581, *The Statutes of the Realm*, vol. 4 (1819): 659–60. This act worked to strengthen previous laws against seditious libel and to clarify the punishments for offenders.

4. *Henry Stanford's Anthology: An Edition of Cambridge University Library Manuscript Dd. 5.75,* ed. Steven W. May (New York: Garland, 1988), p. 187–88, f. 51. The bracketed letters at the end of the poem appear above the "peo-" in the manuscript. Subsequent quotations from this edition will be noted in the text by May's page numbers and the manuscript folio numbers. In all of the quotations, I follow May's transcriptions exactly whenever possible.

5. See May, Introduction, *Henry Stanford's Anthology,* xxxix–xlii. May posits that the section of the manuscript to which the libel belongs was copied very late in Elizabeth's reign (xli), but the ambiguous past tense of the poem indicates a loss, either of the subject herself or of the illusion of her virtue, which might complicate the dating. Although rumors about Elizabeth's illegitimate children also circulated after her reign, I would guess that the poem belongs to her reign.

6. Harold Love argues that, in the seventeenth century, manuscript circulation of certain types of literature, especially news items and libels, was considered a kind of publication; see *Scribal Publication in Seventeenth-Century England* (Oxford: Clarendon Press, 1993). Love nevertheless acknowledges that "inherent in the choice of scribal publication—including the more reserved forms of entrepreneurial publication—was the idea that the power to be gained from the text was dependent on possession of it being denied to others" (183).

7. Ruth Hughey, ed., *The Arundel Harington Manuscript of Tudor Poetry,* 2 vols. (Columbus: Ohio State University Press, 1960), 2:64.

8. Mary Thomas Crane articulates the complexity of early compilation practices, especially in humanist circles, in *Framing Authority: Sayings, Self, and Society in Sixteenth-Century England* (Princeton, N.J.: Princeton University Press, 1993).

9. Crane, *Framing Authority* (4), notes how the sixteenth-century educational practice of gathering commonplaces encouraged "a version of authorship that was collective instead of individualistic," and this tradition may have contributed to the understanding of personal anthologies as safe havens for seditious or critical texts.

10. "Aetos" appears to refer to the Greek word for *eagle,* which was a common symbol for kingship in the early modern period. Natural philosophers describe the eagle's need to file down its continuously growing beak in order to avoid starvation, and the poem's comment on tyranny or on a specific tyrant builds partly upon this image. For a description of the eagle, see *Batman uppon Bartholome, his Booke, De Proprietatibus Rerum* (1582), 177.

11. May, Introduction, *Henry Stanford's Anthology*, viii–xvi. May has identified Stanford as the compiler of the Cambridge anthology (viii–ix), even though Stanford's name (or initials) only appears in the manuscript twice.

12. May, Introduction, *Henry Stanford's Anthology*, xvi–xx.

13. Arthur Marotti's recent book, *Manuscript, Print, and the English Renaissance Lyric* (Ithaca: Cornell University Press, 1995), details the many ways that early lyrics circulated and emphasizes the importance of nonauthorial mediation to the framing, collecting, and interpretation of these lyrics.

14. May, Introduction, *Henry Stanford's Anthology*, xi–xii, xvi.

15. Folger Shakespeare Library MS L.a. 885.

16. Early modern herbals describe "calamus" as a reed used for thatch (and probably for brooms) and for the making of pens. See *The First and Seconde Partes of the Herbal of William Turner* (1568), 64. The poem's author is probably comparing the Pope's abuses of power, perhaps in the form of pardons and other purchasable written privileges, with the queen's abuse of monopoly distribution.

17. Sir Thomas Edgerton defended Elizabeth's royal prerogative, which allowed her to grant monopolies freely, as the "chiefest flower in her garland" during the monopoly debates of the late 1590s. Edgerton is cited by John E. Neale, *Elizabeth I and Her Parliaments, 1584–1601* (New York: St. Martin's Press, 1958), 355.

18. "Shinking" is probably an error for "shrinking" or "stinking."

19. One could argue that many court events were more public than private in that they were performances with an audience somewhat larger than the author and his/her ideal reader, yet these audiences were still more circumscribed and controlled than, say, the audience at a theater, the audience for a printed work, or the audience of potential readers that is often described as the "public." See Marotti's discussion of lyrics as occasional texts, *Manuscript, Print, and the English Renaissance Lyric*, 2–10.

20. May discusses the manuscript circulation of the speech (285).

21. For reference purposes, I cite below the first lines of the poems from the series. May (269) notes that the two Sidney poems, "[R]ing out your belles let mourning shewes be spred, for loue is dead" and "[T]he fier to see my wrong for anger burnes," are from "Certain Sonnets." The poem accompanying the book, which reads "I pray the booke when I am gon," is unique. The verse by W[alter] R[alegh] begins "Calling to mynd myn eye went long about" and the poem on William Parry starts with "William Parrie was ap Harrie by his name." The love

poem that precedes Elizabeth's speech reads "[O]f force I must prayse her I like so well" and the poem that follows is cited in the text.

22. For a discussion of the recontextualization of lyric poetry in compilations, see Arthur Marotti, "The Transmission of Lyric Poetry and the Institutionalizing of Literature in the English Renaissance," in *Contending Kingdoms: Historical, Psychological, and Feminist Approaches to the Literature of Sixteenth-Century England and France,* ed. Marie-Rose Logan and Peter L. Rudnytsky (Detroit: Wayne State University Press, 1991), 21–41.

23. May (286) points out that Stanford probably copied this speech a decade after the queen presented it to Parliament, which could be seen as evidence that Stanford appreciated the speech as literature or as historical record. Many of Stanford's other political entries, however, were transcribed much sooner after the events.

24. This poem is attributed to "W.H.," probably William Hunnis, in all editions of *The Paradise of Dainty Devices.* May, *Henry Stanford's Anthology,* 368.

25. Helen Hackett describes the tendency for authors of court entertainments and literature offering the queen advice on marriage to use a "courteous ambiguity . . . as to whether Elizabeth's virginity or potential marriage is the object of praise." See *Virgin Mother, Maiden Queen: Elizabeth I and the Cult of the Virgin Mary* (New York: St. Martin's, 1995), 97. The Kenilworth entertainment and Sidney's *Lady of May* are relatively well known. Most of these works are exceedingly allegorical in comparison to the poem in Stanford's anthology. Of particular interest to this study is a 1579 New Year's gift to the queen from George Puttenham entitled the *Partheniades.* Three lines cited by Hackett come close to the explicitness of the Stanford plea: "But had shee, oh the twoo ioys shee doth misse / A cesar to her husband, a kinge to her soone / What lackt her highnes then to all erthly blisse" (99). Hackett acknowledges that this straightforward comment is somewhat unusual.

26. May (370) considers Elizabeth's authorship of this poem very doubtful. For the purposes of this study, however, the rumor of authorship is also interesting, for Stanford may have compiled this poem precisely because he thought it was by Elizabeth. The poem is ascribed to Elizabeth in Harleian MS 7392, although the ascription has been added to the work and another ascription has been crossed out.

27. In the 1576 Parliament speech, for instance, Elizabeth claims that were she "a milkemayd wth a pail / on myne arme wherbye my private persen might be

little set by, I would not / forsake y^t single state to match my self wth the greatest Monarch" (p. 87, f. 28v).

28. May, *Henry Stanford's Anthology,* 375–76.

29. May, Introduction, *Henry Stanford's Anthology,* xlii.

30. Ibid., xli.

31. Rupert Taylor, *Political Prophecy in England* (New York: Columbia University Press, 1911), 105–6. The 1581 act of Parliament also included prophecy among the seditious writings against the queen.

"Not as women wonted be"

Spenser's Amazon Queen

Mary Villeponteaux

When Spenser asks Queen Elizabeth to find herself in the "mirrours more then one" provided in *The Faerie Queene*, he actually names only two. "But either Gloriana let her chuse, / Or in Belphoebe fashioned to bee: / In th'one her rule, in th'other her rare chastitee," he writes (3.Proem.5).[1] Twentieth-century critics have provided a list of other mirrors in the poem: Britomart, Mercilla, Acrasia, perhaps even Argante in some sense figure the queen.[2] Why Spenser should choose to acknowledge only Belphoebe and Gloriana remains an interesting question and probably has something to do with the delicate business of representing Elizabeth in a way that meets with her approval. Certainly Belphoebe's permanently virginal state most accurately reflects Elizabeth's image by 1590; but despite Spenser's avowal that Belphoebe represents his queen's chastity, he does not make her the Knight of Chastity or as central and well-developed a figure as the temporarily virginal Britomart. I have argued elsewhere that the portrait of Belphoebe is a literary "mask of youth" through which the poet implicitly criticizes his queen, portraying her chastity as obdurate and sterile in comparison to the complex and dynamic Britomart.[3]

Yet despite the ambiguity with which he portrays her, Spenser proclaims that Belphoebe represents the "rare chastitee" of the queen, as opposed to her rule. This division of Elizabeth into her rule and her virtue reflects the concept of the king's two bodies. As discussed by the Tudor jurist Plowden, the doctrine of the king's two bodies conceptualizes the monarch as a dual self, consisting of a body natural and a body politic. The king might have a weak body or person, but he also has a "body politic" that is strong, even eternal. This crypto-theological doctrine, developed in the Middle Ages, was meant to account for the possibility of rightful heirs to the throne whose bodies were in some way infirm—the king's body politic is "void of Infancy and Old Age, and other natural

Defects and imbecilities," writes Plowden.[4] Part of my argument is that in Spenser's attempts to represent his queen, the private body usually supersedes the public one. I would even suggest that in Elizabethan England in general it was much easier to think of the queen in terms of her body natural. In her own rhetoric, which has been the subject of much discussion in the past twenty years, she often casts herself in terms of personal relationships—she is wife of England, mother of her people, lover of her courtiers. What may account for this is the way that patriarchy constructs its idea of woman as one whose physicality is primary and who exists mainly to fulfill roles in relation to men. Certainly the Renaissance ideal of woman is predicated upon a personal, rather than publicly political, virtue—chastity, which means virginity for the unmarried woman and fidelity for the married so that she can be entrusted to bear the children of her husband, thus fulfilling a dynastic function. The ideal woman has no public side; in fact, even writers who promoted new and liberating ideas about women, such as the importance of women's education, stressed that women should keep their learning and talents within the home. Juan Vives, remembered as a humanist who advocated education for women, still warned in his influential *Instruction of a Christian Woman:* "Wene you it was for nothing that wyse men forbad you rule and governaunce of contreis and that saynte Paul byddeth you shall nat speke in congregatyon and gatherynge of people? All this same meaneth that you shal nat medle with matters of realmes or cities. Your owne house is a cite great inough for you."[5] The domestic rather than the public realm is the proper one for women.

Thus, although the doctrine of the king's two bodies was meant to allow for such oddities as the presence of the "weak and feeble body of a woman" on the throne (to quote Elizabeth herself), in fact the "body natural" of the female monarch seems to have exercised a strong hold over the popular imagination, and over Spenser as he wrote *The Faerie Queene.* The impact of gender on the concept of the king's two bodies has been approached from another perspective by Susan Frye, who identifies the way that Elizabeth's own rhetoric challenged the expected genders of the body natural and body politic. Frye analyzes the contest for the representation of Elizabeth and finds that, in her subjects' discourse from the earlier decades of her reign, there is a tendency to focus rhetorically on her sex— to depict her as a woman first, one who happens to be monarch as well—

and to emphasize the private virtues befitting a woman, primarily chastity. Yet in her public discourse Elizabeth combats this by reversing the expected gender of her two bodies. Rather than representing herself as a woman, but also a prince—thus identifying a female body natural and a male body politic—Elizabeth most often refers to herself as a single sex or as two bodies politic, as in the Golden Speech, when she claims both "the glorious name of a king" and the "royall authoritie of a queen."[6]

In the proem of book 3 Spenser seems to take part in this struggle by announcing his own intention to split his depiction of Elizabeth into bodies natural and political. Yet a complex depiction of the public, political queen—her rule—does not occur in the poem, despite the appearance of female rulers such as Belge, or Irena. We do not necessarily expect to see political rule depicted in great depth since, according to the Letter to Raleigh, private moral virtue, rather than "polliticke vertues," was to be the province of the first twelve books of the projected *Faerie Queene*. Certainly no complex depiction of Elizabeth's rule occurs in the poem, although her private virtue of chastity is depicted in depth through figures like Belphoebe and Britomart. However, in book 5, most overtly political of all the books of *The Faerie Queene*, we do encounter two female rulers: Radigund and Mercilla. Mercilla is one of the clearest representations of Queen Elizabeth in the poem. This fictional virgin queen, whose iconography reflects the real-life queen, presides over the trial of Duessa, commonly regarded as Mary Queen of Scots. Radigund, the monstrous Amazon queen, might also represent Mary in the topical allegory since her overthrow is followed closely by Duessa's trial.[7] Yet Radigund also reflects aspects of Elizabeth, although this sort of representation could never be openly acknowledged by the poet. Spenser's language in discussing Radigund, and the way she functions as a double both for Belphoebe and for Britomart herself, suggest a connection between the queen of Radigund and Queen Elizabeth. The similarity is not really based in styles of government, although Radigund's queenship does elicit the narrator's one direct comment on the rule of woman:

> Such is the crueltie of womenkynd,
> When they haue shaken off the shamefast band,
> With which wise Nature did them strongly bynd,
> . . . .

But vertuous women wisely understand,
That they were borne to base humilitie,
Unlesse the heauens them lift to lawfull soueraintie.

(5.5.25)

Critics normally locate the importance of the Radigund episode in the exact issue treated in this passage: several scholars have tried to deal with the seeming contradiction between Spenser's disdain for women's rule in this passage and his praise of past women rulers in book 3.[8] Others have seen Radigund as a mirror of Elizabeth in that she provides not a reflection but a negative example to encourage analysis: Radigund's tyranny stands in contrast to Elizabeth's rightful queenship. "We must know Radigund to appreciate Elizabeth," as Pamela Joseph Benson puts it, and it is by the conduct of their rules that we know them.[9] Despite the conceptual importance of Radigund's rulership, however, the conduct of her rule is not actually Spenser's primary focus in the poem. We do learn of the Amazon queen's cruelty in her treatment of male captives, but most of what we learn about Radigund focuses on her private role as a woman in love—one whose cruelty is motivated by a lover's rejection, one who seeks to woo the unwilling Arthegall and fights Britomart to the death to keep him. The "body natural" (or in Radigund's case, the body unnatural) supersedes the body politic of this female regent, just as it does in other instances of the representation of Elizabeth.

Thus I am proposing to read the connection between Elizabeth and Radigund not from the point of view of their conduct as rulers but from the point of view of Radigund's role as an unnatural woman, one who symbolically functions to block the union of Britomart and Arthegall, and one who belongs to a race of women popularly believed to pervert generation by cutting off their breasts, committing infanticide, and the like. The use of Amazons to represent Queen Elizabeth is an interesting and complex topic in itself, and one that it might be worthwhile to consider before looking more closely at Spenser's Amazon queen. Queen Elizabeth did not compare herself to an Amazon, but her subjects frequently did, as several scholars have demonstrated. The one occasion where Elizabeth is popularly believed to have represented herself as an Amazon was at Tilbury, but as Frances Teague has shown, we have insufficient evidence to be sure that event ever actually occurred, despite the many colorful accounts of Elizabeth arrayed like a warrior, fearlessly addressing the troops.[10] Popular figures in Elizabethan drama, Amazons were almost always portrayed positively on stage, possibly because they potentially alluded to the queen.[11] Many Elizabethan writers made direct comparison between Elizabeth and Amazons, as Winfried Schleiner has demonstrated.[12] Again, these representations almost always look flattering on the surface, a good example being James Aske's *Elizabetha Triumphans*, a celebration of the defeat of the Armada and one of our few contemporary sources for the story of Elizabeth addressing the troops at Tilbury. Aske describes Elizabeth as "an Amazonian Queene" and compares her to Penthesilia "beating downe amain the bloodie Greekes" as part of his panegyric; Schleiner also lists other contemporary and later accounts of this moment, all of which draw the Amazonian comparison.[13]

However, despite Schleiner's and Jackson's focus on heroic and noble Amazons, not all Elizabethan depictions of the Amazons are so positive.[14] The Amazonian legends have a distinctly negative side, well-documented in some sources yet repressed in most contemporary accounts that clearly allude to Elizabeth. An interesting instance that may be the exception to this rule is the popular *Palace of Pleasure*, William Painter's retelling of classical and continental stories, which contains a notably ambivalent account of Amazonia. Published first in 1566–67, with second and third editions published in 1569 and 1575, Painter's second volume opens with an epistle to the reader in which he describes the Amazon story as one which derives its value from displaying "a strange or miraculous port, (to our present skill) of womens government," a statement which seems clearly to allude to the "present skill" of a woman on the English throne.[15] Despite this apparent acknowledgment of the connection between Elizabeth and the Amazons, Painter's account fails to offer the expected unqualified praise of warrior women. It begins with attention to the features of Amazons celebrated by Elizabethans when they represent their queen in terms of courage, strength, and so forth. Painter describes the Amazons as "most excellent warriers, very valiaunt," and after recounting how they came to power and the lands they ruled, he refers to them as "these miraculous women living after this maner in peace and justice."[16] Nevertheless, his story soon turns from accounts of the valor and victories of a well-governed people to the side of the Amazon legend that proves these women monstrous: their sexual and maternal behavior.

Painter tells how the Amazons, in order to perpetuate their race, "married" with men of a neighboring country, but only in order to breed: the husbands come to the Amazons' country at certain times of the year solely to have intercourse with the women. The men then go back to their own country, having fulfilled their function. Painter also dwells on that horrifying legend about the Amazons' treatment of their infants: they would keep their daughters and train them in arms, riding, and hunting, but the sons they would either send back to their fathers, or else "they murdred them, or brake their armes and legs in sutch wise as they had no power to beare weapons, and served for nothynge else but to spin, twist, and to doe other feminine labour. And for as mutch as these Amazones defended themselves so valiantly in the warres with bowe, and arrowes, and perceyved that their breastes did very mutch impech the use of that weapon, and other exercises of armes, they seared up the right breasts of their yonge daughters."[17] It is noteworthy that Painter chooses to report the Amazons' destruction of the breast here, in relation to their unnatural treatment of their children, since the amputated breast is a central feature of the myth. Painter does report that the name "Amazon" is derived from this practice and means "without the breast," but by subordinating that part of the story to the larger account of the Amazons' cruelty to their infants, he makes the perversion of the maternal role central to the definition of what an Amazon is.

He goes on to focus on another negative aspect of these women by recounting the story of Thalestris, an Amazon who begged "carnal copulation" of Alexander the Great, hoping to bear a daughter and heir. This conclusion to the story leads Painter into a series of questions about the Amazons that are quite different in tone from his opening praise; for instance, he asks, "What monstrouse sexe was this that durst . . . to fight with that terrible personage Hercules? . . . What queene (nay what stalant [stallion]) durst sue for company of meanest man? and yet one of these presumed to begge the match of the mightiest monarch that ever ruled the world."[18] Thus the Amazon, although a type that could be and sometimes was employed in the praise of Elizabeth, also has a monstrous side of which Elizabethans were well aware. Not only do Amazons overturn patriarchy, but the specific enactments of that upheaval are infanticide, the mutilation of children (and destruction of female body parts used for nurturing children), and sexual misconduct. The praise of Elizabeth as an Amazon would thus seem ambivalent at best, linking her leadership and valor with the violation of patriarchy and its values. It is probably not coincidental that Raleigh, in his second-hand account of Amazons in "The Discovery of Guiana," is careful to deny the legendary infanticide as well as the mutilation of the breasts: the Amazons who give birth to sons send them back to their fathers, reports Raleigh, and "that they cut off the right dug of the breast I do not find to be true."[19] These mythical Amazonian monstrosities—infanticide and sexual license as well—are also reflected in seditious rumors about Elizabeth that occurred during the later years of her reign. Carole Levin has demonstrated that a common slander against the queen was to accuse her of secret childbirths and even infanticide.[20] F. G. Emmison's records of Essex sedition cases finds that the rumors of the queen's secret pregnancies reached a climax in 1590 with two similar claims from commoners that Elizabeth had borne several children in secret and burned some of the infants at birth. Dionisia Deryck of Chipping Hill said that the queen "has as many children as I," claiming that some had been burned to death at birth. Robert Gardner of Epping had a similar story that closely parallels Amazonian legends: according to the records of his trial, he claimed that Elizabeth and Leicester had had four children: three girls all still alive, but one boy whom they had thrown into the fire.[21]

Thus the flip side of an image Elizabeth often promoted, that of herself as the mother of her people, appears in these tales of the monstrous mother whose maternity proves her a whore and whose offspring become her murdered victims. Although the representation of Elizabeth as a Petrarchan "cruel fair" whose courtiers played the roles of importuning lovers has received a great deal of critical attention, the dominant impression created by contemporary references to the queen is that her subjects thought and spoke of her as a mother. This metaphor seems to have come forth readily from Elizabeth's subjects, as in Sir Philip Sidney's infamous letter protesting the queen's match with the duke of Anjou, wherein he describes her monarchy as one where "the Infants suck the love of their rightful Prince," and warns that the people do not want to change this diadic state of affairs for one in which they are ruled by "a divided company of stars."[22] Similarly, Leicester in his will prays that Elizabeth may "indeed be a blessed Mother and Nurse to this People."[23] Her court is sometimes metaphorically depicted as a nursery, where she presides lovingly over the courtiers whom she nurtures.[24] This maternal metaphor was Elizabeth's own; she used it frequently and effectively. For instance, at the end of a 1563 speech to Parliament in which she declined to answer their petition on the succession, she assured them, "You shall never have a more natural mother than I mean to be unto you all."[25] That she adopts the metaphor in self-defense suggests what might be problematic about it: she may be England's mother, but her lack of actual progeny promised a possible succession crisis. The metaphor may also be a troubled one because the Elizabethans' cultural construction of motherhood itself is so vexed. To cast the queen's relationships with her subjects in terms of maternity is to evoke a host of competing ideas, many of them negative, about what a mother is.

Mary Beth Rose, in a fascinating article on the early modern representations of motherhood, identifies several areas of ambiguity in the cultural construction of maternity. For instance, while marriage and motherhood seem to gain a new prestige as a result of the Reformation, and consequently the wife and mother's role is enhanced, Protestant writers remain insistent on the importance of the father's authority. The power that a woman has in determining paternity, and thus inheritance, is negatively constructed in terms of suspicion and fear of women's supposed sexual liberality. Perhaps most importantly for my argument, Rose also claims that mothers' influence over their children and responsibility for their education, newly valorized as it was, was also frequently represented as a damaging influence, particularly in terms of mothers' supposed tendency toward excess in "cherishing" their children. "Mothers' responsibilities in the lives of their children therefore must be restricted quantitatively, qualitatively, and chronologically," concludes Rose.[26] The ideal mother is an absent or dead mother; a living, present, nurturing mother endangers her sons because she makes private life too appealing and thus keeps them from more manly, active, public pursuits. This captivating mother who prevents her adult sons from entering the public arena may be glimpsed in some of the dangerous women of *The Faerie Queene,* such as Acrasia, whose emasculating domination of knights has been linked to Elizabeth's relationship to her courtiers.[27] There is a cluster of such female figures in the poem, including Cymoent, the archetypal possessive mother, but also Belphoebe, Elizabeth's clearest avatar, in the sway she exerts over Timias, which causes him to become "mindlesse of his owne deare Lord" (4.8.18).

Radigund too belongs to this group. When she captures Arthegall, she strips him of "all the ornaments of knightly name" (5.5.20) in an echo of Acrasia's erasure of her young captive's "braue shield, full of old moniments" (2.12.80); both women emasculate their captives by taking away the name of knight; both hang the captive knights' arms up as a sign of their victory and the knights' idleness.

Thus, to represent Queen Elizabeth as a mother may be a vexed process when viewed from several different angles. The queen who claimed to be a loving mother of her people may evoke fears of the suffocating mother that Rose describes as one negative formulation of motherhood in early modern Europe. Also, when the concept of Elizabeth as mother is grafted onto the concept of Elizabeth as a powerful Amazon, the resulting image might be one of perversion and cruelty. As Susan Frye has convincingly argued, a central ideological issue in the representation of Elizabeth was the definition of "virtue," since *virtu*, the most desirable attribute for a ruler, is by definition and etymology masculine: active, vigorous, manly.[28] Feminine virtue normally means chastity alone for Elizabethans, an essentially passive attribute threatened by vigor and activity, as the many exhortations to women to stay home and stay quiet would suggest. The Amazons are good examples of *virtu*—the word is actually used to describe Elizabeth when she is praised as a Penthesilia in *Triumphalia de vitoriis Elizabethae* (1589)—but that manliness destroys their feminine virtue; the two cannot easily coexist. Similarly, if Elizabeth is a mother, she is a woman of essentially private virtue whose influence may actually damage the public selves of her (male) children; a mother who is also a public figure exercising manly virtues poses the possibility of monstrosity. Finally, the claim that Elizabeth is England's mother is also a claim that she uses to deflect the question of her marriage; she is mother to her people instead of being mother to an heir who could divert a succession crisis. I propose that the unnatural Amazon Radigund picks up some of these anxieties about the queen's failure to "mother," a failure that of course had serious political implications in Elizabethan England.

Certainly the queen's lack of issue is an unspoken difficulty for Spenser in *The Faerie Queene*, as he creates an unacknowledged portrait of Elizabeth in the character of Britomart—unacknowledged for many reasons, perhaps most pressingly because Britomart's destiny is cast in terms of generation: Merlin foretells that her "womb's burden" will take her from the field of battle. But in other senses—in her androgyny, her power, and not the least in her role as exemplar of the queen's signature virtue, chastity—Britomart is obviously an avatar for Elizabeth.[29] Yet her destiny as Arthegall's wife and the mother of British monarchs draws attention to Elizabeth's refusal to play the role of wife and dynastic mother. In 1590 it was too late to urge Elizabeth to marry and bear children, but it was not too late to offend her by suggesting that she should have done so.[30]

If Britomart "shadows" Elizabeth, then so does her alterego Radigund. The feisty virgin, after fighting such male heroes as Guyon and Marinell in book 3, and winning against Arthegall himself in book 4, finds her ultimate challenge in facing and defeating the Amazon queen Radigund in book 5. The struggle between them is clearly cast in terms of an inner struggle that Britomart undergoes, wherein Radigund represents some aspect of Britomart that must be eliminated before the knight can retire from the field and fulfill her truly important role, that of mother to the future generations of British kings. Critics describe that aspect of Britomart allegorized in Radigund in a variety of ways: Radigund may represent Britomart's violence, her domineering ways, her unwomanliness, her "shadow."[31] I would like to add to this list the idea that Radigund represents sterility, and to claim also that the battle in canto 7 foregrounds the vexed issue of maternity that plagued Elizabeth's reign and her people's imaginations. This interpretation of the conflict represented by Britomart vs. Radigund—procreation vs. sterility—is reflected in the Amazon's name. The name Radigund seems derived from that of Saint Radegund, an allusion which strikes a strange note: why should Spenser's evil Amazon bear a saint's name?[32] But Saint Radegund remained a virgin despite her marriage to Clotaire; this aspect of her story highlights Radigund's representation of Queen Elizabeth—like Radegund a virgin queen—as well as the way Radigund functions in the plot and in the allegory. She serves to block Britomart's maternal destiny in the plot, and allegorically she represents aspects of Britomart's chastity that might be resistant to that destiny. It is fitting, in terms of the allegory as well as in terms of Elizabeth's representation, that Britomart's final enemy should be depicted as a force that perverts generation and blocks procreation; the other "Britomart books" of The Faerie Queene, books 3 and 4, contain prominent myths of procreation, although Britomart's course always seems to move along the periphery of these tales until her encounter with Radi-

gund in book 5. But the two previous books include the Garden of
Adonis, centerpiece of the Legend of Chastity and obviously central to
the allegory of Britomart; the marriage of the Thames and Medway with
its epic catalog of "Neptune's seed" followed by the Ocean's offspring;
and even Scudamour's account of the Temple of Venus, in which the
presiding Venus is described as the creator of the world because she is the
source of the desire that can only be quenched "in generation."

Britomart's dream vision in Isis Church the night before the battle with
Radigund highlights the procreation theme. Often read as an allegory
about justice and equity, the vision can also be read as an allegory about
sexuality, and procreation in particular. In one of Spenser's sources for the
episode, Plutarch's *Moralia*, Isis is described as "the female principle of
Nature"; she "is receptive of every form of generation." She "inclines
always to the better and offers to it opportunity to create from her and to
impregnate her with effluxes and likenesses in which she rejoices and is
glad that she is made pregnant and teeming with these creations."[33] In her
dream, the knight of chastity sees herself impregnated and delivered of a
child, apparently under the auspices of this generative goddess Isis, since
Britomart has "reposed" herself "Vnder the wings of Isis all that night"
(5.7.12). In the course of the dream, Britomart undergoes a transformation from virgin priestess—wearing the garb earlier described as belonging to Isis's chaste priests—to a bejeweled and scarlet-robed queen who
must face and accept the threatening force of a crocodile, later identified
as Arthegall by the same priests. As the pregnant and scarlet-clothed
woman who faces a combative serpent, Britomart recalls the woman
"robed with the sun" of Revelation who gives birth to a male child
"destined to rule all nations with an iron rod." The child is saved from a
devouring dragon who stands in front of the woman as she is about to
give birth (Revelation 12).[34] After Britomart is "dis-maid" by the crocodile in her dream, she grows great with child and gives birth to a lion who
subdues all other beasts, a potent symbol of the victorious British kings
described by Merlin in book 3. Isis's priests interpret the dream as a
prediction of her marriage to Arthegall and their subsequent offspring.[35]
Britomart becomes a queen in her dream, a reflection of Queen Elizabeth
dressed in a scarlet robe and gold crown, but she is a fantasy Elizabeth,
one who becomes pregnant and provides the kingdom with the much-
desired heir. Since this initiatory dream occurs as a prelude to the fight

with Radigund, it seems allegorically to suggest that when Britomart overcomes Radigund, she overcomes a bar to the fulfillment of that procreative destiny depicted in the dream. As an other-Britomart, Radigund is also an other-Elizabeth; one might argue that Britomart is Elizabeth as the poet wishes she were; Radigund is Elizabeth as she is.

In fact Britomart's subsequent fight with Radigund is a battle not only over Arthegall; it is also a battle with herself. Throughout the episode, the two warriors are paralleled through the typical Spenserian devices of repeated phrases and pronoun ambiguity, so that their similarity is repeatedly emphasized. Of course, they are parallel in often-noted obvious ways as well, in that both are female knights in martial conflict with men; both conquer Arthegall in battle after he sees their beauty. The usual critical account of their similarity highlights the contrasts between the two, which the ground of sameness allows us to see. But the two appear more similar than different, and the basis for their similarity resides partly in their lack of feminine virtues. For example, Radigund's lack of femininity is highlighted when the narrator tells us that, when she received news of Britomart's arrival, she was not troubled and confused "as women wonted bee" (5.7.25), just as Britomart wants revenge when she learns of Arthegall's infidelity, rather than lamenting "with loude alew, / As women wont" (5.6.13). As Sheila Cavanagh has pointed out, Spenser uses the metaphor of the cud-chewing cow to depict both figures, an image he uses for only one other figure in the epic, the obsessively jealous and possessive Malbecco.[36] A direct allusion to the way both women shun their "natural" procreative function comes in 5.7.29, when the two first clash in battle. The two

> spared not
> Their dainty parts, which nature had created
> So faire and tender, without staine or spot,
> For other vses, then they them translated,
> Which they now hackt and hewd, as if such vse they hated.
> (5.7.29)

Of course Spenser alludes here to the etymology of *Amaʒon*, "without the breast"; notably, Britomart is implicated in this tradition of mutilation that suggests the rejection of the feminine body. Both Radigund and Britomart seem to "hate" the use of the breast that nature ordained, that is, the feeding of young. Both become so ferocious in this particularly gory battle that the ground is soaked with blood, and another antiprocreative image occurs:

> And on the ground their liues did strow,
> Like fruitles seede, of which vntimely death should grow.
> (5.7.31)

When Britomart finally defeats Radigund, the description of what happens almost spells out the idea that Britomart has defeated a part of herself. She cleaves Radigund's head, and "her proud person low prostrated on the plaine."

> Where being layd, the wrothfull Britonesse
> Stayd not, till she came to her selfe againe.
> (5.7.34)

What appears to have actually happened is that Radigund has been "laid low" by Britomart's stroke, and Britomart comes up to the Amazon's prostrate form and beheads it—just to make sure. But the pronoun ambiguity suggests that Britomart's "proud person" has been laid low, and when that happens she comes to herself again, becomes the self she has been before and must be again to fulfill her dynastic destiny—a lovelorn woman rather than a warfaring knight. The beheading of Radigund is unnecessary to the fight; Britomart has already pierced through the Amazon's helmet "to the very braine" (5.7.33). But the beheading is necessary because of what it symbolizes. Britomart, in order to come to herself again, must remove from herself what Radigund represents: the masculine, public self of rule and war. Applicable here is the common Renaissance analogy that equates the head's ruling the body with the man's ruling the family and the monarch's ruling the nation. In removing Radigund's head in order to come to a self that will allow the fulfillment of her dynastic function, Britomart cuts off a masculine, public function, which we can connect with the *virtu* that makes the Amazon both heroic and monstrous, and may do the same in the case of the queen.

Britomart is indeed a queen in book 5, but only temporarily—she rescues Arthegall and restores the rule of men yet reigns herself as princess in that land for a while, a contradiction that has exercised critics for years. She leaves the princess job, however, because of her pain and sorrow at the departure of Arthegall, a departure to which she must submit because she "tendred chiefe" *his* honor (5.7.44). She seems now to play the ideal woman's part as the Renaissance understood it, in which a woman's private life and virtues are essential to the honor of husband or father. The last we hear of her in *The Faerie Queene*, she remains in "languor and unrest" after Arthegall's departure. I think that Britomart is a figure through whom Spenser has fantasized a powerful queen who could also be a dynastic mother. Yet her end, characterized not by power and action but by words such as "heauinesse" and "languor," suggests to me specifically the "wombe's burden" that Merlin predicted would take Britomart from the field of battle, and in general terms it suggests the loss of power that attends Britomart's destruction of her "other self," the Amazon queen.

This is another kind of queen: not the fantasy queen Britomart in whom Spenser tries to reconcile the body politic with the woman's body natural—that is, to reconcile the idea of a monarch's rule with patriarchy's understanding of wife-and-motherhood. Radigund represents a different kind of fantasy about Elizabeth, one which also privileges her "body natural." But in this case, the body is unnatural, and this woman is a nightmare queen who rebels against a woman's "natural" roles as wife and mother as in the seditious gossip I reported earlier. Rather than being subjected to a man as his wife, Radigund makes men her subjects. Rather than remaining passively chaste, Radigund, like the Amazon Thalestris, actively woos a man. Rather than bearing children, she "hates" the use that nature intended for her body. When Britomart "comes to herself" after defeating Radigund, she also ceases to be Elizabeth's avatar; just as Radigund is replaced by Duessa in canto 9, Britomart is replaced by Mercilla, a virgin queen. Subject now to a man whose honor she holds above her own, languishing and heavy, Britomart prepares for the destiny Elizabeth rejected: mother of British kings.

Notes

1. All quotations from *The Faerie Queene* refer to A. C. Hamilton's edition, cited by book, canto, and stanza. *Spenser: The Faerie Queene*, ed. A. C. Hamilton (New York: Longman, 1980).

2. For the Argante connection, see Judith Anderson's "Arthur, Argante, and the Ideal Vision: An Exercise in Speculation and Parody," in *The Passing of Arthur: New Essays in the Arthurian Tradition*, ed. Christopher Baswell and William Sharpe (New York: Garland, 1988), 193–206.

3. "*Semper Eadem:* Belphoebe's Denial of Desire," in *Renaissance Discourses of Desire*, ed. Claude J. Summers and Ted-Larry Pebworth (Columbia: University of Missouri Press, 1993), 29–45.

4. Edmund Plowden, *Commentaries or Reports* (London, 1816).

5. Juan Luis Vives, *Instruction of a Christian Woman*, trans. Richard Hyrde (London, 1529).

6. Susan Frye, *Elizabeth I: The Competition for Representation* (New York: Oxford University Press, 1993), 13.

7. See Carol Schreier Rupprecht's article on Radigund in *The Spenser Encyclopedia*, ed. A. C. Hamilton (Toronto: University of Toronto Press, 1990), 580–81.

8. For instance, James E. Phillips Jr., "The Woman Ruler in Spenser's *Faerie Queene*," *Huntington Library Quarterly* 5 (1942): 217–34, and Susanne Woods, "Spenser and the Problem of Woman's Rule," *Huntington Library Quarterly* 48 (1985): 141–58.

9. Pamela Joseph Benson, *The Invention of the Renaissance Woman* (University Park: Pennsylvania State University Press, 1992), 295.

10. See Frances Teague, "Queen Elizabeth in Her Speeches," in *Gloriana's Face: Women, Public and Private, in the English Renaissance*, ed. S. P. Cerasano and Marion Wynne-Davies (Detroit: Wayne State University Press, 1992), 63–78. Teague discusses three of Elizabeth's putative speeches, including the Tilbury address on pp. 67–69.

11. Gabriele Bernhard Jackson, "Topical Ideology: Witches, Amazons, and Shakespeare's Joan of Arc," *English Literary Renaissance* 18 (Winter 1988): 40–65.

12. Winfried Schleiner, "*Divina Virago:* Queen Elizabeth as an Amazon," *Studies in Philology* 75 (Spring 1978): 163–80.

13. James Aske, *Elizabetha Triumphans* (1588; rpt. Amsterdam and New York: De Capo Press, 1969). See pages 23–24.

14. See Celeste Turner Wright's 1940 essay, "The Amazons in Elizabethan Literature," *Studies in Philology* 37 (July 1940): 433–56. She provides innumerable examples of both positive and negative depictions of Amazons.

15. William Painter, *The Palace of Pleasure*, 4 vols. (1567; rpt. New York: AMS Press, 1967), 2:6.

16. Ibid., 208–9.

17. Ibid., 210.

18. Ibid., 212.

19. *The Works of Sir Walter Ralegh* (New York: Burt Franklin, 1829), 8:409.

20. Carole Levin, "Power, Politics, and Sexuality: Images of Elizabeth I," in *The Politics of Gender in Early Modern Europe*, ed. Jean R. Brink, Allison P. Coudert, and Maryanne C. Horowitz (Kirksville, Mo.: Sixteenth Century Journal Pubs., 1989), 95–110.

21. F. G. Emmison, *Elizabethan Life: Disorder* (Chelmsford: Essex County Council, 1970), 57.

22. Philip Sidney, *Miscellaneous Prose of Sir Philip Sidney*, ed. Katherine Duncan-Jones and Jan Van Dorsten (Oxford: Clarendon Press, 1973), 54.

23. Philip Sidney, 3d Earl of Leicester, *Letters and Memorials of State . . .*, ed. Arthur Collins (London, 1746), 1:71.

24. See for example Sir Robert Naunton, *Fragmenta Regalia*, ed. John S. Cerovski (Washington: Folger Books, 1985), 78, or p. 57.

25. J. E. Neale, *Elizabeth I and Her Parliaments, 1559–1581* (London: Jonathan Cape, 1953), 109.

26. Mary Beth Rose, "Where Are the Mothers in Shakespeare? Options for Gender Representation in the English Renaissance," *Shakespeare Quarterly* 42 (Fall 1991): 301.

27. Patricia Parker, *Literary Fat Ladies: Rhetoric, Gender, Property* (London: Methuen, 1987), 54–66. See also, for a Jungian analysis of the enveloping mother in book 3, Jonathan Goldberg, "The Mothers in Book III of *The Faerie Queene*," *Texas Studies in Literature and Language* 17 (1975): 5–26.

28. Frye, *Elizabeth I*, 14.

29. Some recent articles that make this claim are Mary R. Bowman's " 'She There as Princess Rained': Spenser's Figure of Elizabeth," *Renaissance Quarterly* 43 (1990): 509–28; and Julia M. Walker, "Spenser's Elizabeth Portrait and the Fiction of Dynastic Epic," *Modern Philology* 90 (1992): 172–99.

30. John King proposes that in the 1580s and 90s the cult of the virgin queen developed as a direct result of the failure of the Alençon match. But this celebration of the virgin goddess does not change the fact that, for Spenser, marital love is the dominant definition of chastity—an awkward framework for praising Gloriana, or Belphoebe (as King points out, p. 67). See "Queen Elizabeth I: Representations of the Virgin Queen," *Renaissance Quarterly* 43 (1990): 30–74.

31. The idea that Radigund represents some aspect of Britomart herself is

commonly asserted. See for instance A. C. Hamilton's discussion in *The Structure of Allegory in "The Faerie Queene"* (Oxford: Clarendon Press, 1961). He depicts Arthegall's submission to Radigund as a reenactment of his earlier "fall," when he submitted to Britomart and thus to woman's beauty and power (p. 183). Angus Fletcher refers to the "potential Radigund" in Britomart, that is, her violence (*The Prophetic Moment: An Essay on Spenser* [Chicago: University of Chicago Press, 1971], 248; see also the discussion on pp. 279–80. Elizabeth Bieman's essay on Britomart in book 5 supplies another reading, in which Radigund's destruction signals the advent of real womanhood for Britomart. See "Britomart in *The Faerie Queene* V," *University of Toronto Quarterly* 37 (1968): 156–74. Carol Schreier Rupprecht uses the term "shadow" to describe Radigund, which she goes on to explain as "the unacknowledged and undermining tendencies within herself [Britomart]," in her article on Radigund in *The Spenser Encyclopedia*, p. 580.

32. For a full discussion of Spenser's Radigund and Saint Radegund, see Thomas H. Cain, *Praise in "The Faerie Queene"* (Lincoln: University of Nebraska Press, 1978), 153–54. Cain reads the hagiographical allusion as ironic but also notes that Saint Radegund, as a patron saint of France, reminds us that Radigund is an enemy of the British nation which Britomart and Arthegall's union will establish. Saint Radegund's French patronage may also forge a link between Spenser's Radegund and Mary Stuart, who was briefly queen of France.

33. *Plutarch's Moralia*, ed. and trans. Frank C. Babbitt (1936; rpt. Cambridge, Mass.: Harvard University Press, 1962), 5:129–30.

34. Kenneth Gross points to this parallel in *Spenserian Poetics: Idolatry, Iconoclasm, and Magic* (Ithaca: Cornell University Press, 1985), 177.

35. For a different interpretation of Britomart's dream, see Julia Walker, pp. 192–97. Walker's conclusion that Britomart becomes "not a mother through 'fleshly force' but an icon" (197)—ultimately, Mercilla herself—is different from mine. However, both our interpretations are based on a recognition of the difficulties inherent in representing a female monarch, one who must be both "public queen and private virgin" (196).

36. Sheila T. Cavanagh, *Wanton Eyes and Chaste Desires: Female Sexuality in "The Faerie Queene"* (Bloomington: Indiana University Press, 1994), 165.

The

Image

of the

Queen

Fair Is Fowle

Interpreting Anti-Elizabethan

Composite Portraiture

Rob Content

Warnings against the public use of images to criticize Queen Elizabeth were issued periodically during her reign. A royal proclamation of 1563, to cite the earliest example, opened by announcing a broad extension of official control over royal image-making:

> Hir majestie perceiveth that a great number of her loving subjects are much greved, and take great offence with the errors and deformities allready committed by sondry persons in this behalf [i.e., royal portraiture], she straightly chargeth all hir officers and ministers to see the observation hereof, and as soon as maybe to reform the errors allready committed, and in the meantyme to forbydd and prohibit the showing and publication of such as are apparently deformed until they are reformed which are reformable.[1]

The tactical approach of this passage is striking in two respects. The first of these is its framing of the court's action as a response to popular demand, hence obscuring any suggestion that the new queen might herself have taken offense at any of these putative "errors and deformities." Secondly, the discourse of deformities is itself remarkable, importing a distinctively medical set of connotations into a discussion of image-making. For "deformities," whether reformable or unreformable, alludes variously to the effects of such blemishing diseases as smallpox and leprosy and to the range of birth defects which were at once sensationalized and deplored as "monstrous" in sermons and ballads. Printed versions of these often moralizing reports were in fact sometimes supplemented with the circulation-enhancing feature of illustrative woodcuts of the queen.

The figuring of unofficial royal portraits as deformed in such ways carried particular weight in the earliest years of Elizabeth's reign, when concerns about her health and fertility were already high. The recent deaths of the young queen's royal siblings left her the sole surviving direct heir of the sickly Tudor line. Worries about her own viability had reached a panic stage only the year before as she suffered from a near-fatal case of small-pox. This concern in turn prompted added pressure upon Elizabeth to produce children, pressure from the 1563 Parliament as well as from the members of her Privy Council who nervously recalled their inability to agree upon a successor during the crisis of her illness. Whether repre-sented as monstrous offspring or as sickness-marred visages, unofficial images of the queen were thus assimilated into anxious discussion of the royal succession, where they were cast among such other threats to queen and kingdom as fatal pregnancies, foreign assassins, and domestic traitors.

In thinking about those unofficial portraits which survived such stren-uous efforts of censorious control, it is important to be aware that they represented acts of defiance not only of these rhetorical impositions. The makers of subversive images were subject to considerable risk of punish-ment, including not only the confiscation and destruction of the offending works, but the loss of reputation and liberty. The more explicit and harsh a critique of the queen, the more necessary therefore that the critic should be shielded from discovery by the spies and informers employed by her "officers and ministers." It should not surprise us when examples of anti-Elizabethan portraiture were hidden in unpublished manuscripts, and circulated among a limited and identifiable audience of their makers' acquaintance. In the pages that follow, I consider two such examples, each of which mocks the official equation of criticism with monstrousness by reversing its implications and "deforming" the queen's image.

Early in 1580 Philip Sidney famously absented himself from Elizabeth's court for a period of "rustication" at the country house of his sister Mary, the Countess of Pembroke. Sometime during the next year or so of internal exile, Sidney completed the manuscript of a lengthy politically charged fiction known as the *Old Arcadia* (to distinguish it from his much-revised *New Arcadia* of 1584).[2] This work was not published, and seems not to have been intended for an audience beyond the circle of readers surrounding Mary.[3]

Critical discussion of the *Old Arcadia* has regularly alleged that the four Eclogues which interrupt the pastoral romantic narrative of the Duke Basilius and his two daughters operate as a critical commentary on Eliz-abethan court culture and its politics.[4] It is not necessary, before developing this allegation further, to decide just how directly the motivation for such a critique might have arisen from Sidney's own recent experience as an opponent of Elizabeth's plan to marry the French duc d'Alençon. In a letter to the queen, datable approximately to October of 1579, Sidney had presented a series of objections to her plan, at once appealing to her own established general pattern of prudential decision making and detailing the particular faults of Alençon. Whether Sidney's subsequent absence from court was a precautionary move taken on his own initiative, or was mandated by the queen, or was simply a chronological coincidence, remains undetermined and perhaps undeterminable. But certainly as a witness to the queen's exaction of a harsh penalty against John Stubbs for having publicly attacked the marriage plan by writing and publishing *The Discoverie of a Gaping Gulf Whereinto England is Like to Be Swallowed by Another French Marriage*, Sidney would have been convinced of the present danger of forthright criticism.

The *Gaping Gulf* affair (so termed by Robert P. Adams in language designed to highlight its civic drama and notoriety)[5] seems to have taken political England by surprise. The queen's determination to make an example of Stubbs brooked no opposition, legal or rhetorical. On November 3, 1579, in the marketplace at Westminster, a cleaver was driven through Stubbs's right wrist with a heavy mallet. After removing his hat with his remaining hand, Stubbs declared his loyalty to Elizabeth (and was then conveyed to prison, where he remained until October of the next year). William Camden observed the crowd's reaction:

The Multitude standing about was deeply silent: either out of an Horrour at this newe and unwonted kind of Punishment; or else out of Commiseration towards the man, as being of an honest and unblameable Repute, or else out of Hatred of the Marriage, which most men presaged would be the Overthrow of Religion.[6]

Failing to reform Stubbs, Elizabeth chose brutally to deform him.

The dangerous circumstances in which would-be vocal critics of Elizabeth found themselves during the Alençon marriage negotiations are *not* reproduced in the setting of the *Old Arcadia*'s First Eclogues. Instead, Sidney's fiction imagines a setting in which a thoughtful critic is permitted to pronounce sharp commentary upon Arcadian political culture. Standing in for seriously endangered real-world critics like Stubbs is a "grave [Arcadian] shepherd" called Dicus. The only offense which Dicus risks is that of confounding the conventional timidity of his audience, his only punishment their conventional dismay. And indeed the shepherd's double portrait—both verbal and visual—of a monstrous composite Cupid, does shock the deferential sensibility of the gathered Arcadians, who hiss and stamp their feet, thinking Dicus "had spoken an unpardonable blasphemy."[7]

And it is true that the portrait of Cupid which emerges both in Dicus's verse eclogue and on the "painted table" which he wears on his breast is genuinely iconoclastic. Cupid is depicted here not as a god but as a "false knave." The portrait presents him in an original and peculiar "new form, making him sit upon a pair of gallows, like a hangman . . . painted all ragged and torn, so that his skin was bare in most places, where a man might perceive all his body full of eyes, his head horned with the horns of a bull, with long ears accordingly, his face old and wrinkled, and his feet cloven."[8] This portrait is not merely unflattering but in its chief elements demonic, a conclusion echoed in the eclogue: "His horned head doth seem the heav'n to spite: / His cloven foot doth never tread aright."[9]

With these last familiar anatomical cues, Dicus implies that those who worship this monstrous composite Cupid are idolatrous minions of the devil, and this accusation is underwritten by the composite imagery itself.[10] Demonic composites played a well-established role in the satirical iconography of reformation and counterreformation illustrated polemic. In the simplest and most straightforward of examples, a pair of horns were pinned to a portrait head. But even in much more complexly allegorized scenes, such as those simultaneously depicting several episodes in which gargoylean eccentricities and Brueghelesque intricacies of invention elaborated the symbolic weight of demonic association, the same fundamental notion was conveyed: that when one's opponents in the controversy spoke, they did so as mouthpieces of Satan.

Examples of demonic composite forms were available in widely circulated prints. To the head of an ass might be appended a woman's torso, a pair of heavily scaled legs, one hoof, one hooked claw, one stump, and a thick tail ending in a dragon's mouth. Johannes Cochläus's 1529 "Martinus Lutherus Septiceps," for example, illustrates a particularly significant semantic feature of composite-creatures, namely the multiplication of particular organs or limbs; the reformer's seven heads suggest a multiplicity of conflicting loyalties, hence his unreliability and the incoherence of his identity.

Demonic composites such as these, most of them produced during the three decades prior to the reign of Elizabeth and in forms suitable for easy reproduction and wide distribution, represent a key source of monstrous imagery upon which later controversialists, including Sidney, were able to draw. By choosing to isolate Dicus—the honest shepherd willing to expose and decry the demonic monstrosities which other Arcadians have standardly affected not to notice—Sidney plays a politically pointed variation on the tale of the emperor's new clothes. Only Geron, another honorable shepherd, backs Dicus in his "blasphemous" accusations and braves the conventional silence of the Arcadian crowd, which included those "of great as of mean houses." With this defiance, moreover, Dicus challenges the views of Duke Basilius himself. The usual effect of the duke's presence at such performances, as the Arcadian narrator describes it, was to "[animate] the shepherds the more exquisitely to seek a worthy accomplishment of his good liking."[11] But Dicus confounds this expectation. He offers his "invective song" not only in contrast to the waste of poetic wit and energy which had preceded it, but as an explicit corrective to the duke's noncomprehending laughter at the graphic image of the monstrous Cupid:

Dicus, as if it had been no jesting matter, told him plainly that long they had done the heavens wrong to make Cupid a god, and much more to the fair Venus to call him her son—indeed, the bastard of false Argus, who, having the charge of her deflowered Io (what time she was a cow), had *traitorously* in that shape begot him of her; and that the naughtiness of men's lust had given him so high a title.[12] [Italics added.]

Dicus's diagnosis features a developing analysis of the self-regarding motives of idolatry. It begins with a solemn indictment of those who would lightly invoke the divine pantheon as an appropriate site for an unworthy candidate. But the stakes are then raised further when mention of treason translates the wrongdoing into the civic realm of complicity with a political evil.

Sidney invented the tale of the illicit and traitorous coupling of Argus with Io, but the theme of "contrary couplings" had been taken up by

Stubbs in the *Gaping Gulf,* addressing the threat to England's interests implicit in the Alençon match. The marriage of Elizabeth to a popish prince, Stubbs charged, would be as "ugly before God and his angels [as if] an Hebrew should marry a Canaanite." Citing St. Paul, Stubbs deplored the prospective marriage as a "contrary coupling together" reminiscent of "the uneven yoking of the clean Oxe to the unclean Asse, a thing forbidden in the lawe."[13] In a more grotesque example, Stubbs invoked the unnatural mating of a lion and a toad, a coupling derived from the fleur-de-lis in Elizabeth's coat of arms and the "old French coat of crawling toads."[14] Dicus's revelation of a profane, indeed criminal, composite lineage for Cupid rebuffs those courtly flatterers who had not only offered idolatrous comparisons of Elizabeth with figures of deity, but in so doing had condoned a betrayal of England's welfare.

Still another twist remains in Dicus's analysis. This consists in detecting lust at the motivational root of the unseemly (and absurd) elevation of Cupid to the status of a god. With this accusation, Sidney exposes the charade of the Petrarchan conventions in terms of which Elizabeth expected her flattery to be framed.[15] The collusion of poets and painters in the deification of Cupid / Elizabeth is targeted in the opening lines of the shepherd's eclogue itself:

> Poor painters oft with silly poets join
> To fill the world with strange but vain conceits:
> One brings the stuff, the other stamps the coin,
> Which breeds naught else but glosses of deceits.[16]

By the time Sidney went to work on the *Old Arcadia,* Elizabethan court poets and painters had long collaborated in celebrating the queen's alleged divinity. The most germane single example, both because of the subject of its own allegorical scheme and because it was so prominently displayed in Whitehall Palace after its completion in 1569, is Hans Eworth's portrait of "Elizabeth I and the Three Goddesses" (figure 1). In this monumental painting, Elizabeth is glorified as the true winner in a contest with Juno, Minerva, and Venus (at whose knee stands Cupid, naked and young as in the conventional representations disputed by Dicus). The queen is depicted trumping the individual virtues of the goddesses with the rarer combination of her own.

Roy Strong's suggestion about the political valence of this work helps

Figure 1. "Elizabeth I and the Three Goddesses," 1569. Attributed to Hans Eworth (1520–1574?). *Courtesty of Royal Collection Enterprises.*

to explain the grounds of Sidney's hostility toward the efforts of court artists to influence the queen's decision making by exalting her:

In concept [this portrait] relates directly and closely to the type of emblematic drawings which appear in Hoefnagel's *Patientia,* a book of allegorical drawings with Dutch, French, and Spanish verses which Radermacher commissioned in the same year. The position it was accorded on the walls of Whitehall, where it was to be seen by all visitors to the palace, must have contributed to the increasing frequency of allegorical and emblematic elements—totally absent before 1569— as a feature of royal portraiture. What is also important is that the cult, in terms of allegorical portraiture, began not within the native tradition but within that of the Protestant exiles: for them Elizabeth's role as the leader of Protestant Europe was already greater than that as mere ruler of the small impoverished kingdom of England.[17]

A decade later, with marriage to Alençon a distinct and much-feared possibility, Sidney must have wondered whether Elizabeth was even determined to maintain her hold on her small kingdom.

The eclogue of Dicus, thus interpreted as political commentary, exposes the vanity of hoping to prevail upon the queen by flattering her, however mightily. By portraying the process of composite-making itself as one which produces monsters, Dicus moreover mocks the logical absurdity of figuring Elizabeth as a composite of all princely excellences. The relevant lines from the eclogue sardonically express Sidney's jaded insight into "state" portraiture: "Yet bears [Cupid] still his parents' stately gifts, / A horned head, cloven feet, and thousand eyes."[18]

The *Old Arcadia*, as noted earlier, is a work which its author did not seek to publish, and the response *within* the work itself to Dicus's assault on celebratory allegorization reveals much about Sidney's reluctance to risk a general public audience for it. The critical thrust of Dicus's eclogue prompts another young shepherd called Histor immediately to warn "with great vehemency . . . all hearers to take heed how they seemed to allow any part of [Dicus's] speech against so revengeful a god as Cupid, who had even in his first magistracy showed against Apollo the heat of his anger."[19] The relevance of official sanction against unpleasing images is emphasized by Histor's choice of the context of "magistracy" as a metaphor for the threat posed by Cupid's anticipated displeasure.

By linking the motif of monstrosity with the sanctions available for the enforcement of official displeasure, Sidney was also echoing the dilemma which, as author, he described himself as suffering in the prefatory letter dedicating the *Old Arcadia* to his sister:

[I]t is done only for you, only to you; if kept to yourself, or to such friends who will weigh errors in the balance of goodwill, I hope, for the father's sake, it will be pardoned, perchance made much of though it have deformities. . . . a young head not so well stayed as I would it were (and shall be when God will) having many fancies begotten in it, if it had not been in some way delivered, would have grown a monster, and more sorry I might be that they came in than that they gat out. But his chief safety shall be his not walking abroad.[20]

The language of "error" and "deformity" with which Sidney here describes his authorial motives echoes the 1563 royal proclamation in which concern was expressed for the grief of those of the queen's subjects prone to "take great offence with the errors and deformities" of unofficial portraits.

Persecution of errors and deformities in royal representation, the polit-

ical valence of "contrary couplings" in the period 1578–81, the vengeful-
ness of official magistracy, and accusations of treason against loyal cit-
izens: it is the invocation of these particular politically charged matters in
the *Old Arcadia*'s First Eclogues which have led me to conclude that
Sidney's monstrous Cupid is not merely his own vivid contribution to the
anti-Petrarchanism of the early 1580s, but an anti-Petrarchan trope turned
anti-Elizabethan caricature.

I turn now to a second example of monstrous composite-imagery. Like
Sidney's, it mocks the imposition of constraints upon Elizabeth's representation. Unlike Sidney's, however, its satire is pictorial rather than verbal.
This second composite monster is found in the manuscript of a late-
sixteenth-century poem by William Wodwall chronicling major events in
the reign of Queen Elizabeth through the year 1590.[21] This remarkable
pen-and-ink drawing (figure 2) depicts a hideous composite-bird.[22] The
manuscript, entitled *The Actes of Queene Elizabeth Allegorized*, recounts in
six cantos six major periods of religious and political controversy during
Elizabeth's reign: the Northern Rebellion, the Ridolfi plot, the Jesuit mission, the Babington conspiracy, a crisis of pride exemplified by sumptuary
excess, and the Armada. Wodwall interprets each crisis as the fulfillment of
a series of presignifying events, monstrous births prominent among them.
It is the crisis of pride which he illustrated with the monstrous fowl.

In its anatomical variety and the multiplication of its plumage ruffs,
this fowl retains features of the demonic aspect of reformation composite-
imagery. The use of birdlike devils was, moreover, familiar in illustrations
providing allegorical warnings against personal vanity. A woodcut from
the 1509 edition of Sebastian Brant's *The Ship of Fools* provides an example. Here a woman observing her image in a mirror is seated upon a plank
held up by the energies of a crouching demon, complete with three-
clawed toes and a sharply curved beak, and crowned with a hornlike crest
of plumed feathers.

Another source, native to England, upon which Wodwall may have
drawn is the well-populated ballad genre in which monstrous births,
including examples of individuals both human and animal born with
gross malformations, were interpreted as divine portents. A surviving example from c. 1570 described "A meruaylous straunge deformed
Swyne" imported from Denmark which possessed the fore parts of a

Figure 2. Pen-and-ink drawing from the manuscript
of William Wodwall's "Queen Elizabeth Allegorized,"
c. 1600. *Courtesy of the Bodleian Library, Oxford*
(MS. Eng. hist. e 198, fol. 85r).

swine, the ears of a lion, the hind parts of a ram, and misshapen clawlike
feet.[23] This may be compared to a prose broadside dated 1562 which
detailed the monstrous features of a pig littered near Hampstead:

It hath a head contrary to all other of that kynd; it hath a face without a nose or
eyes, sauing a hole standing directly betwen the two eares, which eares be broad
and long, lyke the eares of a bloude-hound, and a monstrous body, like vnto a
thing that were flean, without heare. It hath feet very monstrous with the endes of
them turned vpwards, lyke vnto forked endes.[24]

William Wodwall's caricature conforms in the incongruous combination of its head, body, and feet to the template of a ballad monster as

Figure 3. "Strange Birds in Lincolnshire," 1586. German woodcut illustration. *Courtesy of the British Library [1750.c.1(27)].*

established by the examples of the Denmark and Hampstead swine. Wodwall's fowl is also a creature "contrary to all other of [its] kynd." Its single eye is deeply hooded, as would be typical of a bird of prey. The dagger-shaped bill which extends from its chin and throat, however, most resembles those of such carnivorous aquatic birds as terns, grebes, and herons; the threateningly curved raptorial claws of the bird's feet echo this predatory aspect. The bill and eye together, abstracted from the layered ruffs in which they are embedded, suggest the profile of a stork. Contained within the two topmost layers of the bird's gaudy plumage are what appear to be pointed blades or armorial spikes, each centered against a single symmetrical feather. The overall impression made by this image arises from the juxtaposition of two distinguishable patterns of features. On the one hand, this is a creature of dense and elaborate decorative plumage, a creature of fashion; on the other, it is a creature of formidably threatening weapons, both offensive and defensive.

The fantastically large and layered rufflike plumage, which extends entirely around the bird's neck and is distributed in three distinct layers, corresponds to the elaborate multiply tiered ruffs of late Elizabethan fashion. Indeed, this plumage seems to parody the multiplication of sharply tipped layers of ruffs, decorated with slashes and spots, in portraits of the queen and other women beginning about 1585. Through the use of starch and setting-sticks, ruffs of this period could be stacked up in as many as three tiers and could be made wide enough to seem like fanning wings. As several studies of late Elizabethan elegant costume have concluded, the fashion of wearing such birdlike ruffs persisted in the face of vociferous protest. Phillip Stubbes, in his 1585 *Anatomy of Abuses,* notoriously alleged that the ruff had been invented by the devil himself.

The wit of Wodwall's drawing lies particularly in its innovative turn on the conventional moralizing of the monster ballad genre. The main part of such a ballad would usually be devoted to detailed reports of the deformities of the creature, with only the concluding verses rehearsing a standard call for the most generalized of public reforms and the long survival of the queen and her government in spite of a sinning and unrepentant citizenry. The ballad of the monstrous Danish pig is entirely typical in this respect, closing with the lines: "God grant our gracious souerain queen / Long ouer vs may raigne; / And this life past, with Christ our Lord / Heauens ioyes she may attaine!"[25]

Ballad number 23 in the Shirburn collection,[26] however, provides an example in which the moralizing ambition has quite overwhelmed the reporting. The resulting shift in this ballad's object of critique is suggested by the title: "Pryde's fall: or a warning to all *English* women, by the example of a strang monster, borne of late in *Germany* by a proude marchant's wife in the city of *Geneua.*" Spoken from the point of view of the chastened merchant's wife herself, this work narrates a downfall from youthful insouciance and vanity:

My beauty made me thinke
myselfe an Angell bright,
Framèd of heauenly moulde,
and not an earthly wight.
For my soule's happynes
(God's holy bible booke),
I had my lookinge glasse
where I most pleasure tooke. (verse 4)

Later verses proceed to describe a royally pampered pregnancy:

No cost was spar'd, that might
stand me in any steed.
My nurses, young and fayre,
fyt for a royal Queene,
Gaue all attendance there,
as it was dayly seene. . . .
Never had marchant's wife
of Ladyes such a traine. (verses 8 and 9)

Soon there appears the scourge of the monstrous birth itself:

It had two faces strange,
and two heads paynted fayre;
On the browes, curlèd lockes
such as our wantons weare.
One hand held right the shape
of a fayre lokcing glasse,
In which I tooke delight
how my vaine beauty was.
Right the shape of a rod,
scorginge me for my synne. (verses 10 and 11)[27]

Subsequent verses describe the ruffs with which this monstrous creature was born endowed ("About the necke, flaunting ruffes / it had most gallantlye, / Starchèd with whyte and blewe / seemely vnto the eye") and the red roses which decorated the insteps of its "pinckèd shoes."

These verses were printed with an accompanying woodcut whose two faces may be thought to resemble that of Elizabeth herself. Many of the woodcut's details were left unmentioned in the text, except under the covering line "Every part had the shape / of fashions daylye worne." Details thus unspecified in the text include the pair of scaly tails which seem to hang from the monster's lower back, the human face inset at its navel, and the hooded third eye set in the forehead of each of its faces. All of these pictorial elements have precedents in composite-demon iconography. But more important than that for interpreting Wodwall's composite-bird in the context of an attack on court fashion is the association between fashion excesses and composite-imagery. The spiked ruff attached at the neck of the monster's right head in the "Pryde's fall" woodcut immediately recalls the sharp spikes of the Wodwall fowl's own triple-ruff.

Interpreted in the context of protest against the elaboration of dress in courtly and royal portraiture at the time of his manuscript's composition, Wodwall's drawing may be understood in either of two complementary ways. It may stand as a unique generic innovation in which the monster ballad, with its conventional praise of the queen, has been subverted by conflating the report of a monster with the identification of the queen *as* such a monster. Alternatively, the drawing may operate as an instance of what Wodwall knew to be a recognizable generic counter-convention in which the type of illustration ordinarily attached to a monster ballad would be recognized as a more generalized expression of sociopolitical dissent. As in the contre-blason, where the conventional aim of celebrating (by anatomizing) the harmonious virtues or beauties of the beloved is deliberately subverted with a sequence of incongruous and individually horrific details, the Wodwall drawing turns the elaborately gowned portrait against its type, making a monstrous bird-woman out of the elements and associations of fashionable dress.

In 1948, George Orwell and Reginald Reynolds described the drawing as a "daring caricature of the Queen as an old lady, satirising at the same time her love of fine clothes and the fashions of the period."[28] The text of Wodwall's *Actes* does not seem to me, however, to support so direct an interpretation of the caricature's target. (The words "Queene Elizabeth Allegorized" appear as part of the poem's title—which is displayed across the top of every facing pair of manuscript pages—and do not seem to have been specially repositioned to serve as a label for the drawing.) As an application of the image's general satire against prideful display, its critique would nonetheless extend to the queen's own exemplary portraiture.

It is worthwhile emphasizing the remarkable explicitness with which Wodwall's drawing, so interpreted, targets such display as an object of satirical representation. Vanity is represented in a mode associated with monstrous births and as such subjected to the weight of portentous associations which such births were standardly made to bear. A style of dress characteristic of the emblematic iconography of the queen's official portraits is ridiculed. By supplying the parodic image with a daggerlike beak, spiked head-feathers, and threatening claws, a charge of fierce intolerance is added to the critique. Neither turkey nor stork, neither fish nor (any single) fowl, but a foul crossing of species, Wodwall's composite-bird is not only grotesque but dangerous as well, not only a horror but a harpy.

So interpreted, the drawing protests the excesses of royal eulogists and censors alike. One surviving image of Elizabeth in particular seems representative of the celebratory portrait type which the message of the Wodwall fowl could have challenged. This is the full-length oversize portrait delivered to Elizabeth Hardwick, Countess of Shrewsbury, in 1599. Produced in the royal workshop of Nicholas Hilliard, the painting is noteworthy for its employment of the deliberately inaccurate "Mask of Youth." This formalized facial pattern was mandated during the final decade of the queen's reign in preference to depictions which represented her likeness in a more realistic manner.

Roy Strong has drawn attention to the outmoded aesthetic represented by the "Hardwick" portrait.[29] An understanding of how the embroidered imagery of the gown works would seem to depend upon a familiarity with the use of monstrous composite-images to mock the queen. Royal embroiderers regularly turned to the natural world for motifs with which to embellish the brilliant fabrics of Elizabeth's gowns, as in the botanical imagery of the one she wears in the "Welbeck Portrait" of c. 1590. But the menagerie of beasts, real and imaginary, which populate the queen's skirt and bodice in the "Hardwick" painting are unmatched, in number and variety, elsewhere in the catalog of her portraits. The bolder creatures strut, soar, and sport across the broad surfaces of the "Hardwick" gown, while the mildest peer from its folds. In one detail (figure 4) of the gown, no fewer than five naturalistically precise representations of birds, as well as two flying insects (a golden moth, an iridescent-winged butterfly), and

Figure 4. The "Hardwick" Portrait of Queen Elizabeth (detail), 1599(?).
Workshop of Nicholas Hilliard. *Courtesy of the National Trust Photographic
Library.*

a toothy sea-monster (above and to the left of the queen's wrist) can be found. The overall effect is at once lively and reassuring, the ferocity of water-dragons and other predators invariably muted with hints of a grin, and showy displays of flower and vine providing refuge and cover for the more delicate and vulnerable members of this peaceable kingdom.

A design so patently allegorical offers a relatively rare opportunity for extensive and systematic interpretation. The abundance of birds in the design provides a natural point of departure for this effort, for Elizabeth's personal imagery had long featured them. The phoenix and the pelican, important as emblems of regeneration and self-sacrifice respectively, had been introduced as early as 1575 to signify the constant devotion of the heirless queen to the welfare of her people. Both these birds were featured prominently thereafter in Elizabeth's own jewelry and in medallions produced as mementos of her favor. In visual and literary contexts, other celebratory conceits were of course common as well. Elizabeth was standardly compared—for her beauty—to a rose, a star, or the moon, and—for the rarity of her virtues—to a pearl or unicorn; but comparison between the queen and the phoenix seems to have been more widespread than any other of these celebratory tropes. The court panegyrist Thomas Churchyard made regular use of it, as early as 1578 in the entertainment which celebrated Elizabeth's progress to Suffolk and Norfolk, and again repeatedly in several poems of his 1593 *Challenge.* Elkin Calhoun Wilson identified a number of broadside ballads utilizing the phoenix figure to praise the queen. More than a dozen examples can be drawn from the literature of courtly encomia as well, representing the works of writers including John Lyly, Thomas Nashe, George Whetstone, and Nicholas Breton.[30] The aviary of the "Hardwick" gown embroidery seems to extend this pattern of incorporating birds into the imagery of royal celebration, making of the queen's body-on-display a world inhabited with swans, tanagers, darters, cuckoos, and the like.

That this should be a world in which fiercer creatures also dwell compounds the interest of the gown's program. Frances Yates's study of the queen's Astraea cult draws on a source whose import may be extended to interpretation of the wide variety of sea-monsters which share the space of the "Hardwick" gown with flying birds and insects. The following passage from Giordano Bruno's 1584 *La Cena de la Ceneri* provides a clue to the significance of ocean-dwelling life in the queen's iconography:

Of Elizabeth I speak, who by her title and royal dignity is inferior to no other monarch in the world. . . . If her earthly territory were a true reflection of the width and grandeur of her spirit this great Amphitrite would bring far horizons within her girdle and enlarge the circumference of her dominion to include not only Britain and Ireland but some new world, as vast as the universal frame.[31]

Elizabeth's claim to imperial dominion over the seas which separated England from Ireland and from New World lands is implicit in Bruno's allusion to Amphitrite; the "Hardwick" gown in its turn offers a visual illustration of this claimed dominion, one which extends beyond the queen's more familiar oceanic associations with pearls and the tide-influencing moon to encompass and master any hostile creatures which may rise into view on the world's varied surfaces.

The program of the "Hardwick" portrait's bestiary can in this way be assimilated to those of other late Elizabethan allegorical state paintings. The better-known "Ditchley" and "Rainbow" portraits, for example, each represent spectacularly elaborated fantasies of the queen's mastery over real and potential opposition. In the former work, the queen's gigantic proportions associate her with cosmic control of the elements of sunshine and thunder, and locate her in a "universal frame" to which she alone has access. The "Rainbow" portrait, likewise the work of the court allegorist Marcus Gheeraerts, promotes the "Mask of Youth" face pattern into an ethereal realm of ageless beauty; but on the sublunary side, the multiple ears and eyes it pictures on the queen's gown remind viewers of the queen's "intelligencers," the agents who supplied her with information.[32]

Like the "Rainbow" and the "Ditchley," the "Hardwick" portrait is an image of dominance, representing Elizabeth as having status and resources sufficient to overwhelm any challenge to her authority. Bruno's claim that the queen would bring "far horizons within her girdle" is literalized in the "Hardwick" gown's bloodless bestiary, wherein many species of wild and free-flying birds and several types of monstrous predators are reconciled, coexisting in a mutually good-humored harmony which serves to decorate the wide world of the queen's royal body itself. The programmatic imagery of this state portrait shows the queen wearing the same imperial crown as the wooden lion which surmounts the throne to her right, and she remains similarly at ease among the lesser beasts—the birds and monsters—of her own kingdom. Wild and threatening as these creatures might at first appear, the queen masters them. They cannot escape partial occlusion in the folds of her gown. Rise above the oceans or raise up their wings as they may, they cannot move until she moves. All creatures are thus reconciled under the queen's domain, the frightening monsters defanged, the free-flying birds constrained by the limits of the world-wide spaces she encompasses. The illusory "Mask of Youth" is here conjoined with an equally illusory gown of peace.

The "Hardwick" portrait's exercise in the control of royal iconography should not guide us only to identify the official vision and viewpoint which Elizabeth and her image-makers wished to have displayed. It should also prompt us to recognize critical representations of the queen which the "Hardwick" portrait's visual program of pacific birds and monsters sought to neutralize. Such a program, calculated in its imagery and displayed as a show of royalist orthodoxy, would supplement the official proclamation of sanctions against "unreformed" unofficial royal image-makers.

Such sanctions yielded cautiously articulated responses from both Philip Sidney and William Wodwall, each of whom revealed his frankly deformed image to a restricted audience. But having granted that the productions of these two dissidents remained in limited circulation (hence protected from confiscation and available to us today), we may explore the possibility that they represent the exceptional survivors of a wider and more public strain of dissent against the Elizabethan court's control of the queen's image.

Notes

My thanks to anonymous readers at Duke University Press and at Oxford University Press, whose queries and suggestions contributed greatly to my research and to revision of this essay. In particular I acknowledge with gratitude the Duke Press reader who referred me to the 1586 German report of "Strange Birds in Lincolnshire" printed by Georg Lang.

1. Cited in Bernard Denvir, *From the Middle Ages to the Stuarts: Art, Design, and Society before 1689* (New York: Longman, 1988), 124.

2. For these datings, I follow the conclusion of Jean Robertson, ed., *Sir Philip*

Sidney: "The Countess of Pembroke's Arcadia" ("The Old Arcadia") (Oxford: Clarendon Press, 1973), xv–xvii. Katherine Duncan-Jones, Sidney's most recent scholar-biographer, concluded that while much of the *Old Arcadia* was written "during the spring and summer of 1580 . . . , many of the Eclogue poems were already written by 1580, though perhaps not yet fully framed or organized" (*Sir Philip Sidney, Courtier Poet* [New Haven: Yale University Press, 1991], 174–76).

3. This audience may have constituted a coterie in the sense influentially articulated by Arthur Marotti in his *John Donne, Coterie Poet* (Madison: University of Wisconsin Press, 1986).

4. For a discussion of the reception history of Sidney's two Arcadias as politically charged texts, see Annabel Patterson, *Censorship and Interpretation: The Conditions of Writing and Reading in Early Modern England* (Madison: University of Wisconsin Press, 1984), 36–51.

5. Robert P. Adams, "Opposed Tudor Myths of Power: Machiavellian Tyrants and Christian Kings," in *Studies in the Continental Background of Renaissance English Literature: Essays Presented to John L. Lievsay,* ed. Dale J. B. Randall and George Walton Williams (Durham, N.C.: Duke University Press, 1977), 78.

6. William Camden, *The History of the Most Renowned and Victorious Princess Elizabeth,* ed. Wallace T. MacCaffrey (Chicago: University of Chicago Press, 1970), 138–39.

7. Robertson, ed., *Sir Philip Sidney: "The Countess of Pembroke's Arcadia,"* 65.

8. Ibid. The wearing of such an image, which is for Dicus an act of mock-fealty, parodies the court practice of proclaiming loyalty through the display of royal medallions, painted miniatures of the queen, and her favored color schemes.

9. Ibid., 66.

10. Composites form a portion of the category of grotesques. In a useful brief account of Tudor pictorial grotesques, David Evett distinguishes herms, masks, motifs of vegetation, and monsters. Within the last of these categories can be found deformed human beings, deformed animals, and, finally, individual portraits which combine anatomical features ordinarily distributed among individuals of several distinct types or species. It is this final subcategory to which I refer as composites here.

11. Robertson, ed., *Sir Philip Sidney: "The Countess of Pembroke's Arcadia,"* 56.

12. Ibid., 64–65. For the originality of this representation of Cupid's lineage, see Robertson, 429–30.

13. Lloyd E. Berry, ed., *John Stubbs' "Gaping Gulf" with Letters and Other Relevant Documents* (Charlottesville: University Press of Virginia, 1968), 6 ff.

14. Ibid., 67.

15. Important early studies in this now well worn trail of investigation include Leonard Forster, *The Icy Fire: Five Studies in European Petrarchism* (Cambridge: Cambridge University Press, 1969); Stephen Greenblatt, *Sir Walter Raleigh: The Renaissance Man and His Roles* (New Haven: Yale University Press, 1973), and Louis Adrian Montrose, " 'Eliza, Queene of shepheardes,' and the Pastoral of Power," *English Literary Renaissance* 10, no. 2 (Spring 1980): 153–82, and " 'Shaping Fantasies': Figurations of Gender and Power in Elizabethan Culture," *Representations* 1, no. 2 (Spring 1983): 61–94.

16. Robertson, ed., *Sir Philip Sidney: "The Countess of Pembroke's Arcadia,"* 65.

17. Roy Strong, *Gloriana: The Portraits of Queen Elizabeth I* (New York: Thames and Hudson, 1987), 69.

18. Robertson, ed., *Sir Philip Sidney: "The Countess of Pembroke's Arcadia,"* 65.

19. Ibid., 66. Histor's tale of the disastrous love of princess Erona of Lydia, which itself illustrates the political chaos brought about by cupidinous love in a person of royal status, makes up the only significant digression in the whole of the *Old Arcadia*. With this held in mind, Histor's earlier warning looks very much more like a protest against the *directness* of Dicus's critique of Cupid than like a disagreement with its critical *content*.

20. Ibid., 3. While the text of this letter was first printed with Fulke Greville's 1590 quarto edition of the *New Arcadia*, which had been left incomplete at Sidney's death in 1586, the letter's cautionary content seems to me to tie it to the unpublished *Old Arcadia*. (Annabel Patterson notes the "obvious conflict between the discretion involved in the letter, the emphasis on the text's 'safetie' in 'not walking abroad,' and its appearance as the preface to a *published* work," [*Censorship*, 35].) A further difficulty in accepting the letter's link to the 1590 edition is that the letter does not even hint at the radical incompleteness of that text, which Sidney apparently abandoned in mid sentence, part of the way through the third of an expected five books.

21. So far as I have been able to determine, little is known about Wodwall, who is not mentioned in the *Dictionary of National Biography*. Sixteenth-century readers of his poem, the manuscript of which takes up 111 small quarto pages, may not have extended much beyond the circle of those who contributed its commendatory verses. It was briefly described by John Bruce in a contribution to

Notes and Queries in 1869. The manuscript was acquired by the Bodleian Library, Oxford, in 1939, where its shelf mark is MS. Eng. hist. e. 198.

22. The legend printed at the bottom edge of the drawing refers to a ballad in which the significance of the fate of this particular composite was elaborated: "Seaven of these foules or byrds were found and taken in Lyncolnsherre, at Croley, 1588, whereof foure died in shorte space after they were taken, the other three lyved longer, as it is to see in the ballet printed of them." I have not been able to identify any ballad, either by surviving text or by title, which mentions or treats any such material. Nor can I shed light from other sources on the geographical specificity of the legend's assertion that such fowl were found "in Lycolnsherre, at Croley." My review of local historical records has revealed no special associations or memorable happenings in connection either with the small town of Crowle in north Lincolnshire nor that of Crawley in nearby Bedfordshire. There is, however, a German print image of a bird, dated 1586, which illustrates an extended prose account of "Frembden vogeln" found in "Engelandt in der Grosschaft von Licolne" (figure 3). This image, while far more naturalistic, is sufficiently like Wodwall's drawing that it must be considered a possible source for his report of the discovery of strange fowl at Croley. If this is so, then in addition to changing the year from 1586 to 1588, Wodwall rendered his source image more threatening by substituting bladelike spikes for simple quills, less birdlike by simplifying the creature's facial features and plumage, and altogether abstracted from any terrestrial setting by eliminating the planted and stony ground on which the German bird stands.

23. Joseph Lilly, *A Collection of Seventy-nine Black-Letter Ballads and Broadsides Printed in the Reign of Queen Elizabeth between the Years 1559 and 1597* (London: Joseph Lilly, 1867), 186–87.

24. Ibid., 112.

25. Ibid., 189–90.

26. The extant copy of Shirburn 23 is part of the Huth Collection of broadside ballads in the British Library (collection number and shelf mark 28).

27. Andrew Clark, ed., *The Shirburn Ballads, 1585–1616, Edited from the MS* (Oxford: Clarendon, 1907), 134–38.

28. *British Pamphleteers, Volume One: From the Sixteenth Century to the French Revolution* (London: Allan Wingate, 1948), 262. I am grateful to Scott Lucas for drawing this volume to my attention.

29. Strong, *Gloriana*, 150.

30. Hyder Edward Rollins, *The Phoenix Nest* (Cambridge, Mass.: Harvard University Press, 1953), x.

31. Francis A. Yates, *Astraea: The Imperial Theme in the Sixteenth Century* (Boston: ARK Paperbacks, 1985), 85–86.

32. Strong has supplied this persuasive interpretation, citing Henry Peacham's translation from Cesare Ripa's emblem handbook, *Iconologia*, the first edition of which appeared in 1593: "Be seru'd with eies, and listening eares of those, / Who can from all partes giue intelligence / To gall his foe, or timely to prevent / At home his malice, and intendiment." *Gloriana*, 159.

Bones of Contention

Posthumous Images of Elizabeth and Stuart Politics

Julia M. Walker

Two posthumous representations of Elizabeth from the 1620s, Thomas Cecil's engraving of a youthful queen in armor (figure 1) and Marcus Gheeraerts's painting of an aged Elizabeth with Time and Death (figure 2), give us evidence of an imaginative and political opposition between which other posthumous representations of the queen can be read. These two portraits provide a key to the multivalency of Elizabeth's image in the third Stuart decade, showing how potent a marker for political commentary Elizabeth remained. As James tried to arrange a Spanish marriage for his son Charles, the various reactions of a number of factions in English politics are interestingly concentrated in these two images of the dead queen. In the Cecil print the gloriously armed queen subdues the seven-headed beast of Revelation, a monster which is visually linked to the Spanish Armada depicted in the background: a political stance which recalls the dangers of Spain and thus implicitly opposes the Spanish match. The Gheeraerts portrait, on the other hand, is a deliberate parody of the 1588 Armada portrait (figure 3), a record of one of Elizabeth's greatest triumphs. In the portrait of the 1620s the queen is no longer triumphant and powerful, but old, tired, indeed clearly dead. This portrait unmakes the composition and iconography of the Armada portrait, arguing with striking visual effect that the age of Elizabeth is long past and that those who form new paradigms of power should not seek for her precedents in the dust of the tomb. That both the royalist and populist factions turned to images of Elizabeth to make a statement about the proposed Spanish marriage of Charles Stuart gives evidence of just how powerful a political icon the queen remained, even two decades after her death.

The heart of this reading of two posthumous representations of Elizabeth I lies in the disparity between the royal revision of her position in English history, best exemplified by the removal of her body from under

Figure 1. Truth Presents the Queen with a Lance, c. 1622. Thomas Cecil print. *Courtesy of the British Museum.*

the altar of the Henry VII Chapel in Westminster Abbey and its relocation in the marginal space of the north aisle, and the populist celebration of her reign evinced by the memorials in parish churches within the City of London. These well-thought-out and significantly documented representations of the dead queen provide the larger cultural and historical context for my reading of two images of Elizabeth from the 1620s, the first a luxury product for the nobility, unique and not widely circulated, while the second is a more populist artifact, mass-produced and thus more widely known. Like the memorial texts, the two images show us that the split between discrete royal dissing and populist praise of the queen continued from 1606 through the 1620s.

    In the removal of Elizabeth's body from its place of priority under the main altar of the Henry VII Chapel of Westminster Abbey and the relocation of her body with that of her sister Mary in a joint grave in the north

Figure 2. Elizabeth with Time and Death, c. 1622. Attributed to Marcus Gheeraerts, oil on panel. *Courtesy of the Methuen Collection, Corsham Court.*

aisle of that chapel,[1] we see the most lasting, powerful, and ultimately public representation of the deceased queen's identity.[2] The author of this revisionist history through monuments, James had himself buried under the altar with the first Tudor, Henry VII, after erecting a literally concrete version of his own claim to the throne by building an enormous monument to his own mother, Mary Stuart, and placing her tomb in the south aisle of the chapel along with Margaret Beaufort (mother of Henry VII) and James's own paternal grandmother, the Countess of Lennox. In the

Figure 3. Elizabeth I: The Armada portrait, 1588(?). Attributed to George Gower, oil on panel. *By kind permission of the Marquess of Tavistock and the Trustees of the Bedford Estates.*

light of these successful architectural revisions, the words that James caused to be carved on Elizabeth's tomb bear careful reading, especially when compared to the texts appearing in memorials to the queen in London parish churches.

Of all the texts generated in response to the reign and person of Elizabeth I, the most literally lasting may be the texts James I caused to be carved on her tomb in Westminster Abbey. Distanced from the central monument of Henry VII and instead represented as being one with her sister and rival, Mary Tudor,[3] Elizabeth's tomb bears three Latin texts. Only a short Latin verse acknowledges Mary's presence in the tomb, although the substance of that verse would hardly have pleased either Tudor queen: "Partners both in throne and grave, here rest we two sisters, Elizabeth and Mary, in the hope of one resurrection." The more formal Latin epitaphs for Elizabeth appear at the head of the tomb, which is the south end:

AN ETERNAL MEMORIAL

Unto *Elizabeth* Queene of *England, France,* and *Ireland,* Daughter of
Henry the eighth, Grandchild to *Henry* the seventh, great Grandchilde
to King *Edward* the fourth, the Mother of this her country, the Nurse
of Religion and Learning; For a perfect skill in very many Languges,
for glorious Endowments, as well of minde as body, and for Regall
Vertues beyond her Sex
a Prince incomparable,
James, King of Great Britain, France and Ireland, heir of the virtues
and the reign,
piously erects this good monument

and at the foot of the tomb, also in Latin, we find:

Sacred unto Memory:
Religion to its primitive sincerity restored, *Peace* thoroughly settled, *Coine* to the
true value refined, *Rebellion* at home extinguished, *France* neere ruine by intestine
mischiefes relieved, *Netherland* supported, *Spaines* Armada vanquished, *Ireland*
with Spaniards expulsion, and *Traitors* correction quieted, both *Universities* Reve-
nues, by a Law of Provision, exceedingly augmented, Finally, all *England* en-
riched, and 45. yeares most prudently governed, *Elizabeth*, a Queene, a Con-
queresse, Triumpher, the most devoted to Piety, the most happy, after 70. yeeres
of her life, quietly by death departed.[4]

The words James caused to be carved on Elizabeth's newly marginalized
tomb are (literally) politically correct, if one overlooks the significance of
the tomb's revised location, the spacing of the phrase "Principi incom-
parabili," and the left-handed compliment about her gender. As a foreigner, replacing a popular monarch who had always and ever stressed
her Englishness, James needed to choose his words with care as he described both himself and the monarch whose death gave him the throne of
England. If gender and virginity were her weak points, nationality was
his, as we see in the change from "England" in the lines about Elizabeth to
"Great Britain" in the lines James tacked on about himself. Evidently,
even in 1606, he still needed this emphasis, just as he had in his 1604
speech to Parliament where Lancaster-York references were evidently
prompted by the resistance of the House of Commons to the idea of union
with Scotland under a Scots king.[5]

As a site of state ceremonies, Westminster Abbey—especially the Henry VII Chapel, the space most distant from the western entrance—is a fine record of royal and noble agendas; the people of London, however, would have had no influence on the monuments in the Abbey and very little if any occasion to see them. We must turn, therefore, to the parish churches to see the remains of Elizabeth as represented by her subjects. The Civil War, the Great Fire, the Blitz, and the IRA have sequentially removed all traces of memorials to Elizabeth in London parish churches. Fortunately, the 1633 edition of Stow's *Survey of London* is itself a sort of Elizabeth text, as it records all of the texts on all of the memorials to the queen in parish churches within the City of London. That these representations of Elizabeth are very different from those found in the semiprivate space of the Henry VII Chapel is telling. James's revision of Elizabeth had its effect within the court circles and dominates the larger frame of English history as read from monuments, but the parish church memorials—erected between 1607 and 1631—give us a reading of the queen more consistent with the representations produced in her lifetime than with those commissioned by her successor.

When we compare the two sorts of representation—the officially political and semiprivate and Latin with the populistly political and public and vernacular—we find informative differences. In only nine of the thirty-two churches listed do we find any direct reference to the official epitaphs, and those are always conflated and always translated and almost always shortened. There is some disagreement among scholars as to the earliest revival of Elizabeth's popularity after the political reality of a male monarch with children had ceased to be in itself a cause for uncritical populist approval. Neville Davies and others place the revival of Elizabeth's popularity around 1607, while Sir Roy Strong tells us that—after the flurry of images generated in 1603—the 1620s marked the next "revival of interest shown in her as reflected in the engravings. . . . There was little or none before that date as the country was entranced with the phenomenon of a royal family replacing a virgin queen. That revival coincided with the decline in popularity of Stuart rule and the outbreak of the Thirty Years War. Elizabeth then became a golden age ruler and the posthumous heroine of the Protestant cause."[6] Davies, however, quotes Bishop Goodman's account of celebrations of Elizabeth's accession day, arguing that as early as 1607 there "is evidence . . . some of it in plays and poems

that . . . the memory of Queen Elizabeth was being revived with affection."[7] Carole Levin, in her 1994 study of Elizabeth, has it both ways,
suggesting that the initial popularity and "mood of thanksgiving" following James's coronation lasted only a few years. Levin explains: "James'
Scottishness, his favorites, his extravagances, his policies, especially peace
with Spain, all led to dissatisfaction. Within two or three years of Elizabeth's death there began to be a nostalgia for 'good Queen Bess' and the
glories of her reign that swelled by the 1620's."[8] The later dates correspond with the dates listed in the 1633 edition of Stow's *Survey of London*[9]
for the restorations of the churches as they are listed.[10] The two greatest
drawbacks to Stow's listing, however, are that it does not say when the
memorial to Elizabeth was erected, giving only the date(s) for each
church's general restoration, nor does it mention where in the church the
memorial is placed.[11] The fact that only the 1633 edition of the *Survey* lists
the tomb texts can be used in support of their currency, but it could also
suggest that they had become such a conventional feature of churches that
they needed to be cataloged.

Of the thirty varied inscriptions in Stow's list, two sorts evince the
populist presentation of the Cecil print: those that speak of Elizabeth as a
warrior and those that speak of Elizabeth's immortality in a way which
passes conventional Christian discourse. Much less popular is Elizabeth's
famed learning. Only three of the memorials listed quote any version of
the problematic lines from the Westminster tomb. The memorial in St.
Anne Blackfryers praises her for "perfect skill in very many Languages,
for glorious Endowments, as well of mind as body, and for Regall Vertues
beyound her Sex."[12] Similarly, the monument in St. Martin's Vintry translates the end of the line: "inbuded with rare Ornaments of Body and
Minde, in all Princely Vertues above the Sex of Women."[13] Only slightly
more promising is the memorial in St. Mary le Bow, which adds the
ambiguously placed Westminster line: "A Prince incomparable,"[14] here
referring both visually and grammatically to Elizabeth. No other church
memorials evince the need to praise Elizabeth's intellectual accomplishments. Although six churches have a poem which refers to Elizabeth as
the "Queen of Armes, of Learning, Fate, and Chance,"[15] the phrasing
seems to group learning with the latter two entities, leaving only "Armes"
to be mentioned singularly.

To represent Elizabeth as a woman warrior while she was alive was a delicate proposition. Spenser, perhaps, comes the closest when he gives us Britomart in *The Faerie Queene*.[16] For all that we make much of the speech at Tilbury, we have no portraits of Elizabeth dressed in any form of armor during her lifetime. Even in the Armada portrait (1588) she is clad in one of the most elaborate of her fictive dresses, with a large pearl revising the iconic statement of her father's large codpiece (see figure 3).[17] After her death, however, we have the c. 1622 engraving entitled "Truth Presents the Queen with a Lance." Here Elizabeth is mounted on a war-horse, dressed in armor and holding a sword and shield in her left hand as she receives the said lance with her right. Behind her is the Armada victory, exactly as it is represented in the Armada portrait. It is this representation of Elizabeth as Amazon, barely acknowledged in the conventional words of the Westminster tomb, that we find significantly exaggerated in the London church memorials. In the twenty-two-line poem in St. Mildred's Breadstreet she is praised for both "Policy and Armes" which "Did all concurre / in her moste happy raigne, / to keepe Gods Church and us / from plotted harmes, / Contriv'd by Romish wits, / and force of Spaine." Along the same theme, the following poem was the single most popular on memorials, appearing in eleven[18] churches:

> Spaines rod, Romes ruine
> Netherlands reliefe,
> Heavens Jem, Earths Joy,
> Worlds wonder, Natures Chiefe.
> Britaines blessing, Englands splendor.
> Religions Nurse, the Faiths Defender.

Since "ruine" is not a rhyme word, we can infer that being "Spaines rod" was even more significant an accomplishment than having contributed to the "ruine" of Rome, although the two were certainly not unrelated in English minds. And in a poem which appeared only in All Hallowes at the Wall, the martial elements of Elizabeth's reign are even more specifically exaggerated.

> Read but her Reigne,
>   this Princesse might have beene
> For wisdome called
>   Nicaulis, Sheba's Queene,

Against Spaines Holifernes,
    Judeth shee,
Dauntlesse gain'd many
    a glorious victory:
Not Deborah did her
    in fame excell,
She was a Mother
    in our Israel.

An Hester, who
    her person did ingage,
To save her people
    from the publike strage;
Chaste Patronesse
    of true Religion,
In Court a Saint,
    in Field an Amaʒon,
Glorious in Life,
    deplored in her death,
Such was unparallel'd
    ELIZABETH. (emphasis mine)

Here her reign itself is represented as a text: "Read but her Reigne," the poem begins. Furthermore, the text of her reign is represented as being filled with allusions to biblical texts of women leaders—the Queen of Sheba, Judith, Deborah, Esther. Of course Elizabeth had been compared to these biblical women throughout her reign—indeed, Helen Hackett, in her 1995 study, states that "biblical heroines like Deborah and Judith dominated early Elizabethan royal iconography."[19] I would suggest, however, that this Judith reference moves beyond the boundaries of the conventional, or at least moves into another convention.

For a quick fix on what I'm suggesting to be two Judith paradigms, let us briefly digress back to two medieval French representations of the biblical character. In the thirteenth-century sculpture on the north portal of the cathedral at Chartres, there is an archivolt devoted to the Judith story. There, however, Judith is represented as a humble widow doing the will of the elders of the city, completing a task which was only possible for her because she was a beautiful woman. Later in the same century, when Blanche of Castile—who had been shown the newly completed Chartres sculptural program early in her marriage—collaborated with her son Louis IX on the stained glass for the Sainte-Chapelle, a much different representation was crafted. The Sainte-Chapelle windows graphically celebrate Judith's physical triumph over Holofernes; the bloody head is clearly visible both at the moment of decapitation and later—most unusually—displayed on the tip of Judith's sword. The archivolt at Chartres gives us a very different version of the story, with the most often reproduced voussoir figure being that of Judith kneeling, dressed in sackcloth, putting ashes on her head, the humble servant of the patriarchy who is never shown holding the head of the dead enemy.

While I am in no way arguing for any sort of influence between these two French representations of Judith and the various constructions of Elizabeth as a Judith figure, I do want to annex distinction between them. Early in her reign Elizabeth is the dutiful woman most unusually called on by God to serve her people in a public way. The Judith figure of the All Hallowes at the Wall memorial text, however, fits better the fierce paradigm I described from the Sainte-Chapelle windows. Both representations are based on the biblical narrative, but the choice of emphasis makes an enormous difference. In the memorial in All Hallowes at the Wall, Elizabeth is called a Judith who "Against Spains Holafernes . . . Dauntlesse gained many a glorious victory." Arguably the strongest female figure in Hebrew scripture (although banished from most Protestant Bibles before the seventeenth century), Judith is one of the very few women in the Western canon celebrated and revered for killing a man. To describe Elizabeth as a Judith who kills Holofernes is to go far beyond the more traditional biblical type of Deborah.[20] Deborah, of course, also went into battle, although she did not fight; and even the story of Esther, traditionally paired with the Judith narrative in medieval iconography, is here given more active overtones than the biblical text—if not popular tradition—will support, by the phrase "her person did ingage, To save her people." A martial reading of the text is made inescapable by the strongest lines in the poem; near the end of this memorial, Elizabeth is called "In Court a Saint, in Field an Amazon." This representation of the dead queen is so far removed from the formal language of the Westminster tomb that we cannot read it as merely popularized or simplified: this is corrective.[21] To conflate the hagiographic with the classical in so uncompromising a statement is to oppose the official Westminster representation of Elizabeth as an accomplished but unique woman. Among the ranks of saints many heroic women can be found, and, of course, the ranks of Amazons are wholly female. In this memorial verse we are asked to read her reign as we would read the stories of other great women warriors. She is "unparallel'd," but not alone.[22]

Similarly, we find in the inscriptions dealing with her immortality a sense of Elizabeth being one of a select company while having no peer among contemporary mortals of either gender. "Vertue liveth after death, / So doeth Queene Elizabeth" (from the church of St. John Baptist) can be read as a simple statement of Christian life after death, as can the passage from the Gospels about the girl that Jesus raised from the dead, "She is not dead, but sleepeth" (in St. Martin's Orgars, St. Michael Queenhithe, and St. Michael Querne), although I do think the Arthurian overtones of these deserve some consideration. As for the most radical statements—"Queene Elizabeth both was, and is alive, what then more can be said? In Heaven a Saint, in Earth a blessed Maid" and "She was, and is / what can there more be said? / On Earth the Chiefe, / in heaven the second Maid"—each appears only once, in St. Michael Crookedgate and St. Mary Aldermary respectively. Both statements, however, so similar in syntax, appear in the political writings of the period as examples of public feeling about the queen, leading me to the conclusion that their representation as church memorials was the result, rather than the source, of their popularity. Frances Yates, in her nearly canonical study *Astraea*,[23] makes much of these texts in the literature of the period, as does Roy Strong.[24]

Even this brief consideration of the parish church memorials allows us to see how the wealthy merchants in the parish churches may indeed have fallen back on older protocols when they tried to express their recognition of Elizabeth's place in the universal order. Stow's descriptive record of the monuments is not analytical (except in a relative sense—i.e., this is the biggest or the finest or the most ornate monument), but to the reader who has some knowledge of church architecture it is clear that many of these monuments were constructed both physically and imaginatively to replace the lately displaced Lady chapels. Current scholarship on Elizabeth questions the easy equation between the cult of the virgin and the cult of

Gloriana; in particular, Helen Hackett's 1995 book raises a number of valid objections to this simple reading of a complex relationship. Hackett, however, limits herself to literary representation—which makes her scorn for Yates and Strong a bit overstated, as they rely heavily on the portraits. While Hackett makes a compelling case for revising our thinking on the notion that Elizabeth filled a sort of "post-Reformation gap in the psyche of the masses, who craved a symbolic virgin-mother figure,"[25] I would suggest that a text inscribed in a church cannot be evaluated in exactly the same light as a literary text. Scholars have long cited the tag line of Elizabeth's apotheosis: "on Earth the first maid; in Heaven the second." But the cultural artifacts recorded in Stow allow us to see that this concept—even if problematic—may have been literally a social construction.

So we see that the texts of the people differ from the texts of James Stuart. Each set of representations grows from social and political circumstances of which we are aware in other contexts. Reading Stuart history as we read the tombs of the Tudor queen gives us another slant on the issue of the feeling of Londoners for their king. Reading the texts of the memorials in relation to the texts of the Westminster tombs gives us some insight into the political uses men can make of powerful women, even in death. We see this dual agenda—with the same class-defined split—more radically furthered when we examine two images of the dead queen. The Cecil engraving is a very strong populist statement, with the elements of Elizabeth the warrior foregrounded in a historically apocalyptic context. Elizabeth is seated—one could hardly say mounted—on the horse which tramples the seven-headed dragon described in Revelation, as she receives her lance from Truth, interestingly framed by a cave of light. That the dragon is related to both Spain and the papacy is suggested by the background of the Armada fleets, very clearly influenced by the representation of that conflict in the Armada portrait. This gives an apocalyptic overtone to Elizabeth's victory over Spain and makes the engraving an extremely strong statement of Elizabeth's power both in life and after death. A spray of Tudor roses springs from the top of the queen's helmet, a symbol both of eternal feminine life and of the dynasty of which she was arguably the flower; that there are three roses in the spray could be a conventional gesture to the Trinity or a more specific reference to the three generations of Tudor monarchs. Elizabeth holds a sword and shield in her left hand, while she accepts the lance with her right, a traditional prelude to righteous action. When we look at the queen's portraits from the late 1560s until her death, we see that no consistent use was made of the symbolism of left and right hands, although we might argue for the increasing importance of the traditionally empowering right hand. In the 1569 allegory of Elizabeth and the Three Goddesses, she holds the scepter in her right hand, but the more important prop, the apple-colored orb, is held in her left. In the 1572 Allegory of the Tudor Succession, Elizabeth leads Peace with her left hand while she gestures with her right hand, while in the 1583 Siena Sieve portrait, she holds the sieve in her left hand, while her right hand hangs limp at the base of that Virgilian column. In the Armada portrait, however, her right hand rests on the globe, and in the 1603 Rainbow portrait, the rainbow is extended in her right hand.

We need to keep this inconsistency in mind as we read the Gheeraerts painting Elizabeth with Time and Death. Both of Elizabeth's hands are occupied here, with the left holding a neglected book and the right holding her drooping head. However fabled her learning might have been, it is evidently of little benefit or comfort to her now. In fact, as hard as it may be for us to acknowledge in the late twentieth century, the appearance of the book itself may have negative connotations. In the Westminster tomb text, Elizabeth's learning was problematically represented, and in the parish church memorials—as I have already remarked—it was not a popular topic for praise of the queen. More significantly, none of the portraits after the very early 1560s have a book or books in their iconography. Only in the portrait of Elizabeth as princess, painted in the late 1540s during the reign of her brother, do we find her learning foregrounded. There we find a small book clasped in both of her hands and a much larger book on a lectern at her right elbow. Her left hand supports the small book, while her right rests on top of it, almost in the manner of one taking an oath. Here we see Elizabeth's learning as her defining characteristic, a very proper and safe characteristic for one who was only second in line for the throne after a younger brother who was still publicly figured as carrying on the dynasty. In the years during which Elizabeth constructed her own royal image through her portraits, we find no evidence that she or any of her nobles who might have commissioned portraits wanted to stress her extraordinary learning. Her hands hold gloves, fans, flowers, if not more iconographically charged objects, but no books. That Elizabeth with Time and Death features the queen holding a book suggests one of two implicit statements. The most obvious is that her learning, unnatural in her sex as all have observed, has taken the place of her more natural activities as a woman and thus she is left not with the fruit of her body in the form of heirs mourning at her tomb, heirs which might have benefited her nation, but with an effete and somewhat inappropriate way to pass eternity by reading, an activity which evidently gives her little satisfaction. The more convoluted explanation of that book in her left hand would be as a reference to the portrait of her as a princess, a role which the Stuarts would suggest she should never have abandoned. When the early portrait was painted, and indeed for most of Elizabeth's reign, no Stuart supporter would have described her as anything other than an educated, illegitimate daughter of a king. In the Elizabeth with Time and Death, the book held limply in her left hand has sinister implications on many levels.

Similarly, the queen's head held in her right hand is at odds with the other right-handed actions in the portraits, as this pose suggests not action or control, but the abandonment of all active pursuits, including learning. Although her body is oriented to her right as it is in the Allegory of the Tudor Succession, the Siena Sieve portrait, the Armada portrait, the Ditchley portrait, the Rainbow portrait, and in Cecil's engraving, her head is turned to her left, her sight-line down and to the left, as though she had just lowered the left hand holding the book. Death, the more prominent of the two background figures, looms over her left shoulder, and—even though it requires considerable contortion—both of the putti hold the crown with their left hands. Again, the orientation toward the sinister is difficult to overlook.

Formally, I believe, the painting is a deliberate revision of one of the most powerful of Elizabeth's portraits, the Armada portrait. Here, as in the 1588 painting, we see the queen seated before a table (a pose not used in any of the other portraits) with two important elements of the composition over her right and left shoulders. Rather than the English and Spanish fleets and that God-sent storm, however, we see Time behind her on the right, mirroring the queen's pose by propping his head with his left hand as he supports himself with his right arm, his hourglass broken before him, and Death leaning over her left shoulder holding an emptied hourglass in his right hand, his left arm over the back of her chair. The chair and pillow are similar to the Armada portrait chair and pillow, although in the earlier portrait the pillow is behind the queen's left side as mere decoration, while in the posthumous portrait the pillow becomes a seemingly necessary support for her right arm. Not only are the pillow and the chair structurally similar to those in the Armada portrait, but they are very nearly the same rich shade of crimson. With the exception of that earliest portrait of the Princess Elizabeth, painted during the reign of her brother Edward and over which she would have had little if any control, this is the only portrait of Elizabeth in red—a color she would have avoided wearing for its obvious links to sexuality[26]—although it is sometimes present in details of the paintings: in the orb she holds in Elizabeth and the Three Goddesses, the rose and intaglio of the Phoenix portrait, and in the table covering as well as the cushion and chair of the Armada portrait. The Armada portrait figures forth Elizabeth's greatest achievement in the eyes of both her successor and her subjects: victory over Spain. It is her Crécy or Agincourt, all the more significant because the sceptered isle itself was actually threatened by invasion and all the more remarkable because, as Venus said of Carthage, *dux femina facti*. The victory was marked by an explosion of images and symbols of the queen,[27] and became a key element of the memorial texts celebrating her reign. That the Cecil engraving is organized around the mythology of the Armada victory shows us how important it would have been for those who wished to diminish Elizabeth's reputation to diminish the memory of that victory. The subliminal elements of the Gheeraerts portrait are as powerful as any of the iconography used for or by Elizabeth in her own portraits. Here, however, the power of art works toward a very different end.

If we see this posthumous portrait of Elizabeth as a disempowering remake of the Armada portrait, the representation of her face becomes a fascinating issue, for what we see here is not the face of the Armada portrait, but essentially the face of one of the other two portraits we know Elizabeth agreed to sit for: the Darnley portrait painted by Zuccaro in 1575 and used as a face pattern for many royal portraits of the next decade, most famously in reverse for the Siena Sieve portrait. If the intent behind Elizabeth with Time and Death was to represent the queen negatively, why not use the older face from the Armada portrait or the even older and more worn—indeed, haggard—1590s face of the Ditchley portrait, both also painted from life? I would suggest that the use of the younger and arguably most famous face of the queen anteriorizes the agenda of the

1620s painting to Elizabeth's reign not only in life, but in her prime. In "Elizabeth with Time and Death" we see an exhausted and depressed woman, a woman at the mercy of forces she cannot control. That the portrait was long misidentified as having been painted during Elizabeth's troubles with Essex is, I think, a significant error. Yes, the dead Elizabeth might arguably look exhausted (although this doesn't say much for the power of resurrection), but to represent the queen as wornout and losing control in a revision of her Armada portrait with an only slightly aged version of the Darnley face is to call into question—to call with great subtlety but also with profound effect—the power she held and used in life.

The political potency of the Armada in each representation of the queen cannot be understated, for not only was this the defining victory of the last Tudor's reign, but it was an icon for a hotly debated political issue in the early 1620s: the possibility that Charles Stuart might make a Spanish marriage.[28] It is not my goal to examine the complexities of the proposed Spanish match in this essay; rather I want to make the fairly obvious connection between the various factions' feelings about the relationship between Spain and England and the Armada allusions in the two images of Elizabeth from the 1620s.[29] Gardiner speaks of the House of Commons' 1621 opposition to the possibility that "a Spanish Infanta was to become the future Queen of England, and the mother of a stock of English kings. In the course of nature her child would within forty or fifty years be seated on the throne of Henry and Elizabeth."[30] But James, in his attempt to stop protests from the Commons—an attempt which culminated in the dissolution of 1621—also cited Elizabeth, but as an authority for restraining debate in the House, as she did in both 1588 and 1593. Gardiner comments:

To an historian, the dates of these transactions speak for themselves. In ordinary times the House had protested against the Queen's assumptions, and the protestation had not remained without effect. In times of excitement, as in 1588 . . . and in 1593, when the shouts of triumph were still ringing in the ears of her subjects, she had had her way. Such a view of the case, however, was not likely to be taken by James. The right to interfere had been maintained by his predecessor. His dignity would suffer if he abandoned it on any pretext whatever. The Commons, on the other hand, fell back on the necessities of their position, and the almost uninterrupted practice of earlier generations.[31]

As the situation worsened in the summer of 1622, the question of the opinion of the people, as well as the opinion of the House of Commons, arose. Gardiner argues:

Little as the English people knew of what was passing at Rome and at Madrid, they were well aware that James had lowered the dignity of the English crown till the laws of England had been made a subject of treaty with foreign statesmen and foreign priests. In the eyes of his contemporaries he had been guilty of sacrificing the national independence, the great cause of which Henry VIII and Elizabeth had been the champions. In the eyes of posterity, he is guilty of defiling the sacred cause of religious liberty by making bargains over it for Spanish gold and Spanish aid.[32]

Cogswell presents a somewhat less empassioned version of the same situation, when he speaks of Buckingham's lack of popularity as directly related to his active advocacy of the Spanish marriage: "The remarkable level of abuse in [a number of popular] poems of 1622–3 was clearly due much more to the policies he advocated than to the speed of his elevation."[33] Cogswell continues:

Evidence of mounting opposition to the Spanish match can also be found in the streets of London. Booksellers who attempted to move DuVal's *English Spanish Rose* found that customers vied with one another for the wittiest explanation of the frontispiece which depicted Christ bringing Charles and the Infanta together. . . . The mood was apt to get much uglier when live Spaniards appeared. In the summer of 1621, Londoners greeted the Spanish envoys and their servants with "many Insolencies of rude and savage barbarisme". . . . Moreover, local magistrates were loathe to interrupt the hail of catcalls and stones. Eventually James himself had to intervene in order to instill some sense of "respect and civillity" into the urban population.[34]

Perhaps the most telling of the public reactions is John Reynolds's 1624 pamphlet *Vox Coeli, or News from heaven,* in which he wittily presents a discussion (later "published in Elisium") among Henry VIII, Edward VI, Mary and Elizabeth Tudor, Anne of Denmark, and Prince Henry on the topic of Charles's proposed marriage to the Infanta. In this text Elizabeth speaks of the victory of her country "against the pride and malice of Spane, who grew mad with anger and pale with griefe, to see this his great and warlike armado beaten, foyled, and confounded," while lamenting that James has now let "my royall-navy lye rotting."[35]

With so specifically Spanish a conflict between the king and his subjects, we should not be surprised to find references to and the iconic display of the Armada used by both sides. As Woolf contends: "The conclusion seems unavoidable that Elizabeth was, as a propaganda symbol and source of precedents, valued as much by King and Court as by Parliament and Puritanism."[36] While Woolf suggests, as does Gardiner, that James tried to usurp the precedent set by Elizabeth's control of debate in the Commons, he sees the populist response to this 1621 strategy as a misrepresentation, or misguided representation of Elizabeth. "Along side the ghost of Elizabeth the wise and cautious, there now grew up—or rather returned—a *doppelganger:* Elizabeth the Protestant warrior and uncompromising enemy of the Antichrist of Rome and his minions. This was an image unacceptable to the eirenic and peace-loving James."[37] Woolf refuses to allow that James might have seen any image of Elizabeth as a threat, even those obviously constructed to be critical of his Spanish policies. Speaking of the "Foxean image of [Elizabeth as] the lost Deborah" as "being revived in response to the *perceived foreign policy failures* of the 1620's" (emphasis mine), Woolf still claims that this image was not critical of James, but merely "intended to set the King straight."[38]

Setting James and Charles "straight" on the subject of a Spanish marriage is certainly the very least that can be said of the Cecil print. The parish church references to Elizabeth as a Deborah, a Judith, and "Spaines Rod" take on fresh significance in the context of the Spanish marriage conflict. Likewise, it seems more than a possibility that Elizabeth with Time and Death was commissioned not merely as a parody of the queen at her most powerful, but as a dismissal of Spain as the natural enemy of England and English monarchs, substituting instead the more universal Time and Death. Elizabeth's victory over the Armada is figured as ultimately pointless, in that the greater forces which finally overtook her know no national boundaries.

As emphatically as the revision of the Westminster tombs and the texts written for her marginalized memorial, this portrait gives us a graphic example of the politically potent dissing of Elizabeth I by her powerful survivors. Here we see the power of art furthering the agenda of the

Stuarts and their supporters who needed, for a variety of pressing reasons, to erase the shadow of a generally popular queen by representing her as unnatural, alone, powerless, and ingloriously dead. That the portrait has the trappings of regal glory keeps it from appearing an open desecration of the memory of the queen; that these trappings are all so seductively familiar and yet so ultimately sinister makes it a very powerful tool of negative propaganda, a disrespectfully revisionist view of both a monarch and a reign.

Notes

1. See my essay, "Reading the Tombs of Elizabeth I," in *English Literary Renaissance* 26, no. 3 (Fall 1996): 510–530.

2. Elizabeth's burial took place before James entered London, and her body was placed—according to both Millington's diary (Thomas Millington, *The True Narration of the Entertainment of his Majesty from his departure from Edinburgh till his receiving at London*, in *Stuart Tracts 1603–1693*, ed. C. H. Frith [New York: Cooper Square Publishers, 1964], 15) and Camden's *Reges, Reginæ, Nobiles . . .* (London: Excudebat Melchi Bradwoodus, 1603), no page number—in the crypt beneath the altar of the Henry VII Chapel of Westminster Abbey, "in the Sepulchre of her grandfather" (Millington 15) Henry VII, where her father, Henry VIII, had initially planned his own tomb (H. M. Colvin et al., eds., *The History of the King's Works*, vol. 3, 1485–1660, Part 1 [London: Her Majesty's Stationery Office, 1975], 219).

Camden states that Elizabeth was buried "eadem crypta cum Henrico 7." This, along with Millington's diary and a 1606 treasury sheet from the Westminster Abbey Muniments Room (WAM 41095) listing cost for the moving of Queen Elizabeth's body as "Item: more for removing of Queene Elizabeth's Body . . . 46 shillings 4 pence," contradicts all later references to the tomb. James was evidently very successful in diverting attention from his revisionary tomb building. Indeed, when I first pursued this research, I was shown any number of works, including the *Official Guide* of the Abbey and a nineteenth-century history from which much of it was taken. In this text, *Historical Monuments of Westminster Abbey* (London: John Murry, 1876), the author—Arthur Penrhyn Stanley, Dean of Westminster—goes so far as to state that the body of Elizabeth was carried, doubtless by her own desire, to the North Aisle of Henry VII's Chapel, to the unmarked grave of her unfortunate predecessor. At the head of the monument raised by her successor over the narrow vault are to be read two lines full of a far deeper feeling than we should naturally have ascribed to him—"*Regno consortes et urna, hic obdormimus Elizabetha et Maria sorores, in spe resurrectionis.*" The long war of the English Reformation is closed in those words. In that contracted sepulcher, admitting none other but those two, the stately coffin of Elizabeth rests on the coffin of Mary. The sisters are at one: the daughter of Catherine of Aragon and the Daughter of Anne Boleyn repose in peace at last. (163–64)

As an example of Victorian sentimentality, this is striking; as an example of logical political and historical analysis, it is willfully naive. Sources dating back to the latter half of the seventeenth century refer to Elizabeth's present tomb as her only memorial in the Abbey, and in this century Edward Carpenter, in the modestly entitled *A House of Kings: The Official History of Westminster Abbey* (New York: John Day Company, 1966), unproblematically states: "Queen Elizabeth was buried in the unmarked grave of her sister Mary" (142).

3. The monument that James ordered for the two sisters cost a total of 765 pounds (*Westminster Abbey Official Guide* [London, 1988], 69). In *The History and Antiquities of Westminster Abbey* (London, 1856), however, I found the following statement about Elizabeth's tomb: "Walpole has stated, from an office book in the Earl of Oxford's collection, that the whole cost £965 'besides the stone'" (110). As an index to the relative value of that sum, I think it is worth noting that in July 1587 Elizabeth spent 321 pounds, 14s for the funeral ceremony of Mary Stuart, Queen of Scots, at Peterborough. James spent, therefore, little more than twice as much on Elizabeth—and, economically, her sister—as Elizabeth spent on James's mother. *The Scottish Queen's Burial at Peterborough* (1589), in *An English Garner,* vol. 8, ed. Edward Arber (London: Archibald Constable, 1896).

In the south aisle of the chapel James ordered built a tomb for his mother, Mary Stuart, originally buried in Peterborough Cathedral, but brought by Royal Warrant to Westminster "that the 'like honor might be done to the body of his dearest mother and the like monument extant to her that had been done to others and to his dear sister the late Queen Elizabeth'" (*Official Guide,* 76). "Like" does not here mean "same." Elizabeth's tomb is, in the conservative words of the official guidebook, "plainer and less sumptuous than that of Mary Queen of Scots" (69). The latter's, being very much larger, took much longer to complete and was much more expensive. The last recorded figure is an estimate of work yet to be done costing 2,000 pounds. The court and household records of James's reign provide us with further insights as to James's agenda. For one thing, James seems to have been financing the building of Elizabeth's tomb out of the household accounts of his own wife.

In a letter from the queen's court dated 4 March 1604 to Sir Thomas Lake I found the statement that the queen's own accounts could not be paid, but "Rather than fail in payment for Queen Elizabeth's tomb, neither the Exchequer nor London shall have a penny left." The writer went on to "rejoice to falsify the prophecy that no child of Henry VIII should be handsomely buried" (*Calendar of State Papers* 1603–1610, ed. Mary Anne Everett Green (HM's Stationery Office, 1858; rpt. 1967), 14/13, no. 8). And yet it seems that neither London nor the king are leaving their bills unpaid, but rather the queen's.

By his placement of his own mother, Mary Stuart, in line with Henry VII's mother Margaret Beaufort, James foregrounds the claim of the Queen of Scots to the throne upon which Elizabeth sat. Even as he builds a tomb honoring the Virgin Queen, James reminds the public that virgins do not found or further the greatness of dynasties. Later Stuarts continued this architectural statement of the unity of fruitful dynasty, as the tombs of Charles II, William and Mary, and Queen Anne lie in the south aisle, continuing the line from Margaret Beaufort which was interrupted by those two barren (and now marginalized) Tudor queens.

4. John Stow, *The Survey of London*, "Begunne first . . . by John Stow, in the yeere 1598. Afterwards inlarged by . . . A.M. [Antony Munday] in the yeere 1618. And now completely finished by A.M. H.D. [Henry Dyson] and others, this present yeere 1633. Where-unto . . . are annexed divers Alphabetical Tables, etc. . . . Printed by Elizabeth Purslow, and are to bee sold by Nicholas Borne, at his Shop, at the South Entrance of the Royall Exchange. 1633." Spelling of s/f, u/v, i/j modernized from Stow's transcriptions of both translations.

5. James chose to address the concerns of the people by stressing both historical and dynastic inevitability of his reign in a speech to his first parliament on 22 March 1604. He argues: "First, by my descent lineally out of the loynes of Henry the seventh, is reunited and confirmed in mee the Vnion of the two Princely Roses of the two Houses of LANCASTER and YORKE, where of that King of happy memorie was the first Vniter, as he was also the first groundlayer of the other Peace. . . . But the Vnion of these two princely Houses, is nothing comparable to the Vnion of two ancient and famous kingdomes." From *The Political*

Works of James I, ed. Charles H. McIlwain (Cambridge, Mass., 1918) cited by Marie Axton in *The Queen's Two Bodies: Drama and the Elizabethan Succession* (London: Royal Historical Society, 1977), 133.

6. Roy Strong, *Gloriana: The Portraits of Queen Elizabeth I* (London: Thames and Hudson, 1987), 164.

7. H. Neville Davies, "Jacobean *Antony and Cleopatra,*" *Shakespeare Studies* 17 (1985): 128.

8. Carole Levin, *The Heart and Stomach of a King: Elizabeth I and the Politics of Sex and Power* (Philadelphia: University of Pennsylvania Press, 1994), 168–69.

9. Even though the material I cite was added by A.M., H.D., and others, I will still refer to Stow as the author. Stow's survey lists ninety-seven churches within the City of London, thirty-two with memorials to Elizabeth.

10. Dates, sometimes inclusive of five or more years, are given for twenty-nine of the thirty-two churches, the earliest being 1605 and the latest 1633; fifteen of those churches with specific restoration dates were remodeled in the 1620s. A listing of restorations with specific dates shows that most of the construction did indeed take place in or around the 1620s:

1605–1609:	1
1610–1614:	2
1615–1619:	3
1620–1624:	8
1625–1629:	7
1630–1633:	5

11. Nor is it possible to ascertain whether an Elizabeth memorial was already in place in a church which was restored in the 1620s.

12. Stow, *Survey of London,* 826–27.

13. Ibid., 854.

14. Ibid., 840.

15.   Here lies her Type, who was of late,
       The prop of Belgia, stay of France, State,
       Spaines foile, Faith's shield, and Queene of
       Armes, of Learning, Fate, and Chance:
       In briefe, of Women ne're was seen,
       So great a Prince, so good a Queene.

This poem appears in St. Lawrence Jurie, St. Martin's Orgars, St. Maudlin's Oldfishstreet, St. Michael Queenhithe, St. Michael Querne, and St. Michael Woodstreet.

16. See my essay "Spenser's Elizabeth Portrait and the Fiction of Dynastic Epic," *Modern Philology* 90 (1992): 172–99.

17. See Andrew Belsey and Catherine Belsey, "Icons of Divinity: Portraits of Elizabeth I," in *Renaissance Bodies: The Human Figure in English Culture c. 1540–1660*, ed. Lucy Gent and Nigel Llewellyn (London: Reaktion Books, 1990), 11–35.

18. All Hallows the Great, St. Bartholomew Exchange, St. Bennet Grace-Church, St. Botolph Billingsgate, St. Clement's Eastcheap, St. Katherine Cree-Church, St. Mary Aldermary, St. Mary Woolchurch, St. Maudlin Milkestreet, St. Mildred Poultrey, and St. Thomas Apostle.

19. Helen Hackett, *Virgin Mother, Maiden Queen: Elizabeth I and the Cult of the Virgin Mary* (New York: St. Martin's Press, 1995), 87.

20. Interestingly, Elizabeth is never (to my knowledge) referred to as a Jael, a woman who also kills to save her people and who fulfills Deborah's prophecy in Judges. But Jael was merely the "wife of Heber," not a leader.

21. Especially as James was so fond of the French poet Du Bartas, who authored a popular mini-epic out of the Judith narrative (which was translated for James), we can read as deliberate the king's absence of Judith references in his rhetoric supposedly praising the late queen.

22. Since Stow lists the dates for the restoration of All Hallowes at the Wall as 1627–29, it is interesting to speculate whether this praise of Elizabeth was generated in relation to the reign of James or of Charles Stuart. This question is particularly interesting if we try to link outbursts of sentiment for Elizabeth, the "Rod of Spain," with popular opposition to suggestions of a Spanish marriage for Charles. I am grateful to Stella Revard, who raised this point after hearing a paper I gave from this project, and I explore the political implications of this in my forthcoming book *Reading the Remains of Elizabeth I: The Politics and Poetics of Posthumous Representation*.

23. Frances A. Yates, *Astraea: The Imperial Theme in the Sixteenth Century* (London: Pimlico, 1993).

24. Roy Strong, *The Cult of Elizabeth: Elizabethan Portraiture and Pageantry* (Berkeley: University of California Press, 1977).

25. Hackett, *Virgin Mother, Maiden Queen*, 7.

26. Remembering that Spenser dresses "fair Eliza" of the April eclogue in scarlet "like a maiden queen," we note that red is not associated only with the evils of sexuality (as in Revelation), but with sexuality in general, as sixteenth-century wedding dresses were often red. Queen Elizabeth's sexuality, of course,

can never be discussed "in general"; for her the issue must always be very specific and very much under her own control.

27. See M. J. Rodrîgues-Salgado and the staff of the National Maritime Museum, *Armada, 1588–1988: An International Exhibition to Commemorate the Spanish Armada: The Official Catalogue* (London: Penguin Books, 1988), 271–85.

28. For a more fully developed version of this argument, see my forthcoming study, *Reading the Remains of Elizabeth I: The Politics and Poetics of Posthumous Representation.*

29. For a variety of evaluations of the politics of the Spanish match, see the following. Samuel R. Gardiner, *History of England, 1603–1642*, vols. 4 and 5 (New York: AMS Press, 1965). Gardiner's strongly opinionated account—for example, he speaks of James and Charles "signing away the independence of the English monarchy [while James's] subjects were regarding the proceedings of their sovereign with scarcely concealed disgust" (4:399)—makes consistent reference to the various appeals to the memory of Elizabeth by both sides. D. R. Woolf, in "Two Elizabeths? James I and the Late Queen's Famous Memory," *Canadian Journal of History* 20 (1985): 167–91, offers equally strong, if divergent, evaluations of the role of Elizabeth's memory in the Stuart monarchy; while claiming that the "good Queen / bad King dichotomy" is far too simplistic (191), Woolf argues that many writers used references to Elizabeth's policies, not to denigrate James but in an attempt "to set the King straight" (190). For less judgmental accounts of the issue see Conrad Russell, *Parliaments and English Politics, 1621–1629* (Oxford: Clarendon Press, 1979), and Thomas Cogswell, *The Blessed Revolution: English Politics and the Coming of War, 1621–1624* (Cambridge: Cambridge University Press, 1989); and for interesting archival discoveries, see Glyn Redworth, "Of Pimps and Princes: Three Unpublished Letters from James I and the Prince of Wales Relating to the Spanish Match," *Historical Journal* 37 (1994): 401–9.

30. Gardiner, *History of England,* 4:246.

31. Ibid., 257.

32. Ibid., 349.

33. Cogswell, *The Blessed Revolution,* 48.

34. Ibid.

35. John Reynolds, "*Vox Coeli,* or News from Heaven," Elisium, 1624. The pamphlet is reproduced in *Somers Tracts,* ed. Walter Scott (London: T. Cadell and W. Davies, 1809), 2:555–96. For a summary of the debated authorship of this pamphlet see Levin, *The Heart and Stomach of a King,* 213 n. 64.

36. Although Woolf differs from my reading of the situation by refusing to see James using Elizabeth in a critical context: "He may have believed that there were those who misunderstood both the Queen and himself, but that is not the same thing. Respect for the memory of one monarch would carry with it readier obedience to her successor. Disrespect was nothing less than *lèse-majesté*, something which James would never brook" (180). Woolf, I must point out, praises James for the elaborate tomb he constructed for Elizabeth.

37. Woolf, "Two Elizabeths?" 185.

38. Ibid., 191.

Secondary Works Cited

Adams, Robert P. "Opposed Tudor Myths of Power: Machiavellian Tyrants and Christian Kings." In *Studies in the Continental Background of Renaissance English Literature: Essays Presented to John L. Lievsay*, edited by Dale J. B. Randall and George Walton Williams. Durham: Duke University Press, 1977. Pp. 67–90.

Adams, Simon. "Eliza Enthroned? The Court and Its Politics." In *The Reign of Elizabeth I*, edited by Christopher Haigh. London: Macmillan, 1985. Pp. 55–77.

———. "Faction, Clientage, and Party: English Politics, 1550–1603." *History Today* 32 (1982): 33–39.

———. "Favourites and Factions at the Elizabethan Court." In *Princes, Patronage, and the Nobility: The Court at the Beginning of the Modern Age*, edited by Ronald G. Asch and Adolf M. Burke. Oxford: Oxford University Press, 1991. Pp. 265–87.

Adler, Doris. "Imaginary toads in real gardens." *English Literary Renaissance* 2, no. 3 (1981): 235–60.

Anderson, Judith. "Arthur, Argante, and the Ideal Vision: An Exercise in Speculation and Parody." In *The Passing of Arthur: New Essays in the Arthurian Tradition*, edited by Christopher Baswell and William Sharpe. New York: Garland, 1988. Pp. 193–206.

Axton, Marie. *The Queen's Two Bodies: Drama and the Elizabethan Succession.* London: Royal Historical Society, 1977.

Bassnett, Susan. *Elizabeth I: A Feminist Perspective.* New York: St. Martin's, 1988.

Bates, Catherine. *The Rhetoric of Courtship in Elizabethan Language and Literature.* Cambridge: Cambridge University Press, 1992.

Bell, Ilona. "Elizabeth I—Always Her Own Free Woman." In *Political Rhetoric, Power, and Renaissance Women*, ed. Carole Levin and Patricia A. Sullivan. Albany: State University of New York Press, 1995. Pp. 57–82.

Bellamy, John. *The Tudor Law of Treason: An Introduction.* London: Routledge and Kegan Paul, 1979.

Bellany, Alastair. "'Raylinge Rymes and Vaunting Verse': Libellous Politics in Early Stuart England, 1603–1628." In *Culture and Politics in Early Stuart England*, ed. Kevin Sharpe and Peter Lake. Stanford: Stanford University Press, 1993. Pp. 285–310.

Belsey, Andrew, and Catherine Belsey. "Icons of Divinity: Portraits of Elizabeth I." In *Renaissance Bodies: The Human Figure in English Culture c. 1540–*

1660, edited by Lucy Gent and Nigel Llewellyn. London: Reaktion Books, 1990. Pp. 11–35.

Benson, Pamela Joseph. *The Invention of the Renaissance Woman*. University Park, Penn.: Pennsylvania State University Press, 1992.

Berry, Lloyd E., ed. *John Stubbs' Gaping Gulf with Letters and Other Relevant Documents*. Charlottesville: University Press of Virginia, 1968.

Berry, Philippa. *Of Chastity and Power: Elizabethan Literature and the Unmarried Queen*. London: Routledge, 1989.

Bieman, Elizabeth. "Britomart in *The Faerie Queene* V." *University of Toronto Quarterly* 37 (1968): 156–74.

Boehrer, Bruce Thomas. *Monarchy and Incest in Renaissance England: Literature, Culture, Kinship, and Kingship*. Philadelphia: University of Pennsylvania Press, 1992.

Bowman, Mary R. " 'She There as Princess Rained': Spenser's Figure of Elizabeth." *Renaissance Quarterly* 43 (1990): 509–28.

Bradshaw, Brendan. "Sword, Word, and Strategy in the Reformation in Ireland." *Historical Journal* 21 (1978): 475–502.

Brooks, E. St. John. *Sir Christopher Hatton: Queen Elizabeth's Favourite*. London: Jonathan Cape, 1946. Boston: Little, Brown, 1991.

Bruce, John. " 'The Actes of Queen Elizabeth Allegorized.' " *Notes and Queries* 4th ser., 3 (1869): 305–7.

Bush, M. L. *The Government Policy of Protector Somerset*. London: Edward Arnold, 1975.

Cain, Thomas H. *Praise in "The Faerie Queene."* Lincoln: University of Nebraska Press, 1978.

Camden, William. *The History of the Most Renowned and Victorious Princess Elizabeth*. Edited by Wallace T. MacCaffrey. Chicago: University of Chicago Press, 1970.

Canny, Nicholas P. *The Elizabethan Conquest of Ireland: A Pattern Established 1565–76*. Hassocks: Harvester, 1976.

———. *Kingdom and Colony: Ireland in the Atlantic World, 1560–1800*. Baltimore: Johns Hopkins University Press, 1988.

Carey, John. "The Ovidian Love Elegy in England." D.Phil. diss., Oxford, 1960.

Carney, Jo Eldridge. "Queenship in Shakespeare's *Henry VIII:* The Issue of Issue." *Political Rhetoric, Power, and Renaissance Women*, ed. Carole Levin and Patricia A. Sullivan. Albany: State University of New York Press, 1995. Pp. 189–202.

Carpenter, Edward. *A House of Kings: The Official History of Westminster Abbey*. New York: John Day, 1966.

Carroll, Clare. "Representations of Women in Some Early Modern English Tracts on the Colonization of Ireland." *Albion* 25 (1993): 379–93.

Cavanagh, Dermot. "'Possessed with Rumours': Popular Speech and King John." *Shakespeare Yearbook* 6 (1996).

Cavanagh, Sheila T. *Wanton Eyes and Chaste Desires: Female Sexuality in "The Faerie Queene."* Bloomington: Indiana University Press, 1994.

Cerasano, S. P., and Marion Wynne-Davies, eds. *Gloriana's Face: Women, Public and Private, in the English Renaissance.* Hemel Hempstead, Herts: Harvester Wheatsheaf; Detroit: Wayne State University Press, 1992.

Chamberlin, Frederick. *The Private Character of Queen Elizabeth.* New York: Dodd, Mead, 1922.

Chantelauze, M. R. *Marie Stuart Son Procès et Son Exécution.* Paris, 1876.

Churton, Ralph. *The Life of Alexander Nowell.* Oxford, 1809.

Clark, Andrew, ed. *The Shirburn Ballads 1585–1616, Edited from the MS.* Oxford: Clarendon, 1907.

Clark, Peter. "A Crisis Contained? The Condition of English Towns in the 1590s." In *The European Crisis of the 1590s,* edited by Peter Clark. London: George Allen & Unwin, 1985. Pp. 44–66.

——. *The European Crisis of the 1590s: Essays in Comparative History.* London: George Allen & Unwin, 1985.

Clifford, Henry. *The Life of Jane Dormer, Duchess of Feria.* London: Burns and Oates, 1887.

Cloulas, I. *Correspondance du Nonce en France, Anselmo Dandino 1578–1581.* Acta Nuntiaturae Gallicae 8. Paris, 1979.

Cogswell, Thomas. "England and the Spanish Match." In *England: Studies in Religion and Politics 1603–1642,* edited by Richard Cust and Ann Hughes. Harlow Essex: Longman, 1989.

——. *The Blessed Revolution: English Politics and the Coming of War, 1621–1624.* Cambridge: Cambridge University Press, 1989.

Collinson, Patrick. *The Birthpangs of Protestant England: Religious and Cultural Change in the Sixteenth and Seventeenth Centuries.* Basingstoke: Macmillan, 1988.

——. "The Monarchical Republic of Queen Elizabeth I." In *Elizabethan Essays.* London: Hambledon Press, 1994.

——. *The Religion of Protestants.* Oxford: Oxford University Press, 1982.

Colvin, Howard, gen. ed. *A History of the King's Works.* 6 vols. London: HMSO, 1963–82.

Compton, Piers. *Bad Queen Bess.* London: Alex Ouseley, 1933.

Crane, Mary Thomas. *Framing Authority: Sayings, Self, and Society in Sixteenth-Century England.* Princeton, N.J.: Princeton University Press, 1993.

Cunningham, Bernadette. "Native Culture and Political Change in Ireland, 1580–1640." In *Natives and Newcomers: Essays on the Making of Irish Colonial Society 1534–1641*, edited by Ciaran Brady and Raymond Gillespie. Dublin: Irish Academic Press, 1986.

Curtis, Mark H. "The Alienated Intellectuals of Early Stuart England." *Past and Present* 23 (1962): 25–41.

Davies, H. Neville. "Jacobean *Antony and Cleopatra*." *Shakespeare Studies* 17 (1985).

Davis, Natalie Zemon. *Fiction in the Archives: Pardon Tales and Their Tellers in Sixteenth-Century France*. Stanford: Stanford University Press, 1987.

———. "The Rites of Violence." In *Society and Culture in Early Modern France*. Stanford: Stanford University Press, 1985. Pp. 152–88.

de la Ferrière-Percy, Hector, and Comte Baguenault de Puchesse, eds. *Lettres de Catherine de Médicis*. Paris, 1880–1909. 2:306.

Denvir, Bernard, ed. *From the Middle Ages to the Stuarts: Art, Design, and Society before 1689*. New York: Longman, 1988.

D'Ewes, Simonds. *The Journals of all the Parliaments during the Reign of Queen Elizabeth*. London, 1682.

Donno, Elizabeth Story, ed. *Elizabethan Minor Epics*. London: Routledge, 1963.

Doran, Susan. "Juno versus Diana: The Treatment of Elizabeth's Marriage in Plays and Entertainments, 1561–1581." *Historical Journal* 38 (1995): 257–74.

———. *Monarchy and Matrimony: The Courtships of Elizabeth I*. London: Routledge, 1996.

Douglas, Mary. *Natural Symbols: Explorations in Cosmology*. New York: Pantheon, 1970.

Duncan-Jones, Katherine. "Much Ado with Red and White: The Earliest Readers of Shakespeare's *Venus and Adonis* (1593)." *Review of English Studies* n.s., 44, no. 176 (1993): 479–504.

———. *Sir Philip Sidney, Courtier Poet*. New Haven: Yale University Press, 1991.

Dworkin, Andrea. *Pornography: Men Possessing Women*. London: Women's Press, 1981.

Ellis, Henry. *Original Letters*. London: Harding, Triphook, and Lepard, 1825.

Elton, G. R. *Henry VIII: An Essay in Revision*. London: Historical Association, 1962.

———. *Policy and Police: The Enforcement of the Reformation in the Age of Thomas Cromwell*. Cambridge: Cambridge University Press, 1972.

———. *Reform and Reformation: England, 1509–1558*. Cambridge, Mass.: Harvard University Press, 1977.

Emmison, F. G. *Elizabethan Life, Vol. 1: Disorder.* Chelmsford: Essex County Council, 1971.

Erickson, Carolly. *The First Elizabeth.* New York: Summit Books, 1983.

Esler, Anthony. *The Aspiring Mind of the Elizabethan Younger Generation.* Durham, N.C.: Duke University Press, 1966.

Evett, David. *Literature and the Visual Arts in Tudor England.* Athens: University of Georgia Press, 1990.

Findlen, Paula. "Humanism, Politics and Pornography in Renaissance Italy." In *The Invention of Pornography,* edited by Lynn Hunt. New York: Zone Books, 1993. Pp. 49–108.

Fletcher, Angus. *The Prophetic Moment: An Essay on Spenser.* Chicago: University of Chicago Press, 1971.

Ford, Alan. *The Protestant Reformation in Ireland, 1590–1641.* Frankfurt: Peter Lang, 1985.

Forster, Leonard. *The Icy Fire: Five Studies in European Petrarchism.* Cambridge: Cambridge University Press, 1969.

Fox, Adam. "Ballads, Libels, and Popular Ridicule in Jacobean England." *Past and Present* 145 (1994): 47–83.

Foxe, John. *Acts and Monuments of John Foxe.* Vols. 6 and 8. New York: AMS Press, 1965.

Frantz, David O. *Festum Voluptatis: A Study of Renaissance Erotica.* Columbus: Ohio State University Press, 1989.

Fraser, Antonia. *Mary Queen of Scots.* London: Weidenfeld & Nicholson, 1969.

——. *The Wives of Henry VIII.* New York: Alfred A. Knopf, 1993.

Frye, Susan. *Elizabeth I: The Competition for Representation.* New York: Oxford University Press, 1993.

Gabel, J. B., and C. C. Schlam, eds. *Thomas Chaloner's "In Laudem Henrici Octavi."* Lawrence, Kans.: Coronado Press, 1979.

Gardiner, Samuel R. *History of England, 1603–1642.* Vols. 4 and 5. New York: AMS Press, 1965.

Ginzburg, Carlo. *Ecstasies: Deciphering the Witches' Sabbath.* Translated by Raymond Rosenthal. New York: Pantheon, 1991.

Goldberg, Jonathan. "The Mothers in Book III of *The Faerie Queene.*" *Texas Studies in Literature and Language* 17 (1975): 5–26.

——. *Sodometries: Renaissance Texts, Modern Sexualities.* Stanford: Stanford University Press, 1992.

Gowing, Deborah. *Willis, Malevolent Nurture: Witch-Hunting and Maternal Power in Early Modern England.* Ithaca: Cornell University Press, 1995.

Gowing, Laura. "Language, Power, and the Law: Women's Slander Litigation in

Early Modern London." In *Women, Crime, and the Courts in Early Modern England*, ed. Jenny Kermode and Garthine Walker. Chapel Hill: University of North Carolina Press, 1994. Pp. 26–47.

Greenblatt, Stephen. *Renaissance Self-Fashioning: From More to Shakespeare*. Chicago: University of Chicago Press, 1980.

——. *Sir Walter Raleigh: The Renaissance Man and His Roles*. New Haven: Yale University Press, 1973.

Gross, Kenneth. *Spenserian Poetics: Idolatry, Iconoclasm, and Magic*. Ithaca: Cornell University Press, 1985.

Guy, John. "Introduction: The 1590s: The Second Reign of Elizabeth I?" In *The Reign of Elizabeth I*, edited by John Guy. Cambridge: Cambridge University Press, 1995. Pp. 1–19.

——. *Tudor England*. Oxford: Oxford University Press, 1988.

——, ed. *The Reign of Elizabeth I: Court and Culture in the Last Decade*. Cambridge: Cambridge University Press, 1995.

Hackett, Helen. *Virgin Mother, Maiden Queen: Elizabeth I and the Cult of the Virgin Mary*. Basingstoke: Macmillan, 1995.

Haigh, Christopher. *Elizabeth I: Profile in Power*. London: Longman, 1988.

Hamilton, A. C. *The Structure of Allegory in "The Faerie Queene."* Oxford: Clarendon Press, 1961.

Hammer, Paul E. J. "Patronage at Court, Faction, and the Earl of Essex." In *The Reign of Elizabeth I*, edited by John Guy. Cambridge: Cambridge University Press, 1995. Pp. 65–86.

Harrington, John P. "A Tudor Writer's Tracts on Ireland, His Rhetoric." *Eire-Ireland* 17 (1982): 99.

Hartley, T. E., ed. *Proceedings in the Parliament of Elizabeth, 1558–1581*. 3 vols. Leicester: Leicester University Press, 1981–85.

Heisch, Allison. "Queen Elizabeth and the Persistence of Patrimony." *Feminist Review* 4 (1980): 45–56.

——. "Queen Elizabeth I: Parliamentary Rhetoric and the Exercise of Power." *Signs* 1 (1975): 31–55.

Helgerson, Richard. *Forms of Nationhood: The Elizabethan Writing of England*. Chicago: University of Chicago Press, 1992.

Hibbert, Christopher. *The Virgin Queen: Elizabeth I, Genius of the Golden Age*. Reading, Mass.: Addison-Wesley, 1991.

Highley, Christopher. " 'A Soft Kind of War': Spenser and the Female Reformation of Ireland." In *Shakespeare, Spenser, and the Crisis in Ireland*. Cambridge: Cambridge University Press, 1997.

Hill, Christopher. "Censorship and English Literature." In *The Collected Essays of Christopher Hill.* Vol. 1, *Writing and Revolution in Seventeenth-Century England.* Brighton, 1985.

Hinton, Edward M. "Rych's *Anothomy of Ireland,* with an Account of the Author." *PMLA* 55 (1940): 91.

Historical Manuscripts Commission. *Calendar of Manuscripts of the Most Hon. Marquis of Salisbury.* London, 1883.

Hoak, D. E. *The King's Council in the Reign of Edward VI.* Cambridge: Cambridge University Press, 1976.

Hotson, Leslie. "Marigold of the Poets." *Transactions of the Royal Society of Literature* n.s., 17 (1938): 47–68.

Hughes, Paul L., and James F. Larkin, eds. *The Later Tudors: 1553–1587.* New Haven: Yale University Press, 1969.

Hume, Anthea. "*Love's Martyr,* 'The Phoenix and the Turtle,' and the Aftermath of the Essex Rebellion." *Review of English Studies* n.s., 40 (157) (1989): 48–71.

Hunt, Lynn. "Introduction: Obscenity and the Origins of Modernity, 1500–1800." In *The Invention of Pornography,* edited by Lynn Hunt. New York: Zone Books, 1993.

———, ed. *The Invention of Pornography: Obscenity and the Origins of Modernity, 1500–1800.* New York: Zone Books, 1993.

Hurstfield, Joel. *Elizabeth I and the Unity of England.* London: English Universities Press, 1960.

Ingram, Martin. "Ridings, Rough Music, and Mocking Rhymes in Early Modern England." In *Popular Culture in Seventeenth-Century England,* edited by Barry Reay. London: Croom Helm, 1985.

Irwin, Margaret. *Young Bess.* New York: Harcourt, Brace, 1945.

Itzin, Catherine, ed. *Pornography: Women, Violence, and Civil Liberties.* Oxford: Oxford University Press, 1992.

Ives, E. W. *Anne Boleyn.* New York: Basil Blackwell, 1986.

———. *Faction in Tudor England.* Historical Association, Appreciations in History 6 (1979): 22.

———. "Henry the Great?" *The Historian* 43 (Autumn, 1994): 8.

Jackson, Gabriele Bernhard. "Topical Ideology: Witches, Amazons, and Shakespeare's Joan of Arc." *English Literary Renaissance* 18 (Winter, 1988): 40–65.

Jardine, Lisa. *Reading Shakespeare Historically.* London: Routledge, 1996.

Jenkins, Elizabeth. *Elizabeth the Great.* New York: Coward-McCann, 1958.

Johnson, Paul. *Elizabeth I, A Biography.* New York: Holt, Rinehart, and Winston, 1988.

———. *Elizabeth I: A Study in Power and Intellect.* London: Weidenfeld and Nicolson, 1974.

Jordan, Constance. "Women's Rule in Sixteenth-Century British Political Thought." *Renaissance Quarterly* 40 (1987): 421–51.

Joubert, Lauren. *Popular Errors.* Translated and annotated by Gregory David de Rocher. Tuscaloosa: University of Alabama Press, 1989.

Kantorowicz, Ernst H. *The King's Two Bodies: A Study in Mediaeval Political Theology.* Princeton: Princeton University Press, 1957.

Kaplan, M. Lindsay. "Slander for Slander in *Measure for Measure.*" *Renaissance Drama* 21 (1990): 23–54.

Kappeler, Susanne. *The Pornography of Representation.* Cambridge: Polity Press, 1986.

Keach, William. *Elizabeth Erotic Narratives: Irony and Pathos in the Ovidian Poetry of Shakespeare, Marlowe, and Their Contemporaries.* New Brunswick, N.J.: Rutgers University Press, 1977.

Kegl, Rosemary. "'Those Terrible Aproches': Sexuality, Social Mobility, and Resisting the Courtliness of Puttenham's *The Arte of English Poesie.*" *English Literary Renaissance* 20 (1990): 179–208.

Kelly, Henry Ansgar. *The Matrimonial Trials of Henry VIII.* Stanford: Stanford University Press, 1976.

King, John N. "The Godley Woman in Elizabethan Iconography." *Renaissance Quarterly* 38 (1985): 41–84.

——. "Queen Elizabeth I: Representations of the Virgin Queen." *Renaissance Quarterly* 43 (1990): 30–74.

——. *Tudor Royal Iconography.* Princeton: Princeton University Press, 1989.

Lambert, Sheila. "State Control of the Press in Theory and Practice: The Role of the Stationers' Company before 1640." In *Censorship and the Control of Print in England and France, 1600–1910,* edited by Robin Meyers and Michael Harris. Winchester: Saint Paul's Bibliographies, 1992.

Latimer, Hugh. *Sermons and Remains of Hugh Latimer.* Edited by George Corrie. Cambridge: Cambridge University Press, 1845.

Lee, Patricia-Ann. "A Bodye Politique to Governe: Aylmer, Knox, and the Debate on Queenship." *The Historian* 52 (1990): 242–61.

Lennon, Colm. *Sixteenth-Century Ireland: The Incomplete Conquest.* New York: St. Martin's Press, 1995.

Leti, Gregorio. *Historia o vero vita di Elisabetta regina d'Inghilterra.* Amsterdam, 1693.

Letton, Jennette, and Francis. *Young Elizabeth.* New York: Harper and Brothers, 1953.

Levin, Carole. *The Heart and Stomach of a King: Elizabeth I and the Politics of Sex and Power.* Philadelphia: University of Pennsylvania Press, 1994.

——. "Lady Jane Grey: Protestant Queen and Martyr." In *Silent but for the Word:*

Tudor Women as Patrons, Translators, and Writers of Religious Works, edited by Margaret Hannay. Kent, Ohio: Kent State University Press, 1985. Pp. 92–106.

——. "Power, Politics, and Sexuality: Images of Elizabeth I." In *The Politics of Gender in Early Modern Europe,* edited by Jean R. Brink, Allison P. Coudert, and Maryanne C. Horowitz. Kirksville, Mo.: Sixteenth Century Journal Publications, 1989. Pp. 95–110.

Levine, Mortimer. "The Place of Women in Tudor Government." In *Tudor Rule and Revolution, Essays for G. R. Elton from His American Friends,* edited by D. J. Guth and J. W. McKenna. Cambridge: Cambridge University Press, 1982. Pp. 109–23.

——. *Tudor Dynastic Problems, 1460–1571.* New York: Barnes and Noble, 1973.

Lilly, Joseph, ed. *A Collection of Seventy-nine Black-Letter Ballads and Broadsides Printed in the Reign of Queen Elizabeth Between the Years 1559 and 1597.* London: Joseph Lilly, 1867.

Lloyd, E. Berry, ed. *John Stubbs's "Gaping Gulf" with Letters and Other Relevant Documents.* Charlottesville: University of Virginia Press, 1968.

Loades, David. *Mary Tudor: A Life.* Oxford: Blackwell, 1989.

——. "Philip II and the Government of England." In *Law and Government under the Tudors,* edited by C. Cross, D. M. Loades, and J. J. Scarisbrick. Cambridge: Cambridge University Press, 1988. Pp. 177–94.

——. *The Politics of Marriage: Henry VIII and His Queens.* Stroud, Gloucestershire: Alan Sutton Publishing, 1994.

——. *The Reign of Mary Tudor: Politics, Government and Religion in England 1553–58.* 2nd edition. Harlow: Longman, 1991.

Logan, Marie-Rose, and Peter L. Rudnytsky, eds. *Contending Kingdoms: Historical, Psychological, and Feminist Approaches to the Literature of Sixteenth-Century England and France.* Detroit: Wayne State University Press, 1991.

Lossky, Nicholas. *Lancelot Andrewes the Preacher (1555–1626).* Oxford: Oxford University Press, 1992.

Love, Harold. *Scribal Publication in Seventeenth-Century England.* Oxford: Clarendon Press, 1993.

MacCaffrey, Wallace T. *Elizabeth I.* London: Edward Arnold, 1993.

——. *Elizabeth I: War and Politics, 1588–1603.* Princeton: Princeton University Press, 1992.

——. *Queen Elizabeth and the Making of Policy, 1572–1588.* Princeton: Princeton University Press, 1981.

MacKinnon, Catherine A. *Toward a Feminist Theory of the State.* Cambridge, Mass.: Harvard University Press, 1989.

Marcus, Leah. *Puzzling Shakespeare: Local Reading and Its Discontents.* Berkeley: University of California Press, 1988.

Marotti, Arthur F. *John Donne, Coterie Poet*. Madison: University of Wisconsin Press, 1986.

——. " 'Love is not Love': Elizabethan Sonnet Sequences and the Social Order." *Journal of English Literary History* 49 (1982): 396–428.

——. *Manuscript, Print, and the English Renaissance Lyric*. Ithaca: Cornell University Press, 1995.

——. "The Transmission of Lyric Poetry and the Institutionalizing of Literature in the English Renaissance." In *Contending Kingdoms: Historical, Psychological, and Feminist Approaches to the Literature of Sixteenth-Century England and France*. Detroit: Wayne State University Press, 1991.

Martienssen, Anthony. *Queen Katherine Parr*. New York: McGraw-Hill, 1973.

Maxwell, Constantia. *Irish History from Contemporary Sources, 1509–1610*. London: Allen and Unwin, 1923.

May, Stephen W. *The Elizabethan Courtier Poets: The Poems and Their Contexts*. Columbia: University of Missouri Press, 1991.

McCabe, Richard A. "Edmund Spenser, Poet of Exile." *Proceedings of the British Academy* 80 (1993): 73–103.

——. "Elizabethan Satire and the Bishops' Ban of 1599." *The Yearbook of English Studies* 11 (1981): 188–93.

McClintock Dix, E. R. *Printing in Dublin Prior to 1601*. Dublin: C. O. Lochlainn, 1932.

McCullough, P. E. *Sermons at Court: Politics and Religion in Elizabethan and Jacobean Preaching*. Cambridge: Cambridge University Press, 1997.

McLane, P. E. *Spenser's "Shepheardes Calender": A Study in Elizabethan Allegory*. Notre Dame: Indiana University Press, 1961.

Merrix, Robert P. "The Vale of Lillies and the Bower of Bliss: Soft-core Pornography in Elizabethan Poetry." *Journal of Popular Culture* 19, no. 4 (1986): 3–16.

Meyers, Robin, and Michael Harris, eds. *Censorship and the Control of Print in England and France, 1600–1910*. Winchester: Saint Paul's Bibliographies, 1992.

Montrose, Louis Adrian. "Celebration and Insinuation: Sir Philip Sidney and the Motives of Elizabethan Courtship." *Renaissance Drama* n.s., 8 (1977): 3–35.

——. "The Elizabethan Subject and the Spenserian Text." In *Literary Theory/Renaissance Texts*, edited by Patricia Parker and David Quint. Baltimore: Johns Hopkins University Press, 1986. Pp. 303–40.

——. " 'Eliza, Queene of shepheards,' and the Pastoral of Power." *English Literary Renaissance* 10 (1980): 153–82.

——. "Gifts and Reasons: The Contexts of Peele's *Araygnement of Paris*." *English Literary History* 47 (1980): 433–61.

——. "Of Gentlemen and Shepherds: The Politics of Elizabethan Pastoral Form." *English Literary History* 50 (1983): 415–59.

——. " 'Shaping Fantasies': Figurations of Gender and Power in Elizabethan Culture." In *Representing the Renaissance*, edited by Stephen Greenblatt. Berkeley: University of California Press, 1988. Pp. 31–64.

Morgan, Hiram. "Extradition and Treason Trial of a Gaelic Lord: The Case of Brian O'Rourke." *The Irish Jurist* 22 (1987): 285–301.

——. "The Fall of Sir John Perrot." In *The Reign of Elizabeth I*, edited by John Guy. Cambridge: Cambridge University Press, 1995. 109–25.

——. *Tyrone's Rebellion: The Outbreak of the Nine Years War in Tudor Ireland.* Woodbridge, Suffolk: Boyden Press, Royal Historical Society, 1993.

Murdin, William. *Burghley's State Papers.* London, 1759.

Murdin, William, and Samuel Haynes, eds. *A Collection of State Papers Relating to Affairs in the Reign of Queen Elizabeth from 1542 to 1596 left by William Cecil, Lord Burghley.* London: William Bowyer, 1740–59.

Naunton, Sir Robert. *Elizabeth: Fragmenta Regalia.* Edited by John S. Cerovski. Washington: Folger Books, 1985.

Neale, J. E. *Elizabeth I and Her Parliaments.* Vol. 1. London: Jonathan Cape, 1953.

——. *Queen Elizabeth I.* London: Jonathan Cape, 1934.

Norbrook, David. "The Emperor's new body? *Richard II*, Ernst Kantorowicz, and the Politics of Shakespeare Criticism." *Textual Practice* 10, no. 2 (1996): 329–57.

——. *Poetry and Politics in the English Renaissance.* London: Routledge and Kegan Paul, 1984.

O'Dowd, Mary. "Gaelic Economy and Society." In *Natives and Newcomers: Essays on the Making of Irish Colonial Society, 1534–1641*, edited by Ciaran Brady and Raymond Gillespie. Dublin: Irish Academic Press, 1986. Pp. 120–47.

O Riordan, Michelle. *The Gaelic Mind and the Collapse of the Gaelic World.* Cork: Cork University Press, 1990.

Orwell, George, and Reginald Reynolds, eds. *British Pamphleteers.* Vol. 1: *From the Sixteenth Century to the French Revolution.* London: Allan Wingate, 1948.

Outhwaite, R. B. "Dearth, the English Crown, and the 'Crisis of the 1590s.' " In *The European Crisis of the 1590s*, edited by Peter Clark. London: George Allen & Unwin, 1985. Pp. 23–43.

Parker, Patricia. *Literary Fat Ladies: Rhetoric, Gender, Property.* London: Methuen, 1987.

Parthenophil and Parthenophe: A Critical Edition. Edited by Victor A. Doyno. Carbondale: Southern Illinois University Press, 1971.

Patterson, Annabel. *Censorship and Interpretation: The Conditions of Writing and*

Reading in Early Modern England. Madison: University of Wisconsin Press, 1984; rpt. with a new introduction, 1990.

Peck, D. C. " 'News from Heaven and Hell': A Defamatory Narrative of the Earl of Leicester." *English Literary Renaissance* 8 (1978): 141–58.

Peck, Linda Levy. "Peers, Patronage, and the Politics of History." In *The Reign of Elizabeth I,* edited by John Guy. Cambridge: Cambridge University Press, 1995. Pp. 87–108.

Perry, Maria. *The Word of a Prince.* Woodbridge, Suffolk: Boydell Press, 1990.

Peter, John. *Complaint and Satire in Early English Literature.* Oxford: Clarendon Press, 1956.

Phillips, James Emerson. *Images of a Queen: Mary Stuart in Sixteenth-Century Literature.* Berkeley: University of California Press, 1964.

———. "The Woman Ruler in Spenser's *Faerie Queene.*" *Huntington Library Quarterly* 5 (1942): 217–34.

Plowden, Alison. *Lady Jane Grey and the House Suffolk.* London: Sidgwick and Jackson, 1985.

———. *Marriage with My Kingdom: The Courtships of Elizabeth I.* London: Macmillan, 1977.

Pollard, A. F. *England under Protector Somerset.* London: Kegan, Paul, Trench, Trubner & Co., 1900.

———. *Tudor Tracts 1532–1588.* Westminster: Archibald Constable, 1903.

Pollen, J. H., ed. "Papal Negotiations with Mary, Queen of Scots during Her Reign in Scotland, 1561–1567." *Scottish Historical Society* 37 (1901): 61.

Prescott, Anne Lake. "Pearl of the Valois and Elizabeth I." In *Silent but for the Word: Tudor Women as Patrons, Translators, and Writers of Religious Texts,* edited by Margaret Hannay. Kent, Ohio: Kent State University Press, 1985. Pp. 61–77.

Prothero, G. W., ed. *Select Statutes and Other Constitutional Documents Illustrative of the Reigns of Elizabeth and James I.* 4th ed. Oxford: Clarendon Press, 1913.

Quinn, David B. "Government Printing and the Publication of the Irish Statutes in the Sixteenth Century." *Proceedings of the Royal Irish Academy* 49 (1943–44), sec. C, 45–130.

Rait, R. S., and A. I. Cameron. *King James's Secret.* London, 1927.

Read, Conyers. *Lord Burghley and Queen Elizabeth.* London: Jonathan Cape, 1960.

Redworth, Glyn. "Of Pimps and Princes: Three Unpublished Letters from James I and the Prince of Wales Relating to the Spanish Match." *Historical Journal* 37 (1994): 401–9.

Rex, Richard. *Henry VIII and the English Reformation.* New York: St. Martin's Press, 1993.

Ridley, Jasper. *Elizabeth I.* London: Constable, 1987.

——. *Henry VIII: The Politics of Tyranny.* New York: Fromm, 1986.

Robertson, Jean, ed. *Sir Philip Sidney: The Countess of Pembroke's Arcadia (The Old Arcadia).* Oxford: Clarendon Press, 1973.

Rodrîgues-Salgado, M. J., and the staff of the National Maritime Museum. *Armada, 1588–1988: An International Exhibition to Commemorate the Spanish Armada: The Official Catalogue.* London: Penguin Books, 1988.

Rollins, Hyder Edward. *The Phoenix Nest.* Cambridge, Mass.: Harvard University Press, 1953.

Rose, Mary Beth. "Where Are the Mothers in Shakespeare? Options for Gender Representation in the English Renaissance." *Shakespeare Quarterly* 42 (Fall 1991): 301.

Rosen, Barbara, ed. *Witchcraft in England, 1558–1618.* Amherst: University of Massachusetts Press, 1991.

Rupprecht, Carol Schreier. "Radigund." In *The Spenser Encyclopedia,* ed. A. C. Hamilton. Toronto: University of Toronto Press; London: Routledge, 1990. Pp. 580–81.

Russell, Conrad. *Parliaments and English Politics, 1621–1629.* Oxford: Clarendon Press, 1979.

Samaha, Joel. "Gleanings from Local Criminal Court Records: Sedition amongst the 'Inarticulate' in Elizabethan Essex." *Journal of Social History* 8 (1975): 69.

Saunders, J. W. *A Biographical Dictionary of Renaissance Poets and Dramatists, 1520–1650.* Sussex: Harvester Press; New Jersey: Barnes and Noble Books, 1983.

Sawday, Jonathan. *The Body Emblazoned: Dissection and the Human Body in Renaissance Culture.* London: Routledge, 1995.

Scalingi, Paula Louise. "The Scepter or the Distaff: The Question of Female Sovereignty, 1515–1607." *The Historian* 42 (1978): 59–75.

Scarisbrick, J. J. *Henry VIII.* Berkeley: University of California Press, 1968.

Schleiner, Winfried. "*Divina Virago:* Queen Elizabeth as an Amazon." *Studies in Philology* 75 (Spring 1978): 163–80.

Scott, James C. *Domination and the Arts of Resistance: The Hidden Transcript.* New Haven: Yale University Press, 1990.

——. *Weapons of the Weak: Everyday Forms of Peasant Resistance.* New Haven: Yale University Press, 1985.

Scott, Mary M. M. *The Tragedy of Fotheringay.* London, 1895.

Sedgwick, Eve Kosofsky. *Between Men: English Literature and Male Homosocial Desire.* New York: Columbia University Press, 1985.

Seymour, William. *Ordeal by Ambition: An English Family in the Shadow of the Tudors.* London: Sidgwick and Jackson, 1972.

Sharpe, Jim. "Social Strain and Social Dislocation, 1585–1603." In *The Reign of Elizabeth I,* edited by John Guy. Cambridge: Cambridge University Press, 1995. Pp. 192–211.

Shell, Marc. *Elizabeth's Glass.* Lincoln: University of Nebraska Press, 1993.

Shephard, Amanda. *Gender and Authority in Sixteenth-Century England.* Keele, Staffordshire: Keele University Press, 1994.

Shuger, Debora K. *Habits of Thought in the English Renaissance: Religion, Politics, and the Dominant Culture.* Berkeley: University of California Press, 1990.

——. *The Renaissance Bible: Scholarship, Sacrifice, and Subjectivity.* Berkeley: University of California Press, 1994.

Smith, Lacey Baldwin. *Henry VIII: The Mask of Royalty.* Boston: Houghton Mifflin, 1971.

——. *Treason in Tudor England: Politics and Paranoia.* Princeton, N.J.: Princeton University Press, 1986.

Smith, Preserved. *Erasmus.* New York: Dover Publications, 1962; reprint of 1923 ed.

Smith-Rosenberg, Carroll. "Writing History: Language, Class, and Gender." In *Feminist Studies / Critical Studies,* edited by Teresa de Lauretis. Bloomington: Indiana University Press, 1986. Pp. 48–49.

Somerset, Anne. *Elizabeth I.* New York: Alfred A. Knopf, 1991.

Stanley, Arthur Penrhyn. *Historical Monuments of Westminster Abbey.* London: John Murry, 1876.

Starkey, David. *The Reign of Henry VIII: Personalities and Politics.* Hampshire: George Philip, 1985.

——, et al. *The English Court: From the Wars of the Roses to the Civil War.* London: Longman, 1987.

Strauss, Walter R. *The German Single-Leaf Woodcut, 1550–1600.* Vol. 2. New York: Abaris Books, 1975.

Strickland, Agnes. *Memoirs of Elizabeth.* Philadelphia: Blanchard and Lea, 1853.

Strier, Richard, and Donna B. Hamilton, eds. *Religion, Literature, and Politics in Post-Reformation England, 1540–1688.* Cambridge: Cambridge University Press, 1996.

Strong, Roy. *The Cult of Elizabeth: Elizabethan Portraiture and Pageantry.* Berkeley: University of California Press, 1977.

——. *Gloriana: The Portraits of Queen Elizabeth I.* New York: Thames and Hudson, 1987.

——. *Portraits of Queen Elizabeth I.* Oxford: Clarendon Press, 1964.

Taylor, Barry. *Vagrant Writing: Social and Semiotic Disorders in the English Renaissance.* New York: Harvester Wheatsheaf, 1991.

Taylor, Rupert. *Political Prophecy in England*. New York: Columbia University Press, 1911.

Taylor-Smither, L. J. "Elizabeth I: A Psychological Profile." *Sixteenth-Century Journal* 15 (1984): 47–70.

Teague, Frances. "Queen Elizabeth in Her Speeches." In *Gloriana's Face: Women, Public and Private, in the English Renaissance*, edited by S. P. Cerasano and Marion Wynne-Davies. Hemel Hempstead, Herts: Harvester Wheatsheaf; Detroit: Wayne State University Press, 1992. Pp. 63–78.

Thane, Elswyth. *The Tudor Wench*. New York: Harcourt, Brace, 1932.

Thorp, M. "William Cecil and the Antichrist: A Study of Anti-Catholic Ideology." In *Politics, Religion, and Diplomacy in Early Modern Europe: Essays in Honor of De Lamar Jensen*, edited by Malcolm Thorp and Arthur J. Slavin. Kirksville, Mo.: Sixteenth Century Journal Publishers, 1994.

Thurley, Simon. *The Royal Palaces of Tudor England*. New Haven: Yale University Press, 1993.

Tillyard, E. M. W. *The Elizabethan World Picture*. New York: Macmillan, 1944; [missing] University Press, 1992.

Villeponteaux, Mary. "*Semper Eadem:* Belphoebe's Denial of Desire." In *Renaissance Discourses of Desire*, edited by Claude J. Summers and Ted-Larry Pebworth. Columbia: University of Missouri Press, 1993. Pp. 29–45.

von Klarwill, Victor. *Queen Elizabeth and Some Foreigners*. New York: Brentano's, 1928.

Walker, Julia M. "Reading the Tombs of Elizabeth I." *English Literary Renaissance* 26 (1996).

——. "Spenser's Elizabeth Portrait and the Fiction of Dynastic Epic." *Modern Philology* 90 (1992): 172–99.

Warnicke, Retha. *The Rise and Fall of Anne Boleyn*. Cambridge: Cambridge University Press, 1989.

Williams, Gordon. *A Dictionary of Sexual Language and Imagery in Shakespearean and Stuart Literature*. 3 vols. London: Athlone Press, 1994.

Williams, Neville. *Elizabeth the First: Queen of England*. New York: E. P. Dutton, 1968.

Williams, Penry. *The Tudor Regime*. Oxford: Clarendon Press, 1979.

Wilson, Elkin Calhoun. *England's Eliza*. Cambridge, Mass.: Harvard University Press, 1939.

Woods, Susanne. "Spenser and the Problem of Woman's Rule." *Huntington Library Quarterly* 48 (1985): 141–58.

Woolf, D. R. "Two Elizabeths? James I and the Late Queen's Famous Memory." *Canadian Journal of History* 20 (1985): 167–91.

Wormald, Jenny. *Mary Queen of Scots: A Study in Failure*. London: G. Philip, 1988.

Wright, Celeste Turner. "The Amazons in Elizabethan Literature." *Studies in Philology* 37 (July 1940): 433–56.

Wright, Pam. "A Change in Direction: The Ramifications of a Female Household, 1558–1603." In *The English Court from the Wars of the Roses to the Civil War*, by David Starkey et al. London: Longman, 1987. Pp. 159, 168.

Yates, Frances A. *Astraea: The Imperial Theme in the Sixteenth Century*. London: Routledge and Kegan Paul, 1975.

Notes on Contributors

Ilona Bell is a professor of English at Williams College. She has written numerous articles on English Renaissance poetry, Elizabethan women, and Queen Elizabeth. Her forthcoming book is titled *Elizabethan Women and the Poetry of Courtship* (1998). She is completing a manuscript on Elizabeth I and the politics of courtship.

Hannah Betts is a doctoral student at Lincoln College, Oxford, where she is researching the Elizabethan blazon. She has held lectureships at Lincoln College and Pembroke College, Oxford. Her research and teaching interests lie in Renaissance literature and in critical theory.

Sheila T. Cavanagh is an associate professor of English affiliated with the faculty in Women's Studies at Emory University. She is the author of *Wanton Eyes and Chaste Desires: Sexuality in "The Faerie Queene"* (1994) and of numerous articles on Elizabethan literature. Currently she is working on a project concerning women and violence in the early modern period.

Rob Content teaches English at Trinity College in Washington, D.C.

Susan Doran is Reader in History at St. Mary's University College, a college of the University of Surrey. She has written articles and books on Tudor England including: *Monarchy and Matrimony: The Courtships of Elizabeth I* (1996), *England and Europe, 1485–1603*, 2nd ed. (1996), and *Princes, Pastors, and People: The Church and Religion in England, 1529–1689* (1991).

Christopher Highley is an associate professor of English at Ohio State University. His book *Shakespeare, Spenser, and the Crisis in Ireland* will be published by Cambridge University Press. He is currently working on recusant representations of Britain.

Carole Levin is a professor of history at SUNY–New Paltz. She has published *Propaganda in the English Reformation: Heroic and Villainous Images of King John* (1988) and *The Heart and Stomach of a King: Elizabeth I and the Politics of Sex and Power* (1994) as well as three co-edited collections, *Ambiguous Realities: Women in the Middle Ages and Renaissance* (1987), *Sexuality and Politics in Renaissance Drama* (1991), and *Political Rhetoric, Power, and Renaissance Women* (1995). She is the recipient of the SUNY Chancellor's Award for Excellence in Teaching.

Peter E. McCullough studied at UCLA and Princeton, and has held a Junior Research Fellowship at Trinity College, Oxford. Author of *Sermons at Court: Politics and Religion in Elizabethan and Jacobean Preaching* (1997) and articles on Andrewes, Donne, and Milton, he is now the Sohmer-Hall Fellow in English Renaissance Literature at Lincoln College, Oxford and University Lecturer in English.

Marcy L. North is an assistant professor of English at Florida State University. She is the author of "Ignoto in the Age of Print: The Manipulation of Anonymity in Early Modern England," and she is currently finishing a book on the motivations for anonymous authorship in early modern print and manuscript culture.

Mary Villeponteaux is associate professor of English at the University of Southern Mississippi. She has published several articles on Spenser and is at work on a book about the construction of gender in *The Faerie Queene*.

Julia M. Walker is associate professor of English and coordinator of women's studies at SUNY-Geneseo. She has edited *Milton and the Idea of Woman* (1988) and authored *Medusa's Mirrors: Spenser, Shakespeare, Milton, and the Metamorphosis of the Female Self* (1997) as well as numerous articles on Donne, Milton, Spenser, Ovid, and Christine de Pizan. She is currently completing *Reading the Remains of Elizabeth I: The Politics and Poetics of Posthumous Representation.*

Index

Library of Congress Cataloging-in-Publication Data

Dissing Elizabeth : negative representations of Gloriana / edited by Julia M.
Walker.

p. cm.

Includes bibliographical references and index.

ISBN 0-8223-2060-6 (acid-free paper).—ISBN 0-8223-2074-6 (pbk. :
acid-free paper)

1. Great Britain—History—Elizabeth, 1558–1603—Historiography.
2. English literature—Early modern, 1500–1700—History and criticism.
3. Elizabeth I, Queen of England, 1533–1603—Public opinion.   4. English
language—Early modern, 1500–1700—Rhetoric.   5. Public opinion—Great
Britain—History—16th century. 6. Monarchy—Great Britain—Public
opinion.   7. Queens—Great Britain—Public opinion.   I. Walker, Julia M.,
1951–   . II. Series.

DA355.D57   1998

942.05′5—dc21   97-29433